PROPHECY IN
CROSS-CULTURAL
PERSPECTIVE

SOCIETY OF BIBLICAL LITERATURE
Sources for Biblical Study

Edited by
Burke O. Long

Number 17
PROPHECY IN CROSS-CULTURAL PERSPECTIVE

by
Thomas W. Overholt

PROPHECY IN
CROSS-CULTURAL PERSPECTIVE:
A Sourcebook for Biblical Researchers

Thomas W. Overholt

Scholars Press
Atlanta, Georgia

PROPHECY IN CROSS-CULTURAL PERSPECTIVE
A Sourcebook for Biblical Researchers

Thomas W. Overholt

© 1986
The Society of Biblical Literature

Library of Congress Cataloging in Publication Data

Overholt, Thomas W., 1935–
  Prophecy in cross cultural perspective.

  (Sources for Biblical study; no. 17
  Bibliography: p
  Includes index.
  1. Prophets—Addresses, essays, lectures.
  2. Prophecy—Addresses, essays, lectures. I. Title.
  II. Series.
  BL633.088 1986   291.6'3   85-19590
  ISBN 0-89130-900-4 (alk. paper)
  ISBN 0-89130-901-2 (pbk. : alk. paper)

54593

Printed in the United States of America
on acid-free paper

For Sally

CONTENTS

PREFACE

This book is one of the products of an interest in the cross-cultural study of prophecy that goes back fifteen years or more. During that time, I have received help and encouragement from a number of individuals and institutions, and it is my pleasure now to acknowledge a few of those debts. I have benefited greatly from conversations over several years with Robert R. Wilson. These, and his book on the social setting of Israelite prophecy (Wilson, 1980), have been important in helping me formulate the problems in cross-cultural study of prophecy and in extending my interests beyond 19th and 20th century millenarian movements among American Indians and Melanesians. My debt to Burke O. Long is also great. As Old Testament editor of the "Sources for Biblical Study" series, it was he who proposed the possibility of a cross-cultural sourcebook on prophecy. In addition he made valuable suggestions about the structure and content of the book and offered careful and constructive criticisms of the manuscript. He has, in a word, been a good editor. I am also grateful to Robert C. Culley, Frank S. Frick, Sam D. Gill, and David L. Petersen for reading and commenting on portions of the manuscript.

The use of a word processor makes editing and revising easier, but by no means lightens everyone's workload. Hearty thanks are therefore due Carolee Cote, secretary of the Philosophy Department at the University of Wisconsin-Stevens Point, for intelligent, good-humored, accurate, and efficient work over several years, through equipment breakdowns and changes, and on top of her other duties.

Institutional assistance has also been important. A sabbatical granted by the University of Wisconsin-Stevens Point during the spring of 1984 allowed me to bring the project substantially to completion. And though it is now over a decade in the past, I want to express my gratitude to the Society for Values in Higher Education, from which I received a postdoctoral fellowship for cross-disciplinary studies which allowed me to spend an academic year (1973–74) studying anthropology at the University of Arizona. The benefits which have accrued to me from that year have been many and great.

Stevens Point, Wisconsin
Thomas W. Overholt
January, 1985

ACKNOWLEDGEMENTS

Grateful acknowledgment is made to the following publishers and individuals for permission to reprint copyrighted materials used in Chapter II:

Pages 1–40 of Franz Boaz, *The Religion of the Kwakiutl Indians*, Part 2 (New York: Columbia University Press, 1930) are reprinted by permission of the publisher.

Section 2.1 is reproduced from *The Ojibwa Indians of Parry Island, Their Social and Religious Life* by Diamond Jenness, National Museum of Canada Bulletin No. 78, Anthropological Series, No. 17 (Ottawa, 1935), by permission of the National Museum of Man, National Museums of Canada.

Selections from A. Irving Hallowell, *The Role of Conjuring in Saulteaux Society* (Philadelphia: University of Pennsylvania Press, 1942) are reprinted by permission of the publisher.

Section 2.3 is reproduced from John M. Cooper, "The Shaking Tent Rite among Plains and Forest Algonquians," *Primitive Man*, vol. 17 (1944) by permission of the publisher, The Catholic University of America Press.

The *Plains Anthropologist* has granted permission to reprint from Wesley R. Hurt, "A Yuwipi Ceremony at Pine Ridge," vol. 5 (1960); S. E. Feraca, "The Yuwipi Cult of the Oglala and Sicangu Teton Sioux," vol. 6 (1961); and Alice B. Kehoe, "The Ghost Dance in Saskatchewan," vol. 19 (1968).

Section 4.1 is reproduced from *Navajo Texts* by Edward Sapir and Harry Hoijer, copyright 1942, by permission of the publisher, the Linguistic Society of America, and the authors' literary executors, Philip Sapir and Mrs. Harry Hoijer.

Selections from Alexander H. Leighton and Dorothea C. Leighton, *Gregorio, the Hand-Trembler*, Peabody Museum Papers, vol. 40, no. 1, are reprinted with the permission of the Peabody Museum of Archaeology and Ethnology, Harvard University.

Excerpts from William Morgan, "Navajo Treatment of Sickness: Diagnosticians," are reproduced from *American Anthropologist* 33 (3):394–5, 1931, and excerpts from Leland C. Wyman, "Navajo Diagnosticians," are reproduced from *American Anthropologist* 38 (2):238–9,

Acknowledgments

240–2, 243, 244–5, 1936, both by permission of the American Anthropological Association.

Material from Franc J. Newcomb's "The Navaho Listening Rite," *El Palacio Magazine*, vol. 45 (1938) is reproduced by permission of the Museum of New Mexico.

Section 6 is reprinted from *Trances, Healing and Hallucinations* by Felicitas Goodman, Jeannette H. Henney, and Esther Pressel, copyright 1974, by permission of John Wiley & Sons, Inc., and the author, Esther Pressel.

Selections from "The Shaman's Tent of the Evenks and the Origin of the Shamanistic Rite" by A. F. Anisimov are reprinted from H. N. Michael, editor, *Studies in Siberian Shamanism*, copyright 1963, by permission of the Arctic Institute of North America.

"Gwek, the Witch-Doctor and the Pyramid of Dengkur" by P. Coriat is reprinted by permission from *Sudan Notes and Records*, vol. 22, 1939.

Selections from *The God of the Matopo Hills* by M. L. Daneel, copyright 1970, are reprinted by permission of Mouton Publishers.

Selections from *Spirits of Protest: Spirit-Mediums and the Articulation of Consensus Among the Zezuru of Southern Rhodesia (Zimbabwe)* by Peter Fry, copyright 1976, are reprinted by permission of Cambridge University Press.

Selections from *The Religion of an Indian Tribe* by Verrier Elwin, copyright 1955, are reprinted by permission of Oxford University Press.

Selections from "Kamoai of Darapap and the Legend of Jari" by Matthew Tamoane are reprinted from Garry Trompf, editor, *Prophets of Melanesia*, copyright 1977, by permission of the Institute of Papua New Guinea Studies.

Selections from *Road Belong Cargo* by Peter Lawrence, copyright 1964, are reprinted by permission of Manchester University Press.

CHAPTER I
INTRODUCTION: PROPHECY IN CROSS-CULTURAL PERSPECTIVE

Central to the book which you hold in your hands are descriptions, drawn largely from anthropological field studies, of prophet-like figures whose collective activity spans several centuries and circles the globe. I assume that such accounts will be useful to persons interested in biblical prophecy. The figures described are sufficiently different from the biblical prophets, however, to make the truth of this assumption less than self-evident, and so some words of introduction are in order.

Points-of-View on the Prophets

During the past century, an enormous literature has been produced about the biblical prophets and prophetic books. Though inevitably there has been a great deal of repetition, these works also display a variety of specific interests in their subject. Among the most prominent of these have been the religion of the prophets, their place in the history of Israelite religion and institutions, the preservation of their words and of stories about them (literary, form, and redaction criticism), and the origins of Israelite prophecy in relation to similar phenomena in surrounding cultures.[1] In short one may adopt various points of view toward the prophets, and the choice one makes on this matter will to some extent determine what one looks for and finds.

The various points of view are not necessarily mutually exclusive. For example, K. Koch's two-volume survey of Israelite prophecy (1983, 1984) stresses the intellectual basis of the prophets' message. He defines his task in terms of introducing readers "to the thinking of Israel's prophets" (1983:vii), and prefaces his concluding assessment of the "prophetic achievement" with the assertion that "a prophet wants to be taken seriously for the sake of his message, not because of his behaviour as a human being" (1984:190). Still, during the course of his exposition Koch utilizes whenever necessary historical, literary critical, and other ap-

---

[1] There are a number of surveys available of the history of scholarship; cf., for example, Fohrer (1961, 1962, 1980), Limburg (1978), McKane (1979), Neumann (1979), and R. Wilson (1980:1–14).

proaches to the material. It is worth noting that the explicit adoption of a point of view allows Koch to couch his discussion in terms which might otherwise seem bizarre ("metahistory," "auras of action that create destiny," "graduated monotheism," and the like) in the service of an effort to elucidate a way of thinking quite different from our own.

It is necessary that an author adopt a point of view towards his or her subject, and inevitable that, having done so, aspects of the topic which others consider important will be omitted from consideration. For example, R. Coote (1981) takes a redaction critical approach to Amos, stressing the message conveyed by the authors of each of the stages that can be identified in the present book. In doing so it seems reasonable to argue that only in the second stage of the development of the Amos tradition was the question of the prophet's authority raised as an important issue (1981:23–4, 41; cf. Am 7:10–7). From a more sociological point of view, however, it would seem safe to assume that Amos's claim to authority would have been of great importance to his original audience as well. To cite a final example, M. Silver's (1983) analysis of the economic context and its implications for the prophets' activities displays their calls for social reform in a decidedly negative light, and will be thought by some to ignore the contributions of the prophets to the development of Israelite and Jewish religion.

In recent years there has been a growing interest in applying data and theories from anthropology and other social sciences to the study of Old Testament prophecy, though not everyone has approached this task in the same way. One kind of study is exemplified by Robert Wilson's *Prophecy and Society in Ancient Israel* (1980), which makes extensive use of comparative materials. Indeed, it seems fair to say that the long second chapter on "prophecy in modern societies," which draws heavily on anthropological field studies of a wide variety of contemporary cultures, is the key chapter in the book. According to Wilson, the relative fullness of our knowledge about these cultures allows certain observations to be made about such matters as how individuals become intermediaries (a "neutral, general title" which he adopts for a range of prophet-like figures; 1982:27–8), the characteristic behavior of intermediaries, and the social functions which such persons perform. The generalizations which emerge from this investigation are then used to interpret prophecy in ancient cultures such as Mari and Israel about whose history and sociology we are much less fully informed. A similar focus on comparative data characterizes the articles in an issue of *Semeia* (21:1981), entitled "Anthropological Perspectives on Old Testament Prophecy."

Other studies, such as R. P. Carroll's *When Prophecy Failed* (1979) and D. L. Petersen's *The Roles of Israel's Prophets* (1981), draw heavily on sociological theory.[2] Interested primarily in the predictive aspects of prophecy, Carroll is confronted by a paucity of information in the Old Testament both about society's responses to prophetic oracles and about the complex relationships between prophets and society. He seeks to bridge this gap in our knowledge by employing the social-psychological theory of cognitive dissonance to illuminate the social dynamics of such responses. For his part Petersen uses role theory[3] to enhance our understanding of prophetic behavior and to help distinguish among the several terms (e.g., prophet, seer, man of God) which we encounter in the Old Testament.[4]

Turning to anthropology for assistance in understanding Old Testament materials poses the major problem of becoming conversant with some aspects of anthropological theory and practice, as well as with a variety of field studies. Special difficulties accompany the latter task. One is simply access. The relevant studies and reports are mostly outside the humanities, insuring that they will be to some degree unfamiliar to students of the Bible. This problem is exacerbated by the sheer quantity of these studies and their publication by a wide variety of presses, both commercial and governmental. Another difficulty is assessing the reliability of field studies, since methods and objectives of field anthropologists have changed over time and differ among individuals, who carry out their researches with varying skills. Here the reader must depend upon his or her own critical faculties, being alert for underlying assumptions (for example, is some sort of evolutionary hypothesis employed?), biases (are nonliterate peoples viewed as "primitives" or "savages"?, is there a tendency to concentrate on material culture?, etc.), and the imposition on the material of inappropriate categories of analysis.[5] The texts

[2] Cf. also B. Lang's *Monotheism and the Prophetic Minority* (1983a). I discuss one of the essays from this volume in Chapter IV.

[3] "Role" is a metaphor derived from the theatre, where it refers to behavior inherent in a certain "part" in a play rather than to the actor who happens to be cast in that part. Similarly, when studying social roles (e.g., teacher) one focuses on characteristic activities of teachers (e.g., preparing for class) rather than on specific teachers. Cf. Petersen's chapter on "role theory and the study of prophecy" (1981:16–34).

[4] The number of studies employing social scientific theories and/or data in biblical interpretation is growing, and is not limited to the prophets. N. Gottwald's massive *The Tribes of Yahweh* (1979) is a well-known example. In addition one might mention Wilson (1984); Andreasen (1983), on the queen mother; Bourdillon (1977), on prophecy; Chaney (1983) on peasants in premonarchic Israel; Donaldson (1981) and Oden (1983), on kinship in the Patriarchal narratives; and R. Wilson (1977) on genealogy. For historical surveys cf. J. Rogerson (1978) and Lang (1984); for a "preliminary bibliography" cf. Lang (1983b).

[5] Particularly on the second of these cf. Berkhofer (1979) and Gill (1982a:1–14, 1982b:1–9). Knowledge of the history of the discipline and of anthropologists' own critiques of developments within it is useful in making critical judgments about sources. Cf., for example, Beattie (1964), Epstein (1967), Evans-Pritchard (1964), Fisher and Werner (1978),

in Chapter II, with their introductions and notes, are an attempt to address these problems of access, familiarity, and evaluation of sources.

This book, then, provides students, biblical scholars, and other interested persons with a selection of texts representative of various prophet-like individuals found among traditional peoples and of the sort of material available about them. These texts can be useful in themselves, as windows into particular cultures, and can also serve as a basis for a cross-cultural comparison of specific religious and social phenomena. The introduction and notes to the texts provide bibliographic references to assist those who might wish to pursue farther some aspect of the discussion. The texts also enrich our appreciation of the complex settings and social processes that characterize acts of intermediation, and in so doing create an occasion to reflect on how our knowledge of ancient Israel might be enhanced by a disciplined examination of anthropological source materials.

The volume is primarily a sourcebook, and not an explicit comparison of biblical prophets with intermediaries from other cultures. The texts of Chapter II, therefore, form the heart of the book. And yet, the presumption is that the often exotic phenomena which the texts describe *can* be compared with each other and with biblical prophecy. But how can this be done?

Methodological Considerations

One of the issues of method to which biblical scholars and historians of religion have over the years returned is the comparison of apparently similar phenomena across cultural lines (cf. Culley, 1981). J. Z. Smith (1971–72, 1982) has described various attempts at comparison since the time of Classical Greece, observing in the process that no one has worked out any "rules for the production of comparisons" (1982:21). It is not important for our present purposes that I attempt a definitive statement on this matter. Nevertheless, I should state as clearly as possible what I consider the most fruitful approach, and acknowledge some of the possible pitfalls.[6]

Persons who set out to employ materials and methods from the social sciences in biblical research make certain assumptions, for example, ". . . that biblical documents are social products, i.e., communications of people in networks of social relations, and that the writings when seen

---

Geertz (1973), Harris (1968), Hultkrantz (1968), Schapera (1962), Voget (1960), Watson-Franke and Watson (1975).

[6] For a more detailed and theoretical discussion of "social scientific method in biblical studies" the reader is referred to the essays by Malina, Gottwald, and Theissen in Gottwald (1983:11–58).

in their social contexts through the use of self-conscious methods of study will be much more intelligible than if the social settings are ignored, or referred to randomly in undisciplined ways" (Gottwald, 1983b:143). In a somewhat different vein, the British social anthropologist C. R. Hallpike, argues that "intensive study of a few societies, unrepresentatively selected, can illuminate our knowledge of society as a whole." He goes on to speak of "certain fundamental similarities" shared by all societies and cites examples of monographs which have dealt with "fundamental social processes" and others that have elucidated "structural forms basic to human thought and social organization" (1971:134–8). I share Gottwald's assumptions, and my own chance encounter years ago with accounts of the Sioux Indian Ghost Dance and the paths along which that has led me since, predispose me to acknowledge the truth of Hallpike's observations.[7]

The most successful cross-cultural comparisons will likely be those couched in terms of social patterns or structures. This point has been nicely formulated by E. E. Evans-Pritchard (1964:18):

> In comparison what one compares are not things in themselves but certain particular characteristics of them. If one wishes to make a sociological comparison of ancestor cults in a number of different societies, what one compares are sets of structural relations between persons. One necessarily starts, therefore, by abstracting these relations in each society from their particular modes of cultural expression. Otherwise one will not be able to make the comparison.

The appeal is not to innate structures of the human mind, but to structure in terms of real social processes which occur and function similarly in various societies, and which inevitably take on the idiosyncracies of these societies (cf. H. C. Kee's contrasting of the structuralisms of Piaget and Levi-Strauss; 1980:100–05).[8]

A recent example of this general approach is a book by B. Lincoln (1981) which compares the ancient Indo-Iranian cattle, priestly, and warrior "cycles" with corresponding cycles in several East African tribal cultures. For Lincoln comparison "is not a matter of details but of total systems" (1981:163). In this he follows A. Hultkrantz's "ecological approach to religion": in principle,

> ecologically based comparisons cannot properly be used to establish single features of religions. . . . These are far too fickle and may or may not appear in almost any type of environment. Rather, ecological interpretation aims at the organization of such

---

[7] Cf. also Thompson (1972:47–8), Silver (1983:xi), Lang (1983a:58–9, 127).
[8] Similarly, cf. I.M. Lewis (1971:13–5), Hymes (1972:68), MacGaffey (1977–78:178).

facts into patterns and structures. It has as its goal the elucidation
of whole systems of religious belief and behavior, not mere details
(Lincoln, 1981:10; cf. 1–12, 163–77).

Although I adopt a focus somewhat narrower than Hultkrantz's and Lincoln's concern with "whole" religious systems, the same attention to "patterns and structures" leads to fruitful results in a consideration of prophecy.

Voices often warn of the hazards of comparison, and rightly so. One
danger is that in the end one might will simply reduce "the particular to
the general case," (K. Burridge, 1981:101; cf. Blenkinsopp, 1983:32), or,
as E. Thompson (1972:46) puts it, allow abstract typology to submerge
historical context.[9] There are in addition the pitfalls inherent in applying
categories from one discipline to materials belonging to another (cf.
Thompson, 1972:42–6; Meeks, 1983:5–6), and in the temptation "to
equate 'parallelism' with 'proof,' to substitute the citation of parallels for
reasoned argument" (Orlinsky, 1971:7–8).

Caution is, of course, required in any comparative enterprise. Gottwald notes that those who claim the possibility of serious study of a past
society hold "that for certain aspects of social reality we are likely to have
reasonably good data from the past and that, even where we do not,
cautious analogies can be made between better known and lesser known
social entities when the two are *demonstrably comparable in specifiable
ways*" (1983b:143; emphasis added). And J. Z. Smith quotes Wittgen-
stein as a reminder "that comparison is, at base, never identity"
(1982:35). Yet if comparisons with other cultures can never allow us to
infer what *must* have happened in ancient Israel, they may still sometimes allow us to suggest the *kinds of occurrences* that might reasonably
be presumed to have taken place in the social dynamics of a prophet's
functioning. The question of what we in fact do learn from our comparisons is a complicated one to which we will return briefly in Chapter IV.

In order to suggest the kind of comparison I believe to be possible
and important, I have utilized the categories employed by Wilson in his
discussion of anthropological data (1980:42–88). This has a double advantage. First, Wilson deals with these categories of comparison in some
detail, arriving at a theoretical statement about the nature of intermediation which is based on data like those reproduced in this volume. In the
process he cites a considerable amount of literature. The reader who
would like additional help in understanding the kinds of materials presented here may conveniently consult his discussion. Second, Wilson's
book is a convenient example of one way in which the task of cross-
cultural comparison can proceed, using this kind of data. It will become

---

[9] Long (1981b:125) comments in rebuttal: "If reduction of the particular to the general
is a danger, so is its opposite: losing the general in the particular."

apparent, and this is perhaps the single most important point to understand as one begins to read these texts, that the comparisons being made center on the social dynamics and functions of intermediation, and not on what specific intermediaries said.

It follows that the reader will find little by way of direct discussion of biblical materials here. I hope, however, that he or she will gain some appreciation of the rich resources available for such a comparative task, and will be moved to pursue the rewards of reading the Bible and anthropological materials in a way that stimulates dialogue between them. Such study may lead to a better understanding of the Bible, and perhaps also of our human situation. M. Eliade may be permitted a final word on the nature of the documents you are about to read:

> The correct analyses of myths and of mythical thought, of symbols and primordial images, especially the religious creations that emerge from Oriental and "primitive" cultures, are, in my opinion, the only way to open the Western mind and to introduce a new, planetary humanism. These spiritual documents—myths, symbols, divine figures, contemplative techniques, and so on— had previously been studied, if at all, with the detachment and indifference with which nineteenth-century naturalists studied insects. But it has now begun to be realized that these documents express existential situations, and that consequently they form part of the history of the human spirit. (1977:12)

Terminology

A problem encountered when one undertakes to study "prophecy" cross-culturally is the identification of those roles within traditional societies which offer the most promise for comparison with biblical prophets. Here it is not safe to rely on terminology alone, since the various terms and the roles they describe tend to overlap. Too strict distinctions based on these terms may thus mask important similarities among the various roles.[10]

The term "prophet" is at home in the Jewish, Christian, and Islamic religious traditions, and is only occasionally used by anthropologists in their discussions of specific non-Western cultures. When it is used, it often refers to persons who communicate the future on the basis of some contact with the world of spirits (e.g., Spier, 1935; Suttles, 1957; Evans-Pritchard, 1956; Middleton, 1963), from which we can sometimes infer that the author was impressed by the similarities between the role being described and prophecy in the biblical or Islamic tradition (cf. Rigby,

---

[10] I.M. Lewis (1981:25–7) suggests that such distinctions may in large part be due to differences in orientation between American cultural anthropologists and British social anthropologists.

1975). Sometimes the term is used as a label in more general studies of religious movements and leadership (e.g., Emmet, 1956; Guariglia, 1958; Bernardi, 1959; Jules-Rosette, 1978; Köbben, 1960; Koppers, 1959, 1960; Schlosser, 1950).

"Shaman" is a term applied to a large and widespread class of religious practitioners. Shamanism seems to have its "cultural-historical origin" in pre-literate hunting societies (cf. Hultkrantz, 1973:35–7; Nachtigall, 1976), though it can be found in other types of societies as well. There have in fact been attempts, notably by Kapelrud (1967) and Goldammer (1972), to show that specific elements in Old Testament narratives (e.g., communication with the spirits of the dead Samuel in 1 Sam. 28) are comparable to known elements in shamanism.

Shamans have been variously described. Eliade (1964:4–6) defines the shaman as one who "specializes in a trance during which his soul is believed to leave his body and ascend to the sky or descend to the underworld," who has mastered his spirits so as to communicate with them and receive their assistance. Hultkrantz likewise sees ecstasy as a "central, outstanding feature" of shamanism, important because it "opens the door to the other world" and enables the shaman "to create a rapport with the supernatural world on behalf of his group members" (1973:27, 31, 34; cf. L. Peters and D. Price-Williams, 1980).

The latter point leads Hultkrantz (1973:34) to distinguish between "the prophet who feels called upon to pronounce the will of god, or the powers, [and] the shaman [who] manifests solidarity with his own people and carries out their wishes and demands."[11] Still, I. M. Lewis (1981:32–3) has no difficulty using the two terms together. Arguing against "excessive terminological rigidity," he sets forth a definition of shamanism based on the work of Shirokogoroff (excerpts from which appear in Chap. II, 8): "A shaman is an inspired prophet and healer, a charismatic religious figure, with the power to control the spirits, usually by incarnating them. If spirits speak through him, so he is also likely to have the capacity to engage in mystical flight and other 'out of body experiences'."

According to a detailed analysis by R.O. Manning (1976), shamanism can be considered a "profession," and among those persons designated by this term are many who warrant inclusion in a body of material such as that collected here. Additional texts depicting shamans may be found in J. Halifax (1979).

One finds similar prophet-like individuals among religious functionaries known as "mediums," or "spirit mediums," terms which have been particularly favored by British social anthropologists. The actions of such

---

[11] Kapelrud (1967) seems to be making a similar distinction. In his opinion the *nabi*-guilds, which were of Canaanite origin and were only in minor respects different from shamanism, persisted among the Israelites down to the exile.

a person "are believed to be dictated by an extra-human entity which has entered his body or otherwise affected him," and which is above all intent upon communicating something to an audience (Firth, 1969:x-xi). This description is certainly reminiscent of what was just said about shamanism. I.M. Lewis (1981:26–9) in fact criticizes Firth for his overly-scrupulous distinction between "spirit possession," "spirit mediumship," and "shamanism," which he sees as an example of the relatively common tendency of anthropologists to reify "cultural categories and religious and emotional phenomena."

Finally, a word should be said about "diviners." Divination is itself widespread, and its techniques are extraordinarily varied. The latter frequently involve the manipulation and interpretation of physical objects, e.g., the patterns of cracks resulting from placing bones in a fire (ancient China, Cree Indians of Eastern Canada), inspection of the liver of sacrificial animals (ancient Mesopotamia), and the like. Basic to the process is the communication of information (future events, the location of lost or stolen property, the cause of illness) from the spirit world to humans, and it is worth noting that the diviner's message is often not tied in any mechanical way to the manipulations.

It is difficult and perhaps unnecessary to make absolutely clear distinctions among these various roles. In the introduction to *Spirit Mediumship and Society in Africa*, Beattie and Middleton make reference to "divination through spirit mediumship" (1969:xxiii). Indeed, Rigby, like Lewis, argues against "rigid distinctions" among a variety of religious roles, including "prophets, diviners, priests, and mediums" (1975:117). The texts in Chapter II describe practitioners of these various roles. Ojibwa "conjurers" of the shaking tent, Navajo hand-tremblers, and Sioux Yuwipi men are perhaps best classified as diviners, though in their ability to summon and use the assistance of various spirits they resemble shamans. Handsome Lake and Wovoka were leaders of American Indian revitalization movements, but Wovoka was clearly acting the role of a Paiute shaman (Overholt 1982:11–8). There are Siberian shamans and African spirit mediums represented here as well.

Practitioners of these distinct-yet-overlapping roles are comparable because their chief function is the communication of messages or information from the world of the spirits to that of humans.[12] Because they share certain features related to this function, Wilson has proposed calling all these figures "intermediaries" (1980:27–8). Even this term, it must be admitted, is not altogether satisfactory. The priest is also an intermediary of a sort, though his concern to repair and maintain proper relationships between the divine and human worlds centers rather more

---

[12] In a recent article Ringgren (1982:1) defines "prophecy" simply as "the proclamation of divine messages in a state of inspiration."

on the established institutions of the cult than on the communication of direct messages from the deities. The sorcerer or witch is involved in manipulating power to the detriment of others and is thus not an "intermediary" in our sense; yet shamans (who are intermediaries) often engage in similar practices. The distinction between the "intermediary" and the mystic, who is normally little concerned to communicate to others the insights gained from religious experience, is perhaps more absolute. While the activities of biblical prophets may resemble some of these intermediaries more than others, in the strict sense comparability rests on the general social patterns that emerge from studying all of them. In the comments and discussions which follow I will take a somewhat broad and flexible approach to the terminology, most often using "intermediary" and "prophet" as comprehensive, generic terms.

Categories of Comparison

The texts in Chapter II make it abundantly clear that the experience of intermediation is a dynamic process which incorporates actions and responses on the part of both human and divine participants. Although this general idea is familiar to those who have studied biblical prophecy, the social aspects of this process have not been so well recognized.

A fuller understanding of these matters requires that we view the intermediary in a broad cultural context. The kind of sociological and historical information that would make this possible, notoriously scanty for ancient Israel, is more readily available for cultures of more modern times. In this volume we are limited in the amount of detail that can be provided about the cultural setting of the various intermediaries described, but the social aspects of intermediation will be evident in the accounts themselves. The introductions, notes, and bibliography will be of help to those who wish to pursue the matter farther.

The texts reproduced below describe actions and mirror beliefs of persons whose cultures stand at a real distance from us, sometimes temporally and spatially and always in terms of specific cultural content. One does not read of the ecstatic dances of the Siberian shaman or of the assembled Sioux Ghost Dancers, of the shaman's spirit journey to the underworld or of the return of the buffalo and the supernatural destruction of whites which characterized Wovoka's vision and preaching, and feel at once on familiar ground. Nor is it immediately apparent what these and other religious phenomena have in common with each other. In view of this difficulty let me suggest three categories which should be helpful in comparing the following accounts (cf. Wilson, 1980:42–88).

The making of an intermediary

To function as an intermediary entails recognizable, unusual (i.e., non-ordinary) actions and claims. Gwek, the Nuer prophet, displayed possession behavior which included balancing on his head atop a pyramid, nocturnal "yelling and chattering in an unknown tongue," and "turning himself into a goat" (Coriat, 1939:226). The Tungus shaman wore an elaborate costume, played upon a drum, and danced until he or she fell into a trance. All lay claim to some direct communication with a deity.

Such behavior raises the question of the intermediary's mental state, which has sometimes been explained in terms of psychopathology. Eliade (1964:23–6) gives examples of interpretations which assume mental disease or nervous disorder among those destined to become shamans. However, the question is what such symptoms, when they are present, tell us. Consider, for example, the contribution of society itself to the creation and maintenance of "mental illness." From this point of view deviant behavior can be seen to be largely the product of role-playing, which as part of a social system has certain involuntary aspects.

> The individual plays his role by articulating his behavior with the cues and actions of other persons involved in the transaction. The proper performance of a role is dependent on having a cooperative audience. The proposition may also be reversed: having an audience that acts toward the individual in a uniform way may lead the actor to play the expected role even if he is not particularly interested in doing so (Scheff, 1966:56).

Likewise, the intermediary's behavior is, broadly speaking, both defined and affirmed by his or her society. And if this behavior seems to mirror one or another kind of illness, then one must at least say with Eliade that the intermediary is ". . . above all, a sick man who has been cured, who has succeeded in curing himself. Often when the shaman's or medicine man's vocation is revealed through an illness or an epileptoid attack, the initiation of the candidate is equivalent to a cure" (1964:27; cf. also I.M. Lewis, 1981:32). Of great importance is that a person manifesting such (prescribed) behavior is not treated by society as being simply "mentally ill," but as being in possession of powers at least potentially useful to the community. R. Wilson has noted certain common social characteristics of such persons (cf. 1980:46–8 and the literature cited there).

Since not everyone who acts abnormally is considered an intermediary, one must ask about indigenous explanations of this phenomenon. How do members of a society choose among various persons whose behavior might seem to qualify them for the role? Usually one finds something that is accepted as evidence of supernatural designation. This commonly takes the form of personal experiences, such as visions or being possessed by a god. These are often accompanied by symptoms of physical illness, as in the case of Black Elk (Neihardt, 1961:20–47) and Handsome Lake (Parker, 1913:20–6), or by extraordinary behavior such as is common among African spirit mediums (cf. Beattie and Middleton, 1969:50–64, 73–6, and *passim*).

The contemporary Sioux "medicine man," Petaga (Pete Catches), told Arthur Amiotte, whose vision quest he was directing, "I did not ask for my office. My work was made for me and given to me by the other world, by the Thunder Beings. I am compelled to live this way that is not of my own choosing, because they chose me" (1976:29; cf. Ohnuki-Tierney, 1976:178–9). Similarly, B. Myerhoff (1974:99) tells us that the call of a Huichol shaman (*mara'akame*) "comes to the young boy spontaneously in a vision or dream, without any physiological inducement, without deprivation or drugs. But his success in fulfilling the call is far from assured, and actual assumption of the office may not occur until he is well into middle age."

Alternatively, one might be designated by an already-accredited intermediary (cf. Wilson, 1980:51). But this need not exclude supernatural designation. Black Elk, for example, reported his visionary experiences to older shamans for confirmation (cf. Neihardt, 1961:160–5). Even when hereditary transmission is acknowledged as a factor in the selection of a shaman, direct contact with the spirits, as well as more traditional instruction, seem to be requisites for public recognition (Eliade, 1964: 13–23; cf. U. Knoll-Greiling, 1952–53).

In addition every intermediary must ultimately be accepted by some social group in order to carry out his or her duties. An absolutely solitary intermediary would be a contradiction in terms. Social context will therefore always include a "support group," i.e., a clientele, a group of believers and followers, who acknowledge the intermediary's validity and authority. Such groups vary in composition, size, and the power they wield within a given society.[13]

A support group is both an enabling (it grants authority) and a constraining (it has expectations) force in the intermediary's performance. At one level this means that some persons support a specific prophet. At a more fundamental level members of an audience, regardless of the extent to which they agree with the content of what the intermediary says, recognize and affirm the role they see him or her performing. This is evident even in cases where the individual can muster very little apparent support, since no one can be judged a false prophet, failed shaman, or the like unless the institution itself be recognized as valid.

It is, in the final analysis, the group that distinguishes between valid and invalid actions and claims, between authenticity and illness. The process by which this takes place may be quite formal, such as the sha-

---

[13] I. M. Lewis (1971) has discussed this latter point in terms of a distinction between "peripheral" and "central" possession, on which see below.

manic contests reported by Shirokogoroff (cf. Chap. II, 8.3), or casual, as among certain classes of American Indian diviners. In either case accepted criteria are employed. Society's power in the selection of intermediaries is demonstrated in the cases of Qaselid (Chap. II,1) and Yali (Chap. II,15), who where recognized in the absence of any apparent claims on their part.

The texts which follow provide us, therefore, with two perspectives on the coming into being and functioning of an intermediary. From the standpoint of the participants themselves we can see that the making of an intermediary involves some manner of supernatural designation. But we can also see that the social group in which the intermediary operates must in some way validate his or her role.

Behavioral characteristics of the intermediary

Societies authenticate intermediaries partly on the basis of stereotypical behavior such as may be observed in actions accompanying spirit possession, the diviner's manipulation of objects, the arctic shaman's trance-journey, and speech patterned in form and/or content. Among the Tungus the shaman is expected to be able to correctly recite lengthy lists of clan spirits; Black Elk's great vision was dominated by transformations of persons and objects and by symbols like the circle and the number four, all elements common in and valued by the traditional Sioux culture; the audience attending a performance by an Ojibwa shaking tent diviner expects the arrival of specific spirits, who can be recognized by their voices and certain personality characteristics. Indeed, a shamanistic performance can be viewed as a whole series of stereotypical actions (e.g., Ohnuki-Tierney, 1976:179–80), and it is precisely the stereotypical character of such performances which allows the shaman to communicate recognizable meanings to those who observe and participate.[14]

The intermediary's dreams or visions provide further illustration. At first glance these might seem to be the most personal, and therefore idiosyncratic, of experiences. They tend, however, to be highly stereotypical, and the social dynamics which account for this are easy to specify. First, it is probable that visions are generally valued by persons in the intermediary's society. Hallowell (1942:7), for example, notes that in traditional Northern Ojibwa culture certain kinds of dreams were considered necessary for the successful living of life (cf. Wallace, 1959).

---

[14] For example, Haeberlin (1918) has described a shamanistic pattern among the Coast Salish of northwestern North America, one detail of which is that when during the course of a curing ceremony the shaman sang the song of the captured guardian spirit, the patient knew the ceremony had been a success and began to dance and sing. This shamanistic pattern persisted even in the period of intense pressure from intruding whites, and was an important factor in the acceptance by some Indians of the new Indian Shaker religion (cf. Waterman, 1930; M. Smith, 1954; Amoss, 1978).

Second, members of the society recognize that visions have certain uses and value them for that reason. Chief among these functions is contact with the gods or spirits (cf. Lanternari, 1976:322; Jenness, 1935:47; Mendelsohn, 1962; Napier, 1962), and this results in the vision's serving also to legitimate personal power (cf. Amoss, 1977, and Hallowell's discussion of the Ojibwa "shaking tent" in Chap. II, 2) and determine the course of future activities (Lanternari, 1976:322; Jenness, 1935:47–8).

Third, even the specific imagery of visions is quite likely to have been heavily influenced by the society of which the intermediary is a member (cf. Wallace, 1959; Lanternari, 1976; Ridington, 1971). There are many examples of patterned dreams among American Indians. Speaking of the Ojibwa, V. Barnouw (1977:8) says that the fasting visions of young boys and girls "had a rather stereotypical character," the elements of which he briefly sketches. D. Jenness (1935:49–50, 54) says that "in earlier times" the "visions seem to have conformed to a more or less stereotyped pattern," and mentions that fathers typically instructed their sons on what kind of vision to seek. Among the Iroquois there was a "particular type of culturally patterned dream" that was eligible for the guessing rite at the Midwinter Ceremony (Shimony, 1961:182).

Particularly striking confirmation of the stereotypical content of visions comes from cases where the recipient immediately knew how to interpret what was seen. Early in the account of his inaugural vision Black Elk describes a tepee made of clouds with a rainbow door through which he could see "six old men sitting in a row." The oldest of these spoke to him. "His voice," says Black Elk, "was very kind, but I shook all over with fear now, for I *knew* that these were not old men, but the Powers of the World" (Neihardt, 1961:25, emphasis added). At the time of this vision, Black Elk was nine years old. Even allowing for subsequent reflection (Black Elk was 67 when he gave his account to Neihardt), it would seem reasonable to assume that the basis of his "knowledge" about its imagery was traditional Oglala Sioux cosmological conceptions. Or again, consider Don Talayesva, a Hopi Indian from Arizona. After having been initiated into the kachina society (ca. 1898, when he was approximately eight years old), Don's father instructed him to go to the housetop each morning and "pray to the Sun god as he appeared in the east." He did so, and one night in a dream he saw "a strange being . . . in the form of a middle-aged man," who spoke in "a friendly voice" and identified himself as the Sun god. Several years later in a rite connected with the Soyal ceremony Don watched a group of masked dancers (kachinas) enter the kiva[15] and was able to identify one as "representing the Sun god that I had seen in my dream as a boy" (Simmons, 1942:87, 174). One has the impression that Hopi Indians in Don's day knew what

---

[15] An underground chamber in which religious and other activities took place.

the Sun god looked like and expected that when the person and situation were correct he might make an appearance in a dream. We might place in this same category the cases (described below, Chap. II, 1) in which an individual of the Kwakiutl tribe determines through a dream precisely where in the body his or her sickness is located and who will eventually cure it.

Or consider the following two cases. In the spring of his eighteenth year Black Elk undertook a vision quest which resulted in what he referred to as his "dog vision" (Neihardt, 1961:187–91). Several generations later another Sioux Indian, Arthur Amiotte, embarked upon a similar quest (1976). To read these two accounts is to be struck by their similarities, both in the things seen and the order in which they appeared. Both men saw two figures slanting down from heaven toward them, butterflies, birds sitting in a pine tree, soaring eagles, and multitudes of small Sioux children, and both experienced a variety of storm phenomena. Similarly, Myerhoff tells us that among the Huichol Indians of northern Mexico there are several identifiable patterns of peyote visions. Those of the common people were primarily "'for beauty,'" and typically include animals, beautiful colors, and sometimes creatures from the myths. The shaman's dreams, on the other hand, are thought to have "deep meaning" and to contain messages from the gods (1974:165–6; cf. 40–4, 226–7). The contents of the latter seem to be fairly standard, including such things as the revelation of the names by which specific things are to be called during the pilgrimage for peyote (cf. 1974:185–6, especially footnote 25; 219–20). Yet a third type of "culturally structured and recurrent" visionary experiences, quite horrible in their contents, is connected with the eating of "bad peyote" (1974:216–7).[16]

This phenomenon is not limited to American Indians. A. Popov gives us an account of the inaugural trance of a Siberian shaman, during which the "escorting spirit" is supposed to have said nothing, leaving the future shaman "to find out everything himself" (1968:137). This characterization is actually not quite accurate, since when something was judged too difficult to "guess," the escorting spirit explained it specifically (cf. 1968:139). Still, for the most part the candidate was asked to offer an interpretation ("guess") of what he saw, and was highly successful in doing so ("My companion and the old woman slapped their knees in astonishment. 'You are a good guesser!'"; 1968:139–40). This suggests the stereotypical nature of the vision: the candidate already knew the theory and symbolism of shamanism, including where a shaman goes

---

[16] To give one example, "a common ⟨hallucination⟩ is the experience of a man encountering a huge agave cactus in the desert, thinking it is a woman and making love to it" (Myerhoff, 1974:217; for a summary account of the Huichol peyote pilgrimage, cf. Myerhoff, 1976).

during his trance-journies, what he sees there, and what he himself is supposed to do. It might be added that, after regaining consciousness, the future shaman launched into a series of stereotypical activities, including a search for a proper tree from which to construct his drum (1968:145). V. Elwin reports that among the Hill Saora of east-central India shamans typically say that in their visions things are bright when the gods come, but black when the ancestors arrive (1955:476–7).[17]

Thus the group exercises a certain control over the intermediary's behavior, since recognition implies operable criteria of discrimination between authentic and inauthentic behavior, and to win recognition one must conform in some measure to those criteria. The shamanic contest described by Shirokogoroff (Chap. II, 8) is an exceptionally clear example of the evaluation of candidates in terms of how well they met the expectations of the group. Of course, when "society" is said to have an important role in determining the behavior of an intermediary, that term must not be understood in any monolithic way. For while some group support is required for every intermediary, acceptance by the whole community is not. Doubters and rivals are frequent.

The intermediary has room for individual expression, however. Intermediaries within a group are not simply carbon copies of one another. They may be possessed by (or be masters of) different spirits, have different skills, or display idiosyncrasies of costume or behavior. But there is always general conformity to an accepted pattern of behavior. Even actions which seem on the surface altogether out of control can on closer examination usually be located within a larger pattern (cf. Wilson, 1980:63–4.).

The texts in Chapter II describe intermediaries acting in ways characteristic of the roles they have assumed, and reveal, often by implication, the social expectations that accompany their activities.

The Social Functions of Intermediation

In discussing "the social function of intermediation" Wilson (1980:69–86) employs the distinction between "central" and "peripheral" intermediaries in order to designate the relative position of these figures with respect to the society's central institutions. The notion is that differences in social position will entail differences in social function.

The distinction is borrowed from I. M. Lewis's study of possession, or ecstasy. According to him, certain instances of possession may be seen to be "peripheral" on any of three grounds: the possessing spirits "play

---

[17] Cf. also MacGaffey (1977–78:192), who points to the presence of imagery associated with the traditional cults of local tutelary spirits in the visions of the Kongo prophet, Simon Kimbangu. Kane (1974) gives an account of social factors in ritual trance experiences among members of a snake-handling sect in the Southeastern United States.

no direct part in upholding the moral code" of the society, they are foreign spirits originating outside the society in which their victims reside, and/or their "favorite victims" are women and members of other disadvantaged groups within the society (1971:32). Peripheral cults thus embrace disadvantaged groups within a society, and this affects their social functions, which are mainly to raise the status of the intermediary and to press the claims of the deprived group.[18]

But possession also occurs among the more powerful and established segments of society. In such cases it serves to strengthen and legitimize the authority of religious leaders and is "sternly moralistic" in the sense of upholding the established order of the society (cf. Lewis, 1971:29–36; Wilson, 1980:83–6). At this point we can notice a possible overlap in function. Peripheral possession cults can also contribute to overall social stability by giving both the intermediary and his/her support group an acceptable means to vent frustrations and an avenue by which to achieve at least part of their social program.[19]

Such a social-functional analysis is neutral with respect to the reality of the possessing spirits. Lewis makes this point when he says that "the adoption of this sociological line of inquiry does not necessarily imply that spirits are assumed to have no existential reality. Above all, it is not suggested that such beliefs should be dismisssed as figments of the disordered imaginations of credulous peoples. For those who believe in

---

[18] Lewis gives many examples (cf. 1971:66–126). Similarly, Hilger tells us that in Araucanian society (Ardean Highlands of South America) women are scarcely permitted to speak and are limited in expression of certain feelings to a kind of social singing. There is, in fact, only one approved role, shamanistic intermediary of a spirit, in which a woman is allowed to be verbally dominant (cited in Hymes, 1972:45).

[19] One must be cautious when using these categories. First of all, they are highly contextual and take on concrete meaning only with reference to the relation of specific individuals to the various centers of power within a given society. This means, of course, that depending on the point of view from which an intermediary is considered, s/he may be either central (e.g., in the eyes of members of the primary support group) or peripheral (e.g., in the eyes of a given dominant majority within the society). Secondly, there is the problem of translating Lewis's categories, which he uses to describe two types of possession by spirits with their corresponding social manifestations, to discussions of Old Testament prophecy. There is still serious dispute over whether, or to what extent, the Old Testament prophets exhibit possession behavior and may be considered ecstatics (Wilson, 1979 and 1980, can be found on the affirmative side of this debate; Parker, 1978, and Petersen, 1981:25–30, on the negative), and one can therefore question whether it is possible to speak of possession cults in the Old Testament (cf. Long, 1982:251). Even though Petersen has been able to make a strong case for the structural similarity of Lewis's peripheral possession cults to the activities of the "man of god" and the "sons of the prophets" in the Elijah and Elisha narrative, he recognizes the need to proceed with caution in the use of these categories (1981:43–50).

Still, the distinction is useful in that it allows for a more balanced view of the social functions of intermediaries.

them, mystical powers are realities both of thought and experience"
(1971:28). We assert simply that such experiences have tangible social
settings and effects.

The Ghost Dance of 1890 provides a convenient illustration of some
of these points. This movement (cf. Chap. II, 6) had its beginnings
among the Paiute Indians of western Nevada and spread rapidly among
tribes from the Great Basin to the Plains, all of which had by this time
undergone severe cultural stress as the result of white encroachment on
their traditional homelands. Lewis has said that "in its primary social
function, peripheral possession . . . emerges as an oblique aggressive
strategy" (1971:32), and the Ghost Dance was certainly that (though
"oblique" may in this instance be something of an understatement). Its
leader, Wovoka, offered a program for the elimination of the whites and
the improvement of living conditions without the necessity of actually
taking up arms. But if from one point of view Wovoka's message was
considered socially disruptive, it can also be seen as an attempt to foster
stability by bringing about specific social changes. The prophet, among
other things, demanded of his followers that they abandon the traditional
patterns of inter-tribal raiding and warfare.

From the point of view of whites, Indian groups (such as the Navajo)
which did not accept it, and doubting members of groups which did, the
Ghost Dance can be seen as a peripheral cult. But it seems safe to say
that to its adherents it was something more. For while they certainly
recognized their position as peripheral to the emerging dominant culture
and saw the Dance as an opportunity to rectify that situation, viewed
from the inside the Dance had a distinctly central function as well,
namely the reassertion of traditional values and the maintenance of a
stable society based upon them (cf. Overholt, 1978).

As for Wovoka himself, he experienced an enhancement in social
status in his home group and fame which extended far beyond the realm
of his own Paiute people. His improved economic position, directly at-
tributable to his wide-spread reputation, continued for decades after the
end of the movement itself.

Very much the same pattern emerges in the new religious movement
begun among the Seneca Indians by Handsome Lake (cf. Chap. II, 5).
As a result of his revelation and teaching, Handsome Lake's personal
status as a leader of his people was greatly enhanced, and was even recognized in a letter by President Jefferson (Wallace 1972:270–2). In a decade and a half of activity Handsome Lake moved aggressively to deal
with the threatened collapse of Seneca culture following the increased
white American dominance of the late 18th century. He advocated a program which both affirmed elements of traditional Iroquois culture and
encouraged social changes designed to cope with the new situation. For
its adherents the movement pointed toward a new situation of social sta-

bility, or, to use the term employed by Wallace in his general study of "revitalization movements," a new "steady state" (1956).

The activities of Wovoka and Handsome Lake are examples of what are often called millenarian movements, or crisis cults.[20] Such movements may be identified as a special class of peripheral cult, characterized by a cohesive group structure and a definite program of action to ameliorate the deprivation which the members experience. In addition the intermediary often plays an especially important role in the leadership of such cults (cf. Wilson 1980:76–83).

The intermediary's social functions thus seem to cluster around the maintenance of social stability and/or the promotion of social change. Frequently the very fact that a person functions as an intermediary has the result of enchancing his or her social position. Clearly, these functions are not mutually exclusive, as the texts in Chapter II will show.

Some years ago M. Eliade noted that there is often a structural equivalence among "hierophanies" that were widely separated in time. "The process of sacralizing reality is the same," he said, though "the *forms* taken by the process in man's religious consciousness differ" (1964:xvii). Similarly, I have tried to suggest some underlying similarities in the cultural processes of intermediation.

Chapter II contains descriptions of intermediaries in a variety of cultures, arranged by geographical location. According to the program outlined above, the similarities among these men and women should be sought in patterns of social interaction and behavior, rather than in the specific messages they communicate to their audiences. However, one aspect of "message," the social process of its preservation and transmission, is of particular interest to students of biblical prophecy. We will turn specifically to that topic in Chapter III. Finally, Chapter IV will take up briefly the question of what students of biblical prophecy might reasonably hope to learn from such comparisons, and will describe several specific cases in which comparative materials have been utilized in the interpretation of Old Testament prophecy.

[20] There is an enormous literature on these movements which is well worth the attention of anyone interested in biblical prophecy. LaBarre (1971) is an excellent, though by this time dated, survey of this literature. In addition, see the especially important studies by Wallace (1956), Lanternari (1963, 1974), and Burridge (1969). For an application to early Christianity, cf. Gager (1975).

CHAPTER II
TEXTS

The texts presented in this chapter are divided into fifteen sections, some of them lengthy. Precisely because the Old Testament generally omits social details, I have thought it important to include a great deal of such description in these accounts, hoping that this will facilitate an appreciation of the complexity of the social dynamics of intermediation. The editing of the texts has therefore been limited to excerpting materials from still longer selections (indicated by elipses) and minimal changes in punctuation and vocabulary. Foreign words have frequently been eliminated from the text in favor of a translation. Parentheses containing initials standing at the end of a reference note indicate that the note was found in the original text; e.g., (A.I.H.) = A. Irving Hallowell.

An introduction to each section seeks to place the reading in its appropriate ethnographic and historical context. Where possible, something is said about how the text came to be recorded. There are also suggestions for further reading. Because of disparities in the amount of information available to us, and because of special issues which may arise in connection with a given selection, these introductions differ somewhat in length and detail.

Finally, as an aid to reading and comparison, a system of marginal notation calls attention to certain features in the text. The outline given below is based on the "categories of analysis" described in Chapter I. Numbers from this outline stand in the margin opposite portions of the text that illustrate a given characteristic of intermediation. The system is not intended to be an exhaustive analysis of the texts, since the various characteristics often overlap, and such instances cannot always be indicated. Furthermore, some of the characteristics, such as "upholding the established social order" (3.2), tend to be part of the general dynamics of the situation, and do not find expression in just a single paragraph. This stabilizing function of intermediation comes through clearly in Hallowell's *analysis* of his shaking tent data (pp. 71–4 below), and can be glimpsed specifically in various curing ceremonies. But in a broader sense, much of what an intermediary does can be construed as undergirding the society's world view and values. In short the system of notation is meant only to be suggestive. A definitive analysis of a given text would require more careful reflection in light of its specific cultural and historical setting.

Key to the marginal notations:

1.0 THE MAKING OF AN INTERMEDIARY
    1.1   the shaman-to-be is ill
    1.11   initiation effects a cure
    1.2   supernatural designation
    1.21   dreams/visions
    1.3   designation by an accredited intermediary
    1.31   intermediary's role is hereditary
    1.32   formal instruction/informal learning from others
    1.4   group evaluation
    1.41   acceptance by the group
    1.411   faith of the patient
    1.42   rejection by the group
2.0 BEHAVIORAL CHARACTERISTICS
    2.1   stereotypical behavior
    2.11   dreams/visions
    2.12   costume
    2.13   patterned public performance
    2.2   group evaluation/participation
    2.21   contests between intermediaries
    2.3   individuality vs. pattern
3.0 SOCIAL FUNCTIONS
    3.1   raised status of the intermediary
3.11   economic gain/other economic considerations relating to status
    3.2   uphold the established social order
    3.21   diagnose/cure illness
    3.3   encourage social change

THE AMERICAS

1

An Insider's View of the Dynamics of Shamanism

Introduction

Living in a series of sea-coast villages along the northern shore of Vancouver Island and the adjacent mainland coast of British Columbia, the Southern Kwakiutl Indians were part of a larger Northwest Coast cultural community extending from extreme northern California to southern Alaska in which "languages and systems of marriage and descent differ, but the main religious ideas and ritual organizations are alike even to the sharing of nomenclature" (Goldman, 1975:20). From Puget Sound north, including the territory of the Kwakiutl, rugged coastal mountains and dense rain forests caused the people to be dependent upon the sea and rivers for transportation and a major portion of their livelihood. There was no agriculture, and while the Kwakiutl were adequate as hunters of land animals, it was fish (five species of salmon, plus herring, halibut, cod, smelt, and candlefish), sea mammals, and vast flights of migratory waterfowl which provided the main resource base for a highly-developed sedentary culture (cf. Drucker, 1965:1–9).

Much of what is known about traditional Southern Kwakiutl culture is the result of the work of the famous anthropologist, Franz Boas, whose study of these people began in 1885 and continued until his death in 1942. Boas himself made a dozen visits to the Kwakiutl, and in addition trained George Hunt, a half-blood Indian, "to write his language phonetically and serve as informant and field worker" (Goldman, 1975:10; cf. Boas, 1930:part 1, ix-xviii). Hunt in fact did much of the field work, sending reports to Boas in Kwakiutl with an interlineal, literal translation into English, and thus served as a "'mediator' between the alien worlds of the Indian and the 'Western' scholar" (Goldman, 1975:vii). In the end the Boas-Hunt collaboration resulted in nearly ten thousand pages of published, and a large quantity of unpublished, materials on the Kwakiutl, a truly monumental work of ethnography. But as Goldman comments,

> It is not its size alone that gives the Kwakiutl ethnography its prodigious value; it is its authenticity. Unlike many modern field studies that exhibit the writer's methods and theoretical alle-

giances more than they do their subject, the Boas and Hunt ethnography is in the words and imagery of the Kwakiutl. By freeing
ethnography from its confused and labyrinthine entanglement
with the alien psyche and intellectual predilections of the ethnographer, Boas and Hunt created the foundations for a genuine ethnology. (1975:vii-viii)

Codere, who began her own fieldwork among the Kwakiutl twenty-one
years after Boas' last visit, also has high praise for the results of this
lengthy collaboration, saying that "only in field work is it possible to be
closer to an actual alien culture" (Boas, 1966:xxx).

Among the Hunt and Boas texts, there is an account which illustrates
quite vividly the complicated social dynamics of shamanic activity. The
narrative is in fact autobiographical, with George Hunt describing events
that occurred "about 1870 or 1874," when he was in his early teens (Boas,
1966:xxix, 121, 125). According to the story, the young Hunt, who goes
by his Kwakiutl name Giving-Potlatches-in-the-World, was skeptical
about shamans and decided to undertake a test of their integrity. Toward
this end, when the opportunity presented itself, he submitted to instruction by some shamans, and subsequently performed his own curing ceremonials, acquiring the shaman's name, "Qaselid." Qaselid's cures were
spectacularly successful. Even so, the new shaman's skepticism about the
profession, especially as practiced by others, was not altogether overcome.

Altogether, Hunt gave Boas four accounts of these events, of which
the one reprinted here is the longest and the last. According to Boas, the
discrepancies among the accounts illustrate Hunt's "vacillating attitude"
about the experiences and how to report them. His final assessment,
however, is that "the principal inference to be drawn from (them) is that
notwithstanding the knowledge of fraud, a deep-seated belief in the
supernatural power of shamanism persists, even among the sophisticated" (Boas, 1966:123, 125).

In the section on shamanism in his *Kwakiutl Ethnography*
(1966:120–48) Boas summarizes a number of accounts of how various
men and women became shamans. A feature relatively common to them
is the report that prior to his or her initiation the person was sick, was
visited by a supernatural power in a dream, and as a result, was cured of
the illness. Often the type of sickness is not specified. Of the cases in
which it is two involved smallpox, one an apparent intrusion of a supernatural power into the person's body, and a fourth was said to have been
"pretended." Hunt described his own experience to Boas in 1900: "When
I was about thirteen years old, I fell into the fire in a fit and burnt myself
badly. After this I was subject to fainting fits. . . . I had to be held, because I acted like one wild. When I recovered I felt as though I had been
in another world and told my friends what I had seen." After about ten

months of such attacks, a man in the form of a killer whale appeared to him in a dream and announced that on the next day he would perform his first cure. A markedly different case was that of an old shaman who transmitted his powers to his son, becoming powerless in the process. It seems to have been primarily the "head" (or "full," or "chief's") shaman, who could both cure and throw disease, whose "office" was hereditary. Such shamans had "a definite position in the political organization of the tribe," viz. they belonged to the chiefs of the various tribal subdivisions, whom they protected by "throwing disease into" their enemies (Boas, 1966:145–6).

Hunt's narrative of his own shamanic experiences is remarkable for its length and the amount of detail it provides for us. It serves as a good illustration of the categories of analysis described in Chapter I.

There is a vast literature on the native cultures of the Northwest Coast of North America. Specifically on the Kwakiutl, a volume edited by H. Codere (Boas, 1966) provides a useful compendium of Boas' writings, at the center of which is a previously unpublished manuscript on "Kwakiutl ethnography." Codere also includes an evaluation of Boas' contribution to ethnography (xi-xxxii) and a lengthy bibliography of his publications (423–31). Those who wish to pursue the topic of Kwakiutl religion further may also consult two excellent recent studies, Goldman (1975) and Walens (1981). An interpretation of the Qaselid narrative can be found in Levi-Strauss (1963:169–76). For a discussion of the sucking technique in shamanic curing cf. Bahr (1977).

The text is excerpted from Boas (1930:part 2, 1–40); stories about four other shamans can be found in the following pages of that volume (41–56). As an aid to the reader, I have further subdivided the many lengthy paragraphs, and have added the section titles. The footnotes will give some hints as to the world view in terms of which Kwakiutl shamanism must ultimately be understood. Where the text renders a name in both Kwakiutl and in translation, the former has been eliminated. Whenever possible, Goldman's simplified orthography, omitting diacritical markings and certain phonetic symbols, has been utilized. The capitalization of elements in hyphenated names, which sometimes seems inconsistent, follows the printed text.

Text (Boas, 1930: part 2, 1-40)

Qaselid's "motivation"

I desired to learn about the shaman, whether it is true or whether it is made up and (whether) they pretend to be shamans.[1] Now I knew the

---

[1] Consistently throughout his narrative, Hunt voices his skepticism about the genuineness of the shamans—they only pretend to be sick when they wish to be intitiated, they

one who is referred to as a great new shaman of the Nakwaxdax[2], who has the name Making-alive and about the shaman of the Lalasiqwala, who has the name Bringing-Life-out-of-Woods, for they were my intimate friends, the two shamans. And so I went to the Nakwaxdax who were living at Hanging-at-Mouth.

Qaselid's commissioning and initiation

Now as soon as night came I heard a shaman singing his sacred song in the woods at (a place) not far from the rear of the village. Then I asked Causing-to-be-well, the head chief of the Nakwaxdax, for it was his house where I stayed, "Who, indeed, is the shaman singing his sacred song behind the houses?" said I to him. Then he said, "It is the new great
3.21   shaman Making-alive, who is going to cure this Place-of-Home-Coming, the son of Potlatch," said he. "We are all about to go in with the women and the children to this house of Potlatch, for that is where Place-of-Home-Coming is lying down sick," said Causing-to-be-well to me. It was

---

use sleight of hand tricks when performing their cures, and the like (cf., for example, pp. 32, 39–40, 41–2, 54–5). Indeed, he himself resorted to such a trick in his own curing ceremonies. We should be cautious about taking these expressions of doubt at face value, however.

Boas notes that for several reasons it is difficult to get reliable testimony from a shaman. First of all, both they and their audience are perfectly aware that tricks are employed in the ceremonies. Though the exposure of these does "not weaken the belief in the 'true' power of shamanism," shamans are eager to bolster their power by a dramatic use of them. Another important reason for the "difficulty in obtaining truthful statements is based on the relation between Indian and white. The Indian likes to appear rational and knows that shamanistic practices are disbelieved by the whites. So he is liable to assume a critical attitude, the more so the closer his contacts with the whites. This is still further emphasized by the attitude of the Canadian government and the missionaries, who relentlessly persecute most of the Indian practices" (1966:121).

Taking specific note of the skepticism displayed by the first sentence of this text, Boas comments that "at other times, when in a more communicative mood, his (Hunt's/Qaselid's) belief in his own experiences stands out very clearly." He then reports their discussion of these matters in 1900, which has been mentioned above. One specific example relating to the second difficulty may be noted. In the 1900 conversation Hunt described his cure at Ft. Rupert of a man named Calumniated, during the course of which he retrieved the mummy of a dead shaman and integrated it into his performance of a sucking cure. This detail does not appear in the present text, and Boas commented that Hunt "was particularly afraid that the use of the corpse might become known and would cause trouble with government and the missionaries" (1966:123). However, it bears repeating that at the end of his discussion of Hunt's various accounts of his own shamanic experiences Boas concludes that "a deep-seated belief in the supernatural power of shamanism persists, even among the sophisticated" (in the ranks of whom he, presumably, includes his informant). Indeed, the assumption that there can be genuine shamans is explicit at the very end of the present text (cf. p. 58).

[2] "Nakwaxdax" and "Lalasiqwala" are the names of Kwakiutl "tribes" (i.e., separate village units; cf. Boas 1966:37–41). Other such names, like "Gapenox" and "Koskimo," will appear as the narrative proceeds, and can be recognized by their context.

not long that Causing-to-be-well stopped speaking, saying his words to me when four men came wearing red cedar bark around their heads and round red cedar bark tied around their necks. Their faces were black-   2.12
ened with charcoal. They wore belts of flat red cedar bark. As soon as they came into the house they stood up inside of the doorway. Then spoke not aloud one of them when he said, "We come walking that we may all go into the house to witness our friend Making-alive, as he will try to make alive this our friend Place-of-Home-Coming," said he. Then three of them said, "Get up quickly," while they all were covered with eagle down.[3] Then they went out of the house and they never laughed. I asked Causing-to-be-well, "Who are these four men? What are they? Cannibal dancers?"[4] said I to Causing-to-be-well. Then he answered me laughing and said, "These are our great shamans, the four who came walking to us. That one has the name Fool, who spoke first, and that is Cause-of-Falling-down and Bringing-Life-out-of-Woods and Life-Owner. These are our great, feared shamans for they can throw (sickness)," said he to me.

Then Causing-to-be-Well asked me to get ready also, for he was get-ting ready with his wife to go to witness (the performance). Now we went out of the house and we went into the house of Potlatch. Then we were asked by Fool to sit down in the middle of the left hand side of the house. Then came in all the men and all the women and children and not even one of them was smiling as they came in and they did not talk loud. Only they did not come in, the menstruating young women. As soon as they were all inside the four shamans took a board for beating time and put it

---

[3] The use of eagle down was an important feature of shamanic and other ceremonials among the Kwakiutl, though I have found no direct discussion of the reason for this. Goldman (1975:121) comments that it is "a symbol of wealth," and in a caption Walens calls it "the visible manifestation of supernatural power . . . an essential part of Kwakiutl ritual" (1981:plate 13). It seems worth noting that eagles "have an important place in the Kwakiutl metaphorization of their world, and the characteristics of eagle behavior provide a direct analogy to the behavioral and motivational principles of human action" (Walens, 1981:106–8). In the description of his first cure given in 1900 Hunt/Qaselid told Boas of being provided with neck and head rings covered with eagle down, and said, "As soon as the down touched me I felt as though I had been hit over the head. Later on the people told me that at this moment I had run back into the woods. I did not know what was happening" (1966:122).

[4] The cannibal, or *himatsa*, dancer is a central figure in the Kwakiutl winter ceremoni-als. According to Walens, the time of these ceremonials "is in every sense a special time . . . when the motion of the universe is brought to a stop, when all events become coter-minous, when the Mouth of Heaven opens and the powerbeings come from their worlds dressed in their costumes, the blinding light of their power streaming from their bodies as from the sacred quartz crystals and filling the room as does the eagle down trailing from their headdresses. This is the time when the spirits display their beauty and their power before the men of their covenant, and when they give to men the knowledge necessary to rule the world (1981:138; cf. 37–163 and Boas, 1966:171–298, Goldman, 1975:86–121).

down in the rear of the house in front of the song leaders. And also this, the shamans took batons and distributed them among the song leaders. That one also, Fool, took eagle down and feathered all the song leaders and all the spectators. As soon as he had finished, the song leaders beat fast time. They had not been doing so very long when they lifted their batons. It was not very long before they again beat fast time. Then it was not very long before they lited their batons. Then the shaman came singing his sacred song on the right hand side of the house. Now the four shamans went out of the door of the house and the song leaders beat fast time again. Again they lifted their batons. Now came singing his sacred song the shaman, at the seaside of the house. Again beat fast time the song leaders. It was Fool who was leading, coming into the house at the door.

3.21   Then the new shaman came next to him singing his sacred song. Behind him came the three shamans like the attendants of the cannibal
2.13   dancer, whom we call, "those upon whom he leans." Now they went around the fire in the middle of the house. They went around four times as he was singing his sacred song and swinging his rattle. Then he sat down in front of the place where Place-of-Home-Coming was sitting, the sick one. The four shamans went by twos standing on each side of Place-of-Home-Coming, who was naked. Now Making-alive felt of the chest of Place-of-Home-Coming while he was just all the time singing his sacred song; but not for a long time had Making-alive been feeling of the chest of Place-of-Home-Coming when Fool asked Skin-dressing-Woman, the mother of Place-of-Home-Coming, to take a new dish with fresh water in it as a dish for wetting (the mouth) of the shaman. Now Skin-dressing-Woman took a new dish, which was ready on the floor, to give to Fool. Then Fool put down the dish, the receptacle for wetting (the mouth), at the right side of Making-alive. Then Making-alive put his right hand into the water that was in the dish, the receptacle for wetting (the mouth), and he scooped up the water and put it into his mouth while he was pressing with his left hand on the chest of Place-of-Home-coming. As soon as he had the water in his mouth he blew it on the place that was being pressed by him. Then the shaman sucked it. And so he was sucking for a very long time when he lifted his head and took out of his mouth the blood in his right hand, and he squeezed the blood so that it dripped into the water in the dish, the receptacle for wetting (the mouth).

2.13   When the blood was all out, he stood up and sang his sacred song, going around the fire in the middle of the house. Then he stretched out
3.21   his left hand, opening out his fingers and something stuck, (that looked) like a worm, in the middle of the palm of his hand. That was referred to by Fool as the sickness. Then he went around (the fire) and threw upward the sickness. He sat down near the sick man and blew on his chest; but not really for a long time had he been blowing when he stopped. He

sucked only once, for he obtained right away the sickness. When they do not get the sickness when they suck the first time, then they only get the sickness when they have sucked four times. Then Making-alive arose. Around him were standing the four shamans and I saw that they secretly talked to one another. Now they probably finished their talking. Then Making-alive sang again his sacred song and walked out from among the four shamans. He walked around the fire in the middle of the house, swinging his rattle while the song leaders were not beating fast time. As soon as he came to the place from which he had started and where were standing the four shamans, he gave his rattle to Fool. Fool told the song leaders to go ahead and beat time on the boards.

Then Making-alive pressed both his hands against his stomach as he was going around the fire in the middle of the house, as though he were a drunk man. Now he tried to vomit.[5] Four times he went around the fire in the middle of the house, then he vomited blood and he caught it with his left hand. Now there was among it what was referred to by Fool as quartz, among the blood when Making-alive opened his fingers. Then Fool dipped a cup into the water and poured it into his hand in the middle of the quartz crystal[6] so that the blood came off. Then it was shining. Now he held on the palm of his hand the quartz crystal, as he stretched out his left hand. Then Fool and the three other shamans followed him as he went around the fire in the middle of the house and Fool said as they walked following Making-alive, "Do you not now wish to become a shaman and to let this great shaman go ahead and throw this quartz crystal into the stomach of the one who wishes to become a shaman?" said he. Then not one man answered him. Now Fool told the song leaders to go ahead and beat fast time on the board. As soon as the song leaders were beating fast time on the board Making-alive pressed to-

2.13

1.2

[5] Vomiting is a frequently encountered phenomenon in Kwakiutl religion. A shaman may vomit, as here, in the course of a curing ceremony, and vomiting may play a part in the making of a shaman. An example of the latter is the case of Fool. Before he became a shaman, he befriended a wolf, who later appeared to him as a supernatural being and still later participated with other wolves in curing Fool of smallpox by rubbing his body with white foam they had vomited and then licking it clean. The special wolf then "vomited his supernatural power into him at the pit of his stomach (and) in a dream . . . explained to him that now he was a shaman" (Boas, 1930:41–5). At the Grease Feast candlefish oil drops into the wildly blazing fire from a "vomiter beam" near the ceiling of the house, and the guests are nauseated from the quantity of oil they are expected to consume. Vomiting seems to be a symbol of "transformation," which Goldman judges to be "perhaps the central idea of Kwakiutl religious thought." Candlefish oil is considered to be a "female substance," and thus the analogy between vomiting and birth is "a rather obvious association for the Kwakiutl." However, for them "vomiting does not . . . merely replicate the idea of birth. It transforms the idea of birth into the masculine process of killing, and then of restoring to life" (Goldman, 1975:161–2, 201).

[6] The Kwakiutl consider quartz crystals, often vomited by a wolf, to be a source of beneficient power (Walens, 1981:109).

gether his hands and threw the quartz crystal. Fool who was following (him) looked upward watching the quartz crystal. Then he said it was flying about in the house. Now Fool came and stood still in front of the place where I was sitting. He said, "O shamans, important is what has been done by the supernatural quartz for it went into this our friend here, into this Giving-Potlatches-in-the-World," said he, naming my Indian name. "Now this one will be a great shaman," said he. Then all the men turned their faces looking at me where I was sitting. As soon as he finished all went out, the men and women and children, out of the house.

Now we all went into our houses for it was late at night. And so I was ready to lie down when the old woman, whose name was Throwing-away came and sat down near (the place) where I was sitting. She whispered as she said, "Go outside that we may talk together at the seaside (of the house) there," said she, as she arose and went out. But I went out also, not far from her. As soon as I had gone out of the door of the house I saw two men standing at the seaside of the house. Then came the one, that Making-alive, and took hold of my right hand and said, "Come, friend, and let us go," said he, as he pulled me to walk behind the houses. Now we went into the woods and we sat down at the foot of a thick spruce tree.

Now I heard men whispering together. Then spoke one of the men, behold, it was Fool, and he said, not loud, "We have come, we have come, friends invited by Healing-Woman with our great friend Giving-Potlatches-in-the-World, that he now may come to be among us, in our quality of shamans. Now, friends, let us pray our great friend to accept what I am going to say, that our great friend may not make ashamed this new shaman Making-alive who threw into his stomach the quartz which makes great shamans as it goes into the stomach, for he only does not feel it yet. So now he will reply to what I have said to him," said he to me. Now I did not see Cause-of-Falling-down, as he was sitting near to where I was sitting on the ground, for it was very dark that night. Then he spoke and said, "Go ahead friend Giving-Potlatches-in-the-World, go on and take this what makes it easy to obtain property, only waiting for the amount of payment for shamanistic services from the chiefs, when their children are sick and (what is paid) to us shamans here. Let us now have you for a chief and do come among us," said he. Then spoke Qasnomalas. He said, "Good was your word, Cause-of-Falling-down, when you said that we should have our great friend as a chief. Now let him know all the secret ways of the shamans, in case he should answer kindly our speech as we were trying to get him to come among us," said he.

Now I replied to their speeches. I said, "Good are your words, friends, for now you say that I shall be among you. And so I shall look into my heart tonight. I shall tell you tomorrow night," said I to them.

1.41

1.42

3.11

1.32

Then all the shamans begged me not to talk about what they had said to me. Then spoke Making-alive. He said, "O, friend Giving-Potlatches-in-the-World, do not by any means fail to hold these words of our friends here, else it would be a shame if you should not join me, I mean this, that you should really make up your mind to come among us that you may be always happy as we all are in this way," said he. Now we stopped our speeches for a while after this. 1.3

We all went home to our houses. Then at once I went to bed. For a long time I did not go to sleep that night for I was thinking what was to be my answer to the words of the shamans to me. Then it occurred to me that I was the principal one who does not believe in all the ways of the shamans, for I had said so aloud to them. Now I had an opportunity by what they said that I should really learn whether they were real or whether they only pretended to be shamans. Now I made up my mind to go among them and I went to sleep after this.

As soon as day came in the morning I arose and went out of the house. When I went out, one of the young men who has the name Gwayosdedzas, saw me coming walking and he came and stood on the ground where I was standing. Then he questioned me. He said, "Have you not felt the quartz crystal of the liars, the shamans, the one that they referred to that was thrown into your stomach?" said he to me. He meant that he really did not believe the shamans and he said this aloud to them. Then I said to him, "I did not feel it." He said, "You will never feel it, for these are just great lies what the shamans say," said he as he left me. 1.4

Then I went into our house and saw Causing-to-be-well who was building a fire. Then he called me to sit by his side. He whispered and questioned me. He said, "What did you dream of last night? I mean this, what was done by the new shaman Making-alive to you?" said he. And I said I had had no dream. Then he laughed. He said, "You will never dream about the ways of the true shaman-maker for those are just lies what the shamans say," said he. Then I laughed. I said to him, "Now I shall wait for what is going to happen with what Making-alive did to me. I shall not feel it," said I to him. 1.42

Now I found out that all the shamans of the Nakwaxdax were angry with Making-alive, because he said that he had thrown the quartz crystal into my stomach, for I was a visitor, and so it was said that all the shamans would be ashamed if I did not feel that anything had happened to me. Now I really made up my mind to go among the shamans for they had said that they all would teach me all their ways. As soon as I had finished my breakfast with Causing-to-be-well I went out of the house and I walked towards the north end of the village of Hanging-at-Mouth. As soon as I came to the end I went into the woods and I went behind the houses coming back. As soon as I came to the rear of the house of Causing-to-be-well an old woman came to head me off. The woman came 1.42

out of the woods, for she was a shaman woman whose name was Qulen-tsesamaga. She asked me to go into the woods following the trail, "that you go and talk with our friends," said the woman to me. Now the woman went home to her house.

I walked following the trail into the woods. I arrived at the foot of a thick spruce tree. Then I saw Fool hiding at the foot of the tree. As soon as I had gone to the place where he was hiding he requested that we should go into the woods; and so Fool went ahead. I followed him. Then we arrived at the lake of the river of Hanging-at-Mouth. And so I saw a house there, the house of the Cannibal Dancer who disappears in winter when the Nakwaxdax have their winter ceremonial, and the one to which those go who pretend to be sick, who wish to be made shamans by Healing-Woman.

We went in at the door of the house, the house, the receptacle of the supernatural power, for that is the name of the house, and I was asked by Fool to go and sit down in the rear of the house where were sitting Making-alive and Qasnomalas and Cause-of-Falling-down and Bringing-Life-out-of-Woods and Life-Owner and Togomalis and the women shamans, Shaman-Woman and Qulaltalidzemga. As soon as I was seated, Fool spoke. He said, "He has come, our great friend here, friends. He came here, he came into this great place where we are sitting, this which is not known to all the uninitiated men, the secret ways of the shamans. So let us listen to the way of the mind of our great friend Giving-Potlatches-in-the-World. Now you will reply, friend Giving-Potlatches-in-the-World, for really our friends wish that you come among us," said he. Immediately I replied to his words. I said, "Now you all listen to what I am going to say, friends. And so I shall know all the ways in which the shamans act. Evidently you will teach them to me, for I have resolved in my mind to go among you," said I to them.

1.32

Then replied chief Endeavoring-to-Invite who is not a shaman, for he is only a song leader (a wise man), for he gives advice to the shamans what they are to do. But chief Causing-to-be-well is different; he owns the shamans on the opposite side of the numaym[7] of Endeavoring-to-Invite which is the numaym Sisenle. Causing-to-be-well is chief of the numaym Tsitsemeleqala. Then Endeavoring-to-Invite said, "O, friends, now we got this our great friend. Take care, friends, and let us begin to teach him the beginning of the ways of the one who wishes to be a shaman, the one who faints and who trembles with his body when the quartz crystal is thrown into his stomach. Now go on, friend Life-Owner, and try to pretend to faint that it may be seen by Giving-Potlatches-in-the-World here from you," said he.

1.32

---

[7] The numayma (literally, "one kind") are subdivisions within each village, and represent "the ultimate units bound together by strict social obligations" (Boas, 1966:37).

Then Life-Owner sat down on the right hand side of the house. For   1.32
a long time lasted his breathing. Then he was turning on his back and he
stretched out. Then he trembled with his body. Then four shamans went
and took hold of him as he went around in the house and he cried, "Haai,
haai, haai," trembling with his body. As soon as he reached near the door
of the house he stopped. Then Life-Owner stopped breathing as he lay
down on his back.

One of the shamans, that Fool, spoke, for he was holding Life-   1.32
Owner. He said, "The breath of our friend here has jumped out. Now I
shall feel of him, friends," said he, as he sat down by the side of Life-   3.21
Owner, on his right hand side. Then he felt of the middle of the lower
end of his sternum, and of his navel. For a long time he was feeling of it.
Then he blew on what he referred to as a swelling inside at the upper
end of the stomach of Life-Owner. But he had not been blowing very
long at his stomach when Life-Owner began to breathe. Then he trembled with his body. Now Fool arose and spoke. He said, "O friends, now
listen that you may know why our friend did thus. This came into his
stomach, this supernatural power," said he. Then I was told by Cause-of-
Falling-down, that I should watch all the actions of Life-Owner, for this
was the first of the ways of the shamans, the way Life-Owner was acting.

Then Qasnomalas arose and sat down by the side of Life-Owner who
was still lying down on his back on the floor. Then Qasnomalas felt of the
upper part of his navel. He blew on it. He had not been blowing long
when Life-Owner opened his eyes and sat up. Then he spoke, He said,
"O friends! What may have been my way of being thus or (my) being
made foolish," said he. Then Qasnomalas just said, "You were dead; you
were just brought to life by our friend Fool," said he. Then sat down
Qasnomalas with Life-Owner, for he was now well.

Then Fool spoke. He said, "This is the beginning. Now friend, you   1.32
will lie down among the graves every night, always, so that they may
believe that you are a shaman." Then next is the fainting, the trembling   2.1
of the body, always at night; the singing of two sacred songs for healing
the sick; the singing of two sacred songs for trying to catch the soul of the   2.13
sick one who is nearly dead; the singing of two sacred songs for putting
the ring of hemlock and of white shredded cedar bark on the sick one;
the blowing on the top of the head of the sick one when his soul is not   3.21
right; the feeling of the stomach of the shaman when the cause of his
shamanism is not right; the feeling when he tries to find the sickness of
the patient; the feeling for the child of a pregnant woman when the child
does not lie properly in the womb of the woman, for that is always a
reason for calling the shaman and he goes to put right the child; then
also when is eating the shaman.

As soon as a person walks behind him, then the shaman at once falls   1.32
on his back and trembles with his body. Then he bites the edge of his

2.13 tongue and he sucks out the blood and pretends to vomit. Then he says
that it jumped into him the soul of the man who walked behind his back
while he was eating; no matter whether it was a woman or a child or even
a dog; then he falls on his back and trembles with his body and he pretends to vomit the blood of his tongue. Then for a long while he tries to
get it and he vomits out the soul. As soon as he has vomited what he
refers to as the soul, the man, the owner of the soul, sits down and the
shaman sets the soul on top of his head. Then he sings his sacred song.
As soon as he has finished singing his two sacred songs, he blows on the
top of the head of the man. As soon as he has finished the shaman presses
it down with both hands. Now he says that the soul has gone down at the
crown of the head of the man, for that is referred to by the shamans as
the doorway of the soul of the man, the crown of the head. Therefore the
shaman does this.

1.32   As soon as the child of a chief is very ill and also when a chief is very
ill, they give up trying in vain to give medicines of various kinds. Then
3.21 he sends his attendant to ask the shaman to come and cure him. Right
away the shaman who has been named follows the one who was sent that
2.13 he may go and try to cure (the patient). As soon as they enter the house
the shaman is asked by the father of the patient to sit down on the right
hand side of the sick one. The shaman just stares at the sick one who is
now naked. When he has been there awhile feeling about the stomach
or the chest of the sick boy, the shaman speaks. He says, "Great is the
sickness here. Now clear our house that I may try to obtain supernatural
power in the woods towards evening," says he as he arises and goes out
of the house.

1.32   Then he goes into the house of the dreamer, for the dreamer does
not cure sick persons, for he is not given the power by the shaman-maker
3.21 to cure sick persons, but he is given the power to feel the sickness. They
are not called by the name shaman for this is just their name, dreamer,
a common name. However a creature of the shamans is the dreamer, for
he listens all the time for the sayings of the sick people when they point
out with the first finger where they feel very ill in the chest or in the
stomach, and all this is found out by the dreamers and they go to tell all
this to the shamans of their numaym. For this reason I call the dreamer
the eyes of the shamans, for as soon as he finds out everything about the
sickness of a sick man, he at once calls secretly all the shamans to go into
the woods. As soon as all the shamans are seated on the ground the
dreamer speaks. He tells the shamans the place of the sickness seen by
him in the person who is very sick. As soon as he has finished telling
them, one of the shamans speaks. He asks his friends about the kind of
sickness that the patient will have, whether a fly went into him or
whether it is the reason of the winter ceremonial or whether it has been
thrown by a shaman or whether it is sickness or whether the shaman-

maker went into him. "Now you will pick out one of those named by me," says he. Then all the shamans are just quiet. One of them speaks after this. He says, "O friends, I think it is a sickness that makes lie down the patient," says he. Then he takes eagle down and gives it to the shaman who is to cure the sick person, the one who goes to feel of the sick person. That is the reason why he goes to the house of the dreamer, that he is to call secretly all the shamans to go into the woods and also to listen to the dreamer when he tells them where the sickness of the sick person is.

After this has been done the shaman is called who had gone to feel of the sick person, and he succeeds in one attempt to suck (out the sickness), if he makes the down stick on the palm of his left hand, (the down) which is pretended to be the sickness. "Now you will go around the fire in the middle of the house singing your sacred song as you are going." When he arrives at the starting place, he presses on his mouth the blood-covered down which is sticking on, the pretended sickness and he draws it into the mouth and swallows it. "Then you blow on the place where it is sticking. Then clasp your hands together and the song-keepers will beat fast time." Then he throws up what is referred to as the sickness, the blood-covered down, but he has just swallowed it. Then it is believed by those who do not know the ways of the shamans. That is the reason why the down sticks on his hand, the blood, for long before this the shaman put the down between the inner upper lip and the gums before he goes in. It is not apparent although he rinses his mouth before he begins to heal (the sick). It does not come off. As soon as he has made the cure, the first thing he does is to bite the edge of his tongue and when he sucks the sick person the blood comes out of his tongue. Then the shaman raises his head. Then the down mixed with blood comes. (There are) many shamans who suck the sick person and the blood comes out from the gums. This is an easy way to obtain the blood when it is this way with the blood of the gums. It is a good shaman who does this, but it is difficult when the shaman bites the edge of his tongue for it is very painful, and for a long time it does not stop bleeding, even a long time after he has stopped sucking the one who is being healed, although he rinses out his mouth with cold water. The blood does not stop flowing. But it is very easy to get blood from the gums, for the blood only comes when the shaman sucks strongly. After he has stopped sucking, the gums stop bleeding. After he has sucked he rinses out his mouth with cold water and immediately the gums stop bleeding after that.

Now the killer-whale is the shaman-maker of the shamans who have for their chief Endeavoring-to-Invite, the head chief of the numaym Sisenle of the Nakwaxdax; and it is said, otherwise is Causing-to-be-well, who (also) owns shamans, for Causing-to-be-well is the chief of the numaym Tsitsemeleqala of the Nakwaxdax. It is said, the toad is the one

[right margin markers:]
1.32
2.13
3.21

1.32

(who) makes his shamans. It is said, the Magic-of-the-Woods is the shaman-maker of the shamans of chief Owner-of-Throwing-away- (Property), for Owner-of-Throwing-away is the head chief of the numaym Chiefs'-group of the Nakwaxdax. It is said that Warrior-of-the-world is the shaman-maker of the shamans of chief Potlatch, for Potlach is the head chief of the numaym Great-ones. It is said that Quick-moving-Woman, the Mouse-Woman, is the shaman-maker of the shamans of Haqalal, the head chief of the numaym Temltemlels.

1.32   And one each is the dreamer of each of the chiefs of the various numaym who watches for the kinds of sickness of all the men and the
3.21   women and the children, and he informs the shamans regarding the sick persons who have been seen by him. And so therefore, the shamans know early the place of the sickness in the body of the person. This is often done by the shamans when they say that they dream of the sickness that is said to be on the left hand side of the chest of the person; for, indeed, the shaman just follows the words of the dreamer. It is he, the dreamer, who tells the shaman what is heard by him, spoken about the feeling of weakness of the people when they talk that they think that they do not keep together with their souls. Then the shaman says right away that he dreamed that he tried to catch his soul.

1.32   Immediately the man referred to by the shaman as the one who has no soul begs the shaman to have mercy on him and to try to get his soul
1.411 that it may come back to him. As soon as night comes he builds a fire in the middle of the house of the person who has no soul, and then is set right by the shaman the soul of the man. And so this is the reason why I say that the ways of the shaman are (according to) what is said by the dreamer; for the one who has the name Made-to-be-Foolish is the dreamer of the shamans of Endeavoring-to-Invite whom I now joined, for Made-to-be-Foolish is the son of Fool, the shaman. Made-to-be-Foolish is the only one who owns the right to get the bodies to be eaten by the cannibal dancers of the Nakwaxdax, when the Nakwaxdax have their winter ceremonial in winter.

1.32   Now I was told just to follow the instructions given by the shamans to me, according to everything that I talked about in this writing. Now I
2.1   really resolved to pretend to be a shaman. Now I fainted and, before it was really daylight in the morning, I went to the graves and I sat down and was waiting for those to wake up who belong to the Kwakiutl. As soon as I saw one man walking along I arose so that he should see me. Then I started and went home. Now that man talked about seeing me among the graves.

The first cure

3.21   I had not been doing this long before I went to Landotter-Point, the village of the Lalasiqwala. As soon as I had thrown my anchor stone into the water the late chief of the Lalasiqwala, the late Getting-Rich, came. He spoke and said, "Welcome, child; welcome, you have come, you have come being sent for to come to this my grandson Food-Owner, who dreamed about you that you would come and take out his great sickness, this one who is now given up by the shamans of my tribe, the Lalasiqwala. Now he said that he had a dream last night that you came to take out this his sickness. Therefore I come to beg of you, Giving-Potlatches-in-the-World, to go tonight,"—for although he is not a shaman, that one of whom the sick person dreams, generally the sick person gets well quickly for, indeed, he himself believes in his dream, although that man is not a shaman who comes to take out the sickness,—said the late Getting-Rich to me. Now the Lalasiqwala did not know that I was trying to become a shaman. 1.411

Now I always kept with me a little eagle down which is to represent the sickness sucked out of the patient. As soon as it was getting dark in the evening many men came in their canoes to get me. I had already taken the eagle down and put it under my upper lip between (the lip and) the gums. As soon as this was done I went aboard the canoe and when the canoe arrived on the beach of the house of the late Getting-Rich, then all the men went ashore and they all went into the house of the late Getting-Rich. I was the last. When all the men had gone in we went in with the late Getting-Rich and his late elder brother, the late Qomoxsala. For these were the great shamans of the Lalasiqwala, both of them. Now the fire was in the middle of the house and they were all inside, the men and the women and the children, in the house. And so he was the first, the late Qomoxsala. I was next to him. The last was the late Getting-Rich. Then we walked and went to the place where Food-Owner, the sick young man, was lying in the middle of the rear of the house. 2.3

Then the late Qomoxsala asked me to sit down at the right hand side of Food-Owner. Then I saw that he was really weak, for his breath was really short. Then the late Qomoxsala spoke. He said, "Now go on, Food-Owner, point out where in your dream Giving-Potlatches-in-the-World took out your sickness, for it is he who has come and sits by your side," said he to him. Now Food-Owner opened his eyes and looked at me, for he had his eyes shut when I sat down by his side. I almost did not hear him when he spoke. He said, "Welcome, have mercy on me that I may live, father," said he as he pointed with the first finger of his right hand to the lower end of his ribs. "I dreamed that here you took out something like a worm," said he. 1.411

At once I pressed on it with my right hand. I said to him, "Now I shall try to get it out so that you may get well," said I to him. And the wife of the late Getting-Rich, who had the name Xaneyos, came and put down a wash basin with fresh water on my right hand side, (this basin 2.13

3.21

has the name "the shaman's receptacle for wetting"), and also a cup full of fresh water. Then I took the cup and I rinsed my mouth with the water of the cup and after I had done so I tried to suck out what was referred to by Food-Owner as the sickness that I had taken out in his dream. Now I tasted the blood that came out of my gums. Not very long had I been sucking when I lifted my head. I spat the blood into my hand, mixed with the down intended to represent the sickness, into my right hand. Then I squeezed the surface of the down. Then I arose and I opened my right hand and sang the sacred song made by Cause-of-Falling-down for me. Now the blood-covered down stuck on my right hand as I went around the fire in the middle of the house. Then the Lalasiqwala beat fast time, for they all saw that what they called the sickness, sticking to my hand. Now Food-Owner also saw it. Therefore he wished to sit up. Now Food-Owner was sitting on the floor. Just at his sides were the late Getting-Rich and his late wife Xaneyos holding him. As soon as I came to where he was sitting I asked him to look at his former sickness. And so he said that this was the way of his dream, said he. Then I took off the blood covered down and wrapped it in shredded white cedar bark and I went and buried it in the hot ashes of the fire in the middle of the house. Now I finished after this.

    Now all the Lalasiqwala were surprised at what I had done for Food-Owner, for he said right away that he was very hungry in the morning, and he also said that there was no pain in his right side, indeed, because he believed strongly in his dream about me. As soon as I sat down, the late Qomoxsala went and sat down by the side of the head of Food-Owner and they whispered together and talked together. After they had finished their talking, the late Qomoxsala arose and spoke. He said, "O you slaves, Getting-Rich and you, Xaneyos, don't stay in this way in the house. Arise and let us sing our sacred songs to thank our master for his words, for he said that he felt the sickness taken out by this great shaman. Now he is alive," said he and all the Lalasiqwala sang their sacred songs. After they had finished singing, the late Getting-Rich took a well made neck ring of the cannibal dancer, of thin red cedar bark, for Food-Owner was a cannibal dancer. He told his tribe that he would now put the ring around my neck for my shaman's neck ring, "and also the name Qaselid, for the shaman's name of this great shaman, for he has pulled Food-Owner out of what would have been his grave box," said he as he came and put around my neck the red cedar bark. Now we finished after this. Now I was known by all the tribes as a great shaman on account of Food-Owner who became at once quite well: and now he was a strong man again.

Marginal notations: 2.3, 1.411, 1.41, 1.41

Aid from a "dreamer"

Now I was walking along late at night, when I saw a small canoe coming to the beach and a single man in it. I went down to the beach to meet him for he was just sitting still in his small canoe as though he hesitated whether he should come ashore or not. Then I went up to him. Behold, who should it be but Made-to-be-Foolish, the dreamer of the shamans of the Nakwaxdax. As soon as he recognized me he spoke to me secretly. He said, "O friend, this is the work I do traveling in the night, trying to find out the sickness among the various tribes that I may go and tell our friends at Hanging-at-Mouth, so that they may dream. Now I only wish to come and tell you about chief Calumniated, for now he is very ill and they have already made his grave box. I mean that you may dream this night about what I told, and that you tell your dream in the morning," said he. Then he started and paddled away. Now he went home to Hanging-at-Mouth, and he also told what had been seen at Fort Rupert—that Calumniated was now very ill,—to the shamans. Made-to-be-Foolish did not tell the Nakwaxdax that he had come to Fort Rupert and he also did not tell that Calumniated was now very ill, for that is the way for Made-to-be-Foolish to act, because nobody in his tribe knows where he goes when he goes paddling, for he generally starts in the night. But then the shamans know. . . .

Rivalry over shamanic secrets

This is the reason why I do not believe in all the doings of the shamans of all the tribes. I mean this, I went to the Koskimo. When I arrived at the beach of the house of Great-Mountain I was invited in by him. Immediately his wife got ready to give me to eat. And after I had eaten, Great-Mountain told me that all the Koskimo would go in with their wives and children into the house of Beginning-to-Give-Potlatches, for he felt strongly about his sick princess Woman-Made-to-Invite and   3.21 that all the shamans had tried in vain to cure her, said he. Immediately I asked Great-Mountain, "In what part of the body does Woman-Made-to-Invite feel the sickness," said I to him. Then he said, "She also feels it at the lower part of the chest at the upper end of the stomach," said he.

As soon as it was evening, there went to call four of those who are referred to by the Koskimo as real shamans who have gone through (everything), that is Hadaho and Place-of-Getting-Rich and Great-Dance and Post-of-World. As soon as the four shamans had gone out to walk and   2.3 call at the house of Great-Mountain, I took some down which I always kept with me and I wrapped it up so that it was round like a worm. As soon as I had done so I went and put it under my upper lip in the space between it and my gums, and this was the reason why I had done so, because the four shamans asked me to go and look on, for they did not yet know that I was believed to be a shaman by the Lalasiqwala and the Kwakiutl.

Now Great-Mountain asked me to go with him and his wife, and we went into the house of Beginning-to-Give-Potlatches. Then we were asked to sit down at the right hand side of the door of the house. Now I saw Woman-Made-to-Invite lying down on a new mat in the middle of the rear of the house. When all the men and women who did not menstruate and the children had come in Beginning-to-Give-Potlatches arose

1.41   and spoke. He said, "Welcome, supernatural ones, for you have come to fight for my child with the Evil-Bringing-Woman. I mean this, supernatural ones, now you will really suck it out," said he.

Now none of the shamans of the Koskimo went near Woman-Made-

2.13   to-Invite, the sick woman, for they kept together sitting down in the middle of the right hand side of the house. They do not act in the way as

3.21   is done by the Nakwaxdax, for the song leaders beat fast time four times before the shaman comes into the house. And so the first to stand up was Hadaho, and he sat down at the right hand side of Woman-Made-to-Invite. Then they took off the shirt of Woman-made-to-Invite and immediately Hadaho pressed his right hand on the lower end of the chest, not making a sound. Then Beginning-to-Give-Potlatches took a small dish and poured fresh water into it. After he had done so Beginning-to-Give-Potlatches called the four late shamans, old women, to go and pray that the shaman might cure her. The name for the four women is "Those-who-Pray-for-the-Shaman". Now two women sat down on the right hand side of Hadaho, and two sat down on his left.

2.13   And when the four who pray for the shaman were ready, Hadaho put his right hand into the water in the small dish and he put the water into

3.21   his mouth and took it in his hand. Now he rinsed his mouth. As soon as he had finished, he bent his mouth to the upper end of the stomach of the sick woman. As soon as he began to suck the women began to pray speaking together, the four praying-women of the shaman. They said, "Go ahead, go ahead, curer, curer, curer, who begs for our true friend. You, supernatural power, supernatural power, go ahead, go ahead! Now have mercy of her, use your supernatural power that you may make her alive with your true life-bringer of your supernatural power. Supernatural power, go ahead, go ahead, curer, curer, curer."

As soon as the shaman lifted his head, for this is referred to by the

2.13   Indians as lifting the head, when he stops sucking the sick woman, then again the four women said together, "Now it has come, now it has come,

3.21   now it has really come. You have obtained what made sick our friend," said they. Then the shaman pressed with his right hand his mouth and he took out of his mouth saliva and put it on his hand. He squeezed the saliva which is called by the shamans of the Koskimo "mixed with sickness." He put his hand into the water in the small dish and he squeezed it in the water so that all the saliva should come off. Hadaho just squeezed what was referred to as the sickness with his right hand. Then he lifted his hand and he opened his hand and blew upon it once. Then he blew upward what is referred to as the sickness. This was all that Hadaho did. Then Hadaho arose and went and sat down where he had first been sitting, but the four women never moved from where they were sitting . . .

> Hadaho's performance is repeated by the other three shamans. The only variation comes when the second of these, Post-of-World, raises his head from the patient's stomach and exclaims, "Now I have at last found your great sickness, this rotten material. And so I have come and obtained this matter." In the process of putting "what he referred to as matter" into the dish of water, he tilted his hand so that it could "be seen by all the spectators."

. . . Now the shamans had finished. Then it came to my mind that I would try to find out the strength of the shamans, whether it was real or whether they only pretended to be shamans as the shamans of the Nak-waxdax did who are no real shamans, for they only act as though they were shamans. Then I told Great-Mountain that I wished to feel of Woman-Made-to-Invite, said I to him. Immediately Great-Mountain **1.41** arose and told the Koskimo what I had said. All the Koskimo just thanked me for what I had said, for Woman-Made-to-Invite was just sitting on the mat, for the four women were still sitting where they had first been sitting, before they were called to come and pray. Now I arose and went **2.13** and sat down by the side of Woman-Made-to-Invite. I felt where it was seen by me that she was felt of by the four shamans. I saw that it was truly swollen after the sucking of the shamans; for when they suck **3.21** strongly they bite and pull with their heads. Therefore the marks of the sucking are really blue. Then I asked the sick woman to lie on her stomach. She obeyed what I said to her. Then I felt of the lower end of her shoulderblades on her back.

After I had been feeling I asked Beginning-to-Give-Potlatches to **2.13** draw some water for me. He came carrying a cup full of water and gave it to me. Then I put down the cup with water in it, and I tucked up the sleeves of my shirt and I was barefoot. Then I told Beginning-to-Give-Potlatches that I would try to get the sickness of his princess, said I to him. Immediately he arose and told his tribe what I had said. Then all **1.41** the Koskimo thanked me.

Now I took the water in the cup and rinsed my mouth. After I had rinsed my mouth I spat the water on the floor near the fire in the middle **2.13** of the house. Now the four shamans came who had been taking out the sickness of the woman and sat down on each side of me. Also the four praying women came and sat down where they had been sitting before.

3.21   After I had rinsed my mouth I bent down my head on the back of the sick woman and I did not act roughly when I first sucked, but finally I sucked strongly and I nearly lifted my head. Now I tasted the blood when it came and filled my mouth, coming out of my gums. Now the four women were praying together. Then I lifted my head and I put the blood from my mouth into my hand, among it the down, the pretended sickness. Now I just held the blood in my right hand. As soon as Beginning-to-Give-Potlatches saw the blood as it was dripping down he took a small dish and he came and put it down at my right hand side. Then I

2.3   squeezed the down with my right hand. When all the blood had come out, I passed it from one hand to the other like a worm with a long round body, the down in my hands being covered with blood. Now this was seen by all the Koskimo and by the sick woman. While it stuck on my hand I was singing my sacred song.

2.3   Now I arose and went around the fire in the middle of the house. I turned downward my right hand so that by all the Koskimo might be

2.13   seen the pretended sickness sticking on my hand. After I had gone around the fire I stood up on the outer side of the sick woman. I asked Beginning-to-Give-Potlatches to get a small piece of shredded cedar bark for me. Then he took it, came and gave it to me. I took the shredded cedar bark and wrapped it around the blood covered down. Then I went and buried it in the hot ashes. As soon as I had done so I gave away one

3.11   hundred dollars to the Koskimo, that they might know my name as a shaman, Qaselid. Now I finished that night after this.

Now Beginning-to-Give-Potlatches spoke, after he had been whispering with his princess Woman-Made-to-Invite. He said, "O Koskimo,

1.411   good are these words of this Woman-Made-to-Invite, for she says she feels that the sickness has been sucked out by this Qaselid. Now she is alive, says she." Then all the Koskimo sang their sacred songs and their

1.41   women thanked him for his words. Now I saw that the shamans of the Koskimo, were ashamed, the four reputed ones, on account of what I

1.42   had done, for only they did not sing their sacred songs. Then I was scared of what they might say to me.

Then we all went out of the house and we went home to the house of Great-Mountain, for now it was past midnight. Then Great-Mountain said to me to go and lie down in the bedroom where he sleeps. I obeyed his words. As soon as I lay down, he came and sat by my side. He whispered as he was speaking. He said, "This is the reason why I wish you to

1.42   come and lie down inside, that you may sleep soundly, for these shamans of the Koskimo are now ashamed of what you have done, for you have

2.3   shown the sickness so that it was seen by all the men. Now all the Koskimo are surprised. I mean this, you might be called by the shamans before daylight and they will try to find out what was done by you and why you got the sickness so that it stuck on your hands. It would be best if you would not tell them," said he. "This is it, that you may be ready for them," said he and he lay down. Now it was really sweet in my eyes when I fell asleep, for I was tired; for almost the whole day I had been walking on the trail going through to Koskimo.

Now I did not know that day had come in the morning when Beginning-to-Give-Potlatches came and I was awakened that I might take breakfast in his house. Then at once I arose and went out of the bedroom. I washed my face and, after I had done so, Great-Mountain asked me to sit down where he was sitting with his wife, Nexaxsestalak. He said, "Do not go too quickly, when they call you the first time, for they will come and call you four times, according to the ways of the Koskimo when they invite. Now you will go after that," said he. Now I followed what he had said to me. As soon as he had come back three times to call me I arose and followed him.

When I went into the house I was told by Beginning-to-Give-Potlatches to sit down in the rear of the house and now I saw Woman-Made-to-Invite, as she was sitting down in the middle of the right hand side of the house of her father. Then the six chiefs of the various numaym of the Koskimo came in. They sat down, three on my right hand side and they sat down, three on my left hand side. When they were all seated, dried salmon was taken and was roasted by the wife of Beginning-to-Give-Potlatches. When four dried salmon were all roasted they were broken into pieces and put into four dishes. And when that was done they came and put the dishes down in front of us. Now there was no grease, for the dried silver salmon is very fat. Then water was drawn for me to drink.

After I had done so the chiefs also drank, and when they had done so, Woman-Made-to-Invite arose, the woman who had been sick, and she came and stood in front of me. She took the dried roasted salmon which was in my dish and broke off a small piece from it. Then she turned around to the right and she spoke and said holding the piece of dried salmon in her right hand, "Now since I have been brought back to life by this great shaman, I put this into his mouth so that he may eat first from this for which I invited him," said she as she put it into my mouth. She also said, "You alone will be my shaman, Qaselid, for you have brought me back to life, although I had already been given up by the shamans of the Koskimo," said she and she went back and sat down in her seat.

Now we ate the dried salmon after this. After we had done so each chief spoke in turn, thanking Woman-Made-to-Invite for what she had said to me. And that is why they praised me because Woman-Made-to-Invite really stopped being sick after this. As soon as they had finished speaking to me, all went out of the house and I went into the house of Great-Mountain. And so I was sitting there for quite a while thinking about many things, for I was hesitating and was afraid of the words of all

1.41

3.21

1.41

the chiefs who had praised me. They had made their shamans common
people. That is why I said in my mind that I would go home to Fort
Rupert; and so I told Great-Mountain that I would go home when day
came next morning.

It may be that Great-Mountain told somebody what I had said to
him, therefore a man, named Lelpila, came at once and sat down by my
side as I was lying on my back in the house of Great-Mountain. He whispered as he was speaking to me. He said, "I have been sent to come and
call you to follow me so that we may go to the purifying place in the
woods of our fellow shamans, for they are all there now. Now get up and
let us go through the rear door," said he. Then I at once made ready,
when Great-Mountain spoke. He said, "What are you whispering about,
Lelpila? Are you sent by our friends to come and call him? And don't
you want me to know why you call him? Now, wait for me, Qaselid, and
let us go," said he. Then Great-Mountain was angry because he was not
called also, and also because he did not know why the shamans were
calling me.

Then Great-Mountain went first as we went through the rear door of
his house, as we were going back into the woods. We came to the foot of
a hill and there I saw a cave. Then Great-Mountain went down into it,
for a ladder was standing in it. I was next to him. Lelpila was last. As
soon as I went down I heard something like the rushing sound of a river.
Now I came to the stone floor of the inside and it was like a house which
was dark. Then I was taken hold of by Hadaho and he made me sit down
where hemlock branches were. For a long time none of the shamans
spoke. Now it was getting light as I was sitting down a long time. I could
see the faces of many men and of two women shamans of the Koskimo
and of the Gapenox. Now I saw a large river inside of the place where
we were sitting down.

Then Hadaho spoke and said, "You have come, friend, welcome Qaselid, you have come, for you have come to see the faces of our friends.
These are the supernatural shamans of the Koskimo and Gapenox, these
who are now seen by you, who all have come and are sitting in this
purifying house of the one who gives us supernatural power, for whose
sake we are shamans. I only wish first to speak to our friend here, you,
shamans," said he. As soon as he stopped speaking Great-Dance spoke
and said, "Welcome, friend Qaselid, let me tell you all about our own
ways when we cure a sick man and what we obtain when we cure a sick
man. As soon as we get the soul of the sickness which is a man, then dies
the sickness which is a man. Its body just disappears in our insides. Then
it ceases being sick the place in which it has been, after that; for every
sickness is a man: boils and swellings, and itch and scabs, and pimples
and coughs and consumption and scrofula; and also this, stricture of the
bladder and stomach aches; and all the various kinds of sickness; they are

1.32

all men, for they walk about where we are walking. That is when the
man that is the sickness goes into us, when we meet him. I mean this,
that you can get out the sickness, which is a man, and his body and his
soul; our friend Qaselid, that I may mention it. Now he also will tell us
shamans the reason why the sickness sticks to his hand," said he.

Then all the shamans were silent and they were all waiting for me to
speak and tell them also what kind of a thing a sickness is. For a long
time I kept quiet for I could not plan what to say. And so (I thought) my
name was that of a novice shaman and I could not talk about my secret
ways because I had not yet been a shaman for four winters. I also could
not take pay from the father of the one whom I had cured, because I had
not yet been a shaman for four winters. Now for a long time I felt foolish
in my heart. It may be I was afraid of what had been said by them, or it
was the different kind of smell below, therefore I was as though I was
sleepy where I was sitting and therefore I was really startled when Great-
Mountain spoke with really angry words to the shamans. He said, "O
shamans of the Koskimo and of the Gapenox, it does not seem that your
words are wise, for you know about this novice shaman, Qaselid, that he
cannot talk about what is given to him by the shaman-maker to do," said
he as he told me to go out of the purifying place and he told me to go
first.

Then I arose and went up the ladder. Great-Mountain went next to
me. We went home to his house after that. Not one of the shamans spoke
as we went out. Then we sat down in his house and Great-Mountain
spoke and said, "O son, Qaselid, do not deliberate long why I spoke
angry words to the shamans in the purifying place. That is the reason of
my anger against them that they did not tell what they had done when
they all went secretly into the purifying place and when they came secretly to call you to go to them that they might find all the instructions
given by the supernatural power what you should do. Now I am grateful
that you never replied to their words, for I was angry with the shamans
because I am the head shaman of the shamans, for it was that way with
the first Great-Mountain who came along, beginning at the time when
Qaneqelak made Great-Mountain a shaman at Gose, when Qaneqelak
brought back to life those who had been vomited by the lake-monster.
The only great shaman of the ancestors of the Koskimo was Great-
Mountain. That is his name, for he was the only first chief of the ancestors of the Koskimo. His shaman's name is Togomalis. By force came to
obtain the ancestors of the Koskimo Calm-Water from the Xoyalas.
When were finished the houses of all the Koskimo at Calm-Water, then
Great-Mountain found the purifying place and, therefore, it is really
mine," said he.

Then Great-Mountain forbade me to go home at once, and I obeyed
him. Now I was always invited by Beginning-to-Give-Potlatches to go

2.2

3.11

and eat in his house, for he was glad on account of his daughter Woman-Made-to-Invite, for she was now walking about. Great-Mountain never tried to find out what I had done to the pretended sickness, the down that stuck to my hand. Now all the Koskimo really believed that I was a great shaman after that.

1.41

1.32

2.13

I asked Great-Mountain, "Don't these also tie with shredded cedar bark rings the sick person, that may come back the soul when it has missed (the owner of) his soul? When there is no shredded cedar bark then a ring of hemlock branches is used by the shaman," said I to him. Then Great-Mountain said that a bird is our soul as we are men and women. "When our bird flies away from a man here, then our bodies are not strong. It is just all the time as though we were sleepy. The man just goes down in weakness without cause, for he is not hungry and, therefore, he is lean. Also, he does not feel any sickness in his body. Then he asks the soul-catching shaman, Place-of-Getting-Rich, to feel of him and then Place-of-Getting-Rich feels of the place where our soul is sitting as we are men, on each side of our necks. Then the shaman says that the soul has flown away. Then the man who has no soul just prays the shaman to try to get the bird; (it is the soul that is meant). And when evening comes, then the one who has no bird calls his numaym and all go into this house. When they are all inside then the shaman is called. Evidently at that time he catches the bird, as he comes walking along to the house in which the whole numaym is inside. When the shaman goes in he never sings his sacred song after the manner of the shamans of the Nakwaxdax, when they try to catch a soul, for they sing their sacred songs as they are searching for it. The shaman just stands inside of the doorway. Then he speaks and says, "Truly, by good luck I found this bird of our friend here, for I bring it now, as I caught it," says he, as he comes walking and squeezing it in his right hand. Then he presses with his right hand as he spreads it open on the right hand side of the neck of the man. Then four times he blows on it. This is referred to by the shamans as blowing the bird into (the body). Now it is finished after this," said he.

Now I had discovered everything regarding the ways of the shamans of the Koskimo and Gapenox after this. They did not give up, the two shamans of the Koskimo, Hadaho and Great-Dance, to find out what I had done. So I told Great-Mountain that I would walk to the north side of the point of Xutes. Then Great-Mountain said, "Only take care of Made-to-be-Only-one-in-House, the virgin, the nice daughter of Hadaho, for I suppose that she will be sent by her father to try to inveigle you to tell her what her father tries to find out. You must not tell her, therefore I say to you that I have seen Made-to-be-Only-one-in-House trying to come into my house really dressed up. I mean this, Made-to-be-Only-one-in-House never comes into my house. Go on! I just want you to be careful," said he.

Then I walked to the place where I was going. When I was able to look into Kagik I sat down on the rocks. After I had been sitting there on the rocks for some time two young women came along laughing as they came towards me and they came one on each side of me and sat down on the rocks. It was Made-to-be-Only-one-in-House, the daughter of Hadaho and the daughter of Great-Dance, whose name was Ayaga. Then Made-to-be-Only-one-in-House spoke. She said, as though she recognized me, "What are you thinking as you are sitting here on the rocks?" said she to me. I imitated the ways of the novice shaman of the Nakwaxdax, for they do not dare to laugh for four years. I also did not reply to her right away. Then I said to her, "I just wished to come and sit down on the rocks," said I to her. Then both of them laughed together and Made-to-be-Only-one-in-House spoke again and said, "I know why you came to sit down on the rocks, you long to see your sweet-heart at Fort Rupert. Therefore you are downcast." Now she stopped talking, for Great-Mountain came in sight at the point. Right away he spoke and said, "O Qaselid, come and leave those prostitutes," said he. Immediately I got up and went to him. When I came to the place where Great-Mountain was standing on the rocks, he said, "This is the reason why I told you to be careful, on account of these bad women, for they are the bait of their fathers who wish to find out what they are not allowed to know these two mischievous women of whom their fathers say that they are virgins; but they have been going for a long time with men, when they were not yet nearly menstruating and they were wishing to try to inveigle you. They wanted you to tell them what their fathers are trying to find out," said he. Then he went into his house and we sat down.

Now I told Great-Mountain that I was going to go home when daylight came the next day, said I to him and he allowed me to come home. As soon as daylight came in the morning Great-Mountain awakened me and we quickly took breakfast. As soon as we had finished Great-Mountain took me up to the head of the trail, seven miles from Xutes, traveling in a small canoe. Now Great-Mountain never tried to find out what I had done in the shaman's talk. When we arrived at the trail I stepped out of the small canoe and I started and went on alone and it was not nearly evening when I came here to Fort Rupert. As soon as I entered my house my wife at once gave food to me.

A contest between rival shamans

As soon as I had finished eating, my wife told me what had been said by the one whom the Kwakiutl referred to as the great shaman of the numaym of Those-Having-a-Name of the Great Kwakiutl, that he said I should play with him with our shamanistic power, (I) with him. "I mean that you shall be ready for him tonight," said she to me. Now it was evening when someone came to call to witness the great one who had

2.21

been for a long time a shaman, Aixagidalagilis, who was going to play,
2.3   said the four young men who were not shamans. And when the four
young men went out, the inviters, I took the eagle down which I always
keep with me and I put the round imitation of a worm which represents
the sickness, between my upper lip and my gums. Then I put on my
headring of red cedar bark and also my shaman's neckring of red cedar
bark.

Now I was ready for the callers. They went around four times calling,
then they said, "We come, sent by our tribe that you may be a spectator,
together with your wife," said they. Immediately we arose, I and my
wife, and we followed the four young men. Then we went into the house
of Aixagidalagilis. We were told to sit down in the middle of the right
hand side of the house. Now the four Kwakiutl tribes were all inside with
their women and their children. Now I saw that I was alone, the last one
to enter the house, for immediately the door was barred after I had come
in and I sat down with my wife.

I had not been sitting for a long time when Aixagidalagilis came out
2.12   of his room holding the shaman's rattle in his right hand. He had on his
head a ring of rough red cedar bark and spread out was the neckring of
red cedar bark. He stood up in the rear of his house in front of the song
2.11   leaders. Then he spoke and said, "This was my dream last night; the
shaman-maker said to me that you should come into my house here,
friends. If I should not obey what he said to me I should have bad luck.
2.13   Therefore I thank you that you have all come to my house," said he and
swung his rattle. Now he went around the fire in the middle of the house
and he came up near to the door. Then he sang his sacred song. Now the
supernatural power came to him. He continued going around the fire in
the middle of the house. After he had gone around four times he stood
still in the rear of the house. Then he said, "I am very hungry, I am very
hungry," said he swinging his rattle. Evidently all the men did not understand what he meant by being hungry, and therefore nobody spoke.
Then he said again, "I am very hungry, I am very hungry, I am very
hungry," said he. Then his daughter, whose name was Inviter-Woman,
arose at the right hand side of the rear of the house. "You fools, don't you
understand why my father here, the shaman, says he is hungry? This is
what he means by being hungry, it is your sickness. Go on, take off your
clothes, you who are sick, so that he may take pity on the one who will
do so; for there is nothing to be feared this night, for that is his dream.
3.11   Therefore, you will not pay my father, this shaman," said she.

Immediately undressed one man, whose name was Wawengenol, for
2.13   he was consumptive. And when he had done so Inviter-Woman came
and put on the floor a basin containing water and spread under it a new
3.21   piece of white calico while the shaman was still standing there on the
floor and did not move in the place where he was standing in the rear of

his house. Then Inviter-Woman finished after she had put down the basin on the floor and she told the shaman her father. Now the shaman turned to the right and he went and sat down at the right hand side of Wawengenol. For a long while he felt of the middle of the chest. I heard Aixagidalagilis say that there was no sickness in the middle of the chest. Then he felt of the right hand side of the chest. He had not been feeling long before he felt of the left hand side of the chest. Then he pointed with his first finger to the place where the heart of Wawengenol was beating. Then the shaman spoke and said, "I have now found the place where the sickness is," for I heard all the words of the shaman, for there was only one man between myself and him.

Then he rinsed his mouth with the water in the basin. After he had   2.13
done so he put his mouth to the place where was beating his heart. Four times he blew at it and then he sucked. He was sucking at it for a long time, then he lifted his head. He pressed his mouth with his right hand and then he blew out of his mouth into his hand something really white. Then the shaman said that it was pus sucked out, and mixed with it was what he referred to as the sickness. Then he washed off what he called pus and he squeezed the sickness in his left hand. Then with his right hand he took his rattle and arose on the floor and shook his rattle, then he sang his sacred song. Then he went around the fire. When he came   2.3
in front of Wawengenol the shaman put down his rattle on the floor and he took off his rough head ring of red cedar bark. Then Aixagidalagilis spoke and said, "Now all you friends, now I will show you the strength of the sickness for I shall put the former sickness of this our friend into my head ring," said he as he tucked what he called the sickness into its front part. After he had done so he took his rattle and he told the song leaders to go on and beat fast time. Then the shaman shook the rattle and sang his sacred song, as he walked towards the post of the ridge pole on the right hand side of the door. Then he put the red cedar bark on a smooth place on the post. He said that the sickness had bitten the post. He came walking and went around the fire in the middle of the house. He went straight up to the post and took off the head ring and he pinched off what was referred to as the sickness. He put it into his mouth and swallowed it. He does that way for he says that he puts the sickness into his stomach after he has obtained it. He sucked just once on Wawengenol, for the shaman said that he had taken out the sickness. The shaman never showed the sickness to Wawengenol and to all the spectators.

As soon as he had finished another man whose name was Made-to-   2.13
Give, who belongs to the numaym Laxsa of the Qomoyaye who was also sick of consumption, took off his shirt. Then Made-to-Give spoke and   3.21
said, "Indeed, you my tribe, now we are told by this great shaman to come to this house to be pitied by him. Now I came to beg you, great shaman," said he. Immediately Inviter-Woman took the wash basin and

poured out the saliva and water that was in it where the rain drops from the roof on the right hand side of the house. The reason why Inviter-Woman poured out the water in the wash basin for wetting (the mouth) is that her father tried to guess whether it might be attempted to take the saliva mixed with water; for Inviter-Woman said to me that, when she poured on the ground what her father had sucked out, that she stepped over it four times to take away its supernatural quality, so that her father should not feel the witchcraft of the witches, said she to me. She came carrying the wash basin and put it on a new piece of cotton goods which she spread down on the right hand side of Made-to-Give. Then she put on it the wash basin and she drew fresh water and poured it into the wash basin.

As soon as she had done this she called her father who was just stand-

2.13   ing still in the rear of the house. Immediately her father, the shaman, started, still carrying the rattle. Then he sat down at the right hand side

3.21   of Made-to-Give. He felt of each side of his neck. Then he said that there was no sickness there. Then went down what was being felt by him on each side of the chest. It arrived what was being felt by him down at the lower end of the sternum and the upper end of the stomach. Then the shaman spoke and said, "Now I have found what does this to you, for it is this sickness which stops up the mouth of your stomach," said he. Now the shaman pressed his right hand in the water in the wash basin and he scooped up the water and put it in his mouth and rinsed his mouth. As soon as he had done so he applied his mouth. Now he blew four times and sucked at the upper part of the stomach. When he had been sucking a long time, then finally he lifted his head. He said that he had not succeeded in getting the sickness, "for it is rooted, therefore I find it really difficult to get it. Now go on, please help me, you song leaders, go on and beat fast time that this great sickness may jump out of our friend," said he. As soon as the shaman applied his mouth the song leaders beat fast time; but it was not long before the shaman lifted his head. Then the song leaders stopped beating fast time. Now the shaman spit out the saliva into his left hand and he squeezed it when he put it into the water in the wash basin and he squeezed it so that all the saliva came off from what he referred to as the sickness. Then he arose and squeezed with his left hand what he called the sickness. Then he held in his right hand his rattle and he said that he got the mother of the sickness."

2.13   As he said this he walked around the fire in the middle of the house. When he arrived at the rear of the house he lifted his hand in which he held his rattle, and looked at his rattle. Then the shaman spoke looking

2.3   at his rattle. He said to his rattle, "You say that you are also hungry?" Evidently his rattle answered him saying that it was hungry. I only guess that this was what the rattle said because the shaman said, "Go on, take care that you swallow this great sickness," said the shaman, as he told the song leaders to go ahead and beat fast time. As soon as the song leaders beat fast time the shaman put the beak of the raven carving on his rattle nearest to the knuckle of his second finger and of his first finger. Then his rattle hung down from there while he went around the fire in the middle of the house. When he arrived at the rear of the house he took the handle of the rattle and pulled it off. Then said the shaman to the spectators, "Did you see my rattle as it bit the palm of my hand after it had swallowed the great sickness?" said he. Now also had never seen one of the men what was referred to by the shaman as the sickness. Now he finished after this. And now he sang his sacred song. Then he told the song leaders to sing after him the words of his sacred song.

> "Do those supernatural ones really see it? Those supernatural ones see it plainly, those supernatural ones. No one can imitate our great friends the supernatural ones. Wae."

Now the shaman danced around the fire in the middle of the house and all the shamans started to sing, for that was meant by the words of the sacred song, for Aixagidalagilis said to the shamans that only he was a real shaman. He said that they all only pretended to be shamans, therefore he said this in the last words with which he had danced;

2.13

> "Nobody can see through the magic power,
> Nobody can see through my magic power."

As soon as the sacred song was at an end the shaman sang again, dancing with the sacred song which said this,

2.13

> "We came to this one whom we praise; the one who is praised; the one with supernatural power. Ha ham am am hamai.
>
> We came to witness the one to be witnessed, the supernatural power. Ha ham am am hamai.
>
> We came to ask him to bring us back to life, the one who brings back to life; the supernatural one. Ha ham am am hamai."

As soon as the dance with the sacred song of the shaman ended, he sat down. Now he finished. Now he did not say a word. Then Tsalagilis arose, who belonged to the numaym of the Kukwakum of the Gwetela, and spoke. He said, "It is good that we came together in this house of our great friend Aixagidalagilis for this is not the place to hesitate to speak. He is the one of whom I speak, this new shaman Qaselid, I ask you to take mercy, Qaselid, to take pity and to bring back to life my daughter, Lalakotsayogwa," said he, for Lalakotsayogwa was not sitting among all of those who had come into the house. Therefore, Tsalagilis sent four middle aged men to call his daughter. They had not been gone long when the four men came in with Lalakotsayogwa. Then Lalakotsayogwa went straight to the rear of the house and Inviter-Woman spread

1.41

out a new mat on which Lalakotsayogwa sat down. As soon as she was sitting on it Inviter-Woman took a wash basin and spread a mat under it. She put on to it the wash basin and then she poured fresh water into it.

3.21   When everything was ready she came to call me. I arose and sat down at the right hand side of Lalakotsayogwa. As soon as I was seated Lalakotsayogwa took off her shirt; she only kept her petticoat. Now she pointed to what she referred to as really a kind of heavy hanging sick-

2.2   ness, below her ribs on the right hand side. "This Aixagidalagilis always tried to set right. Then he said he would now take out my sickness, but I am only getting much weaker," said she.

        Then I tucked up both sleeves of my shirt and I asked that four times

2.13   for a long time the song leaders should beat fast time as is done by the Nakwaxdax for their shamans. Immediately they beat fast time. The first time I felt what was referred to by her as her sickness. Now I saw Aixagidalagilis lying down on his back near the place where I was sitting. Now, evidently he tried to find out about me, for he was watching me. When the song leaders had beaten fast time four times, I pretended that my body trembled. I applied my mouth and immediately I sucked. I had not been sucking long when I raised my head and at the same time the song leaders stopped beating fast time. Then my mouth was full of blood mixed with the down, the alleged worm. Then I spat the blood into my hand and I tilted my hand so that all the men and women could see the blood as it ran into the water in the wash basin. As soon as all the blood was out they all saw the alleged worm, the down that stuck on the palm of my right hand.

        Now I stood up after this and went around the fire in the middle of

2.13   the house. Now I was singing my sacred song and also a sacred song against the shamans, made for me by Fool, the shaman of the Nak-

2.3   waxdax. As soon as I arrived at the post, the place to which Aixagidalagilis had stuck his red cedar bark, I took off the alleged worm, the sickness, and I stuck it on to the post. Then I left it and went and felt of the

1.411   woman, Lalakotsayogwa. Then she spoke and said, "For what was felt by you, great supernatural one? I felt it when you took out the sickness that now sticks on the post," said she. Then I arose and went to the post. I took off the alleged sickness, the worm. I asked someone to get a small piece of soft cedar bark for me. Then Inviter-Woman came and gave me the soft cedar bark. I wrapped it around the worm, the alleged sickness, and I buried it in the hot ashes of the fire in the middle of the house. Now this was finished after this. This is my sacred song which was sung.

> "He tried to prevent me from succeeding, the one who does not succeed, the reason of not succeeding, Wo.
>
> Ah, I shall not try to fail, to have no sacred secrets, wa waai wa wahai hawo.

He tried to make me succeed, the one who causes success, the reason for success, wa waai wa wahai hawo. I was purified by the one who purifies, the reason of purification, wo wa waai wa wahai hawo."

As soon as I had ended, my wife Made-to-Spout-in-House arose and called her late brother, Omxid, whose name is Mythical-Person in the winter ceremonial, to go where she was standing. Then Omxid went and stood by the side of my wife. He spoke and said, "O, you great brother-in-law, that is what you do, you, you great supernatural one. Turn to me and listen to my speech to you, brother-in-law. This will be a marriage gift from your wife to you, these two hundred dollars," said he. Immediately Ten-Fathom-Face arose and thanked for the words my wife had said to me. Then one hundred dollars were given to the Qomoyaye; one hundred dollars to the Great-Kwakiutl and the Qomkutes that they might know my shaman's name, Qaselid. Now all the men went out after this.   3.1   3.11

When day came in the morning Tsalagilis called me and my wife to come to his house. Immediately we went and followed him. When we had gone into his house Lalakotsayogwa stared at my wife. She said, "O Made-to-Spout-in-House, take good care of this great shaman, your husband. There is no sickness left, the one that was seen by me buried in the ashes. Now I am alive, master, I am surprised by this, for I was only getting worse when Aixagidalagilis finished treating me," said she. Then she gave us to eat and after we had eaten she did so twice in the house. Then spoke her father Tsalagilis and said, "Indeed, you, Qaselid, and your great treasure, the water of life, are the reasons that my daughter is alive. Now you, now you have brought her back to life. Now take care, look out, you and your wife, for all the men see in the minds of the shamans that they are ashamed for what you did last night. I mean this, that you should be careful of them," said he.   1.411   1.41   1.4

I thanked him for what he and his daughter had said. When I had finished thanking them for what they had said we came home to our house. Then we sat down, (I) with my wife, and my wife spoke and said. "Did you hear what was said to us by Tsalagilis? He asks us to be careful of the shamans, for it might be true that they are envious on account of what you did, for not at all did you make invisible the sickness, for I saw into the inside of Aixagidalagilis last night when you were going with the sickness then sticking to the palm of your hand, to the post. Then I saw he was truly downcast. I mean that we together must be careful on account of him," said she; but I did not meet her sayings to me.   1.4

And so it got dark in the evening, when entered Inviter-Woman my house. She came and sat down beside me. She whispered and spoke and said to me, "Father sent me to come to you secretly to call you to go secretly to talk with him in the back of the village. Then he said you should follow me," said she. Then Inviter-Woman got up and went and sat down beside my wife, Made-to-Spout-in-House. They also whispered talking together. When they had finished talking my wife told me to go into the bedroom. Then she told me why Inviter-Woman had called, that 1.4 she came for me on behalf of her father, Aixagidalagilis, for me to go and talk with him, because he was truly ashamed, as he was being talked about as being ashamed, because he had said that he was the only great shaman, by all those men who hate him. "Go now, follow her, only take care," said my wife to me.

Right away we went out of my house, with Inviter-Woman. She was the one who led, Inviter-Woman. We walked behind the village and we went under a spruce tree. That was where Aixagidalagilis was sitting under the tree. Immediately he spoke and said, "It won't be bad what we say to each other, friend, but only I wish you to try and save my life 1.42 for me, so that I may not die of shame, for I am a plaything of our people on account of what you did last night. I pray you to have mercy and tell me what stuck on the palm of your hand last night. Was it the true sickness or was it only made up? For I beg you to have mercy and tell 1.32 me about the way you did it so that I can imitate you. Pity me, friend," said he.

I did not answer him for a long time, at last I answered him and said to him, "Your saying to me is not quite good, for you said, 'Is it the true 2.3 sickness, or is it only made up?' You do not believe that it was the sickness, in the way you spoke to me, that they were only made up, your red cedar bark that stuck on the post, and your rattle that bit the palm of your hand," said I to him. Then he spoke and said, "Let me tell the way of my head ring of red cedar bark," said he as he took it off, for he always had it on his head. Then he said, "Truly, it is made up what is thought by all the men it is done this way. Go on! Feel the thin, sharp-pointed nail at the back of the head of this my cedar bark ring, for I tell a lie when I say that the alleged sickness which I pretend to suck out from the sick person and which is put into this my head ring of red cedar bark, goes and bites into the post. I only press the nail into the post. Then it looks as though it was truly biting, the sickness that was not seen and that is only made up." Then he talked about his rattle. He said, "And that about the raven rattle used by the shaman for that is why the head of the raven of my rattle is short and round, because in the beginning I wished to do this, to pretend that it bites the palm of my hand. That head of the raven is just tucked between the proximal joints of my second finger and my first finger. All these fools believe that it is truly biting the palm of my hand," said he.[8]

---

[8] It is appropriate to point out again (cf. note 1) that Hunt's account has a certain bias. It would seem wise not to take at face value Aixagidalagilis' "admission" that he was, pure

Then I also spoke and said to him, "O, friend, now, truly, I am surprised at what you say, for you are common, for you say that you only
make up all that you do in your shamanism." Then he said, "It is for the
sake of the amount of pay given to the shamans by the sick person. That   3.11
is why I was tempted. Therefore long ago I pretended to faint at Oseq.
For a long time I lay down as dead on the beach, and then many ravens   1.1
came soaring above me. Then I saw them. It occurred to me to say to
my tribe if they should find me, that all the soaring ravens had become   2.1
men and that so it happened that they instructed Lalepalas,—for this
was his name before he was made a shaman by the raven men, for he
was going to have the shaman's name Aixagidalagilis,—thought I, as I
lay down as dead, for there is no lie that is not believed by the early
men. Now I truly told a lie after that, for now I told those who found me,
when I pretended to come to life, I mean this, I pretended to come to   1.11
life, for I just pretended to faint, as my whole mind began from that time
on to be covetous for the property of the sick men. I mean this, not one
of those is honest who says he is made a shaman by what we call
'Healing-Woman.' It would be wonderful, if a man could talk with the
animals and the fishes. And so the shamans are liars who say they catch
the soul of the sick person, for I know that we all own a soul. When we
are asked to try to catch the soul of the sick person, then I resort to taking
tallow and to pretend that it is a soul. And so the tallow is sitting on the
palm of my hand when I come into the house of the sick person. When
all the spectators see the white thing, the alleged soul, sitting on my
hand, I blow at it and then press on my mouth; and so I draw the tallow
into my mouth and I swallow it. Then I go to the place where the sick
woman sits and I pretend to make the alleged soul sit on her head. Then
I blow on it. Now it is done after that. Then the sick one believes that it
is really the soul, but it is just a lie," said he.

Now I was afraid of him, for he was talking angrily to me when he
was talking. Then his daughter, that is, Inviter-Woman, spoke, for she
was still sitting there just listening to our words, (mine) and her father's.   1.42
She said, "O Qaselid, do have mercy also, tell my father what he means

---

and simple, a fraud. A comment by Walens (1981:24–5) helps put the whole matter of
shamanic tricks ("fraud") into perspective.
  The audience at a curing ceremony knows that the shamans perform tricks, and they are
admired for their ability to do so. However, "if a shaman bungles one of these tricks, he
is immediately killed." There is no paradox here, since it is the fluidity of the shaman's
actions and not his thoughts which is crucial: "the motions of the tricks (reinforced through
their exact duplication by the spirits) . . . effect the cure." Thus, while fluid actions enjoin
the spirits "to use their power to cure," bungled tricks force them "to perform actions that
are (similarly) disjointed, undirected, and destructive." Rather than curing, the shaman
who acts in such a fashion "kills by unleashing uncontrollable chaotic power on the world."
Shamans had reason to fear being "shamed" in front of an audience, as well as to learn and
gain proficiency in new tricks.

that you should tell him, for don't you know that he is troubled by all the talk of the men? I mean this; do have mercy that he may live," said she. Then I said to her, "This is disconcerting at the coming of daylight," for it was now really getting daylight in the morning. "Let us go home, else we might be seen," said I to her. Then I stood up and went home to my house. Then my wife said that she never slept for she was worrying about me, for Aixagidalagilis was a bad man. My wife said I should not agree to go to him, "if he should call for you again," said my wife to me. Then my mind met the wishes of my wife. That made me happy, that he now had told me that he only pretended to be a shaman; and they truly believed, the early men, that he was the only, really great shaman. Then I was glad that I had found out that all he did was made up, for he said that there was no one true shaman among the shamans in this our world here, when he spoke to me.

1.42   Now he was truly an ordinary person after this. I never saw him again. One man came whose name was Naxwalis, who belongs to the numaym True-Name, and told that Aixagidalagilis had started away at night, when it became night again after the time of our talk together under the spruce tree. Nobody knew which way they had gone, he and his wife Hakwagilaogwa and their daughter Inviter-Woman and also their son, whose name was Sparrow. Then said Naxwalis that he went away for shame on account of the talking of all the men, for they said he should be ashamed because he did not let all the men see the sickness of the sick person that he referred to as the thing sucked out of him; for always 3.11   many blankets were paid to him, and a large canoe was paid to him, when the sick one was a respected person. Therefore was very sick the heart of Aixagidalagilis. Then Naxwalis asked me to take care in case I should happen to meet him, for it was really not too serious a matter for him to shoot anyone, whosoever beat him in giving potlatches and in practicing shamanism. Therefore he was really feared. Oh! I have forgotten to mention what he said to me that night under the spruce tree, when Aixagidalagilis said to me, "Don't you know that it is bad to allow all the men to see the sickness, for it blinds those by whom it is seen. Therefore many of the first Indians have one eye shut, those who have seen the sickness. It is like the lightning of the thunder." This is the last of what he said.

1.42   Now I believe he went crazy after this. For almost one year he did not come home to Fort Rupert. Now it was autumn; then he came home. Now he was really crazy, he and his daughter Inviter-Woman. Only his wife Hakwagilaogwa and his son Sparrow paddled as they came home. Then I went to see him. When I went into his house he at once tried to speak; but I did not understand what he said to me. In vain I pitied him, for really I did not understand what he tried to say to me. Then Inviter-Woman was sitting at the right hand side of the fire of their house. She just kept on laughing. When for a short time she stopped laughing then she cried and she herself pulled out her hair. Her mother Hakwagilaogwa told me what troubled her, that a great unholiness had been brought down upon her husband, when he happened to find the double-headed serpent[9] at Oseq, when he went hunting in the evening, with Inviter-Woman steering, for she was menstruating. "Then, it is said, they arrived at Aosayaogum, at the mouth of the river. Then it is said Aixagidalagilis saw something crawling down like an animal creeping among the salal bushes. At once, it is said, your friend took up his gun to shoot it. It is said the aforesaid animal came out of the salal bushes and lay crossways on the rock there near the bank of the river. Then your friend recognized that it was the double-headed serpent, for it had one head at each end. It is said in the middle of it was a large head of a man. It is said your friend saw it plainly and then he no longer knew our world, he and Inviter-Woman. They were dead. And so, it is said, they were brought to life by a handsome man who came. Then, it is said, the man said to your friend, 'I was seen by you. I was going to give good luck to you, but this was the cause of unholiness, the menstruating woman sitting in the stern of your canoe. Therefore, from this day on, you will have trouble until the time of your death,' said the double-headed serpent-man as he disappeared," said Hakwagilaogwa, as she was telling me. "And so from that time on he does not know what he is saying, and also Inviter-Woman," said she.

Now Aixagidalagilis and his daughter Inviter-Woman were just getting worse. They became more crazy. It may have been three winters before Aixagidalagilis died. Then for a short time Inviter-Woman came to her senses. Perhaps six months or seven beginning from the time when her father died she came to her senses. Then Inviter-Woman lived a long time. Then she also died. Now that is the end of the talk about Aixagidalagilis who was believed by all the tribes to be really a great shaman who had gone through (all the secrets). Then I found out that he was just a great liar about everything that he did in his shamanism.

In the house of a shamaness

Then I went to Nimkish at Yilis in the winter. There I was going to stay in the house of Memxo. When we went into his house, his wife spread a new made mat for me to sit on, as they do for the novice shaman; for everything is new, the dish and the dipping dish for grease and new was my eating spoon, because all the tribes believed me to be a true   3.1

---

[9] The *sisiutl* is a serpent with a head on each end and a human face in the center of its body. The Kwakiutl consider it "one of the most terrifying of all beings." On the *sisiutl's* place in Kwakiutl mythology, where it "metaphorizes all-pervading hunger" and Transformer's killing of it represents "the first step for the development of morality," cf. Walens (1981:124–32). For a summary of the *sisiutl's* characteristics, cf. Goldman (1975:236).

shaman, but I only pretended to be a shaman, because I wanted to find out all the ways of the shamans of the tribes.

1.32

The wife of Memxo, herself a shaman, took Quaselid back into the forest to a "house made of spruce branches," so that he could witness her attempt to cure a woman afflicted with "green matter" in the stomach. The shaman claimed that the details of her technique came in a dream from "toad, the great supernatural one," but it was reported to Qaselid's wife that the new techniques which she from time to time introduced into her performances were in fact plagiarized from other shamans: "Your friend Helagolsela invented it with her husband, that she should pretend to be a shaman. Now really she is paid many blankets when she is treating a respected man. Therefore she does this: when she sees a novice shaman who comes from the different tribes she tries to find out all he does." This rumor seems to have been confirmed on the following day, when the shaman, speaking to Qaselid and his wife, said, "This was my thought when I asked you and your husband to come; for a husband cannot disobey, even if it is difficult, what his wife says. I mean to say this to you, Made-to-Spout-in-House; I beg this renowned great shaman, your husband, to add to my power."

1.41

While still talking with the shaman, Helagolsela, Qaselid was summoned by a woman who had "got weak," and was having fainting spells. Entering the room where the woman was lying, "I sat down at her right hand side and I was asked to feel of her chest and stomach. Then I felt of her. When I had just begun to feel of her chest she opened her eyes. She spoke and said, "Oh wonder! You have come, master. Now that you have come in time I have come to my senses." Apparently, Qaselid's presence and touch were enough to effect a cure, and he and his wife were soon on their way home.

The successful shaman remains a skeptic

3.11

. . . When daylight came in the morning we came home to Fort Rupert, and now I had found out all the ways of the shamans of all the tribes, for all of them do as is done by Helagolsela, for she only presses downward with both her hands on the stomach of the sick woman so that may go down what she calls green matter, that she may pass it off. Only lately the new shamans of the Fort Rupert speaking tribes imitate the shamans of the Nakwaxdax who suck. . . . Only one shaman was seen by me, who sucked at a sick man and I never found out whether he was a real shaman or only made up. Only for this reason I believe that he is a shaman; he does not allow those who are made well to pay him. I truly never once saw him laugh. . . . And now is ended the talk about shamans.

2
Contacting the Spirits in the Shaking Tent

Introduction

When Europeans first made contact with them in the mid-seventeenth century, the people whom we today know as the Ojibwa (or Chippewa) were living along the north shore of Lake Huron and around the east end of Lake Superior. During the summer they for the most part gathered in villages at major fisheries, such as Sault Ste. Marie, and dispersed in the winter to live and hunt in smaller family groups. The rigid system of family hunting and trapping territories which came to characterize the Northern Ojibwa seems, however, to have developed in the post-contact period under the impetus of the fur trade.

There was and is no Ojibwa "tribe" in the sense of a unified sociopolitical entity. Deepening involvement in the fur trade stimulated migrations of various groups from their earlier homeland, and by about 1800 there were four identifiable segments of the Ojibwa people. Those who migrated westward through the territory north of Lake Superior are commonly referred to as the Saulteaux (the name itself derives from their former residence at Sault Ste. Marie), or Northern Ojibwa. They lived mainly in small, isolated hunting bands, and in contrast to their kinsmen to the south did not harvest wild rice or make maple sugar. The Southwest Ojibwa traveled through what is today the Upper Peninsula of Michigan and westward into Wisconsin and Minnesota, displacing the Sioux, who had previously inhabited large sections of that territory. They were hunters and gatherers preoccupied with the fur trade, and therefore did little farming. The Southeastern Ojibwa inhabited portions of the Lower Peninsula of Michigan and adjoining areas of Ontario, where they hunted, fished, and engaged in some horticulture. The Bungee, or Plains Ojibwa, who integrated themselves into the bison-hunting economy of the Northern Plains, comprised the western-most group of the Ojibwa people.

Of these four divisions the first two have historically been the most prominent. While there were important cultural differences between them (e.g., villages, such as the one at Chequamegon on the southern shore of Lake Superior, were more permanent and important in the south than the north, while the system of family hunting and trapping territories was rigorously developed in the north, but not the south), they shared a common language and participated in the broad patterns of the Woodland Algonkian culture.[1]

---

[1] This brief historical sketch of the Ojibwa is taken from Overholt and Callicott (1982:24), which may be consulted for citations of sources.

In this section we are concerned with a type of intermediation between humans and spirits characteristic of the Ojibwa and other Indians of the central and northeastern Woodlands of the United States and Canada. Often referred to as "conjuring," Hallowell says that among the Ojibwa it "is an institutionalized means for obtaining the help of different classes of spiritual entities by invoking their presence and communicating human desires to them." The conjurer is thus "a specialist in invocation" (Hallowell, 1942:9). Traditionally, the ability to conjure came as a "dream blessing" received during the puberty fast. It could not be purchased, and was not the result of instruction. As puberty fasting declined, visions received at other times have come to be accepted as legitimate. It is considered dangerous to attempt to conjure without having had proper visions (Hallowell, 1942:19–25).

Though often referred to as a "tent," the conjuring lodge is actually a barrel-shaped structure approximately 4 to 5 feet in diameter and 6 to 8 feet tall, open at the top. It is specially constructed by persons other than the conjurer immediately prior to the performance. Poles are firmly planted in the ground and bound together by hoops made of thinner saplings, and the whole is covered with birch bark, canvas, or some other convenient material. Rattles or bells may be attached, and these sound as the structure shakes (cf. Hallowell, 1942:35–40; Casagrande, 1956).

As we will see, the shaking of the lodge is believed to be caused by the entrance into it of various spirits, with whom the conjurer, and sometimes members of the audience, communicate. But the conjurer is not considered to be possessed by these spirits; Hallowell remarks that they are thought to speak "*to* or *in the presence* of the shaman, rather than enter his body and speak *through him*" (1942:12–3; cf. Cooper, 1944:81).

The main features of this "conjuring complex" (Ray, 1941) have a fairly wide distribution across the northern United States and southern Canada. The shaking tent form of the rite seems to have originated among the Algonkian-speaking peoples of the northeastern Woodlands (including the Ojibwa) and to have been brought to the Plains by other Algonkian groups, such as the Plains Cree, Cheyenne, Arapaho, and Blackfoot (Hultkrantz, 1967; Schaeffer, 1969). Regional variations of course occur, as our Gros Ventre text (2.3 below) illustrates. Eventually, there developed on the Plains a form in which the shaking of the lodge was lost and a feature found only occasionally in the northeast, the binding and "miraculous" release of the shaman (the so-called "Houdini trick"), became prominent. Among the Sioux, this rite was referred to as "yuwipi" (cf. Section 3).

The reconstruction of a "typical" shaking tent rite with which our selection of texts begins (2.1) is taken from Diamond Jenness' study of the social and religious life of a community of Ojibwa Indians on Parry Island, Ontario, located on the northeast coast of Lake Huron's Georgian

Bay. This group was somewhat more acculturated than the Saulteaux, or Northern Ojibwa, of the Berens River in the Lake Winnipeg country of Manitoba, among whom Hallowell began to do fieldwork in 1930. Hallowell was one of the major figures in the study of the Ojibwa, and his writings and those of others who followed him make possible a quite explicit description of the assumptions of the Ojibwa world view in terms of which the conjuring described in the texts can be understood. A convenient introduction to that world view and to the anthropological literature on the topic may be found in Overholt and Callicott (1982:139–66). The Gros Ventres, a name given the Algonkian-speaking Atsinas by French traders, lived in the northern Plains, where they were allies of the Blackfoot confederacy. Their form of the rite has elements in common with both the Ojibwa shaking tent and the Sioux yuwipi. The Gros Ventres text reprinted here was recorded by Fr. John M. Cooper, a contemporary of Hallowell who did extensive research among Algonkians. According to Cooper's informants, the series of events described is supposed to have occurred in the 1880's.

The shaking tent rite has been observed and reported by white visitors among the Indians of the northeastern Woodlands since the earliest days of contact. In his *Relation* for the year 1634 Father Paul le Jeune describes witnessing a performance among the Montagnais of Quebec. In this case the tent was set up inside Le Jeune's cabin, in which the lights had been extinguished. The structure shook violently for three hours, during which time the "juggler" (Le Jeune's term for a conjurer) called upon and spoke with "Genii," asking them about his own and his wife's health, the proximity of game animals, and the amount of snow that would fall during the up-coming winter. There is reference also to flying sparks and the juggler's soul leaving his body (Thwaites, 1897: vol. 6, pp. 163–73). Le Jeune's *Relation* for 1637 returns briefly to the shaking tent, the good Father puzzling over how a man would have enough strength to forcibly move such a sturdy structure for a "long" time (Thwaites, 1898: vol. 12, pp. 17–21). A convenient guide to the early accounts, which are scattered through the *Jesuit Relations* and various travelogues and reports, is Lambert (1955:13–46, excerpted in 1956). Additional information on the rite may be found in Casagrande (1956), Coleman (1937), Densmore (1932), Flannery (1939), and Morriseau (1965:70–81). An interesting side-light is provided by Gary Granzberg and his colleagues, who studied some isolated Cree communities in northern Manitoba whose first experience with television came in December of 1973. Though the shaking tent ceremony had mostly died out by that time, traditional conceptualizations of communication associated with it had a demonstrable effect upon how the people responded to what they saw on TV (Granzberg, *et al.*, 1977).

Two recent books deserve special notice. C. Vecsey has written a full-scale history of Ojibwa religion which provides excellent background for the following texts and includes a section on the shaking tent (1983:103–6). J. Grim (1983) identifies four "patterns" in classical Siberian shamanism ("cosmology," "tribal sanction," "numinous encounter" and its "ritual enactment," and "trance experience") and uses these as the framework for an explication of Ojibwa shamanism, including the shamans of the shaking tent.

Texts

2.1 An ethnologist's reconstruction of a "typical" Ojibwa shaking tent ceremony (Jenness, 1935: 66–7)

3.21   Let us imagine ourselves now in an Indian camp, sharing all the views of the Parry Islanders as to what takes place during a conjuror's seance. Some man has hired him to discover why a relative lies dangerously ill, and, with the assistance of friends, has erected a proper conjuring lodge.

2.13   We idle around until dusk, for . . . the conjuror may not operate in full daylight. At last he approaches, crawls beneath the birch-bark envelope and disappears within. He is speaking. We cannot distinguish the words, but we know he is calling the other *manidos*[2] that always lend their aid. There is a sudden thud, and the lodge rocks violently, for a spirit (*medewadji*: a spirit of the conjuring lodge) has entered it. Another thud and further rocking; then another, and still another. Perhaps a voice says "What do you want me for?," and snapping turtle (*mashikkan*) answers: "We do not want your help." Inside the lodge there are now five or six *medewadji* or *manidos*, souls or spirits of animals like the bear and the serpent, who have assembled together with the spirit of thunder, their chief, and of snapping turtle, longest-lived of all creatures, their interpreter. We cannot see them, but we understand that turtle rests at the bottom of the lodge, feet up, keeping it from sinking into the ground; that thunder is at the top, covering it like a lid; and that the other spirits are perched around the hoop that encircles the frame. They look like human beings about 4 inches tall, but have long ears and squeaking voices like bats.

2.13   Meanwhile the conjuror has been kneeling on the floor of the lodge with his face to the ground, and remains thus (supposedly) throughout the performance. Probably he has omitted to take any tobacco inside with him, and since the *manidos* require a little tribute before they set

---

[2] "*Manido*" (variously spelled *manitou*, *manito*, etc.) is the Ojibwa word for "spirit," and carries with it a connotation of power.

about their task his employer must hand in some tobacco over the top of the lodge. A brief period of silence follows, and the aroma of tobacco smoke floats from the shrine. Then the *manidos* discuss among themselves the cause of the sick man's condition. They decide that a sorcerer has bewitched him, so with a violent rocking of the lodge one of them departs to summon the soul of the offender for trial.

The audience outside the lodge now becomes visibly excited, and the employer of the conjuror draws nearer. Again the lodge rocks as the *manido* brings in the sorcerer's soul. "Is it you who have caused my son's sickness?" shouts the employer. "Is it you?" The soul cannot avoid confessing if the sorcerer is guilty. "Shall we kill him? Shall we kill him?" shout the *medewadji* in their squeaky voices, while thunder closely guards the top of the lodge to prevent the soul's escape. "No, not yet," replies the man, who is generally afraid of being held responsible for the sorcerer's death. "Let him restore my son to health and pay us fitting compensation. How much will he pay?" So the man outside and the soul within bargain with one another until they arrive at an agreement. Then the *manidos* release the soul, which returns to its owner; and the lodge rocks for the last time as they themselves depart. The seance has ended. The exhausted conjuror crawls out from his shelter and retires to his tent. Tomorrow, or the next day perhaps, the relatives of the sick man will pay him for his toil.   3.11

The performance just described explains the general character of these seances; but no two of them were exactly alike, not only because they were held for different needs, but because each conjuror had his special methods. On rare occasions he might even remain outside the lodge (presumably after concealing a confederate within). Sometimes, it is said, his *medewadji* or helping spirits cured sickness by exchanging the soul of the patient with that of a man in perfect health; the latter merely felt indisposed for a short time until his new soul regained strength. Or, again, when a band of Indians were starving, the helping spirits summoned and killed the shadow[3] of a moose or deer; then the next day the hunters killed the animal itself, which no longer possessed a shadow to warn it of danger.

2.13

2.3

2.2 Ojibwa conjuring (Hallowell, 1942)

How a conjurer arrived at the cause of the illness in one . . . case is illustrated in the following account.

W could not pass his urine freely. He had been treated by a conjurer

---

[3] Jenness (1935:18–28) reports that the Parry Island Ojibwa thought that all objects in the world were made up of three parts: body, soul, and shadow. The latter could wander free from the body, observing and reporting what was going on in the vicinity.

but the medicine he had been taking did not help him. When he heard
1.41   that this Indian was going to conjure, W asked him to try to find out why
he did not get better. At the seance W's mother, a woman past sixty
2.13   years, was sitting at his side. After the performance had been going on
for some time and a number of *pawaganak*[4] had manifested themselves,
one of these supernatural beings said, "How is the sick Indian feeling
tonight?" W replied, "Not very good." Then the *pawagan, memengweci,*[5]
sang a song. After this was finished *memengweci* spoke again. "It is some
of my medicine that my grandson (i.e., the conjurer) has been giving
away. I don't know why it should not do its work. Perhaps some of the
old people did something wrong. I'd like to know if I am right about
that." At this one of the men in the audience said, "Why don't you
speak?" He was sitting near W's mother who asked, "Are you speaking to
me?" "Yes," said the other Indian. Then the old woman remained silent
for a little while. Finally she spoke:

"I don't know. Perhaps it is true. A long while ago there were four of
1.41   us playing together—two boys and two girls. I was only a little girl then.
We had made a little wigwam and we were playing that we were camping
like the old folks. Of course I did not know that I was doing anything
wrong. I had a little thimble belonging to my mother and I was sewing.
One of the little boys was lying down and I was lying down, too. His
little penis was standing erect. I took the thimble and shoved it on the
end of his penis. Then I told him to go and piss. He said, 'I can't. I can't.
It's too tight. It hurts.' Then he started to cry a little. So I took the thimble off and we told him not to tell."

After this recital the conjurer said, in his own voice, "I thought there
was something that stopped the medicine from working." (Hallowell,
1942:55–6)

*   *   *

Especially strong conjurers can even summon the souls of the
dead into the lodge, as can be seen from the following account of
a ceremony that took place in 1914. Hallowell's informant was an
eyewitness, having himself cut the poles and helped in the construction of the conjuring lodge.

After sunset William came out of his dwelling. He had his coat on
and carried a blanket and pillow. He used the pillow to kneel on while in
2.13   the conjuring lodge. He went into the lodge and at once it began to

---

[4] Spirits, especially as they manifest themselves in dream experiences and in the conjuring lodge.
[5] One of a class of "semi-human beings," who are said to "live in the rocks" and who "are
met by human beings" (Hallowell, 1942:7).

shake. All the people were seated around it. Before he went in William called me to him and handed me some tobacco wrapped in a handkerchief. He said, "Give this to the people, give everyone a pipeful." I did as he told me and after he was inside I called to him and said I had some left. At this William replied, "That tobacco does not belong to me. It belongs to 'our grandfathers.' Pass it to anyone that wants a smoke."

By this time the tent was shaking harder and the *pawaganak* had started to come in. They named themselves and sang their songs. All the winds were there and, of course, *mikinak*.[6] There were also present *memengweci*, *pijiu* (Lynx) and many others.   2.13

After a couple of hours some one came in singing very, very strongly.   2.13
I heard William saying to it, "One thing I was asked and I don't know the answer. You are one of those that sees many things. You can look around and tell me what I don't know." Then this *pawagan* sang again, a very long song. It was the boss *djibai*.[7] Then this *pawagan* spoke, "I saw something a long, long way back. It's the old people's fault this man here is sick."

Then the boss *djibai* talked to the sick man (J.B.):

D.: How long have you been sick?

J.B.: Quite a long while.

D.: Where are you sick?

J.B.: I'm always feeling pain around my waist. It is as if there were something drawing me together there.

D.: Your father has something to do with this. If you like I'll call him and ask him to come in here.

J.B.: (*half to himself*) I wonder if it can be so?

Then someone whispered to J.B.: It's all right. Go ahead.

So he said: I'd like to hear my father.

The boss *djibai* sang again. All at once, while this was going on, someone else came in the conjuring lodge. The singing stopped and everyone sat very quiet.

Then William spoke: Here is the one you asked for. You can talk to him. (*The tent was shaking very gently now.*)

J.B.: Is that you, father?

F.: Yes, my son.

J.B.: Who are you with?

F.: I'm with my grandchild. Ever since I left, I've always been happy. I've never been hungry. I've never been thirsty. I've never suffered any pain. It is a beautiful country where I am living. When I was alive I always tried to do what was right. Try to do the same thing, my son; don't do anything wrong to anyone. If there is ever anyone who says

---

[6] The "master" or "owner" of the "great turtles" (Hallowell, 1942:7).

[7] "I.e., the master of the spirits of the dead." (A.I.H.)

something bad to you, don't answer. That's the way I tried to act. If you act this way you will be glad. You'll see me some day, too. I see some people I know sitting outside. I see my oldest daughter!

Suddenly another voice, that of a child, came from the conjuring lodge.

C.: I see my mother sitting there. Don't do that, Mother. I don't like to see you do that. (*The woman whose father and adopted daughter appeared in the conjuring tent was crying.*) You hear my voice here. I'm happy. It is always bright like day where I live. It is never dark. There are pretty flowers where I live, it's like a great garden. And there are lots of us. There are great singers there, too. Don't forget what I am telling you. Live right and some day you'll find me.

Then the father of J.B. spoke again:

F.: Have you taken much medicine for your sickness, my son?

J.B.: Yes, but it has not helped me.

F.: There was one time, my son, that I made a mistake. A man died and I dressed him for burial. I pulled his belt too tight. I pulled as hard as I could. That is what makes you sick now. That is the reason the medicine you have taken has not helped you. The medicine cannot work itself down into your body.

J.B.: I hope I will get well now.

F.: My son, I hope you will. It's my fault that you have been sick around your waist.

3.21 Then William spoke again: I don't know what kind of medicine to give this man tomorrow morning. Is there anyone here inside that has some medicine I can give this man?

At this point *memengweci* spoke up: I'll give him a little.

William: You can give it to him tomorrow morning.

M.: No, I'll go and get it now.

So he went out.

J.B.: I wonder how far he has to go.

Pawagan: There is only one place to go.

Someone in the audience: Where is that?

Pawagan: *Memengweciwak* live at *kickabiskan*, high rock.

Soon the *menengweci* was back in the conjuring lodge and said to William: When morning comes you give that Indian this medicine of mine I have brought you and tell him how to use it. (Hallowell, 1942: 57–9)

*　　*　　*

Besides illness, there are other occasions for conjuring, among them to protect the camp from an approaching windigo[8], to ob-

---

[8] A cannibal giant with horrible features and a heart of ice.

tain knowledge of an enemy's movements, to foretell future events, to direct hunters to the location of game, and to locate lost or stolen articles (Hallowell, 1942:64–9). Conjurers themselves view some of their number as fakes, others as extremely powerful. Recognition of the latter seems largely based upon acts of power, or "tricks," which these persons are able to perform, such as locating and/or physically restoring lost objects, making the lodge shake even while tightly bound and quickly escaping from the bonds themselves[9], and the like.

This is in harmony with native theories of supernatural blessings and with a mode of life which offers considerable latitude for the cultivation   2.3 of individual versions of the basic cultural material. The basic philosophy of these people offers ample validation for unique powers of the individual, and the threshold of credulity remains low so long as these powers are expressed in terms of familiar native patterns. And the respect, if not awe, which the demonstration of unique powers meets, is ample moti-   3.1 vation for the individual who craves prestige. It is perhaps the major type of social recognition which this society has to offer. But it can only be won and maintained by actual demonstrations of magic power in competition with others. No doubt this is why it is said that conjurers are so jealous of one another. (Hallowell, 1942:71–2)

*   *   *

Europeans tended to be skeptical of the powers manifested by conjurers, and we have already seen that the Ojibwa did not consider all conjurers to be equal in power. But Hallowell notes that in the native view there was no general skepticism about the performances. Indeed, he reports a number of instances of former conjurers, since converted to Christianity, who until their deaths "asserted that they were not personally responsible for the manifestations" of power (e.g., the shaking of the lodge) that accompanied their performances (Hallowell, 1942:73–4).

Within the framework of native theory any skepticism with respect to the presence of the spirits in the conjuring tent is out of place. On the contrary, a conjuring performance provides perceptual evidence of the reality of spiritual entities, and in aboriginal times conjurers, along with other types of shamans, undoubtedly enjoyed outstanding prestige. For   3.1 the Ojibwa proper William Jones asserts that "nobody had so much influ-

[9] This "Davenport" (or "Houdini") trick is widely, but not universally, reported of shaking tent conjurers (cf. Hallowell, 1942:70 n. 117). It is similar to a principal feature of the yuwipi ceremonies described in Section 3, and indicates some cultural interconnection between the northeastern Woodlands and northern Plains.

ence as one who did the *tcisakiwin*,"[10] and formerly an equivalent statement would have been applicable to the Saulteaux. . . .

In view of such statements, is it possible to maintain that these conjurers were deliberate imposters, charlatans and frauds? I think not. Nor
is it necessary to conclude with the Spiritualists that they told all they
knew, and to draw the inference that the movements of the tent and the
vocal phenomena actually were due to supernormal forces. The problem
is much more complex than either of these antithetical solutions suggest.
To my mind the essential point is this:

As individuals these conjurers had played a role that was set by their
2.1   culture. And they had played it successfully. Their personal statements,
in fact, reflect the thoroughness with which they had identified themselves with it, and consequently the depth of their personal convictions.
1.21   Not only had they dreamed the appropriate dreams that validated their
role in their own eyes; we must assume that they unconsciously invested
2.11   the act of conjuring with an emotional aura which was experienced as if
some objective forces were involved. Such an emotional vortex is not an
unfamiliar psychological phenomenon and while it may verge toward the
abnormal in certain types of personality, individuals with creative artistic
gifts are well acquainted with it. In Western culture, in fact, we still have
a tradition that the poet or musician becomes "inspired." To play a role
successfully that is thoroughly validated by the ideology and values of
any human society is only to act a part in the sense that we all act a part.
The successful conjurer thoroughly identifies himself with his role. The
approved means are part of the total situation and inseparable from it.
When, as outsiders, we raise questions about insincerity and fraud,
therefore, it simply indicates that we find it impossible to penetrate and
understand the behavioral world in which these Indians lived.

In rejecting, as we are inclined to do, all the a priori assumptions
upon which their belief system is based and in terms of which their be-
3.2   havioral world is organized, we are actually indicting the foundations of
their culture, which is irrelevant to the problem of how conjuring functions within that culture. Within the cultural system of the Saulteaux, for
example, *conjuring as an institution* serves a variety of functions and is
an integral part of Saulteaux society as a going concern. From the standpoint of the Indians themselves, therefore, it is not conjuring as an institution that can be challenged, for it embodies too many beliefs and values that are basic to the operation of the social order as a whole. All that
is possible is to differentiate between *genuine* conjurers and those
thought to lack the necessary supernatural validation for their task.

It was not until 1940, after I had spent a number of seasons with the

---

[10] An Ojibwa term for the act of conjuring; also spelled *djisakiwin*.

Saulteaux and written this monograph, that I had an intimate conversation with an Indian that illuminates this differentiation in a very striking manner and bears out the deductions cited above which I had made previously.

This man, whom I shall call M, had conjured only once. What he tried to do was to discover the hidden cause of a young woman's illness. He found that she was sick because her father had used "bad" medicine to make a man he disliked suffer. The illness of the woman was an automatic penalty for her father's aggression. The outcome of the conjuring performance was that the old man not only confessed he had done wrong but immediately fetched the "bad" medicine and turned it over to the conjurer. The woman recovered so that conjuring in this instance was a perfect success.

Imagine my surprise, then, when M spontaneously told me not to believe for one moment that the conjuring lodge was shaken by spirits or that the voices heard were not the vocalizations of the conjurer himself. Such statements, if removed from the context of our total conversation, would suggest that this man was quite clearly an impostor. Yet this is by no means the case. When we consider other things which he also told me in the same conversation I believe that an integral psychological picture is produced which is realistic, despite the fact that it contains features that seem inconsistent from our point of view. It demonstrates, I believe, the insight that can be gained through one man's actual unpretentiousness and thoroughgoing honesty. We can discern a little more clearly how conjuring works as viewed from the standpoint of the conjurer himself.

M was not an impostor from the native point of view, nor from the standpoint of his own ego, because he had a dream revelation that validated his conjuring. M said he had his dream for the first time when he was a baby, in fact he was still on the cradle-board. It was later repeated several times. M dreamed of the West Wind, the main one that blows in the conjuring lodge, he said. He also dreamed of the lodge itself and of growing up to be a man who conjured. (Parenthetically, I may add that M's father was a well-known conjurer.) In his dream, *wisakedjak*[11] came to M and told him of a sick woman who still had years of life ahead of her—if he conjured. After M was married and had two children there was a sick woman in camp whom he recognized as the one he had been told about and he knew he could cure her. So M had a conjuring lodge of eight poles made. He ordered that they be planted very deep in the ground and he said the lodge was not easy to move from the outside.

But as soon as I got inside (he said) and put my hand on one of the

1.21

2.1

[11] An anthropomorphic spirit; the culture hero.

posts it seemed as if the lodge were very easy to move. It is something like beating a drum; it was almost as if it shook itself. I knew just what to do, what songs to sing and everything else. There are more than thirty different songs. The inside of the lodge was not dark; it was as light as

2.11   day. I saw *wisakedjak* plainly before me there. He told me what was the matter with the woman. So I said to her father, "You have done something wrong. You have used medicine you got in the *midewiwin*[12] for bad purposes. You made a man suffer illness for three winters." I told him to give up the medicine at once or else his daughter would die. So the old man gave up the medicine.

        If we take this account at its face value, as I believe we must, it is

2.2   obvious how M's experience was colored by the behavioral world in which he was brought up. No skepticism is evident with respect to the fundamental beliefs of Saulteaux society. M had full confidence in the validity of his dream experiences and their significance for subsequent action. And I see no reason to doubt his vision of *wisakedjak* in the conjuring lodge nor the illumination in the lodge of which he speaks. Yet we know that psychologically speaking these were of the nature of projec-

2.1   tions. But from the standpoint of his behavioral world they were as "real" as anything could be. M was caught up in the whole situation. In fact his success in putting over such a performance without previous experience might almost class as a miracle in itself. But I may add that M is an unusually capable individual in all departments of Saulteaux life and, as estimated from the Rorschach record I obtained, he undoubtedly is a man of very superior mental endowments. Consequently I am ready to believe that the observation of conjuring performances over a long period of years, particularly since his father was a conjurer, may easily have prepared him for the one performance which he undertook. On this occasion he was genuinely "inspired."

        M, then, is anything but an impostor despite his perfectly honest

2.1   statements of the mechanics of tent shaking. Actually, he played the game according to the rules. He had a dream blessing, he conjured without formal tutelage at the proper time and he cured the woman because of the power obtained through his dream blessing. These features are essentially those called for in the cultural blue-print of conjuring in Saulteaux society. The mechanics of shaking the lodge are subordinate to these and unless *we* believe in the possibility of supernatural forces ourselves it must be assumed that the Saulteaux conjurer must integrate the material means employed in manipulating the lodge with his personal inspiration and beliefs. In the case of M, of course, the effectiveness of conjuring as an institution was supported by the cure effected. And M

[12] The Ojibwa medicine society.

himself *stressed* this fact; he did not deny it. Consequently I believe that in the last analysis the point to be emphasized is M's honesty—an honesty, that is to say, of belief as well as of action. It is for this reason that his statements give us a psychologically realistic picture of the Saulteaux conjurer. We have illuminated for us the various factors in the situation that must be reconciled.

At the same time it must be clear that although M was honest with me, he might have been inclined to be less so if he had been a practicing conjurer, or if contemporary Saulteaux culture were less undermined through acculturation. For I believe we must assume that conjuring, as a going concern, of necessity must receive support from the belief that supernaturals manifest themselves in the conjuring lodge according to the prevailing notions already described. But it may be doubted if the conjurer, no matter what his state of mind at the time of any particular performance, can fully believe what the spectators believe. Ordinarily he must maintain a professional reserve on certain points.[13] (Hallowell, 1942:73, 75–9)

*   *   *

Finally, I reproduce in full Hallowell's brief chapter on the "social functions of conjuring."   3.0

In addition to its ostensible and immediate purpose as defined by the occasions upon which it is practiced, conjuring as an institution plays   3.2 an important role in Saulteaux society from a more inclusive point of view. It reinforces values and beliefs that make Saulteaux society a going concern.[14]

In the first place, it provides tangible validation of basic concepts about the nature of the dynamic entities of the cosmos, familiar in belief and myth. By means of it the *pawaganak* become objectified to men through a direct appeal to auditory experience; at the same time they are individualized by a qualitative differentiation of the "voices" issuing from the lodge. Each voice can be identified with the personality, hence the "real" existence of the *pawagan* from whom it is believed to issue. This

---

[13] Hallowell points out that there is a standard response to doubts about the cause of the lodge's movement. While Ojibwa "readily admit" that some individual conjurers have shaken, or tried to shake, the lodge themselves, they insist that something bad (e.g., illness, or information provided during the performance proving unreliable) follows such episodes. Thus, "skepticism is directed toward individuals who practice conjuring rather than toward the institution itself." In addition counter-examples are used to provide support for the traditional view, e.g., extremely old or otherwise physically handicapped individuals who have been known to conjure for hours without becoming exhausted (Hallowell, 1942:79–80).

[14] On this general topic cf. also Hallowell (1934).

auditory association is also promoted by the adoption of the characteristic vocal peculiarities of certain *pawaganak* as heard in the conjuring tent, by story tellers. A narrator, for instance, will imitate the vocal peculiarities of *mikinak* in repeating the myths in which the Great Turtle appears. The songs sung by each *pawagan* also aid in establishing the latter's identity and individuality. Consequently, to doubt the existence of the *pawaganak* is almost tantamount to doubting the evidence of one's senses.

3.2   This objectification and differentiation of the personalities of spiritual beings likewise humanizes them, and this effect is enhanced by the intimacy established between the audience attending a conjuring performance and the *pawaganak*. These spiritual beings are not only heard, but rapport is established between them and the human beings present, principally by the repartee that goes on between members of the audience and *mikinak*. I fancy that there is an important psychological principle involved here. Objectification, without the encouragement of rapport through conversation which promotes a certain sense of intimacy, might tend to set up a cool and detached appraisal of the spirits which might lead to skepticism and disbelief. In short, the situation as defined is ideally adapted to promote the ends which it undoubtedly serves. Tangible support is likewise given to the belief that the souls of human beings survive death when the spirits of the dead are invoked in the conjuring lodge. And in the seance described, one of these spirits spoke of how pleasant a place the Land of the Dead was.

3.2   There is one spiritual being, however, who is never invoked in the conjurer's lodge. This is *kadabendjiget*, the high god. "He" remains remote and aloof from direct contact with the lives of men. His name is seldom mentioned, he is regarded with awe and it is unthinkable that he should enter into intimate and tangible relations with man. But even in this case the conjuring lodge as an institution supports native beliefs in a negative fashion. The high god is conspicuous by his *absence*, this fact emphasizing his status.

3.2   In the second place, by implicitly exposing the dangers involved in a violation of the mores in certain instances, conjuring lends indirect support to the social structure. And directly it reinforces the sanction which is one of the motivating forces for conformity. This sanction operates through the belief that illness will inevitably follow deviations from established codes of conduct. Murder, deceit, incest and the minor sexual perversions, even unnecessarily cruel treatment of animals, are under a disease sanction. Since a conjurer is called upon from time to time to fathom the hidden sources of illness, the exposure of moral turpitude as the basic cause in some instances serves to remind the community of its potency. The disease sanction is thus upheld, and a warning provided for those who may be inclined to depart from traditonal patterns of conduct.

In the third place, the very existence of conjuring as an institution,   3.2
and the possibility of resorting to it when consumed with fear, apprehension, or worry, creates a sense of security and confidence in the face of
the hazards of life. If game is scarce and famine threatens, a conjurer can
be appealed to and, with the aid of his supernatural helpers, he may be
able to direct the hunter to the place where game may be found. By
similar means it is possible for him to secure news about the health or
circumstances of absent persons which will alleviate apprehension.
Furthermore, a powerful conjurer is able to protect a whole community
or specific individuals from malevolent influences. He can determine the
source of magically projected illness and even retaliate in kind if he is
strong enough. Or he may protect a whole community from the ravages
of a *windigo*.

Since conjuring performances are always carried out in public, the   3.2
concrete demonstration in case after case of the way in which the dynamic forces of the universe can be mobilized for the benefit of man
creates a sense of security and confidence. Perhaps this is the reason one
old pagan remarked to me that the Christian religion might be all right
for the next life, but that the Indian religion was better for this one.

Finally, a conjuring performance provides diversion and entertainment for those assembled to witness it, despite the fact that this is not its
ostensible purpose. It might even be characterized as a form of dramatic
art, confined like radio performances to the auditory level. Dramatic
qualities must be particularly striking in those instances where two conjurers are struggling for power or where a *windigo* is being fought. I   2.2
believe that the Saulteaux themselves are not insensible to esthetic qualities in these performances. This is evidenced in their evaluations of the
seances of different conjurers. They do not rate them exclusively in
terms of the truths revealed or the proximate ends believed to be
achieved. A conjurer, for example, who can bring a lot of *pawaganak*
into the tent is not only considered stronger in power than one who
commands fewer spirits, but the performance of the former is judged to
be *better*. That is to say, the Indians appear to *enjoy* a performance
where there is a great variety of *pawaganak* present, where the spirits
are well characterized and where there are funny things said. This requires considerable artistic skill on the part of the conjurer. A good ven-
triloquist will undoubtedly outrank a poor one since voice manipulation
is so essential to success. It is fair to say that a conjuring performance
which is thoroughly satisfying and convincing to the Indians is one which
is on a higher artistic level than one they deem unsatisfactory. One of the
criticisms of the performance described was that the conjurer did not
bring in enough spirits, although, as I have said, his prognostications all
proved correct.

In view of these wider social functions it is not difficult to understand   3.2

why conjuring has persisted up until the present day even in communities where the Indians have been Christianized and in other respects influenced by occidental culture. To my mind, the occurrence of conjuring in such cases is an index of the vitality of native beliefs, attitudes and values despite a veneer of acculturation. When conjuring entirely disappears we can be certain that the behavioral world of these Indians, as constituted in terms of their aboriginal belief system, already will have collapsed. Other institutions of occidental origin will have arisen to perform social functions relative to the new order of life which conjuring previously exercised in Saulteaux society.[15] (Hallowell, 1942:85–8)

2.3 The shaking tent among the Gros Ventre (Cooper, 1944:72–5)

A certain old woman (her great-great-grandchild is still living) had a ghost helper.[16] Her name was 'Woman' but for various reasons she was nicknamed 'Bear Old Woman.' When I was about ten years old a party of Gros Ventres was camped at Lodge Pole, about two miles from the Little Rocky Mountains. One night Cree enemies came and stole all the Gros Ventres' horses except those belonging to one man. This man loaned out his horses as far as they would go around to four of the Gros Ventres who went in pursuit of the Cree.

3.0   Then that evening two of the other men, one of them my father, approached Bear Old Woman. They filled up a pipe just as you do when you go to someone to doctor you, offered it to the old woman, and asked her to find out from her ghost helper who stole the horses and where they were. Bear Old Woman, who had quite a temper, got angry right away as usual and pushed the pipe away as a sign of refusal. Finally one of the young fellows there, a relative of hers, said: 'Well, let me smoke it,' to force her to accept. She angrily grabbed the pipe and had to go through with the rite. When she took the pipe she rubbed her hands on the ground and rubbed dust on the pipe and offered a prayer before smoking. The pipe was then smoked by her and by the two men who had approached her.

Then they began to get things ready. They killed a puppy, singed its hair off at a fire, took its insides out without skinning, quartered it up and boiled it. They put the boiled meat on a plate and got ready some

---

3.1

3.11

[15] It should be mentioned that, though conjurers are paid a fee for their services, conjuring cannot be considered a profession, since no one derives his living from it. Indeed, the fee is relatively small, and it is believed that one must conserve one's power and not conjure "too much" (i.e., even as much as several times a year). The major compensation accruing to a conjurer is prestige; cf. Hallowell (1942:31–3).

[16] It is characteristic of the Gros Ventre form of the rite that only one spirit, always the ghost of a deceased person, appears. This text is a narrative in the first person by one of Cooper's informants.

other kinds of food to give to the old woman. Then the two men filled up a pipe and they together, with a 'servant' went to Bear Old Woman's lodge. On arriving there they set down the plate of dog meat near the head of her bed, the pipe between the incense hearth and the lodge fire, and the other dishes between the lodge fire and the door.

When everything was arranged and Bear Old Woman was still sitting on her bed, she said: 'Whoever is the greatest unbeliever among you, come and tie me up.' One of the four volunteered. Then the old woman got up and went to a place just south of the head of the bed, to a little enclosure made by hanging up a blanket. He hobbled her four fingers with sinew, interlacing it in and out of the four fingers of each hand. Then he tied her hands together behind her back and also hobbled her feet. She was lying on a robe. He gathered the robe around her and tied her with rawhide thongs until only her head stuck out of the robe. And so he left her lying on her back. He returned to his place to the southeast of the old woman and sat down.

2.13

Then Bear Old Woman said: 'All right. Start to sing now.' They sang four tunes without stopping, the song belonging to the old woman's ghost helper. As they were singing the third time they heard an owl and the old woman said: 'Don't receive *that* spirit. He is bad. Continue singing.' So they continued and just as they finished the fourth time the old woman said: 'That is the one. Receive *that* spirit.' The people around heard these two owls.

2.13

When the second owl lighted on top of the lodge, the top shook and the ghost helper spoke: 'What do you want me for?' They said: 'We want you to tell us where our horses are and who has them so we can find them.' The ghost helper answered: 'All right. I'll have to go look for them, but you go ahead and smoke this pipe (the one lying near the incense hearth). When you have smoked up what is in the pipe, refill it and put it back in the same place and wait.'

They had barely started smoking when the ghost helper was back again. So they just dumped out what was left in the pipe and refilled it. The helper said: 'Never mind. I am hungry and want to eat.' But they didn't mind him. The spirit then said: 'Your horses are not very far away from here. Your four friends have already recaptured your horses and are bringing them back.' He also said to my father: 'One of your horses has a thick broad rawhide rope around his neck and is dragging it, and that other man's mare's colt will play out on the trip back home.'

After the helper had said all this, the four men judged that he was through, so they took the pipe and lit it and offered the helper a smoke. The inside of the old woman's lodge was dark as there was no fire. The helper took the pipe from their hands and then they saw it light up rhythmically as a pipe does when it is puffed, and after taking a few puffs the helper said to the men: 'You smoke the rest. I am hungry and want to eat.' They could hear him chewing on the dog meat inside where the woman was. After a while the helper said to the men: 'Here, you can eat the rest of this pup.' The meat had been eaten off of one hind leg of the pup so that just the bones were left. Then the ghost helper said: 'I see this foolish old woman lying here helpless.' Then they heard a noise as if the helper had struck the old woman with the flat of his hand and he was

2.1   heard blowing. The next instant the ghost helper said: 'Here, try to untie this,' and the knotted sinew and rawhide thong hit the chest of the man who had tied her up.

2.1   Then they heard the old woman give a long sigh. She had been in a trance all this time and was just coming out of it. Next the ghost helper said: 'Now I am going to leave you.' And they heard the same racket at the top of the lodge they had heard when he first came in and there was a violent shaking of the whole lodge, especially at the top of it.

        After the ghost helper was gone they kindled the fire again and there

2.13 was light. Bear Old Woman came out of the enclosure and sat down on the bed and prayed with the bowls of food in her hand. Then she and the men ate and afterwards sat around and smoked and chatted. Then the men went home and told what the spirit had said.

        Next morning all the people in the camp, including the children, got up early and went up on the highest nearby ground to look for the four men coming back with the horses. Towards evening of the day the four Gros Ventres who had gone in pursuit of the thieves brought all the horses back, except the one which, as the spirit had said, had played out and could not stand the trip back. And one of my father's horses had a rope around its neck as the ghost helper had said it had. The pursuers had caught up with the Cree and surprised them asleep in a little swamp covered with grass and brush and so took the horses back home. On the return trip they got lost in a bad storm, went in the wrong direction and not until daylight did they discover their mistake and so had to circle their way back. They had neither eaten nor slept during all the two days and nights they had been gone.

3
The Yuwipi Cult Among Contemporary Sioux

Introduction

The rites to which we now turn were performed among Western, or Teton, Sioux Indians living on the Pine Ridge Reservation in southwestern South Dakota. We have already noted the similarity of yuwipi ceremonies to the shaking tent rites of traditional Woodlands culture (section 2). Historically, then, yuwipi can be seen to have ancient roots, and the people themselves insist upon its antiquity. Lame Deer, in his younger days a practicing yuwipi-man, called it "one of our most ancient rites," and spoke of having learned of it from his grandmother, who in turn had been told about it during her own childhood (Lame Deer and Erdoes, 1972:184; cf. Feraca, 1961:155–6). The term "yuwipi" is usually said to mean "they wrap him up" (or, "they roll it up"), referring to the binding of the shaman which is characteristic of the rite (Powers, 1977:144). In addition Lame Deer relates the term to "the tiny, glistening rocks we pick up from the anthills. They are sacred. They have the power" (Lame Deer and Erdoes, 1972:185).[1]

The following texts both mention the visions through which yuwipi-men gain their power, and in this respect they correspond to other "sacred persons" among the Sioux (Powers, 1977:145, 150). Lame Deer suggests that instruction, and perhaps even designation, by a yuwipi-man could also be a factor: "I myself used to practice *yuwipi*, but I don't anymore. I have passed beyond this stage. But I have taught a number of men to become *yuwipis*, and I will teach more" (Lame Deer and Erdoes, 1972:187).

The principal male participants in a yuwipi ceremony prepare themselves by purification in a sweat lodge.[2] The ceremony itself is performed in total darkness, and has as its prominent features the binding and miraculous release of the shaman and the arrival of various spirits, whose presence is discerned by flashing sparks, voices, loud noises, and the like. In Lame Deer's view the binding is a mechanism "to make the spirits appear." Symbolically, the bound shaman is "dead,"[3] and "his spirit could be hundreds of miles away in the far hills, conversing with the

---

[1] Both Lame Deer and Erdoes (1972:183–97) and Powers (1977:143–54) have extended discussions of yuwipi.

[2] Cf. Feraca (1961:156–8) and Powers (1977:147–8). The sweat lodge plays an extremely important part in Sioux religion; cf. Brown (1953:31–43), Lame Deer and Erdoes (1972:174–82).

ancient ones" (Lame Deer and Erdoes, 1972:194–5). The ceremonies are commissioned by individuals who have specific needs, most often sickness or the desire to locate a lost person or object (Lame Deer and Erdoes, 1972:187).

The yuwipi shaman functions as an intermediary, communicating with the spirits that have arrived in the room and conveying their responses to questions brought by persons in attendance (Lame Deer and Erdoes, 1972:196–7; Powers, 1977:151–2). In doing so he not only addresses the present needs of specific individuals, but also provides an important element of cultural continuity both between generations and between the present and the more distant past (cf. Powers, 1977:187, 207).

In addition to the work already cited Powers has a book on yuwipi (1984). Lynd (1889:159) contains an early account of a yuwipi-like rite. Further descriptions of ceremonies may be found in Hurt and Howard (1952), Ruby (1966), and Kemnitzer (1978). Kemnitzer (1970) provides an analysis of the various ritual objects used in the ceremony, and Fugle (1966) attempts to set yuwipi in the context of other Lakota (Sioux) "night cults."

The following texts comprise two accounts by ethnologists of yuwipi ceremonies in which they were participant-observers. The first is brief, and will give the reader a quick impression of the main elements of such rites. The second is a more detailed description. It should be remembered that, while these rites are generally "typical," individual ceremonies will vary depending upon the circumstances which occasioned them, their physical setting, and the training and preferences of the shaman involved.

Texts

3.1 Frank Fools Crow's ceremony (Hurt, 1960:51–2)

3.0

Wesley Hurt attended this ceremony on the Pine Ridge Reservation in January, 1958. The rite was the third in a series commissioned by a young mixed-blood in connection with his campaign for chairmanship of the tribal council. In the first ceremony the main question addressed had been whether he should run for the office at all. The answer was affirmative, and a second rite was held to determine whether he would win the primary election. A fourth was to be held following his election to office, but, since he did not win, it was never held (Hurt, 1960:48, 51).

---

[3] As part of his being bound, the shaman is wrapped in a blanket or star quilt. Traditionally, the Sioux wrapped corpses in similar fashion and placed them on scaffolds, exposed to the elements.

. . . For the final time the lamp was extinguished and the singers and priests began a new series of songs. Above Fools Crow appeared a series of sparks, first forming the pattern of a cross and then flying all over the room. Over the leader a rattle began shaking and one of the Indian guests cried out, "They are here!" This Indian later explained that it was a belief that the rattle untied the bonds of the medicine man. Loud knocks were heard at the door, although the priest was still singing in a muffled voice as if he were still wrapped in the blanket. The rattle began moving through the room and the sparks continued to fly. Fools Crow then asked the guests if they wanted to know the location of any lost article or the answer to anything they had on their minds. One by one, the guests asked such questions as "Where is my lost watch?" or "Will I make a safe journey to New York?" The singing began once more; the sparks and rattles flew around the room and the smell of burning sweet grass pervaded the atmosphere although no coals of the burning grass could be seen. Wind blew on the necks of the participants. The beds were tilted under some of the guests. Fools Crow then told one Indian that his watch had been stolen by a friend or a relative and that he did not want to reveal the name. He informed another guest that she would have a safe journey and in like manner answered the questions of the other guests. 2.13

The medicine man then said he was going to try to answer the candidate's question, which would be difficult and dangerous, and that the guests who did not believe in Yuwipi would have a snake crawl over their laps. The singing started again. A drum was snatched away from one of the singers and began flying about the room making loud noises as it hit the stove pipes, walls, and rafters. Noises from eagle bone whistles were heard all over the room and the rattles and sparks flew about. The 4 altar flags were thrust skillfully into the writer's hands. Into the hands of 2 of the Indians were placed sections of the tobacco pouch "rosary."[4] Fools Crow then spoke to the candidate stating that he would become tribal chairman, not to listen to the bad talk of his opponents, and that the Oglala needed a young man like him to be their leader. The singing continued for a while, and the sparks, drums, and rattles remained active. 2.13

At 9:00 P.M. the lights were on. Fools Crow was sitting on the sage bed facing the sand mound. The rope was tied up in a neat ball. He then took his pipe, smoked it, and drank the water from the wood bowl. The 2.1

---

[4] Powers notes that "*Yuwipi* men often refer to these tobacco offerings as rosaries because each offering is prayed over as it is attached to the string." Offerings of this type are pre-Christian, however, and should not be taken as an indication of missionary influence (1977:149).

4 small flags were taken from the center can, broken, and thrown into the stove. On the sand mound one of the drums was placed. The leader dressed and then disassembled the altar, placing the paraphernalia back in the bag. The bag was taken outside. . . . [5]

2.3   At present at Pine Ridge there are 5 practicing Yuwipi leaders known to the writer. Each has a slightly different altar and ritual. Their
1.21   power is derived from dreams in which they acquire a guardian spirit. For example, Fools Crow's guardian is the red-headed woodpecker, a skull of which he ties to his pipe stem during the rite. Once an individual
2.1   decides to be a Yuwipi leader, he must lead a clean and circumscribed life or misfortune, such as having his family die, will befall him. An attempt at fakery also will bring bad luck. For example, a Yuwipi leader tried to use a mixture of gun powder for producing sparks. This powder blew up and blinded him. Another faker found himself caught in the rafters of his house and had to have help getting down. He ceased to practice after that.

3.2 The Loafer Camp meeting (Feraca, 1961:158–62)

> In June of 1956 Stephen Feraca and a fellow anthropology student attended a yuwipi ceremony at the Loafer Camp Road community on the Pine Ridge Reservation. The etiquette of arranging for such a rite is roughly as follows. A person who desires a shaman's assistance brings him "a pipe or some Durham tobacco." As he smokes, the shaman listens to the petitioner's story, and, if he decides to take the case, "he usually instructs the seeker to prepare a feast for the meeting as well as to obtain the required cloth and tobacco offerings." He also designates the house where the rite will take place (Feraca, 1961:156). Lame Deer says that there is "no real fee" for the shaman's services, but "the sponsor is expected to provide the food" for the feast which follows the ceremony (Lame Deer and Erdoes, 1972:187). While the men purify themselves in the sweat lodge, the women prepare the food for the feast. All are present in the darkened room for the shaman's performance. At this particular meeting there were approximately 30 participants, including 9 adult males, plus women, small children, and a few teenage girls. Teenage boys were conspicuous in their absence. Together, the ceremony in the room and the feast lasted from about 10 P.M. until midnight.

Preparation of the Room

Most of the furniture had been moved outside the house, bedrolls being placed against two of the walls as seats. A large quilt, to be used

[5] Hurt comments that "the general reaction of the Indian guests (to the ceremony) was one of belief and considerable fright" (1960:51).

later in wrapping the shaman, was hanging on a nail in the central pillar of the room. When we entered the room, the house owner's daughter who was also the wife of the principal singer was busily tacking tarpaper and canvas over the windows. The door was open but tarpaper and blankets were ready to be placed over it. Although all Catholic religious pictures had been removed from the walls, a small rosary had been overlooked.

Before shutting and covering the door the devotees had seated themselves on the bedrolls, the men, including the singers with drums, sitting on one side of the room and the women and children on the other side. The men had removed their hats.

Preparation of the Altar and Sacred Area

While the room was prepared and the devotees were seating themselves, the Yuwipi man took his ceremonial articles from an old suitcase and began to arrange them on the wooden floor. On a piece of paper roughly a foot square, earth had been poured and smoothed into a circle by a spotted eagle feather. One large tomato can and 6 smaller ones, all bearing their labels, had been filled with earth and arranged behind the earthen altar along the south wall. Sticks about 2 feet long to which had been tied cloth offerings were placed in these smaller cans. The larger can held a longer stick with the Sioux symbol representing "all that is," a cross within a circle, in this instance quilled. Dangling below the symbol were several spotted tail feathers of the eagle, and surrounding this larger staff were 4 small sticks bearing white and dark blue ribbons.

Why the shaman took the time to arrange these offerings along the wall is inexplicable since he removed all the sticks, with the attached offerings, and held them over the steam bucket brought in from the fire by a singer. The articles were purified as water was poured onto the hot stones in the bucket. The large can with its original offerings and symbol remained immediately behind the earthen altar; the other cans were placed about the room, outlining a rectangle. The shaman maintained a definite pattern in placing the cans with their colored cloths. . . .

2.1

Tied tobacco was arranged on the floor behind the cans. This commonly used ceremonial item consists of minute pieces of cloth, each containing no more than a few grains of tobacco. The miniature bags ideally should be tied with the same piece of string. The length of tied tobacco laid on the floor was more than 30 feet long, each of the more than 400 pinches of tobacco constituting separate prayers and offerings to that number of "little men."

Within the sacred area enclosed by the tobacco strings the shaman arranged a cellophane package of herbs which were not used, 2 small gourds, and a length of braided sweetgrass. A bone whistle, also unused, was placed between the large can and the earthen altar, and a beautifully decorated catlinite[6] pipe with a T-shaped bowl was solemnly placed in front of the altar.

At this point everyone, including small children who had not participated in the sweat bath, filed clockwise, or to the left of the steaming bucket, and returned to their seats. As this purificatory rite was held, the shaman rolled up the sleeves of his rather grimy shirt and repeated some aspects of his vision. He announced that he would make use of lightning medicine or power. . . . The shaman, as he concluded his initial speech, drew the appropriate designs in the earth with his index finger. As 3 of the women returned from the steam bucket, they placed offerings of Durham sacks and razor blade on the altar. The shaman outlined the earth circle with the tobacco strings (sometimes referred to as rosaries) and placed the Durham sacks around the altar after stripping the paper from them.

Sage was passed to the left by the principal singer who also served as an assistant, each person in the room placing a bit over the right ear. After warning me to keep the sage my friend, Oliver Red Cloud, also added that by doing so "the Yuwipi will know you." An aromatic dried flower was handed to each person with which to rub himself as an added protection.

The sacred area and all of the devotees were further protected and purified by the assistant who lit an end of the sweetgrass rope with the lantern and waved it around the room. Everything was purified, including the altar, the prayer cloths, and the heads of everyone present. During this purification the shaman twisted a sun symbol of sage from the pile thrown into the sacred area by one of the men. He placed this symbol on the floor.

The pipe was then filled by the shaman without its being lifted from the floor. With a quick flourish to the 4 directions the first pinch of tobacco was carefully placed in the bowl. With the filling of the pipe the sanctity of the altar and the ceremonial area was assured.

Scarification of the Volunteers

Three women walked in turn into the sacred area, faced the main altar, and held the pipe which was proffered them by the shaman. The method of holding the pipe, bowl facing the devotee, differed from that in sweat bath use. As a woman held the pipe in both hands, stem outward, the shaman cut the minute piece of flesh from her arm with the razor blade. The pieces of flesh were placed in the gourds as offering to the Yuwipi. The blood flowed freely until the shaman's assistant wiped

[6] The red pipestone, considered sacred by the Sioux and other Indian groups, which is found only at the quarry near present-day Pipestone, Minnesota.

the wounds with some sage. The gourds were returned to their place on the floor.

After the ceremony it was learned that the first woman made this sacrifice for a grandson who had already been cured; the second woman for a son who was in the army overseas. The last woman, the wife of the assistant, had pieces of flesh taken from both arms in thanksgiving for her baby who had survived a long illness. . . . [7]

Those men with drums (the flat or one-sided variety is usually in evidence at cult meetings) held them and the beaters in readiness; the shaman was alone in the sacred area. It was understood that all others would remain seated while the lights were out.

First Lights-Out Session

After the sole lantern was blown out, there was perfect silence. A tremendous whack on the principal singer's drum started an indescribable din. The opening phrases of the Yuwipi songs were as high pitched as was possible for the singers. The drumming was purposely discordant, quite unlike dancing songs in which several singers beat one large drum. Everyone in the room particularly the women and children, fairly screeched. The shrilling of the children on the closing phrases of each song cannot be described. After constant singing for perhaps 15 minutes the lantern was lit. The Yuwipi had not yet arrived.

The shaman announced that he would be tied by his assistants and subsequently released by the Yuwipi when they arrived on the scene. He also stated that shiny objects were dangerous and requested the

2.1

---

[7] Two features of traditional Sioux religion are present here: the making of a vow (i.e., an agreement to perform a certain act, if a hoped-for benefit is received, or in order that it may be received) and of offering of one's own flesh. Both were prominent in the Sun-dance, and can be illustrated by an account by Chased-by-Bears, an old Sioux who early in this century told Densmore about his earlier participation in the dance. "My first Sun-dance vow (he said) was made when I was 24 years of age. I was alone and far from the camp when I saw an Arikaree approaching on horseback, leading a horse. I knew that my life was in danger, so I said, 'Wankantanka (traditionally translated "Great Spirit" or "Great Mystery," a complex sacred entity with sixteen aspects; cf. Powers, 1977:45–55), if you will let me kill this man and capture his horse with this lariat, I will give you my flesh at the next Sun-dance.'" He was successful, and that summer danced with the lariat attached to the flesh of his right shoulder and the rawhide figure of a horse to the flesh of his left. Various forms of "piercing" of the flesh of chest and back, as well as the offering of bits of flesh cut from the arms (Densmore records a vow to give 200 such bits, half of which were voluntarily assumed by two of the man's female relatives), were characteristic of the Sioux Sun-dance. Chased-by-Bears articulated the motivation for such offerings as follows: "A man's body is his own, and when he gives his body or his flesh he is giving the only thing which really belongs to him. . . . I must give something that I really value to show that my whole being goes with the lesser gifts; therefore I promise to give my body" (Densmore, 1918:98, 135).

writer to remove his metal rimmed glasses. Mirrors are usually covered
during cult meeting for fear of lightning.

2.1   A rawhide length was produced with which the shaman's hands and
feet were tied while he was standing. He appeared without shoes when
the lamp was lit and his shirt was now removed. The quilt was taken
from the pillar, wrapped around him so that even his head was covered,
and then more rawhide was wrapped around the entire figure. Amid
some muffled grunting he was laid face down on the sage bed with his
head toward the altar. After again waving some lighted sweetgrass
around the altar and the wrapped figure, the assistant took his seat and
picked up his drum. The lantern was blown out.

Second Lights-Out Session

Some piteous moans announced the entrance of the spirits which the
shaman named in a muffled voice. Iktomi, a spidery gnome, was there.
The Rat, Swift Wind, Good Voiced Hawk, Swift Eagle, Holy Medicine,
and Flying About were all present.

Various noises, such as pounding on the walls, were heard while the
devotees sang lustily. The gourds glowed with a blue-green color and
began to fly about the room as the Yuwipi took their offerings. They
struck the four walls, floor, and ceiling often quite close to the heads of
the participants. . . .

When relative quiet was achieved, some of the devotees, in no par-
2.13   ticular order, addressed the spirits through the shaman. Each phrase was
addressed to grandfather(s)[8] and answered by muffled grunts or brief
comments from the shaman. Each of the women who had made sacrifices
recited a lengthly account of their troubles. The owner of the house
spoke about his sick grandchildren. . . .

A rhymed prayer by the shaman, during which the devotees held
2.13   their hands over their faces, was followed by more singing. The song
consisted almost entirely of the typical nonsense syllables but contained
2.1   one important phrase, they go on a special trip. The Yuwipi would soon
leave for the caves, clouds, woods, or water where they reside in order
to bring the required power, medicine, or answers to the shaman. Their
presence continued for a while as was evident from the pounding noises,
moans, and flashing gourds. The drum beat was changed for another
song and then the lantern was lit, revealing the shaman completely free
of all his bonds. The quilt was folded neatly in its original place on the
pillar. The light was quickly extinguished.

---

[8] The term used here means "paternal grandfather," and is "commonly used for a great
many of the figures known to Sioux cosmology. The *Yuwipi* are always addressed in this
manner" (Feraca, 1961:157).

Third Lights-Out Session

The shaman made some brief remarks, some of them laugh-provoking. Several songs were featured during this session. One song attracted our attention since it was addressed to *Wakan Tanka*, proving that the supreme power was not entirely ignored in favor of lesser spirits. . . .

. . . Oliver Red Cloud advised me that if we had brought a dog for the feast the pipe would have danced. At most cult meetings dog meat is the main dish. . . .

The gourds flitted violently about amid pounding and banging on the walls; and then, with a loud swish created by a blanket passed over the heads of the people the Yuwipi took their leave. The lamp was lit and the more formal part of the meeting had ended.

The shaman jested with several persons. One of the singers laughingly revealed that the rawhide used in tying the shaman was rolled into a tight ball in his jacket pocket. The Yuwipi put it there, he said.

After dismantling the altar and the sacred area the shaman returned the ceremonial items to his suitcase. The Durham offerings were thrown to the singers and accepted with thanks. One of the women who had previously addressed grandfather(s) was handed the red cloth that had been tied to one of the sticks. Another woman was given some of the tied tobacco, both of these gifts signifying that the Yuwipi would treat their requests favorably. The writer knows of another occasion when some distraught parents were given a black cloth by the shaman. They would soon receive, he informed them, a letter from the War Department to the effect that their son was dead.

The pipe was passed to an old woman sitting near the altar. She lit it, said "my relatives all," and after a few puffs passed it to her left. Everyone, including very small children, took the pipe and repeated the ceremonial phrase. As in the sweat bath, a chorus of "haus" answered each repetition of the phrase. The pipe was then placed in the suitcase and the feast began.

Plates, cups, and eating utensils were passed to the left by the girls—men's side first. The meal, typical of the full bloods, consisted of boiled beef, soup containing very little meat, store white bread, and crackers soaked in warmed tomatoes. While the devotees were eating, the author was thanked publicly by the house owner for the feast. No one made any remarks about the lack of dog meat.

The plates were removed and the principal singer passed water to the left starting with the men's side. Everyone remained seated as the singer handed each person a dipperful of water from the bucket he carried. Before or after drinking all said "my relatives all" and were answered in the usual manner. With the passing of the water the ceremony was officially brought to a close. The devotees began to leave, some taking their bedrolls with them. It was near midnight.

Conclusion

Most Teton shamans, particularly the Yuwipi men, are jacks of all trades including in their repertoire curing, counselling, finding missing persons or lost articles, and occasionally predicting future events. Despite the many stories of trickery told throughout the Sioux country, the devotees continue to believe in the power of the Yuwipi men, ignoring these stories or in some cases actually accepting the noises and flashes as part of the show. The author has spoken to a young mixed blood who was paid by a shaman to manipulate gourds and to rub his fur covered arms over the faces of the devotees at a Yuwipi meeting. The same singers are often used by a variety of shamans and may themselves be passable magicians. Some of the older and more experienced shamans, among them Yuwipi men, are rather adept at "making the spirits talk" from various points around the room. Often the voices seem to be emanating from the ceiling.

1.42 Certain elements among the Sioux have often tried to expose the Yuwipi men as frauds, usually without success. Horn Chips, now dead, can be considered one of those Yuwipi men who greatly added to the cult's popularity. For one thing his spirits spoke in many different voices, and all his prophecies are said to have been fulfilled. Some years ago, by order of Superintendent Gleason who was in charge of Pine Ridge Reservation, Horn Chips' meeting was held in a lighted room. Indian police were present and the police chief himself carefully tied and wrapped the Yuwipi man. Lights flashed on the ceiling (distracting everyone's attention). Horn Chips was untied when the flashing ceased. It is understandable that many Sioux refer to him as the "real Yuwipi man."

4
Navajo Diagnosticians

Introduction

The Navajo and Apache are Althapascan-speaking peoples who sometime after 1000 A.D. began a migration from the northwestern part of the continent toward what is now the southwestern United States. After their arrival there around 1500 A.D., the two groups began to diverge, the Navajo showing an increasing preference for herding and farming. In this, as well as in other aspects of material and non-material culture, the Navajo were influenced by their new neighbors, the sedentary Pueblo Indians.[1] This influence can be seen in handicrafts like weaving, in creation myths of the "emergence" type, and in elaborate religious ceremonials incorporating sacred dry-paintings and costumed god-impersonators (cf. Kluckhohn and Leighton, 1962:33–44; Luckert, 1975:8–14).

The Navajo have a complex ceremonialism involving two main types of rituals. Blessingway rites are for the purpose of protection and the maintenance of general well-being and harmony. Specifically, they may be employed in emergencies (e.g., to counteract a bad dream), at a girl's puberty ceremony or a wedding feast, to bless a new hogan,[2] to combat errors that may have occurred during the performance of a chantway, and on other such occasions. They are not, however, used for curing. And they are short, the full form taking only two nights to perform. Chantways, on the other hand, are a class of rites concerned primarily with healing. Within this class there are three groups of ceremonials, the largest of which is Holyway.[3] The latter are concerned with illnesses caused by Holy People,[4] each ceremony being associated with a myth which establishes a pattern revealed by a particular Holy Person, conformity to which in the ritual guarantees the patient's cure (cf. Gill, 1977–78). In their full form most chantways take nine nights to perform, and include the construction and ritual use of elaborate dry-paintings on the floor of the hogan.

---

[1] It is thought that the influence became particularly strong after the Pueblo Rebellion against the Spanish in 1680, when residents fled some of the pueblos and took refuge among the Navajo.

[2] The hogan is the traditional Navajo log-and-earth dwelling, and is necessary for the performance of all chantways.

[3] "The suffix '-way' is a translation of the ending of Navajo names for their ceremonials" (Wyman, 1975:3 note 4).

[4] "Holy People are spiritual entities which Navajos identify with the power of creation and the life force of all things" (Gill, 1977–78:145).

The men who conduct these ceremonials are "trained specialists, called 'singers,' because the singing which accompanies every important act in the ritual is held to be the one essential element of the ceremonial. The singers learn by apprenticeship, ratifying their knowledge by payment to the teacher," and since they are so complex, each learns only one or two complete ceremonies (Wyman, 1975:5–6). The singers, then, function rather more as priests than as traditional shamans (cf. Luckert, 1975:5–7).[5]

If the Navajo singers shade off toward a more priestly function, it is in the diagnosticians that we encounter intermediaries of the type represented in this volume. Often referred to in the literature as diviners, their main function is to discover the cause of someone's illness and recommend an appropriate treatment (i.e., chantway) for it. However, diviners may also be called upon to locate lost articles, animals, or persons; to identify witches; to find water when a party is in strange territory; and the like (Hill, 1935:65; Wyman, 1936a:236–7; Newcomb, 1938:46–7). In this one recognizes a similarity to the practices described in sections 2 and 3 above. Kluckhohn distinguishes between singers and diviners by pointing out that the learning of ceremonials falls into the "priestly" tradition, involving "formal instruction in a system of abundant lore." Divination (in the context he is speaking specifically of hand-trembling), on the other hand, falls into the "shamanistic" tradition, characterized by a direct "gift" with no formal instruction and a minimum of lore (1939: 66–7).

Several types of divination are practiced among the Navajo. Hand-trembling, or motion-in-the-hand, involves an involuntary shaking of the arm which ceases when the diviner has arrived at a correct diagnosis and prescription. It is said that this ability cannot be taught or learned, but comes suddenly, like a gift. The case of Gregorio, given below, illustrates these points. Matthews (1902:114–6) gives an account of a "trembling rite" and a reproduction of the dry-painting used in it. In a second type, listening, the practitioner employs paraphernalia, special symbols (incorporated in dry-paintings), and medicines through which he becomes receptive to and can interpret auditory stimuli, thus learning the cause of the illness, the location of a stolen object, etc. (cf. 4.3, below). Star-gazing, a third type, has as its focal point looking intently at a star (in variations, at the sun or the moon) or into a quartz crystal to discover the sought-for information (cf. 4.4). Both star-gazing and listening can be learned, Wyman saying of the latter that "an intelligent man can learn it

---

[5] For a general background and guide to further literature on Navajo religion and ceremonialism cf. Kluckhohn and Leighton (1962:200–52), Wyman (1950, 1970:3–35, 1975:1–13), and Gill (1977–78).

in one night" (Wyman, 1936a:245). Finally, it appears that Navajo diviners sometimes employed plants, like jimsonweed, that produced something of a narcotic effect (Hill, 1938; Kluckhohn, 1944:175–6). In all of
these it is difficult to say that the diviner contacts individual spirits, but
clearly he or she[6] performs an activity that originated with and was sanctioned by such spirits, as the various myths concerning the origin of the
divinatory techniques show (cf. 4.1). Furthermore, in the performance
the diviner establishes a relationship to this realm of power.[7]

Additional accounts of Navajo divination may be found in Morgan
(1931), Wyman and Newcomb (1963), Wyman (1975:172–7), and Benz
and Luckert (1973). Wyman and Newcomb make reference to smoke
divination, a form about which no information had previously been published; a description of the use of this form may be found in the middle
of a chantway myth recorded by Wyman (1975:172–7).

Texts

4.1 A myth of the origin of hand-trembling (Sapir & Hoijer, 1942:73–5)

> This myth names Gila monster as the Holy Person through whom
> humans derived hand-trembling, and also assumes some instruc-
> tion in the transmission of the skill. In a similar myth discussed
> by Wyman, Gila monster, who was at that time a man, was given
> the gift of hand-trembling by seven Holy People and told that the
> coming humans were to practice it. Gila monster says he hadn't
> learned it or practiced it; "the spirit simply entered him, and that
> is the way he got it" (Wyman, 1936b:136).

Now, this (story begins) when we came into being. Now, at that time,
it began, it came into being.

At that time, a certain (person) suddenly became sick, they say. At
that time, then, "By what means will it be known (what ails) him?" one
said. It having happened so, someone spoke thus, they say: "I, my arm
tells me things," he said, they say. And then, "I customarily perform it
over pollen,"[8] he said, they say.

By that means, now, it (i.e., the sick man's fate) was to be made
known, they say. So it happened; (just as) "From here, (his fate) will be

---

[6] Wyman notes that women frequently practice hand-trembling and, sometimes, listening, but not star-gazing (Wyman, 1936a:237).

[7] In his essay on Navajo diagnosticians Morgan says, "the trance appears to be the only
constant of Navajo diagnostics" (1931:396).

[8] "Pollen" (collected from cattails and corn, but also made by crushing the petals of blue
flowers, etc.) is ubiquitous in Navajo ceremonialism. "Matthews summarizes the meaning
of Pollen: 'Pollen is the emblem of peace, of happiness, of prosperity, and it is supposed
to bring these blessings'" (quoted in Reichard, 1950:251; cf. Wyman, 1970:30–2).

made known by means of it," he had said. "You will die," his arm said (to the patient), they say. And then, "Tomorrow (you will die)," it said to him, they say.

Then, "What is it that is doing so to him? What is it that has killed him?" he said, they say. And then, this which stands in him[9] has given him up. It is doing so to him.[10] So then, this that one thinks is known to one. It is known to one's limbs. It is known to one's arms.

"So then, how is (this) known to you?" (someone) said, they say. "It came to pass (from) the one called the Gila monster. This which was shaken off of him, I ate it. From that (which I ate) it has become known to me. Now then, you too may become instructed in (this knowledge)," he said to him, they say. So then, (the shaman) put that which had been shaken off of him[11] on (the learner), they say. And then, "Now then, try it out," he said to (the learner), they say. In accordance with that (ceremony) it seems, in accordance with that, they started to live, they say.

"What knowledge that old man had about (the ceremony)!" he said, they say. And then, "They told each other about it. From where he learned it I don't know but it is indeed true that I know about it," he said, they say.

At that place there, then, another (person) also became sick, they say. That (shaman) there did so to him sure enough. "Now you will move your hands about, my grandson," he said to (the learner), they say. "At some time or other, these earth people, when they are sick, will go behind you for protection," he said, they say. And then, "For that reason, you will always stand before them (to protect them)," he (the learner) was told.

That (learner) over there also shook his hands toward (the patient), they say. "It happens that an evil spirit is indeed doing so to him," he said, they say. And so that same old man (i.e., the shaman) was used again. Right there he restored (the patient) to health. He made a sand painting, they say. He spoke a prayer too, they say. He spoke to the sun by means of this (prayer), they say, saying, "My grandson will get well again."

And so everyone got to be so that their lives depended on him. And so, then, they came to have great love for him as time went on. "This man from over there, what will he say again?" they said as time went on, they say. They lived under his direction, they say.

---

[9] "That is, the soul." (E.S./H.H.)

[10] "That is, the fact that the soul has given him up is responsible for his death." (E.S./H.H.)

[11] "That is, the pollen which had fallen off as his arm shook." (E.S./H.H.)

4.2 The Navajo hand-trembler at work

> Alexander and Dorothea Leighton have given us an extensive account of a particular hand-trembler, Gregorio. The selection printed here describes the on-set of his shaking and gives examples of his practice. (Leighton & Leighton, 1949:53–6, 160)

One day I was lying in the hogan, I wasn't feeling very good. You 1.1
know, some days you feel like you're————, you act like you're going
to sleep, want to lie down. I feel that way. . . . Was laying down northwest side and facing towards the doorway (east) and I went to sleep for a
little while. When I woke up, my legs and feet and whole body was
feeling like was all large, just like when you sit down or laying down and
your legs went to sleep. You know what kind of feeling you got in that
leg. I am all over my body like that. And I can feel something through
the arms there, just like running through the hands, and feel like running out of the end of the fingers. After that my hands start to shaking.
This happened right in the middle of the afternoon. I had hand-
trembling all that afternoon, all that afternoon towards sundown. I don't
keep on Hand-trembling, but stop for a little at a time. Do that till after
dark. After dark I don't know much what I am doing on account of that
body, the way it feel. I was over here on the northwest side of the hogan.
While I was sitting over there that shaking start off again. Then, altogether I thought the sun was shining about me. I feel like the sunshining 1.21
was coming in the door. The sunshining bright like today in little spot
right where I am sitting. That happened just a little while. The sunshine
moved off on the south side very quickly. (Was this in the night?) Yes, in
the dark. The fire is going, not very big. After that sunshine goes away,
that feeling what I got in my body, I could feel it very well. It all start
from the end of the toe and coming up through the knee and on up to
the top of the head. The way it felt in the arms, right through the arms 1.11
and through the end of the fingers. After that it is all gone, I felt very
good. It feel good after that. All the Hand-trembling stopping then. The
next day when I am herding sheep the hand-trembling starts for a little
while, and then it is all over again. I had it like that one day, and then
after that it didn't do it any more. The people round there who were 1.4
with me, they all know, they told me I had the Hand-trembling like the
other people knows how.

Manuel, my uncle, was pretty sick at that time. Manuel heard about
that. He sent somebody down where I was, tell me to come there where 1.41
he is sick. So I went down there and he was pretty sick. There was some
people tried already that knowed how to do this Hand-trembling. There
was a lot of Singers already sung over that man. None of them helped.
Manuel says he heard that I have Hand-trembling. Told me that he

wanted me to try it out. Do it over him, see what I can find out. Says
he'll give me good sheep if I'll do that. Told him that I don't know much
about Hand-trembling. That is just something that I just had it. (He) told
me the best way is for me to try it out. Well, I made up my mind, did it
for this man. Did it for this man quite a while. I found out what he have
to do is get a Singer who would know the Chiricahua Wind Way.[12] (I) say
to the sick man he should get that Singer, one part of the night, one day
and one whole night. If he do this I think he is going to get over it. I told
him that they should get Ricardo. So they went over and got Richardo.
Ricardo sung for this man, sing the way I told him. The man was real
sick when Ricardo started, leg was swell all over on both leg. The people
just take this sick man and carry out in the blanket when he wants to go
out. (Go out for what?) To go to the toilet. So Ricardo sang like that.
After he sing part of the day and night, the man beginning to get well.
He got well pretty quick. From finish the song, just five days after that
the man beginning walking around. So he getting better every day until
he get well. This was towards lambing time again. . . .

(How did the thought of the right Sing for Manuel come to you?)
When you going to do the Hand-trembling, first you close your eyes.
You hold your hand like this (out in front) and start to thinking. You say
a few words in pray. When you closing your eyes you feel like something
like a lightning or sunbeam coming from the heaven. As you close you
eyes, not looking, thought like you seen this sunbeam strike down inside
the hogan, look like everything you seen inside is white and bright. Nobody could see that but you. You don't see that yourself, but thoughts
you having like that. That white doesn't stay long, goes after that. When
you start, you hand start shaking. Then start thinking about the Singer,
think about the Singers' names, take one at a time. You see you pray
already that you going to point the Singer out that will do good for the
patient. As you going along, the Hand-trembling kind of pushes the
Singer off. When you go along like that, sometime you come to the
Singer that the Hand-trembling will push it right inside the hogan, and
the Hand-trembling will kind of point all his medicine, kind of shake it
in, bring it in. That is the way I point out. That is the way I did with his
man, kinda mentioned some Singers and when I came to Ricardo, it
pushed him in. After this white sunbeam, if you think you didn't have
any of that, that is bad luck. Whenever you think you get the white
shining bright, then that is better they say, that is good. When you feel
the patient and everything is black in here (in the hogan), that means is
no good. That mean you going to lose a man some time. . . .

Another day, Harry come over to see me. He says his wife was hav-

---

[12] One of the Holyway ceremonials.

ing a baby and having some kind of trouble. Start four days ago. There is three Singers with the woman now, but those Singers doesn't help any, they doesn't seem to do any good for the woman. Besides, they are doing some Hand-trembling over the woman. These Singers were come from over the mountains. He says the man that did the Hand-trembling says this woman is going to have a dog baby, a puppy, and they got all mixed up in there so they want me to do the Hand-trembling. Told them that I just started. He thinks that I could do it better than those men down there. They sure need a good man for the Hand-trembling over that woman. Says he wants to pay me a saddle horse for do that. I got my horse and went on back over there where the woman is. There were a lot of people there, mens and woman. They told me that the woman already had a pain. Five days ago she had the big pains started, still having the pain. They want me to do it right away. . . . 1.411

3.11

We wait a little while, the woman have big pain again. I start the Hand-trembling again, do the same thing like I did before, pushing down. The woman had the baby right away. The placenta (sic) came along with the baby at the same time. The baby looked good, cried good. I notice the baby was in good shape. Everybody is surprised about that time. After the baby is born, they had another hogan on one side there, and we all go over there. There is just two women helping the baby and mother. I stayed in there for a while. They sent me word from outside and they feed me, then they told me they got this horse for me. I put a rope around this horse and lead it off back home. Was a good black horse that they gave me. . . . 3.11

Bill told us how Gregorio had found a purse for the Kluckhohns. From C.K. we have the following account of the episode:

"My wife had lost her handbag. I hired Gregario to locate it by Hand-trembling. Gregorio went to the hogan, washed his hands and arms, and rolled his sleeves to the elbow. He had to go to the top of a hill. He stood under a tree, facing north, with a bag of pollen. Pollen was sprinkled on his right hand, with lines across the palms to each finger, then some on the back. His hand started to tremble; it was held at a right angle to the ground. Soon he rubbed the palm of his left hand with the palm of his right, and it started to tremble instead. There was a subsequent alternation. His eyes were clenched shut. There were no spoken prayers. His palms were sometimes parallel and touching the ground. There was occasional beating of the dust. He made motions symbolizing the bag with the hands. He said it was in Cottonwood at the trading store; someone had picked it up, a tall white man. 2.1

"He does divination mostly for Indians in their hogans. He says to find anything lost from a person, you have to be where you can see around. He faced north because something was lost in that direction. My *impression* was that he was forcing his arm to move. He is somewhat taciturn."

3.21   Asked about cases, Bill told of a woman whose neck, just below the jaw, was all swollen up, and Sings had done her no good. Gregorio did Hand-trembling and told them to get a Singer from Willow Fence who knew the Snake Way. They did, and she got well. Another case was a boy of four who had fever and pain in his chest. Gregorio told them to get a Singer to do Chiricahua Wind Way, and the boy got well. A local Singer here did that.

> Moving from a focus on a single individual, we now turn to Wy- man's more general discussion of hand-trembling (Wyman, 1936a:243, 238–42).

          Motion-in-the-hand cannot be inherited and cannot be learned. It
2.1   comes to one suddenly, like a gift, and is usually acquired at a chant where there is some doubt about the diagnosis. Anyone present who is sitting and watching the service may suddenly begin to shake. Then he goes to the patient and tries to make a diagnosis. If he is successful he then knows that he has motion-in-the-hand and can practice thereafter. Following this he may go to a medicine man who knows the motion-in-
1.32   the-hand chant, but in the winter only; and for a fee he learns from him the prayers and songs. These may be learned from anyone who knows them; not necessarily from another diagnostician. Before the prayers or songs are learned the novice may practice by having someone else pray and sing for him. There is, then, no period of apprenticeship for motion-in-the-hand. The art may also be acquired at a motion-in-the-hand chant (this is identified with one of the wind chants), where a sand painting containing Gila monsters may be made or where Gila monster songs are sung. When someone hears this animal's songs he may begin to shake. . . .

          It has been said that before the diagnostician begins to work he dis-
2.2   cusses the patient's condition with the family or with other bystanders. All my informants insisted that the diagnostician need not know anything about the case before beginning, and that he always goes to work without preliminary gathering of information. They seemed surprised when I suggested such a thing, saying that he "does not need to" since the infor- mation is supposed to come through supernatural means. On each occa- sion where I saw a man-with-motion-in-the-hand work, including one performance for myself, he started the ritual without preliminary discus- sion. In each instance, however, he had been around enough to gather casually about as much information as he could obtain by further discus- sion.

3.11   After a fee has been stipulated, which is usually small—such as a

ring, bracelet, moccasins, fifty cents, or a dollar—the man-with-motion-in-the-hand washes his hands and forearms and, with one arm bared to   2.13
the elbow, sits crosslegged near the patient. In my case he first placed corn pollen upon me in ceremonial order from right foot to top of the head, but this is ordinarily omitted. Then he sprinkles pollen from his right elbow along the radial margin of the forearm, around the hypothenar eminence, and along the palmar surface of the thumb to its tip; from the tip of each finger along the palmar surface to the center of the palm, beginning with the middle finger; and, finally, in the center of the palm.   2.3
A variant of this procedure is to draw the line from the elbow to the thumb in the form of lightning with four angles, with the apex of the first angle near the elbow, directed toward the ulnar margin of the forearm. Another is to draw a line of pollen from the hypothenar eminence to the ulnar edge of the palm, after placing pollen on the fingers and before finaly depositing some in the center of the palm. Most diagnosticians use the right hand; at least they always start with the right hand. One informant said that a few might use the left hand if they are used to it. Sometimes they begin with the right hand, later clap the hands together, and then use the left hand, letting the right hand rest.

Ordinary corn pollen is used; but if a Gila monster can be obtained it is placed on a buckskin, pollen is sprinkled over it, and then gathered again. This constitutes "live-pollen" and is considered more effective. . . .

During the prayer and after the diagnostician sits with eyes closed   2.13
and face averted, and as soon as the singing begins his extended hand usually begins to shake. Although it was said that the motion of the hand may begin any time, even during the prayer (in which case the prayer is discontinued and a song begun), it more often than not begins at the start of the song. It was also stated that if the motion-in-the-hand is a new acquisition it starts easily, but if it is old there may be a little difficulty in starting it. While the hand is moving the diagnostician thinks of various diseases or causes of disease. When something happens which tells him that he is thinking of the correct one, he then thinks of various chants which might cure the disease; then, of what medicine man[13] might be the best one to give the chant; then perhaps of plant medicines or other therapeutic measures which might be used. After all the desired information has been divined the shaking stops of itself, the singing is discontinued, and the diagnostician opens his eyes and tells those assembled what he has discovered.

It is difficult to describe the motion of the hand and arm. It varies from a fine tremor with the extremity held in one position to rather violent motions of the whole arm through large arcs. The various types of

---

[13] I.e., singer.

motion can best be recorded in the following description of how the diagnostician arrives at the correct diagnosis and prescription. It must first be understood that it is claimed that the motion is involuntary—it starts and stops without volition—and that since the diagnostician closes his eyes and turns his face away from the patient, he does not see what his arm is doing. One informant said that if you do not believe this the man-with-motion-in-the-hand will let you hold the shaking hand, and then the other hand will begin to shake; and that if you hold both his hands then his whole body will shake.

2.1   A common event is for the forefinger to draw a line in the sand of the floor, while the diagnostician is thinking of a cause of disease. If it is not the correct cause the hand rapidly erases the line with a brushing-away motion, and another line is drawn while thinking of another cause; and so on until a line is drawn which is allowed to remain, and the hand performs a rapid pointing or patting motion toward the line. This type of motion tells the diagnostician that he is now thinking of the correct cause, so he ceases to think of causes of disease and begins to think of various chants to cure the disease. Disease is located in the body of the patient by feeling, grasping, or patting various parts of his body, and again a rapid patting motion of the hand on a particular part tells that the disease is located in that part. An informant said that the patient "does not have to tell where the pain is, but you can feel it when you are doing it (motion-in-the-hand), and when you quit and ask him if that is the place where he has pain, he will say 'yes'." The proper medicine-man to treat the patient is selected by thinking of various men who know the selected chant, while the hand points in the directions in which they live. A persistent pointing motion in one direction tells that the man to call is over there.

One method used to discover the cause of sickness and the chant to cure it is interesting in that it is strikingly similar to automatic writing. A picture is drawn in the sand by the moving forefinger; then the diagnostician opens his eyes, looks at it and sees that it is symbolic of some chant or is like a fragment of a sand painting used in some chant. He then knows that it is this chant which is causing the trouble.

To understand this, one of the Navaho theories of disease must be understood. If a Navaho woman is pregnant (five, six, or seven months or more) and she or her husband goes to a war-dance and sees there the rattle-stick or the scalp, or the man who "kills" the scalp, then the unborn baby may later suffer from sickness associated with the war dance and have to have the same chant, i.e., the war dance, to cure it. The malign influence may not attack him until he is as much as sixty years old, or it may begin to operate when he has suffered from some accident and is thus in a weakened condition. The same applies to other chants, to seeing dead animals, especially those struck by lightning, or to eating the flesh of animals which have been exposed to lightning. The lightning influence is especially malign, and a lightning chant is needed to avert it. The malign influence from any particular chant is removed by having the same chant sung over one. All this applies to similar happenings during one's life as well as to prenatal influence. . . .

4.3 Divination by listening (Newcomb, 1938:47–9)

. . . In a country as rugged as the Navajo Reservation there are numerous instances where sheep and horses stray away or are stolen, and sometimes children are lost in the wooded sections. Once in a while grown people go to distant places to obtain employment and months pass during which their family has no word from them. In such cases the Listening Rite is considered most effective in locating the lost animals or children and in obtaining information concerning distant relatives. This ceremony is also used if a Navajo has been having very bad luck and thinks that someone is casting an evil spell over him.   3.0

The medicine-man who undertakes the Listening Rite must possess a variety of "medicines." An important item is a conch shell of the pink and white variety about as large as a man's fist. Just as important is a section of honey-comb or a small wasp's nest containing one or more bees sealed inside, and also there is the "ear-medicine." This "ear-medicine" is a strange mixture. First, the yellow stain must be scraped from a rock that echoes, using an arrow point or a piece of flint—this is called the ear-wax of the listening rock. Ocean foam, mud from the bottom of a salt lake, ear-wax from the ears of a dog, a coyote, a night-hawk, and an owl are all necessary ingredients. These things are mixed to form a soft paste.

The ceremony starts, as do all Navajo rites, by everyone who takes part or witnesses the proceedings taking a bath. This may be a ceremonial sweat-house bath or it may not, there being no set rule. There is no special hogan erected for small ceremonies but some hogan is emptied of its usual contents and the floor is scraped clean and sprinkled with wind-blown sand. There is a small fire built in the center directly beneath the smoke-vent. The medicine-man enters first, muttering a low prayer which is the houseblessing. He also tosses a little pollen to the four directions and up through the opening, then sprinkles a little pollen over himself, putting a pinch on top of his head and another pinch in his mouth.   2.1

All the family enter after the medicine-man and the one who wishes to learn about the lost animal or person, or the one who thinks he is bewitched, sits near the west wall facing the east, the others sit on the northwest side of the hogan. In front of the patient, the medicine man, using white ashes and charcoal, paints the figure of a spotted dog. To the left of the fire a crude figure of a boy or of a girl (according to the sex of the patient) is designed in grey ashes. Sometimes a figure made of pollen is placed beside it. Just inside the door a coyote is painted in grey dust (gathered from coyote tracks) and charcoal. This serves as a door guard. When the painting is completed, two songs are sung, one for the dog and one for the coyote. These are the last words that may be spoken in the hogan. All the people inside must sit very still so that not even the breathing may be heard and keep their eyes fixed on the person in the

2.13   west. He in turn keeps his attention focused on the small figure made of ashes. Early in the proceedings, the medicine-man has selected one of the relatives to accompany him and act as his helper and sponsor—to tell the others what happened while he was in the trance. Now these two steal silently from the hogan and walk six or seven yards toward the east, or far enough to find a small smooth piece of ground. Here the medicine-man makes a small sandpainting, and they both sit on the west side of this, facing the east. Four songs are now sung and a long prayer-intoned—the relative accompanying the medicine man but generally one syllable behind. Then the medicine-man marks both their faces with ocean foam and mud from the salt lake. He also puts small balls of "ear-medicine" into both their ears. After this, neither must make a sound. The medicine-man holds the shell over his right ear while his left hand containing the honey-comb, is held level just in front of his eyes.

2.13   From the shell he first hears a confused murmur of voices as though people were talking in a distant hogan. Sometimes there is the sighing of the wind, or the rippling of water, or the crackling of fire, or people chanting. After a time the sounds become more definite and the medicine-man is able to determine the place from which they are coming. It is from "the house of the bee" that the most exact information is obtained, because the bee follows all trails and knows who has gone along them, but never becomes confused or fails to return to his home. The bee tells them which way to search and what has happened along the trail. If the bee is silent there is no use searching, for the lost will never be found or there is no one bewitching the patient. When voices are heard plainly they are supposed to be the voices of the ones who are casting the evil spells. Then the medicine man attempts to identify these voices so as to find out who stole the horses or sheep; or whom the child may be talking to; or who has bewitched the patient.

4.4 Star-gazing: two descriptions (Wyman, 1936a; Morgan, 1931)

1.32   Star-gazing differs in some important respects from motion-in-the-hand. It can and must be learned, and anyone who wishes may learn it from a practitioner. It was said that an intelligent man can learn it in a day, although most beginners take longer. The complete ritual of star-gazing is somewhat more complicated than that of motion-in-the-hand, even involving the making of a sand painting, although a briefer ritual without the sand painting is often used. This may be because there is need for immediate diagnosis, because the patient cannot afford the complete ritual, or because the diagnostician does not know how to make the sand painting; for he may practice the briefer ritual without knowing the complete one. The fee is somewhat larger than that for motion-in-the-hand, being a blanket, a horse, ten head of sheep, or ten or fifteen dollars, for a small service. Otherwise the general considerations concerning diagnosis by motion-of-the-hand apply to star-gazing.

3.11

In the complete ritual the diagnostician first makes a sand painting in the dwelling, about two feet in diameter. It represents a white star with four points toward the cardinal directions. Between the points of the star are four heaps of sand representing mountains, the southeast mountain being white, the southwest blue, the northwest yellow, and the northeast black. Around the whole, with an opening to the east, is a zig-zag line representing lightning. Then the diagnostician makes ready the dried and powdered lenses from the eyes of the five night-birds with keen sight who acted as lookouts in the legend of how star-gazing was first made known to the people. He dips the tip of his finger in this material and then draws it along his lower eyelids. It is similarly applied to the patient, to the one man who will go out with the star-gazer to assist him, and to anyone else present who is "smart" and may be able to assist by seeing something. The eyes of the five birds mentioned are the main ones, but eyes of other birds may also be used if available. Then the fire is covered and from now on the people who remain inside do not move or make any noise, but they concentrate and try to see something in addition to that which is seen by the diagnostician, sometimes gazing at a star through the smokehole.

2.13

The star-gazer takes one person with him and leaves the house. Outside he prays the star-prayer to the star-spirit, asking the star to show him the cause of the sickness. Then he begins to sing star-songs and while singing gazes fixedly at a star or at the light of a star reflected in a "glass rock" or quartz crystal which he holds in his hand. Soon, it was said, the star begins to "throw out a string of light and at the end of this the star-gazer sees the cause of the sickness of the patient, like a motion picture." If these strings of light are white or yellow the patient will recover; if red, the illness is serious or dangerous. If the white light falls on the house and makes it as light as day around it, the patient will get well. If the house is seen burning or in darkness he will die. If a certain medicine man is the proper one to cure the sickness the star will throw a flash of light in the direction of his home, or on his body if he is present. Places far away may be seen. After the diagnostician has obtained enough information in this way he returns to the house and tells what he has seen. If anyone else has seen anything, his experience is also considered.

Sun-gazing and moon-gazing are done the same way. A star-gazer can diagnose for himself. If he has not yet learned the prayers or songs, someone else who knows them may pray or sing for him while he looks at the stars. It was said that the same prayers, songs, and procedure are always used. One old star-gazer who is now nearly blind says that he can still practice by taking two men with him "to do the looking for him" while he prays and sings, and then making a diagnosis from their report. (Wyman, 1936a:244–5)

*   *   *

2.13   A man is sick. A stargazer is called in. He comes into the hogan. The patient is here. Others are there. He talks to the patient and others. They discuss the illness. The fire is put out. The stargazer chants, then he says, "Everyone must close his eyes. No one must move or speak. Everyone must concentrate on the illness and try to see something." The stargazer takes a man from the hogan, and walks away some distance. He performs movements with his body. Any horses or sheep are frightened away. When there is no noise, the stargazer places a crystal or stone on his hand. He chants. He prays to the Gila monster. He does not pray to a lizard, but a lizard beyond the lizards, a larger one. Then the stargazer holds out his arm and hand in line with the moon or some star, and gazes unwinking at the crystal. Soon he sees something. He closes his hand upon what he has seen in the crystal. Also there may seem to be a line

2.11   of light which is "lightning" from the star to the crystal or to the ground around him so that the ground appears light. The stargazer sees the hogan and the sick man, even though his back is turned to it. . . . He sees a man, or a bear, or a coyote, or perhaps the head of a coyote, or perhaps the bear is biting the patient. Then he goes back to the hogan. The fire is lighted. He asks what the others have seen. This is talked about. He tells what he has seen. Maybe it is a man. Maybe the man is a witch and is making the illness. He must find out who the man is. Maybe it is a coyote. The stargazer puts marks on the floor of the hogan. He lays down a handkerchief. He lays a piece of turquoise, maybe a special stone, maybe a bit of pearl, on the handkerchief. He makes a bag of the handkerchief. He chants and prays. He gives the bag to a man. He tells him to go in a certain direction until he finds a coyote track. He must see how fresh it is, what the coyote was doing, what direction he went. He must open the bag and lay it on the tracks and carefully arrange it in order. Then he must return to the hogan. If the coyote track led away from the hogan, the patient will get well. If the illness is serious the stargazer will prescribe a ceremony and the shaman who can give it. (Morgan, 1931:394–5)

5
Handsome Lake: The Intermediary as Founder of a New Religion

Introduction

With Handsome Lake we are in the relatively unique position of having for an intermediary of a traditional culture not only important contemporary reports of his activity, but also a considerable body of written teachings attributed to him. In this section we will focus on the activity of the man himself, returning in Chapter III to the problem of the transmission and preservation of his teachings after his death.[1]

The Seneca tribe of North American Indians to which Handsome Lake belonged had been a member of the famed Iroquois League, a closely knit confederation of tribes whose origin predates the arrival of Columbus. During much of the 18th century, this confederation was able, through a system of playing off the British against the French, both to maintain its territory and security and to benefit from the material goods of European culture. But all that ended during the American Revolution, which split the confederacy. Neutrality was abandoned, and most of the Iroquois gave their loyalty to the British. The ultimate result was that nearly all of their villages from the Mohawk River to the Ohio country were destroyed, and they were cut off from their allies to the west, who established their own independent confederacy.

The reservation system which was gradually imposed upon the Iroquois during the last decades of the century created what Wallace calls "slums in the wilderness, where no traditional Indian culture could long survive and where only the least useful aspects of white culture could easily penetrate" (1972:184).

The Cornplanter grant on the Allegheny River in northern Pennsylvania was unique among the reservations, because of its relative isolation from white settlement. Though the influences of European material culture were considerable, many of the old social and political customs survived and the annual cycle of traditional religious ceremonials were still observed. It was there that Handsome Lake, Cornplanter's half-brother, resided. Of course, such isolation could only be relative, and the social pathologies that had been making inroads among the Iroquois for years were found also in Cornplanter's town. Excessive consumption of alcoholic beverages was a particularly serious problem.

There was no unanimity of opinion among the Iroquois as to how to

---

[1] Much of this introduction is taken from Overholt (1981). The brief sketch of Iroquois history depends largely upon Wallace (1972:21–236). For further bibliography on Handsome Lake cf. H. W. Turner (1978:94–112).

confront the problems inherent in their historical and cultural situation. Each reservation had its factions, the progressives "advocating the assimilation of white culture" and the conservatives "the preservation of Indian ways" (Wallace, 1972:202; Berkhofer, 1965). Cornplanter may be reckoned with the former group, and by the time of Handsome Lake's vision his village had already come under the influence of Quaker missionaries. These men were non-dogmatic in their approach to religion, and chose to concentrate on offering positive assistance to the Cornplanter Seneca in such practical areas as farming, carpentry, and education. By May of 1799 they had also persuaded the council to ban the use of whiskey in the village (Deardorff, 1951; Wallace, 1972:221–36).

The Gaiwiio ("Good Message"), a record of Handsome Lake's religious experiences and teachings which is still in use among followers of the "Longhouse way" (cf. Shimony, 1961), begins by describing a "time of troubles" in Cornplanter village (cf. 5.1, below). The scene is at first community-wide. A party of Indians had just returned from Pittsburgh, where they had traded skins and game for whiskey. A wild drinking party followed in which village life was disrupted and some families moved away for safety. The focus then shifts to a single sick man, who was held in the grip of "some strong power," and feared that he might die. Realizing that the cause of his illness was whiskey, he resolved never to use it again. Afraid that he would not have the strength to do this, he prayed to the "Great Ruler," and began to be confident that his prayer had been heard and he would live. The sick man was Handsome Lake.

On June 17, 1799, the sick man appeared to die. His body was prepared for burial and relatives summoned, but he revived and reported he had had a vision of three messengers who had been sent to reveal to him the Creator's will and instruct him to carry it to the people. The vision also contained a threat, for Handsome Lake was shown the steaming grave of a man who had formerly been commissioned "to proclaim that message to the world," but had "refused to obey." On August 7 of the same year he received a second revelation in which he was guided on a journey through heaven and hell and given moral instruction. A third revelation occurred on February 5, 1800. Each of these visions was reported and discussed in a council of the people.[2]

Several passages in the Good Message make it clear that Handsome Lake expected to, and did, receive further revelations. In his initial vision the three messengers promised, "We shall continually reveal things

---

[2] This account of the initial visionary experiences follows the chronology reconstructed by Wallace on the basis of a journal kept by one of the Quaker missionaries and other sources. The present form of the Good Message (or, Code of Handsome Lake) as represented in Parker (1913) has some of the revelations out of sequence (cf. Wallace, 1972:359–60, note 5).

unto you," and this promise was repeated in 1809 when in the midst of a personal crisis the messengers came to him and said, "We understand your thoughts. We will visit you more frequently and converse with you" (Parker 1913:25, 47; Wallace 1972:293–4). Although the present form of the Good Message makes it difficult to date specific revelations, there is some internal evidence of such a continuing sequence. Most conspicuous are the place names. The Good Message specifically sets the initial vision in Cornplanter's village, but subsequent sections are said to derive from Cold Spring, Tonawanda, and Onondaga (all in New York; Parker, 1913:46–7, 57, 60–2, 76–80). These localities correspond to known periods of the prophet's activity. Furthermore, there are at least four sections of the Good Message that Wallace links to specific, datable events: a derogatory reference to Chief Red Jacket arising out of a dispute over the sale of reservation land in 1801, a prophecy intended to discourage Iroquois participation in the "war in the west" (1811), and a composite section mentioning the people's reviling of Handsome Lake and his meeting with the Spirit of the Corn which seems to mirror events that took place in the years 1809 and 1815 (Parker, 1913:68, 65–6, 47; Wallace, 1972:260, 293–4, 318). The final sections of the Good Message deal with the revelations and events immediately preceding Handsome Lake's death, which occurred on August 10, 1815, at Onondaga (Parker, 1913:76–80). It is clear that later revelations did not simply repeat the content of earlier ones. They rather seem to have arisen out of Handsome Lake's attempts to deal with new situations, and were doubtless seen by him to be divine responses to his own quest for a solution.

Handsome Lake's first vision contained already the main themes of his subsequent proclamation, for the messengers revealed to him the four great wrongs by which "men spoil the laws the Great Ruler has made and thereby make him angry": drinking whiskey, using witchcraft, using "compelling charms," and practicing abortion. In the Good Message considerable space is given to positive commands relating to social behavior (gossip, drunkenness, sharing, mourning customs, etc.), family life (the care of children, husband-wife relationships, the care of elders), and religion (the traditional medicine societies were ordered to disband, but a number of traditional ceremonies were specifically sanctioned and regulated). In addition it deals in several places with the relationship between Indians and whites (agriculture, schooling, and the Creator's protection of his people against extermination by the whites) and with the status of Handsome Lake himself (disbelief is said to be due to the operation of an evil spirit, and will be punished). A number of these themes are reinforced in the sections of the Good Message recounting the second revelation (the "sky journey"), where Handsome Lake witnessed the suffering of a variety of sinners (drunkard, wife-beater, gambler, etc.) in the house of the "punisher" (Parker, 1913:62–76).

Wallace understands the preaching of Handsome Lake to fall into two distinct phases. The first, covering the years 1799–1801, was characterized by an "apocalyptic gospel" in which the people were summoned to repentance and the recurring themes were world destruction, sin, and salvation. The second phase began in 1801 and featured a "social gospel" in which the main values stressed were "temperance, peace and unity, land retention, acculturation, and a revised domestic morality" (Wallace, 1972:278; cf. 239–302). The response to this message was mixed. In the early years he was able to exercise both political and religious power, and the council at Buffalo Creek in 1801 prohibited the use of liquor and appointed him "High Priest, and principal Sachem[3] in all things Civil and Religious." Over the next few years, however, his political influence declined. In 1807 the Iroquois confederacy was reorganized and the great council fire established at Buffalo Creek, where one of Handsome Lake's chief rivals, Red Jacket, was influential. Handsome Lake and Cornplanter also quarreled, and factions developed in the Allegany band, causing the former to move out and locate first at Cold Spring and later at Tonawanda. But his religious influence remained strong. He made an annual circuit of visitations to other reservations preaching his gospel and winning converts (Wallace, 1972:260–1, 286ff., 296ff.). As Wallace describes it,

> these conversions were not casual matters. The Indians traversed the same mystic path to Gaiwiio as white converts to Christianity; the converts retained an intense devotion to the prophet who gave them strength to achieve salvation. "One of the Onondagas, when asked why they did not leave their drunken habits before, since they were often urged to do it, and saw the ruinous consequences of such conduct replied, they had no power; but when the Great Spirit forbid such conduct by their prophet, he gave them the power to comply with their request" (Wallace, 1972:301, quoting from a contemporary mission newspaper).

What one notices about the Good Message is how directly it spoke to the situation that plagued the Iroquois of Handsome Lake's day. Addressing a people debauched and demoralized by contact with white culture and the loss of their own traditional ways, it accused them of wrongdoing, laying heavy stress on evils disruptive of harmonious community life (strong drink, witchcraft, charms, and abortion). In its commandments great emphasis was placed on the strengthening of family relationships and the regulation of social behavior. In response to the growing influence of white culture there was explicit approval of farming, house-

---

[3] The sachems, who normally held their office for life, were appointed delegates to the council which ruled the Iroquois federation.

building, animal husbandry, and, to a limited extent, education "in English schools" (Parker, 1913:38).

In real life parts of this message evoked a negative response and caused Handsome Lake trouble, particularly his determined attacks against witchcraft and supposed witch-inspired conspiracies. Reaction to the execution of one witch in 1809 caused him to have to leave Cold Spring, a situation reflected in the Good Message: "Now it was that when the people reviled me, the proclaimer of the prophecy, the impression came to me that it would be well to depart and go to Tonawanda. In that place I had relatives and friends and thought that my bones might find a resting place there" (Parker, 1913:47; cf. Wallace, 1972:254–62, 291–4).

The Good Message spoke to the current situation, advocating such important cultural innovations as the involvement of men in farm labor, limited acceptance of white education, and the dissolution of the totem animal societies. The individual autonomy and glorification that had been characteristic of the old Iroquois way were condemned, and family solidarity and restraint advocated in their stead. All this was in response to the collapse of the old hunting and trading system under pressure from encroaching whites, which forced the Iroquois into more intensive agriculture. For where gardening in the traditional culture had been the responsibility of the women, plow agriculture is a man's work and the yearly agricultural schedule demands a stable social order. Handsome Lake therefore preached values that emphasized communal order over individual gratification (cf. Tooker, 1968).

But for all that, the Good Message was rooted in the traditions of the past. Social solidarity was stressed in its ethical commandments, and in particular the old religious values and ceremonies were for the most part retained. Its major new religious concept, the notion of judgment and afterlife in heaven or hell, was compatible with the old beliefs and was introduced "to insure the dedication of the people to conservative ritual." Handsome Lake "was in his own eyes as the messenger of God, necessarily the defender of faith" (Wallace, 1972:318; cf. 251–4, 315–8). As Parker puts it, "Handsome Lake sought to destroy the ancient folk-ways of the people and to substitute a new system, *built of course upon the framework of the old*" (Parker, 1913:114; emphasis added). Eventually, a myth even developed to account for the origin of the conditions that made the Good Message necessary and to fix its place in the overall order of things.

That the message of Handsome Lake gained such wide acceptance among the Iroquois in his own day would seem to be due largely to the skill with which he utilized the old traditions of the people in addressing himself to the crucial problems of the present. And when after his death (1815) some of the traditional Iroquois leaders sought a way to counter the threats of both sectarian Christians and disruptive nativists, they

found it convenient to call upon the memory of Handsome Lake in attempting to define the form and spirit of the old religion. We will return
in Chapter III to that portion of the story.

The Code of Handsome Lake is essentially a collection of prophetic
utterances with scattered biographical sections, particularly for the period of his "call." In this respect it is similar to the prophetic books of the
Old Testament. In the case of Handsome Lake, however, we do have
considerable cultural and historical data from other sources with which
we can reconstruct the social context of his prophetic activity. Wallace
(1972) is the best single resource for someone interested in pursuing this
subject in more depth. Other sources in addition to those cited in this
introduction will be referred to in Chapter III. Elsewhere, I have made
an attempt to compare Handsome Lake with Jeremiah in terms of a general "prophetic process" to which both in large measure conform (Overholt, 1981).

In the Parker edition the text of the Good Message runs to sixty
pages. From this material I have excerpted and organized topically sections that bear on how Handsome Lake came to be a prophet and how
he functioned in that role. Some minor changes have been made in the
text. Parker keeps a number of Seneca words, especially proper names,
often giving the English in brackets; most of these have been eliminated,
and the translation incorporated into the text. In addition I have omitted
Parker's descriptive subheadings from the narrative of Handsome Lake's
commissioning, his section numbers from the body of teachings proper,
and diacritical marks from the Seneca words that remain (e.g., Gaiwiio).

For a full text of the Parker edition, as well as an introduction on
Parker and his work, see Fenton (1968).

Texts

5.1 Handsome Lake's initial revelation and commissioning (Parker,
1913:20–30)

The beginning was in May, early in the moon, in the year 1800.
It commences now.
The place is on the Allegany River, in Cornplanter village.
Now it is the harvest time, so he said.
Now a party of people move. They go down in canoes down the
Allegany river. They plan to hunt throughout the autumn and the winter
seasons.
Now they land at Warren, Pa., and set up camp.
The weather changes and they move again. They go farther down
the river. The ice melts opening up the stream and so they go still farther
down. They land at Pittsburgh. It is a little village of white people. Here

they barter their skins, dried meat and fresh game for strong drink. They put a barrel of it in their canoes. Now all the canoes are lashed together like a raft.

Now all the men become filled with strong drink. They yell and sing like demented people. Those who are in the middle canoes do this.

Now they are homeward bound.

Now when they come to where they had left their wives and children these embark to return home. They go up Cornplanter creek.

Now that the party is home the men revel in strong drink and are very quarrelsome. Because of this the families become frightened and move away for safety. So from many places in the bushlands camp fires send up their smoke.

Now the drunken men run yelling through the village and there is no one there except the drunken men. Now they are beastlike and run about without clothing and all have weapons to injure those whom they meet.

Now there are no doors left in the houses for they have all been kicked off. So, also, there are no fires in the village and have not been for many days. Now the men full of strong drink have trodden in the fireplaces. They alone track there and there are no fires and their footprints are in all the fireplaces.

Now the dogs yelp and cry in all the houses for they are hungry.

So this is what happens.

And now furthermore a man becomes sick. Some strong power holds him.   1.1

Now as he lies in sickness he meditates and longs that he might rise again and walk upon the earth. So he implores the Great Ruler to give him strength that he may walk upon this earth again. And then he thinks how evil and loathsome he is before the Great Ruler. He thinks how he has been evil ever since he had strength in this world and done evil ever since he had been able to work. But notwithstanding, he asks that he may again walk.

So now this is what he sang: the Death chant, the Women's song, and the Harvest song. Now while he sings he has strong drink with him.

Now it comes to his mind that perchance evil has arisen because of strong drink and he resolves to use it nevermore. Now he continually thinks of this every day and every hour. Yea, he continually thinks of this. Then a time comes and he craves drink again for he thinks that he cannot recover his strength without it.

Now two ways he thinks: what once he did and whether he will ever recover.

Now he thinks of the things he sees in the daylight.

The sunlight comes in and he sees it and he says, "The Creator made this sunshine." So he thinks. Now when he thinks of the sunshine and of the Creator who made it he feels a new hope within him and he feels that he may again be on his feet in this world.

Now he had previously given up hope of life but now he begs to see the light of another day. He thinks thus for night is coming. So now he makes an invocation that he may be able to endure the night.

Now he lives through the night and sees another day. So then he prays that he may see the night and it is so. Because of these things he now believes that the Great Ruler has heard him and he gives him thanks.

Now the sick man's bed is beside the fire. At night he looks up through the chimney hole and sees the stars and he thanks the Great Ruler that he can see them for he knows that he, the Creator, has made them.

Now it comes to him that because of these new thoughts he may obtain help to arise from his bed and walk again in this world. Then again he despairs that he will ever see the new day because of his great weakness. Then again he has confidence that he will see the new day, and so he lives and sees it.

For everything he sees he is thankful. He thinks of the Creator and thanks him for the things he sees. Now he hears the birds singing and he thanks the Great Ruler for their music.

So then he thinks that a thankful heart will help him.

Now this man has been sick four years but he feels that he will now recover.

And the name of the sick man is Handsome Lake, a council chief.

Now at this time the daughter of the sick man and her husband are sitting outside the house in the shed and the sick man is within alone. The door is ajar. Now the daughter and her husband are cleaning beans for the planting. Suddenly they hear the sick man exclaim, "So be it!" Then they hear him rising in his bed and they think how he is but yellow skin and dried bones from four years of sickness in bed. Now they hear him walking over the floor toward the door. Then the daughter looks up and sees her father coming out of doors. He totters and she rises quickly to catch him but he falls dying. Now they lift him up and carry him back within the house and dress him for burial.

Now he is dead.

Then the daughter says to her husband, "Run quickly and notify his nephew, Awl Breaker, that he who has lain so many years in bed has gone. Bid him come immediately."

So the husband runs to carry the message to Awl Breaker. And Awl Breaker says, "Truly so. Now hasten to Cornplanter, the brother of the dead man and say that he who lay sick for so many years is dead. So now go and say this."

So the husband goes alone to where Cornplanter lives and when he has spoken the wife says, "Cornplanter is at the island planting." So he goes there and says, "Cornplanter your brother is dead. He who was sick for so many years is dead. Go at once to his bed."

Then Cornplanter answers, "Truly, but first I must finish covering this small patch of seed. Then when I hoe it over I will come." . . .

Now everyone hearing of the death of the sick man goes to where he lies.

Now first comes Awl Breaker. He touches the dead man on every part of his body. Now he feels a warm spot on his chest and then Awl Breaker says, "Hold back your sadness, friends," for he had discovered the warm spot and because of this he tells the people that perhaps the dead man may revive. Now many people are weeping and the speaker sits down by his head.

Now after some time Cornplanter comes in and feels over the body of the dead and he too discovers the warm spot but says nothing but sits silently down at the feet of the dead man.

And for many hours no one speaks.

Now it is the early morning and the dew is drying. This is a time of trouble for he lies dead.

Now continually Awl Breaker feels over the body of the dead man. He notices that the warm spot is spreading. Now the time is noon and he feels the warm blood pulsing in his veins. Now his breath comes and now he opens his eyes.   1.11

Now Awl Breaker is speaking. "Are you well? What think you?"

Now the people notice that the man is moving his lips as if speaking but no words come. Now this is near the noon hour. Now all are silent while Awl Breaker asks again, "My uncle, are you feeling well?"

Then comes the answer, "Yes, I believe myself well." So these are the first words Handsome Lake spoke.

Now then he speaks again saying, "Never have I seen such wondrous visions! Now at first I heard someone speaking. Some one spoke and said, 'Come out awhile' and said this three times. Now since I saw no one speaking I thought that in my sickness I myself was speaking but I thought again and found that it was not my voice. So I called out boldy, "So be it!" and arose and went out and there standing in the clear swept space I saw three men clothed in fine clean raiment. Their cheeks were painted red and it seemed that they had been painted the day before. Only a few feathers were in their bonnets. All three were alike and all seemed middle aged. Never before have I seen such handsome commanding men and they had in one hand bows and arrows as canes. Now in their other hands were huckleberry bushes and the berries were of every color.   1.21

"Then said the beings, addressing me, 'He who created the world at

the beginning employed us to come to earth. Our visit now is not the
1.11   only one we have made. He commanded us saying "Go once more down
upon the earth and (this time) visit him who thinks of me. He is grateful
for my creations, moreover he wishes to rise from sickness and walk (in
health) upon the earth. Go you and help him to recover.' Then said the
messengers, 'Take these berries and eat of every color. They will give
you strength and your people with us will help you rise.' So I took and
ate the berries. Then said the beings, 'On the morrow we will have it
that a fire will be in the bushes and a medicine steeped to give you
strength. We will appoint Dry Pudding and Dipped Tobacco, a man and
his wife, to make the medicine. Now they are the best of all the medicine
people. Early in the morning we will see them and at that time you will
have the medicine for your use, and before noon the unused medicine
will be cast away because you will have recovered. Now moreoever before noon many people will gather at the council house. These people
will be your relatives and will see you. They will have gathered the early
strawberries[4] and made a strawberry feast, and moreover will have
strawberry wine sweetened with sugar. Then will all drink the juice of
the berry and thank the Creator for your recovery and moreover they
severally will call upon you by your name as a relative according as
you are.'

"Now when the day came I went as appointed and all the people saw
me coming and it was as predicted.

"Now the messengers spoke to me and said that they would now tell
me how things ought to be upon the earth. They said: 'Do not allow any
one to say that you have had great fortune in being able to rise again.
The favor of the four beings is not alone for you and the Creator is willing
to help all mankind.'

"Now on that same day the Great Feather and the Harvest dances
were to be celebrated and at this time the beings told me that my relatives would restore me. 'Your feelings and spirits are low,' they said, 'and
must be aroused. Then will you obtain power to recover.' Verily the servants of the Creator said this. Now moreover they commanded that
henceforth dances of this same kind should be held and thanksgiving
offered whenever the strawberries were ripe. Furthermore they said
that the juice of the berry must be drunk by the children and the aged
and all the people. Truly all must drink of the berry juice, for they said
that the sweet water of the berries was a medicine and that the early
strawberries were a great medicine. So they bade me tell this story to

---

[4] "The earliest of the wild strawberries are thought to be of great medicinal value and
are eagerly eaten as soon as ripe. So sacred a plant is the strawberry that it is thought to
grow along the 'heaven road.' A person recovering from a severe illness says, 'I almost ate
strawberries.'" (A. P.)

my people when I move upon the earth again. Now they said, 'We shall   1.21
continually reveal things unto you. We, the servants of him who made
us, say that as he employed us to come unto you to reveal his will, so   2.11
you must carry it to your people. Now we are they whom he created
when he made the world and our duty is to watch over and care for
mankind. Now there are four of us but the fourth is not here present.
When we called you by name and you heard, he returned to tell the
news. This will bring joy into the heaven-world of our Creator. So it is
that the fourth is not with us but you shall see him at another time and
when that time is at hand you shall know. Now furthermore we must
remind you of the evil things that you have done and you must repent of
all things that you believe to have been evil. You think that you have
done wrong because of the Death chant, the Women's song, and the
Harvest song and because you partook of strong drink. Verily you must
do as you think for whatsoever you think is evil is evil.'

"'And now behold! Look through the valley between two hills. Look
between the sunrise and the noon!'

"So I looked, and in the valley there was a deeper hollow from which
smoke was arising and steam as if a hot place were beneath.

"I answered, 'I see a place in the valley from which smoke is arising
and it is also steaming as a hot place were beneath.'

"Then said the beings, 'Truly you have spoken. It is the truth. In that
place a man is buried. He lies between the two hills in the hollow in the
valley and a great message is buried with him. Once we commanded that
man to proclaim that message to the world but he refused to obey. So
now he will never rise from that spot for he refused to obey. So now to
you, therefore, we say, proclaim the message that we give you and tell it
truly before all people.'

"'Now the first thing has been finished and it remains for us to uncover all wickedness before you.' So they said."

"Now the beings spoke saying, 'We must now relate our message.
We will uncover the evil upon the earth and show how men spoil the
laws the Great Ruler has made and thereby made him angry.'

"'The Creator made man a living creature.'

"'Four words tell a great story of wrong and the Creator is sad because of the trouble they bring, so go and tell your people.'

"'The first word is Whiskey (or Rum). It seems that you never have
known that this word stands for a great and monstrous evil and has
reared a high mound of bones. You lose your minds and whiskey causes
it all. Alas, many are fond of it and are too fond of it. So now all must
now say, "I will use it nevermore. As long as I live, as long as the number
of my days is I will never use it again. I now stop." So must all say when
they heard this message.' Now the beings, the servants of the Great
Ruler, the messengers of him who created us, said this. Furthermore

they said that the Creator made whiskey and gave it to our younger brethren, the white man, as a medicine but they use it for evil for they drink it for other purposes than medicine and drink instead of work and idlers drink whiskey. No, the Creator did not make it for you."

So they said and he said. It was that way.[5]

"Now spoke the beings and said, 'We now speak of the second word. This makes the Creator angry. The word is witchcraft. Witches are people without their right minds. They make disease and spread sickness to make the living die. They cut short the numbered days, for the Creator has given each person a certain number of days in which to live in this world.

"'Now this must you do: When you have told this message and the witches hear it they will confess before all the people and will say, 'I am doing this evil thing but now I cease it forever, as long as I live.' Some witches are more evil and cannot speak in public so these must come privately and confess to you, Handsome Lake, or a preacher of this Gai-wiio (Good Message). Now some are most evil and they must go far out upon an abandoned trail and there they must confess before the Creator alone. This course may be taken by witches of whom no one knows.

"'Now when they go they must say:

"Our Creator, O listen to me!
I am a miserable creature.
I think that way
So now I cease.
Now this is appointed
For all of my days,
As long as I live here
In this earth-world.
I have spoken."

"'In this manner all must say and say truly, then the prayer will be sufficient.'"

So they said and he said. It was that way.

"Now the beings spoke again saying, 'This is the third word. It is a sad one and the Creator is very sad because of this third word. It seems that you have never known that a great pile of human bodies lies dead because of this word, the secret poisons in little bundles named compelling charms. Now the Creator who made us commands that they who do this evil, when they hear this message, must stop it immediately and do it nevermore while they live upon this earth-world. It matters not how

[5] Most of the discreet sections within the body of the code end with this or a similar two-sentence refrain. The antecedent of "they" is the messengers, and of "he" Handsome Lake.

much destruction they have wrought—let them repent and not fail for fear the Creator will not accept them as his own.'"

So they said and he said. It was that way.

"'Now another word. It is sad. It is the fourth word. It is abortion.

"'Now the Creator ordained that women should bear children.

"'Now a certain young married woman had children and suffered much. Now she is with child again and her mother wishing to prevent further sufferings designs to administer a medicine to cut off the child and to prevent forever other children from coming. So the mother makes the medicine and gives it. Now when she does this she forever cuts away her daughter's spring of children. Now it is because of such things that the Creator is sad. He created life to live and he wishes such evils to cease. He wishes those who employ such medicines to cease such practices forevermore. Now they must stop when they hear this message. Go and tell your people.'"

So they said and he said. It was that way.

5.2 Examples of Handsome Lake's activity after his commissioning (Parker, 1913:49–50, 52–3, 46–7, 45–6, 55, 44)

"'Now another message to tell your people.

"'The messengers have given the promise to the prophet that he will be able to judge diseases and prescribe remedies. So also he will be able to see far down into the earth as far as runs the elm's root. Then if any trouble comes and anyone asks the help of the prophet, he must give it freely, but they who ask must give an offering of tobacco. Now there will be some in your care who will be taken from your hands for other treatment. No wrong will be done and you must bear no ill will. It is said that the events of all our days are foreknown, so when the time comes for you to exercise your power we will tell you and then you may judge the earth and cure diseases.'"   3.11

So they said and he said. It was that way.

"Now another message for your people.

"Now when my relatives heard all this they said, 'This man must be a clairvoyant.'   2.2

"The news spread and Cornplanter came as a messenger. Now he came to Handsome Lake and said, 'Why, having the assurance of powers, do you not commence now. Come prophesy!' Now he had tobacco for an offering. Then he said, 'My daughter is very sick.'   3.21

"Now the diviner of mysteries did not respond to his entreaty and so Cornplanter went out but soon came running back. This second time he had the same request and pleaded more earnestly, but without avail.

"Then it was said that he would not respond to the cry of a brother and had no hearing for the voice of a brother.

"Again Cornplanter returned and urged his brother.

"Now the people said, 'Have we not something to say to you as well as the messengers of the Creator?'

"Then he answered and said, 'Truly the people say that I will not reason. Verily I am true to my words. Now I can do nothing but try but I have not yet the permission of the messengers.'

2.11 "Now he went into a deep sleep and when he awoke he told his vision. Now he said that the death chant should be sung for the sick woman.

"Now it is said that at that time the first song was in order but every part of the song was silent.

"Now a rumor spread that after all it was not wrong to continue the ceremonial dances once forbidden. So many were sick because they had not observed the commanded method of closing the societies."

This was so when Gaiwiio was new. It was that way. . . .

"Now another message.

"This happened when Gaiwiio was new. It was the time when he dwelt at Cornplanter village.

"A father and son appeared in Cornplanter village. Now the name of the son was Ganiseon. They were on a hunting journey and came from Cattaraugus village with a horse and cart. Now they tarried in Cornplanter village for several nights before again taking up their journey.

"It was during the hunting season that the news spread that some one had returned from the hunting grounds without a companion. It was the young man who had returned. So they questioned him and asked where his father was. He answered, 'My father is lost. I went about searching for my father a number of days. I walked and searched and signalled with gun discharges hoping to find him. I could not find him and became weary waiting for his return.' So he said."

"Now Cornplanter when he heard this said, 'It is apparent to me that the young man has spoken the untruth.' So then they all went to the diviner of mysteries and Cornplanter spoke to him saying, 'It is my opinion that the boy has murdered his own father.' And the prophet answering said, 'They have not yet given me the power to see things but this will I do. Bring a bullet, a knife, and a hatchet that the boy may look upon these things when I speak and perhaps the truth will come. One of these things will move though not touched and he shall be the witness.' So the head men did as bidden and placed the objects as directed. In the middle of the floor they spread a blanket and put the articles upon it. Then they gathered around it and watched, and as they watched he spoke and the bullet moved. Thus it happened. Then spoke Handsome Lake, 'This brings the confirmation of the rumor. Truly the youth has murdered his father, and furthermore I saw that the crime was commit-
2.11 ted between Franklin (Pa.) and Oil City (Pa.). On the south side of a

mountain, where half way up an elm is broken, leaning over on the downhill side to the west lies the body buried in the leaves of the top branches. He, the father, is buried in the leaves.' So he said when he spoke. The chiefs and head-men appointed a delegation to see if all he had said were true. So they went as they had been told and found the body of the father and brought it back with them." It was that way. . . .

"So now another story.

"It happened that at a certain time a certain person did not honor Gaiwiio. At a gathering where Gaiwiio was being told this was done. It was at Cold Spring village.

"A man was standing in the doorway showing disrespect to the pro-   2.1
ceedings within. The prophet was speaking and as he said in closing 'It is finished,' the man in the doorway *daini'dadi*.[6] Now that was the last. The man did not go home to his dwelling and the next day it was rumored that he was missing. A search was made and on the other side of the Allegany in a swamp two days later the man was found. He was sitting above it. He had broken branches and arranged them in the form of a nest upon which he sat devouring snakes. He was not in his right mind. They took him from his nest and soon he died." It was that way.

"Now another story.

"Now it was that when the people reviled me, the proclaimer of the prophecy, the impression came to me that it would be well to depart and go to Tonawanda. In that place I had relatives and friends and thought that my bones might find a resting place there. Thus I thought through the day.

"Then the messengers came to me and said 'We understand your   2.11
thoughts. We will visit you more frequently and converse with you. Wherever you go take care not to be alone. Be cautious and move secretly.'

"Then the messengers told me that my life journey would be in three stages and when I entered the third I would enter into the eternity of the New World,[7] the land of our Creator. So they said." It was that way.

"The day was bright when I went into the planted field and alone I wandered in the planted field and it was the time of the second hoeing. Suddenly a damsel appeared and threw her arms around my neck and as she clasped me she spoke saying, 'When you leave this earth for the new world above, it is our wish to follow you.' I looked for the damsel but saw   2.11
only the long leaves of corn twining round my shoulders. And then I understood that it was the spirit of the corn who had spoken, she the

---

[6] Parker nowhere translates this word, but the gist is not difficult to imagine.

[7] "The heaven described by Handsome Lake was called the New World because it had not been previously known. The generations before had not gone there, not having known the will of the Creator as revealed by the prophet." (A.P.)

sustainer of life. So I replied, 'O spirit of the corn, follow not me but abide still upon the earth and be strong and be faithful to your purpose. Ever endure and do not fail the children of women. It is not time for you to follow for Gaiwiio is only in its beginning.'" It was that way. . . .

"'Now another message for your people.

2.2   "'Some of your relatives and descendants will say, "We lack an understanding of this religion," and this will be the cry of the people. But even we, the servants of the Creator, do not understand all things. Now some when they are turned to the right way will say, "I will continue so for all of my days," but this will not be so for they surely will fall short in some things. This is why even we can not understand all things.'"

So they said. It was that way. . . .

"Now another message.

"Now the messengers commanded him to give attention and he did. Then he saw a great assembly and the assembly was singing:

> 'The whole earth is here assembled,
> The whole world may come to us.
> We are ready.'

"Then said the messengers, 'What did you see when you gave attention?'

"He answered, 'I saw a great gathering of beings and the gathering was singing and the words of the song were:

> 'The whole earth is here assembled,
> The whole world may come to us.
> We are ready.'

2.1   "Then said the messengers, 'It is very true. The beings that you saw resemble human creatures. It is true that they are singing. Now the as-
3.21   sembly is a gathered host of medicines for healing. Now let this be your ceremony when you wish to employ the medicine in a plant: First offer tobacco. Then tell the plant in gentle words what you desire of it and pluck it from the roots. It is said in the upper world that it is not right to take a plant for medicine without first talking to it. Let not one ever be taken without first speaking.'"

So they said and he said. It was that way. . . .

"'Now another message to tell our people.

2.2   "'The religious leaders and the chiefs must enforce obedience to the teachings of Gaiwiio.'"

So they said and he said. It was that way.

5.3 Apocalyptic elements in Handsome Lake's message (Parker, 1913:58–9, 43)

"Now another message.

"Now it is said that you must relate what the messengers say about

the coming end of the earth. Relate how all those who refuse to believe
in Gaiwiio will suffer hardships. Now when the earth is about to end the   1.42
chiefs and head-men will disagree and that will be a sign. So also, the
Overseer of the ceremonies will disagree. Then will the relations know
the truth."

So they said and he said. It was that way.

"Now another message.

"Now we say that you must tell your friends and relatives that there
will be a time when all the earth will withhold its sustaining foods. Then
will come the end of the world and those who refuse to believe in Gai-   1.42
wiio will suffer great hardships."

So they said and he said. It was that way.

"Now another message. . . .

"Now we think that a time will come when a woman will be seen
performing her witch spells in the daylight. Then will you know that the
end is near. She will run through the neighborhood boasting how many
she has slain by her sorcery. Then will you see how she who refused to   1.42
believe in Gaiwiio will suffer punishment."

So they said and he said. It was that way.

"Now another message.

"In that time you will hear many rumors of men who say, 'I have
spoken with the Creator.' So also will you see many wonders but they
will not endure for they will be the work of the evil spirit.

"Verily we say that there will be none other than you who will receive a message from the Creator through us. This truth will be proclaimed when the end comes."

So they said and he said. It was that way.

"Now another message.

"In that time every poisonous creature will appear. These creatures
the Creator has imprisoned in the underworld and they are the creations
of the evil-minded spirit. Now it is our opinion that when they are re-   1.42
leased many people will be captured and poisoned by them. Men will
see these hardships when they fail to believe in Gaiwiio."

So they said and he said. It was that way.

"Now another message.

"Now there will be some who will enter into a sleep. When they lie
down they will be in health and as they sleep the Creator will withdraw
their lives for they are true. To the faithful this will happen."

So they said and he said. It was that way.

"Now another message.

"Now we think that the Creator will stop the earth and heavens. All
the powers of nature will he suspend. Now they will see this who refuse
to believe in Gaiwiio."

So they said and he said. It was that way.

"Now another message.

"Now we think that when the end comes the earth will be destroyed
1.42 by fire and not one upon it will escape for all the earth will be enveloped
in flames and all those who refuse to believe in Gaiwiio will be in it."

So they said and he said. It was that way.

"Now another message for your people.

"'If all the world would repent the earth would become as new again.
Because of sin the under-world is crumbling with decay. The world is
full of sin. Truly, this is so.'"

So they said and he said. It was that way.

5.4 Pronouncements on aspects of Iroquois culture and on the people's
current social and historial situation (Parker, 1913:39–40, 42, 60, 31,
32, 35–6, 39, 49, 68, 65–6, 38)

"'Now another message for you to tell your people.

"'It is not right for you to have so many dances and dance songs.

"'A man calls a dance in honor of some totem animal from which he
desires favor or power. This is very wrong, for you do not know what
injury it may work upon other people.

"'Tell your people that these things must cease. Tell them to repent
and cease.'"

So they said and he said. It was that way.

"'Now this shall be the way: They who belong to these totem animal
1.4 societies must throw tobacco and disband.' So they said. Now in those
days when the head men heard this message they said at once in anger,
'We disband,' and they said this without holding a ceremony as the messenger had directed."

It was that way. . . .

"'Now another message to tell your people.

"'Now the messengers said that this thing was beyond the control of
Indians.

"'At some future day the wild animals will become extinct. Now
when that day comes the people will raise cattle and swine for feast food
at the thanksgivings.'"[8]

So they said and he said. It was that way. . . .

"Now another message. Tell it to those at Tonawanda.

"Now they said to him, 'Watch a certain place.' So he did and he saw
a certain person holding meat in his hands. The man was rejoicing and
was well clothed and fed and his name was Tadondaieha, and he recognized him."

"Then said they to him, 'How is it?'

[8] "Pork is now the principle ceremonial food." (A. P.)

"He answered, 'I recognized Tadondaieha and he held meat in his hands.' So he answered he who talked religiously."

"Then the messengers answered, 'Truly you saw a man with meat enjoying himself. He was joyous because he was a prosperous and successful hunter and gave game as presents to his neighbors. So his neighbors were grateful and thanked him. Now the man you saw has departed from the earth. In his earth-life he cleansed himself each day, visited and enjoyed himself in his best clothing. He was ever good to his fellow-beings and so he is blessed and will receive the reward reserved for him by his Creator."

So they said and he said. It was that way.

"Now another message.

"'The Creator has ordered that man and wife should rear their children well, love them and keep them in health. This is the Creator's rule. We, the messengers, have seen both men and women desert each other when children come. The woman discovers that the man, her husband, loves his child and she is very jealous and spreads evil reports of him. She does this for an excuse before the world to leave him. Thus the messengers say that the Creator desires men and women to cease such mischief.'"

So they said and he said. It was that way. . . .

"'Now another message to tell your people.

"'The married often live well together for a while. Then a man becomes ugly in temper and abuses his wife. It seems to afford him pleasure. Now because of such things the Creator is very sad. So he bids us to tell you that such evils must stop. Neither man nor woman must strike each other.' So they said.

"Now furthermore they said, 'We will tell you what people must do. It is the way he calls best. Love one another and do not strive for another's undoing. Even as you desire good treatment, so render it. Treat your wife well and she will treat you well.'"

So they said and he said. It was that way. . . .

"Now another message.

"'A way that was followed.

"'Sometimes a mother is ready to feed her family. When she is ready to bid them sit down, she glances out and sees someone coming and straightway hides the foods. A woman visitor comes in. Now after some conversation the visitor says she is unwell and goes out. Then the family commences to eat. And the Creator says that who follow such tricks must repent as soon as they hear this message, for such practices are most wicked.'"

"Now the messengers said this."

"'Now the Creator made food for all creatures and it must be free for all. He ordained that people should live in communities. Now when visitors enter a lodge the woman must always say, "come eat." Now it is not right to refuse what is offered. The visitor must take two or three bites at least and say, "Thanks." Tell this to your people.'"

So they said and he said. It was that way. . . .

"Now another message.

"'When a woman sees an unfortunate girl who has neither parents nor settled home and calls her in and helps her repair her clothing, cleanse herself and comb her hair, she does right and has favor in the sight of her Creator. He loves the poor and the woman does right before him. So we, the messengers, say that you must tell your people to continue to do this good thing.'"

So they said he he said. It was that way. . . .

"Now another message to tell your people.

· "'Now some men have much work and invite all their friends to come and aid them and they do so. Now this is a good plan and the Creator designed it. He ordained that men should help one another.'"

"Now another message of things not right.

"'People do wrong in the world and the Creator looks at all things.

"'A woman sees some green vegetables and they are not hers. She takes them wrongly. Now she is a thieving woman. Tell your people that petty thieving must cease.' So they said.

"'Now the Creator gave our life givers (corn, beans, squash) for a living. When a woman sees a new crop and wishes to eat of it in her own house, she must ask the owner for a portion and offer payment. Then may the owner use her judgment and accept recompense or give the request freely.'"

So they said and he said. It was that way. . . .

"'Now another message to tell your people.

"'Now we are of the mind that the cold of winter will take life away. Many will be taken away because of the changing cold. Moreover some will freeze because they are filled with strong drink. Then again when the earth grows warm and warm changes come, many will perish because of strong drink. Now the Creator never intended that variations of weather and season, warm and cold, should cause death.'"

"'The Creator made the waters of the earth, the rivers and lakes. These too will cause death and some filled with strong drink will be swallowed up by the waters.'"

"'And now more. The Creator made fire and this will also cause death and some filled with strong drink will be destroyed by the flames.'"

1.42 "'Verily he has said and ordained that they who disobey Gaiwiio should fall into hardships.'"

So they said and he said. It was that way. . . .

"So they proceeded on their journey[9] and had not gone far when they came to a halt.

"Then the messengers pointed out a certain spot and said, 'Watch attentively,' and beheld a man carrying loads of dirt and depositing them in a certain spot. He carried the earth in a wheelbarrow and his task was a hard one. Then he knew that the name of the man was Red Jacket, a chief.

"Then asked the messengers, 'What did you see?'

"He answered, 'I beheld a man carrying dirt in a wheelbarrow and that man had a laborous task. His name was Red Jacket, a chief.'

"Then answered the messengers, 'You have spoken truly. Red Jacket is the name of the man who carries the dirt. It is true that his work is laborious and this is for a punishment for he was the one who first gave his consent to the sale of Indian reservations. It is said that there is hardship for those who part with their lands for money or trade. So now you have seen the doom of those who repent not. Their eternity will be one of punishment.'"

So they said and he said. It was that way. . . .

"So they proceeded a little ways farther and in a short time they reached a certain spot and stopped.

"Then said the messengers, 'Look toward the setting sun.'

"So he looked and saw. Now as he looked he seemed to see a man pacing to and fro. He seemed to be a white man and in his hand he seemed to have a bayonet with which he prodded the ground. Now moreover he seemed very angry.

"Then said the messengers, 'What did you see?'

"He answered, 'I saw what seemed to be a man pacing to and fro. He seemed to be a white man and in his hand he seemed to have a bayonet with which he prodded the ground, and, moreover, it seemed that he was angry.' So he said when he answered.

"Then the messengers said, 'It is true. He is a white man and in a temper. It is true. Indians must not help him and the head men must honestly strive to prevent their followers from helping him.'"[10]

So they said and he said. It was that way. . . .

"'Now another message.

"'Three things that our younger brethren (the white people) do are right to follow.

"'Now, the first. The white man works on a tract of cultivated ground and harvests food for his family. So if he should die they still have the

---

[9] This unit is from a section of the Code known as "the journey over the great sky-road," in which the messengers gave Handsome Lake a guided tour through the other world.

[10] "The reference is to "the 'war in the west,' probably General Harrison's campaign against Tecumseh in 1811." (A. P.)

ground for help. If any of your people have cultivated ground let them not be proud on that account. If one is proud there is sin within him but if there be no pride there is no sin.

"'Now, the seond thing. It is the way a white man builds a house. He builds one warm and fine appearing so if he dies the family has the house for help. Whoso among you does this does right, always providing there is no pride. If there is pride it is evil but if there is none, it is well.

"'Now the third. The white man keeps horses and cattle. Now there is no evil in this for they are a help to his family. So if he dies his family has the stock for help. Now all this is right if there is no pride. No evil will follow this practice if the animals are well fed, treated kindly and not overworked. Tell this to your people.'"

So they said and he said. It was that way.

"Now another message to tell your relatives.

"'This concerns education. It is concerning studying in English schools.

"'Now let the Council appoint twelve people to study, two from each nation of the six. So many white people are about you that you must study to know their ways.'"

So they said and he said. It was that way.

6
Wovoka, the Indian "Messiah," and the Ghost Dance of 1890

Introduction

The last third of the nineteenth century was for the Indians of the Great Plains and western mountains of the United States a time of acute cultural crisis characterized by increasing white domination and the break-up of their traditional way of life. Repeating a pattern which had already occurred in other parts of the country, armed conflict between Indians and whites led to land cessions and the confining of tribal groups to reservations, the size of which was in many instances further reduced by subsequent cessions. Virtually overnight, the once free-roaming hunters were required to become farmers. Their cultural, economic, and political situation was desperate.

One of the responses to this situation was a millennial movement known as the Ghost Dance of 1890, which had its origin in the visionary experiences of Wovoka, a Paiute Indian, who was often referred to as the Indian "messiah." Wovoka was born about 1856 (Mooney 1896:771) and lived all his life in the Mason valley of western Nevada, about 40 miles northwest of the Walker Lake reservation. Because of his association as a seasonal worker with the family of a nearby white rancher, David Wilson, he was also widely known by the name John (Jack) Wilson. After an initial revelation in about the year 1887, he began to teach the dance to his people. His most important vision, however, came on January 1, 1889, in conjunction with a total eclipse of the sun. On this occasion he felt himself to be taken up into the spirit world, where he met "God" and was given a message to convey to his people (see 6.4 below).

Wovoka taught that the time was coming when the whites would be supernaturally destroyed and all dead Indians would return to the earth. The herds of game animals would also be restored, and the old way of life would flourish again on a reconstituted earth in which there would be no more sickness or old age. In preparation for this great event and to hasten its arrival the Indians were instructed to perform the Ghost Dance ceremonial at regular intervals. The latter involved large numbers of people moving slowly around a central tree, and one of its characteristic features was a trance experienced by many of the dancers, in which they visited the spirit world, conversed with dead relatives, and often caught glimpses of villages of Indians living in the old way. During late 1889 and 1890, this new religion spread rapidly on the Plains. Among the Sioux of South Dakota, the doctrine and practice of the dance took on a note of overt hostility towards the whites, inaugurating an unfortunate chain of events which culminated in the massacre of Chief Big Foot's band at Wounded Knee on December 29, 1890.

Through his public activity, Wovoka gained a reputation for his acts of power, and this stayed with him long after the Ghost Dance movement had, for all practical purposes, come to an end. Seen in its cultural context, it is clear that though for a time he advocated a doctrine which had appeal far beyond the bounds of his own Paiute people, his mode of operation was essentially that of a Paiute shaman.[1] He died in 1932.

Materials on the Ghost Dance are available to us for detailed study largely due to the labors of James Mooney, an indefatigable researcher for the Bureau of American Ethnology. Beginning in late 1890, when the movement was still in full swing, Mooney spent approximately three years in an intensive investigation of the Ghost Dance. By his own account twenty-two months of this time were spent in the field, talking with Indians and whites in Indian Territory (now Oklahoma), the northern Plains, and Nevada. In January of 1892 he was even able to interview Wovoka himself (6.4 below). All told, in those days of railroads and horse-and-buggy he travelled "nearly 32,000 miles" and spent "more or less

---

[1] For a discussion of Wovoka in the context of Paiute shamanism see Overholt (1982:11–8). Dangberg (1968) is perhaps the best biographical sketch of Wovoka.

time . . . with about twenty tribes" (Mooney, 1896:654). The result was his book-length study, which forms part 2 of the Fourteenth Annual Report of the Bureau of Ethnology, published in 1896. Of the man and his contribution Bernard Fontana (1973) says: "James Mooney may well have been one of the greatest of all American anthropologists. Certainly *The Ghost-Dance Religion and the Sioux outbreak of 1890* is one of the finest studies of American Indians ever written, a tribute to the Indian people with whom it is concerned and a lasting monument to its author, an outspoken collector of knowledge in search of truth."

Despite the fact that Mooney was in the field as events were unfolding, it is difficult to be absolutely certain about the exact content of Wovoka's original message. The earliest reports are second- and third-hand, often given to Mooney by delegates from the various tribes who had visited Wovoka and brought his teachings back to their own people. There are indications that the particular perceptions and needs of these men and their tribes often resulted in embellishments of and even substantive changes in the doctrine (see 6.5 below). Even the fact that Mooney spoke with Wovoka himself does not guarantee us an accurate account of the original message, since that interview took place in early 1892, after the occurrence of two important events which may have been responsible for certain modifications in the teaching, viz., the failure of the millennium to arrive in the spring of 1891, as had been widely expected, and the violence among the Sioux which culminated in Wounded Knee. It is possible that by 1892 Wovoka had modified his message in the direction of a decreased emphasis on the destruction of the whites through some natural catastrophe and an increasing elaboration of its ethical content (do not fight, cooperate with the whites, etc.).[2] Nevertheless, the sources give us a reasonably clear picture of Wovoka's functioning as an intermediary, and for our present purposes that is the thing of most interest.

The ordering of the texts printed below will indicate something of the development which the movement underwent. First, in chronological order there are four accounts of encounters with Wovoka. The first selection in 6.5 is of the same type, but the main interest in the two texts there is the way in which the prophet's message was affected by the particular situation and needs of the Sioux. Finally, the texts in 6.6 show how both Wovoka and some who spread his message ceased to be harbingers of an imminent millennium, focusing their attention on problems of everyday life in a continuing world.

Mooney's classic study (1896) is the basic source on the Ghost Dance. For a discussion of specific issues and comprehensive bibliographies see Overholt (1974, 1978, 1982) and Turner (1978:70–94).

---

[2] For a more detailed discussion of this problem cf. Overholt (1974:41–4, 52–6).

Texts

6.1 "Captain Dick's" account, the earliest report of Wovoka's teaching
(Mooney, 1896:784)

> This account is contained in a report to the War Department sub-
> mitted by Captain J. M. Lee in the autumn of 1890. In it Lee
> records a conversation with a Paiute Indian named Captain Dick,
> who recounted Wovoka's teaching as it had been described to him
> by another Indian toward the end of 1888.

Long time, twenty years ago, Indian medicine-man in Mason's valley
at Walker lake talk same way, same as you hear now. In one year, maybe,
after he begin talk he die. Three years ago another medicine-man begin
same talk. Heap talk all time. Indians hear all about it everywhere. Indians come from long way off to hear him. They come from the east; they
make signs. Two years ago me go to Winnemucca and Pyramid lake, me
see Indian Sam, a head man, and Johnson Sides. Sam he tell me he just   1.4
been to see Indian medicine-man to hear him talk. Sam say medicine-
man talk this way:

"All Indians must dance, everywhere, keep on dancing. Pretty soon
in next spring Big Man (Great Spirit) come. He bring back all game of
every kind. The game be thick everywhere. All dead Indians come back
and live again. They all be strong just like young men, be young again.
Old blind Indian see again and get young and have fine time. When Old
Man (God) comes this way, then all the Indians go to mountains, high up
away from whites. Whites can't hurt Indians then. Then while Indians
way up high, big flood comes like water and all white people die, get
drowned. After that water go way and then nobody but Indians everywhere and game all kinds thick. Then medicine-man tell Indians to send
word to all Indians to keep up dancing and the good time will come.
Indians who don't dance, who don't believe in this word, will grow little,
just about a foot high, and stay that way. Some of them will be turned
into wood and be burned in fire." That's the way Sam tell me the
medicine-man talk.

6.2 Porcupine's account of a visit to Wovoka (Mooney, 1896:793–6)

> In the autumn of 1889 Porcupine, a northern Cheyenne from the
> Tongue River agency in Montana, and several other delegates
> from the Sioux, Arapaho, and Shoshoni tribes journeyed to Ne-
> vada, where they visited Wovoka and attended a Ghost Dance
> near Walker Lake. In the spring of 1890 he returned to Montana,
> where on June 15 he made a lengthy report about his journey to
> one Major Carroll at the Tongue River agency (Mooney,
> 1896:784, 793, 817).
> It will be noted that Porcupine continually refers to Wovoka

as "the Christ," which raises the question of possible Christian influences on Wovoka and/or his followers. Mooney addresses this point when, speaking of Wovoka's early life, he states that through his association with the David Wilson family he "gained some knowledge of English, together with a confused idea of the white man's theology" (1896:765). One should not overestimate the importance of this influence, however. Looking beyond superficial traits at the antecedents of the movement and the shape of the expectation it proclaimed, the dance appears thoroughly traditional in its basic values, beliefs, and hopes. Indeed, Alexander Lesser, who has studied the dance as it was appropriated by the Pawnee, suggests that despite the incorporation of some Christian elements the "sancation" of the hope which the doctrine brought ". . . was native to the Indian mind. It was based on the vision, on the direct supernatural experience. In the vision a message came from the deceased, telling the living what to do, telling the living what would happen" (1933:109).[3]

Porcupine's account begins with a description of the long ride on a series of trains and of the various reservations and towns he passed through and the people he met along the way. He continues:

1.4   What I am going to say is the truth. The two men sitting near me were with me, and will bear witness that I speak the truth. I and my
2.2   people have been living in ignorance until I went and found out the truth. All the whites and Indians are brothers, I was told there. I never
3.3   knew this before.

The Fish-eaters[4] near Pyramid lake told me that Christ had appeared on earth again. They said Christ knew he was coming; that eleven of his children were also coming from a far land. It appeared that Christ had sent for me to go there, and that was why unconsciously I took my journey. It had been foreordained. Christ had summoned myself and others from all heathen tribes, from two to three or four from each of fifteen or sixteen different tribes. There were more different languages than I ever heard before and I did not understand any of them. They told me when I got there that my great father was there also, but did not know who he was. The people assembled called a council, and the chief's son went to see the Great Father (messiah), who sent word to us to remain fourteen days in that camp and that he would come to see us. He sent me a small package of something white to eat that I did not know the name of. There were a great many people in the council, and this white food was divided among them. The food was a big white nut.[5] Then I went to the agency

[3] Cf. Overholt (1974:43–4, 46–7) and (1978:193, note 25).
[4] The Pauite of Walker Lake, Nevada (Mooney, 1896:1051).
[5] The nut of the pinon pine was a common food item among Indian tribes of the Great Basin.

at Walker lake and they told us Christ would be there in two days. At the end of two days, on the third morning, hundreds of people gathered at this place. They cleared off a place near the agency in the form of a circus ring and we all gathered there. This space was perfectly cleared of grass, etc. We waited there till late in the evening anxious to see Christ. Just before sundown I saw a great many people, mostly Indians, coming dressed in white men's clothes. The Christ was with them. They all formed in this ring around it. They put up sheets all around the circle, as they had no tents. Just after dark some of the Indians told me that the Christ (Father) had arrived. I looked around to find him, and finally saw him sitting on one side of the ring. They all started toward him to see him. They made a big fire to throw light on him. I never looked around, but went forward, and when I saw him I bent my head. I had always thought the Great Father was a white man, but this man looked like an Indian. He sat there a long time and nobody went up to speak to him. He sat with his head bowed all the time. After awhile he rose and said he was very glad to see his children. "I have sent for you and am glad to see you. I am going to talk to you after awhile about your relatives who are dead and gone. My children, I want you to listen to all I have to say to you. I will teach you, too, how to dance a dance, and I want you to dance it. Get ready for your dance and then, when the dance is over, I will talk to you." He was dressed in a white coat with stripes. The rest of his dress was a white man's except that he had on a pair of moccasins. Then he commenced our dance, everybody joining in, the Christ singing while we danced. We danced till late in the night, when he told us we had danced enough.

The next morning, after breakfast was over, we went into the circle and spread canvas over it on the ground, the Christ standing in the midst of us. He told us he was going away that day, but would be back that next morning and talk to us.

In the night when I first saw him I thought he was an Indian, but the next day when I could see better he looked different. He was not so dark as an Indian, nor so light as a white man. He had no beard or whiskers, but very heavy eyebrows. He was a good-looking man. We were crowded up very close. We had been told that nobody was to talk, and even if we whispered the Christ would know it. I had heard that Christ had been crucified, and I looked to see, and I saw a scar on his wrist and one on his face, and he seemed to be the man. I could not see his feet. He would talk to us all day.

That evening we all assembled again to see him depart. When we were assembled, he began to sing, and he commenced to tremble all over, violently for a while, and then sat down. We danced all that night, the Christ lying down beside us apparently dead.

The next morning when we went to eat breakfast, the Christ was

2.1

with us. After breakfast four heralds went around and called out that the Christ was back with us and wanted to talk with us. The circle was prepared again. The people assembled, and Christ came among us and sat down. He said he wanted to talk to us again and for us to listen. He said: "I am the man who made everything you see around you. I am not lying to you, my children. I made this earth and everything on it. I have been to heaven and seen your dead friends and have seen my own father and mother. In the beginning, after God made the earth, they sent me back to teach the people, and when I came back on earth the people were afraid of me and treated me badly. This is what they did to me (showing his scars). I did not try to defend myself. I found my children were bad, so went back to heaven and left them. I told them that in so many hundred years I would come back to see my children. At the end of this time I was sent back to try to teach them. My father told me the earth was getting old and worn out, and the people getting bad, and that I was to renew everything as it used to be, and make it better."

He told us also that all our dead friends were to be resurrected; that they were all to come back to earth, and that as the earth was too small for them and us, he would do away with heaven, and make the earth itself large enough to contain us all; that we must tell all the people we meet about these things. He spoke to us about fighting, and said that 3.3 was bad, and we must keep from it; that the earth was to be all good hereafter, and we must all be friends with one another. He said that in the fall of the year the youth of all the good people would be renewed, so that nobody would be more than 40 years old, and that if they behaved themselves well after this the youth of everyone would be renewed in the spring. He said if we were all good he would send people among us who could heal all our wounds and sickness by mere touch, and that we would live forever. He told us not to quarrel, or fight, nor strike each 3.3 other, not shoot one another; that the whites and Indians were to be all one people. He said if any man disobeyed what he ordered, his tribe would be wiped from the face of the earth; that we must believe everything he said, and that we must not doubt him, or say he lied; that if we did, he would know it; that he would know our thoughts and actions, in no matter what part of the world we might be.

When I heard this from the Christ, and came back home to tell it to my people, I thought they would listen. Where I went to there were lots of white people, but I never had one of them say an unkind word to me. I thought all of your people knew all of this I have told you of, but it seems you do not.

Ever since the Christ I speak of talked to me I have thought what he 2.2 said was good. I see nothing bad in it. When I got back, I knew my people were bad, and had heard nothing of all this, so I got them together and told them of it and warned them to listen to it for their own good. I talked to them for four nights and five days. I told them just what I have told you here today. I told them what I said were the words of God Almighty, who was looking down on them. I wish some of you had been up in our camp here to have heard my words to the Cheyennes. The only bad thing that there has been in it at all was this: I had just told my people that the Christ would visit the sins of any Indian upon the whole tribe, when the recent trouble (killing of Ferguson) occurred. If any one of you think I am not telling the truth, you can go and see this man I speak of for yourselves. I will go with you, and I would like one or two of my people who doubt me to go with me.

The Christ talked to us all in our respective tongues. You can see this man in your sleep any time you want after you have seen him and shaken hands with him once. Through him you can go to heaven and meet your friends. Since my return I have seen him often in my sleep. About the time the soldiers went up the Rosebud I was lying in my lodge asleep, when this man appeared and told me that the Indians had gotten into trouble, and I was frightened. The next night he appeared to me and told me that everything would come out all right.

6.3 The Cheyenne-Arapaho "messiah letter" (Mooney, 1896:781–3)

> After his visit to Wovoka in January, 1892, Mooney returned to Indian Territory, where he was sought out by Cheyenne and Arapaho friends who pressed him for details of his journey. These groups had sent a delegation of their own to Wovoka in August, 1891, and one of the members of that delegation, a Cheyenne named Black Short Nose, gave Mooney a "written statement of the doctrine delivered by Wovoka" to them which had been "written down on the spot, in broken English, by one of the Arapaho delegates, Casper Edson, a young man who had acquired some English education . . . at the government Indian school at Carlisle, Pennsylvania." Mooney accepted this letter as "the genuine official statement of the Ghost-dance doctrine as given by the messiah himself to his disciples" (Mooney, 1896:778–80). It is reproduced here in his "free rendering," along with a comment made by Mooney on the "revolutionary" nature of Wovoka's ethics.

When you get home you must make a dance to continue five days. Dance four successive nights, and the last night keep up the dance until the morning of the fifth day, when all must bathe in the river and then disperse to their homes. You must all do in the same way.

I, Jack Wilson, love you all, and my heart is full of gladness for the gifts you have brought me. When you get home I shall give you a good cloud (rain?) which will make you feel good. I give you a good spirit and give you all good paint. I want you to come again in three months, some from each tribe there (the Indian Territory).

There will be a good deal of snow this year and some rain. In the fall there will be such a rain as I have never given you before.

Grandfather (a universal title of reverence among Indians and here meaning the messiah) says, when your friends die you must not cry. You must not hurt anybody or do harm to anyone. You must not fight. Do right always. It will give you satisfaction in life. This young man has a good father and mother. (Possibly this refers to Casper Edson, the young Arapaho who wrote down this message of Wovoka for the delegation.)

Do not tell the white people about this. Jesus is now upon the earth. He appears like a cloud. The dead are all alive again. I do not know when they will be here; maybe this fall or in the spring. When the time comes there will be no more sickness and everyone will be young again.

Do not refuse to work for the whites and do not make any trouble with them until you leave them. When the earth shakes (at the coming of the new world) do not be afraid. It will not hurt you.

I want you to dance very six weeks. Make a feast at the dance and have food that everybody may eat. Then bathe in the water. That is all. You will receive good words again from me some time. Do not tell lies.

*   *   *

3.3 The moral code inculcated is as pure and comprehensive in its simplicity as anything found in religious systems from the days of Gautama Buddha to the time of Jesus Christ. "*Do no harm to any one. Do right always.*" Could anything be more simple, and yet more exact and exacting? It inculcates honesty—"*Do not tell lies.*" It preaches good will—"*Do no harm to any one.*" It forbids the extravagant mourning customs formerly common among the tribes—"*When your friends die, you must not cry,*" which is interpreted by the prairie tribes as forbidding the killing of horses, the burning of tipis and destruction of property, the cutting off of the hair and the gashing of the body with knives, all of which were formerly the sickening rule at every death until forbidden by the new doctrine. As an Arapaho said to me when his little boy died, "I shall not shoot any ponies, and my wife will not gash her arms. We used to do this when our friends died, because we thought we would never see them again, and it made us feel bad. But now we know we shall all be united again." If the Kiowa had held to the Ghost-dance doctrine instead of abandoning it as they had done, they would have been spared the loss of thousands of dollars in horses, tipis, wagons, and other property destroyed, with much of the mental suffering and all of the physical laceration that resulted in consequence of the recent fatal epidemic in the tribe, when for weeks and months the sound of wailing went up night and morning, and in every camp men and women could be seen daily, with dress disordered and hair cut close to the scalp, with blood hardened in clots upon the skin, or streaming from mutilated fingers and fresh gashes on face, and arms, and legs. It preaches peace with the whites and obedience to authority until the day of deliverance shall come. Above all, it forbids war—"*You must not fight.*" It is hardly possible for us to realize the tremendous and radical change which this doctrine works in the whole spirit of savage life. The career of every Indian has been the warpath. His proudest title has been that of warrior. His conversation by day and his dreams by night have been of bloody deeds upon the enemies of his tribe. His highest boast was in the number of his scalp trophies, and his chief delight at home was in the war dance and the scalp dance. The thirst for blood and massacre seemed inborn in every man, woman, and child of every tribe. Now comes a prophet as a messenger from God to forbid not only war, but all that savors of war— the war dance, the scalp dance, and even the bloody torture of the sun dance—and his teaching is accepted and his words obeyed by four-fifths of all the warlike predatory tribes of the mountains and the great plains. Only those who have known the deadly hatred that once animated Ute, Cheyenne, anmd Pawnee, one toward another, and are able to contrast it with their present spirit of mutual brotherly love, can know what the Ghost-dance religion has accomplished in bringing the savage into civilization. It is such a revolution as comes but once in the life of a race. 3.3

6.4 An interview with Wovoka (Mooney, 1896:771–3)

> Mooney gives us a colorful account of his journey to visit "the messiah," including a description of his party's becoming "lost on a sage plain on a freezing night in January" on the way to his first lengthy interview (Mooney, 1896:764–76). That interview took place on January 1, 1892. The following excerpt places particular emphasis on how Wovoka came to be an intermediary, and also shows his desire to dissociate himself from the violence characteristic of some of his followers and certain aspects of the reputation he had gained among whites, largely because of sensational reports in the press.[6]

He had given the dance to his people about four years before, but had received his great revelation about two years previously. On this occasion (January 1, 1889) "the sun died" (was eclipsed) and he fell asleep in the daytime and was taken up to the other world. Here he saw God, with all the people who had died long ago engaged in their oldtime sports and occupations, all happy and forever young. It was a pleasant 1.21

---

[6] Many of the reports of the movement which appeared in the eastern press were inaccurate and misleading; cf. Watson (1943). William Fitch Kelley, a young reporter for the *Nebraska State Journal*, was at Pine Ridge during the worst of the trouble. His dispatches, covering the period from November 24, 1890 to January 16, 1891, are available in a convenient collection (Kelley, 1971), and seem to be one of the best examples of white reporting of the dance.

land and full of game. After showing him all, God told him he must go back and tell his people they must be good and love one another, have

3.3   no quarreling, and live in peace with the whites; that they must work, and not lie or steal; that they must put away all the old practices that savored of war; that if they faithfully obeyed his instructions they would at last be reunited with their friends in this other world, where there would be no more death or sickness or old age. He was then given the dance which he was commanded to bring back to his people. By performing this dance at intervals, for five consecutive days each time, they would secure this happiness to themselves and hasten the event. Finally God gave him control over the elements so that he could make it rain or snow or be dry at will, and appointed him his deputy to take charge of affairs in the west, while "Governor Harrison" would attend to matters in the east, and he, God, would look after the world above. He then returned to earth and began to preach as he was directed, convincing the people by exercising the wonderful powers that had been given him.

1.21   In 1890 Josephus, a Paiute informant, thus described to the scout Chapman the occasion of Wovoka's first inspiration: "About three years ago Jack Wilson took his family and went into the mountains to cut wood for Mr. Dave Wilson. One day while at work he heard a great noise which appeared to be above him on the mountain. He laid down his ax and started to go in the direction of the noise, when he fell down dead, and God came and took him to heaven." Afterward on one or two other occasions "God came and took him to heaven again." Wovoka also told Chapman that he had then been preaching to the Indians about three years. In our conversation he said nothing about a mysterious noise, and stated that it was about two years since he had visited heaven and received his great revelation, but that it was about four years since he had first taught the dance to his people. The fact that he has different revelations from time to time would account for the discrepancy of statement.

He disclaimed all responsibility for the ghost shirt[7] which formed so important a part of the dance costume among the Sioux; said that there were no trances in the dance as performed among his people—a statement confirmed by eyewitnesses among the neighboring ranchmen— and earnestly repudiated any idea of hostility toward the whites, assert-

---

[7] The "ghost shirts" were loosely-cut, fringed outer garments of traditional design upon which were painted a variety of symbols. There is some debate over where the connection between this garment and the dance originated, but it is clear that it was among the Sioux that the shirts gained the greatest importance. It was widely believed that these garments would render the wearers invulnerable to the white man's weapons, and Mooney tells the poignant story of how when a woman "shot in the Wounded Knee massacre was approached as she lay in the church and told that she must let them remove her ghost shirt in order the better to get at her wound, she replied: 'Yes; take it off. They told me a bullet would not go through. Now I don't want it any more'" (Mooney, 1896:790).

ing that his religion was one of universal peace. When quetioned directly, he said he believed it was better for the Indians to follow the white man's road and to adopt the habits of civilization. If appearances are in evidence he is sincere in this, for he was dressed in a good suit of white man's clothing, and works regularly on a ranch, although living in a wikiup. While he repudiated almost everything for which he had been held responsible in the east, he asserted positively that he had been to the spirit world and had been given a revelation and message from God himself, with full control over the elements. From his uncle I learned that Wovoka has five songs for making it rain, the first of which brings on a mist or cloud, the second a snowfall, the third a shower, and the fourth a hard rain or storm, while when he sings the fifth song the weather again becomes clear. 1.21

. . . He makes no claim to be Christ, the Son of God, as has been so often asserted in print. He does claim to be a prophet who has received a divine revelation. I could not help feeling that he was sincere in his repudiation of a number of the wonderful things attributed to him, for the reason that he insisted so strongly on other things fully as trying to the faith of a white man. He made no argument and advanced no proofs, but said simply that he had been with God, as though the statement no more admitted of controversy than the proposition that 2 and 2 are 4. 1.21

6.5 Wovoka's message given a militant twist by some of his Sioux disciples (Mooney, 1896:797, 788–9)

> Despite Wovoka's disclaimer to Mooney, some of the delegates tended to stress the connection between him and "Jesus" claimed in the "messiah letter." What is of particular interest are the subtle differences of interpretation that occur in connection with this element. Porcupine's tone is reverential throughout, and when he speaks of the previous coming of the messiah, his manner is matter-of-fact (6.2 above). However, when the Sioux delegates who visited Wovoka at the same time as Porcupine (1890) take up the theme, the tone is decidedly hostile toward the whites. This is evident in the first selection printed below.[8]
>
> There are a number of factors that might account for this hostile turn in the doctrine as it was preached among the Sioux. This was a rather large group of Indians who in the fifteen years ending with the Custer battle of 1876 had been relatively successful in their military encounters with the whites. Many of the old chiefs, Red Cloud, Sitting Bull, Hump, and others, were still alive. The treaty of 1868 had established a great Sioux reservation comprising the whole of the present South Dakota west of the Missouri River, but by 1889 significant portions of this area had

---

[8] For further examples of anti-white sentiments and actions in the Sioux Ghost Dance, see Overholt (1974:55).

been taken over by the whites, including all of the Black Hills
and a broad corridor between that area and the eastern part of
the territory. In addition the Sioux had a number of specific griev-
ances relating to such matters as cuts in rations, delays in mone-
tary compensations promised in the treaties, crop failures, disease, and boundary disputes. In an appendix on the "Causes of
the Outbreak" Mooney presents a collection of documents which
illustrate these conditions (Mooney, 1896:829–42), and a history
of the whole period is admirably presented by Utley (1963). One
has the impression that for many of the Sioux the white conquest
was not yet a psychological reality, and that, consequently, the
"non-progressive" leaders could still command a large following.
On this point the statements by V. T. McGillycuddy, a former
agent at Pine Ridge reservation, and American Horse, one of
the "progressive" chiefs, are informative (Mooney, 1896:831–3,
839–40).

Short Bull, a delegate to Nevada in 1889, was one of the first
Sioux to adopt and advocate the Ghost Dance and one of the last
to give it up.[9] In the autumn of 1890 the situation on the Sioux
reservations was tense, and this is reflected in the second selection, a speech given by Short Bull at Red Leaf camp, Pine Ridge
reservation, on October 31. One significant feature of this speech
is the explicit claim by the disciple to have himself received direct
revelation from God. There is also an explicit reference to the
ghost shirts ("holy shirts") in a context which makes their militant
associations evident.[10]

"From the country where the Arapaho and Shoshoni we start in the
direction of northwest in train for five nights and arrived at the foot of
the Rocky mountains. Here we saw him and also several tribes of Indians. The people said that the messiah will come at a place in the woods
where the place was prepared for him. When we went to the place a
smoke descended from heaven to the place where he was to come. When
the smoke disappeared, there was a man of about forty, which was the
Son of God. The man said:

"'My grandchildren! I am glad you have come far away to see your
relatives. This are your people who have come back from your country.'
When he said he wanted us to go with him, we looked and saw a land
created across the ocean on which all the nations of Indians were coming
home, but, as the messiah looked at the land which was created and
reached across the ocean, again disappeared, saying that it was not time
for that to take place. The messiah then gave to Good Thunder some
paints—Indian paint and a white paint—a green grass (sagebrush

---

[9] A biographical sketch of Short Bull may be found in Overholt (1978:175–6).
[10] For a discussion of the role of disciples in the spread of the Ghost Dance, cf. Overholt (1974:52–6).

twigs?); and said, 'My grandchildren, when you get home, go to farming and send all your children to school. And on way home if you kill any buffalo cut the head, the tail, and the four feet and leave them, and that buffalo will come to life again. When the soldiers of the white people chief want to arrest me, I shall stretch out my arms, which will knock them to nothingness, or, if not that, the earth will open and swallow them in. My father commanded me to visit the Indians on a purpose. I have came to the white people first, but they not good. They killed me, and you can see the marks of my wounds on my feet, my hands, and on my back. My father has given you life—your old life—and you have come to see your friends, but you will not take me home with you at this time. I want you to tell when you get home your people to follow my examples. Any one Indian does not obey me and tries to be on white's side will be covered over by a new land that is to come and over this old one. You will, all the people, use the paints and grass I give you. In the spring when the green grass comes, your people who have gone before you will come back, and you shall see your friends then, for you have come to my call.'"

The people from every tipi send for us to visit them. They are people who died many years ago. Chasing Hawk, who died not long ago, was there, and we went to his tipi. He was living with his wife, who was killed in war long ago. They live in a buffalo skin tipi—a very large one— and he wanted all his friends to go there to live. A son of Good Thunder who died in war long ago was one who also took us to his tipi so his father saw him. When coming we come to a herd of buffaloes. We killed one and took everything except the four feet, head, and tail, and when we came a little ways from it there was the buffaloes come to life again and went off. This was one of the messiah's word came to truth. The messiah said, "I will short your journey when you feel tired of the long ways, if you call upon me." This we did when we were tired. The night came upon us, we stopped at a place, and we called upon the messiah to help us, because we were tired of long journey. We went to sleep and in the morning we found ourselves at a great distance from where we stopped.

*   *   *

(Short Bull said:) My friends and relations: I will soon start this thing in running order. I have told you that this would come to pass in two seasons, but since the whites are interfering so much, I will advance the time from what my father above told me to do, so the time will be shorter. Therefore you must not be afraid of anything. Some of my relations have no ears, so I will have them blown away.

Now, there will be a tree sprout up, and there all the members of our religion and the tribe must gather together. That will be the place where we will see our dead relations. But before this time we must dance the balance of this moon, at the end of which time the earth will shiver very hard. Whenever this thing occurs, I will start the wind to blow. We are the ones who will then see our fathers, mothers, and everybody. We, the tribe of Indians, are the ones who are living a sacred life. God, our father himself, has told and commanded and shown me to do these things.

Our father in heaven has placed a mark at each point of the four winds. First, a clay pipe, which lies at the setting of the sun and represents the Sioux tribe. Second, there is a holy arrow lying at the north, which represents the Cheyenne tribe. Third, at the rising of the sun there lies hail, representing the Arapaho tribe. Fourth, there lies a pipe

2.2 and nice feather at the south, which represents the Crow tribe. My father has shown me these things, therefore we must continue this dance. If the soldiers surround you four deep, three of you, on whom I have put holy shirts, will sing a song, which I have taught you, around them, when some of them will drop dead. Then the rest will start to run, but their horses will sink into the earth. The riders will jump from their horses, but they will sink into the earth also. Then you can do as you desire with them. Now, you must know this, that all the soldiers and that race will be dead. There will be only five thousand of them left living on the earth. My friends and relations, this is straight and true.

Now, we must gather at Pass creek where the tree is sprouting. There we will go among our dead relations. You must not take any earthly things with you. Then the men must take off all their clothing and the women must do the same. No one shall be ashamed of exposing their persons. My father above has told us to do this, and we must do as he says. You must not be afraid of anything. The guns are the only things we are afraid of, but they belong to our father in heaven. He will see that they do no harm. Whatever white men may tell you, do not listen to them, my relations. This is all. I will now raise my hand up to my father

1.2 and close what he has said to you through me.

6.6 The routinization of Wovoka's message (Dangberg, 1957; Kehoe, 1968)

With the failure of the hoped-for millennium to arrive, the Ghost Dance gradually died out as a mass movement. Wovoka's reputation continued to remain high among some Indians, but his mode of activity seems to have changed: extant letters sent him by some of his followers during the period 1909–1911 show him functioning as an elder and dispenser of sacred objects. James O. Long of the Indian Service at Oswego, Montana, was familiar with the contents of some of the correspondence that has not survived. He wrote in 1938 that at no time did Wovoka "send instructions in the dance, or in any way give advice concerning the religion" (Dangberg, 1957:286). As the letters printed below indicate, Wovoka's followers were concerned with how to get on in their lives in this world.

The second selection traces this development a step further. Fred Robinson, author of the first letter, was responsible for the transmission of the dance to a small community of Sioux living in Saskatchewan, descendants of Indians who had fled the United States in the 1860's and 1870's. The Ghost Dance continued to be practiced there down into the 1950's "primarily as an ethical code for Indians, not merely a ritual" (Kehoe, 1968:301). The second selection printed below shows how the believers at the Moose Woods reserve near Saskatoon perceived the lines of authority through which the doctrine was mediated to them.

Moose Woods Reserve
Dundurn [Saskatchewan] Jan 17/09

Jack Wilson

I thought I would write you a short letter today I will tell you who I am Oct 27th 1905 you send me paint 3 can full and some medicine too Jan 29th 1906 you wrote to me and send me (1 tomatoes can) full of paint. I tell you this so you can remember who I am I am staying with the news you tell me all the time till now I have been as far north to a place called Prince Albert and I am telling them about the news and till now I am staying here for winter I came to this place and I am telling every day what they ought to do father will you help me with the heart of the people where the prayers come from I want you to help to make the people straight thought. Help me too How can it be done to grow one church of prayer Help me father that I want them to know forwards the road of life Help me that I want the people on earth to think and go into the road of life The people think they would have their own way and have good time, I am always talking about the everlasting life

1.41

Another thing is pulling the people and you know that I am telling them about the good road and good life and I am telling them too on one side the Bad road and the evil spirit The last one I mention is a man have gone on that side you must hear that There were not many people but this man he divides them into two and he spoil the whole thing You know some people have good time. So he want it like that. He gave me some bad words and he send some to you, his name is Rufus Medicine. As it is hard to get the people in shape and I want you to quit them. The people here have raised $37.00 and send them to you as you have it already now All the people that have paint have raised money for you as what they say, and this fellow is going back to (Poplar Mont) I am going to Prince Albert as they want me over there to tell them of the News. I will be back in a few days again you seems to forget me so long so I write to you You know me well so If you get this letter try and answer me

I am yours faithful worker

I shake hands with you with my Best thought

Fred Robinson

.   .   .

Dundurn,
Sask,
Box 122, 4/8/09

Jack Wilson, Dear father We have a praying meeting last night, And pray to you I stand here to day again praying to you to help this indians I give magepie feathers and medicine out last night, hear me father and look upon me as then own son, help, me, father, send on me good things that I may lived upon this earthes to do Gods Good Will And you, pray for me that I may know the Good ways toward Gods our father, I am going home on April, I like very much to hear from you before I lived this Reserve, Indians are all well, I must come close, by shakings hands with you, wish to hear from you

    I am yours son,

R. W. Medicine

.   .   .

Kyle Post Office
March 17, 1911.

Dear Father:—

    Just a few lines to you this morning to let you know something I wrote to you here lately and told you that I did not get something that you send me Well I made a mistake I did not open the package ever since you send it to me until this morning that is on the 17 of March and when I open it and looked through the medican you send I found in it the paint that you send so I am very sorry I told you the wrong thing I said I did not get it but I hope you will excuse me for it I made a mistake so that is what I want to let you know that I got all you send me. I got a little scared for a while when I found the paint so I am going to send you money because I have foold you so bad and this morning I am sitting in a Mexican man's house and there is a young girl there she is my niece she is very sick so I want you to pray to the Lord to get here well again for me and when she gets well again I want to let every bod know it so that is whey I want you to helpe me and you aske me to come over to see you so I think Im going to come over with Red Star and he told me that he send you money and asked you something but you did not answer him so if you want me to come with him I want you to let me know soon so this will be all for this time so I shake hand with you and hope to stand solid by you

    I am your son

Cloud Horse

P.S. I would like to find out if you have any kind of rules for your medicans that you send me if so let me know too————the feathers let me know please.

.   .   .

Kyle Post Office
Dec 13, 1911

Dear Father:—

    Your letter has been received and I was very glad indeed to hear from you dear father

    Now I am going to send you a pair of mocissions but if they are not long enough for you when you write again please send me your foot measure from this day on—I will try to get the money to send to you. I wish I had it just at present I would send it wright away

I think I might get the money soon enough to send it so that is why I say that so. I will get it just as soon as possible and be sure to send it so if you get a letter from me I may have the money in that letter so dear Father this will be all. I can answer you so for your sake all the Indians out here make fun of me but I allways think dear Father that around me you would give me strength. so if you get the money I want that medican and some good feathers & that paint so that is what I want you to send me.

So this is all for this time I give a good & hard shaking of the hands to you I hope you have pity on me

I remain your son

Cloud Man Horse

(Dangberg, 1957:288–9, 292–3)

*   *   *

In the one community in which his message was well received, Robinson is still remembered. A photograph of him in Indian costume hangs in a prominent position on the wall of the main room of the comunity leader's house. The religion Robinson brought was recognized as a new gospel. In Saskatchewan it competed with the Christian gospels carried by missionaries of several Catholic and Protestant denominations and probably with other Indian-originated cults, as well as with the traditional beliefs of the several tribes. Only the Dakota near Prince Albert seem to have found the Ghost Dance religion more appealing than its competitors. At this date it is impossible to assess how much of the Ghost Dance's appeal here was due to Robinson's personality, how much due to the message itself, but its persistence in the community for over half a century suggests that the Ghost Dance was far more than a "Messiah craze." . . .

The leader of the Saskatchewan Dakota Ghost Dance congregation is proud to be able to repeat the gospel of his religion exactly, he claims, as it was taught to him by Fred Robinson. Robinson himself had explained to his Saskatchewan followers that he taught as he had learned from Kicking Bear, the link with the prophet Wilson. The following version of the chartering legend of the Saskatchewan Ghost Dance was given to me as a condensation of the complete legend, which is said to require more than two hours to narrate. A younger member of the Ghost Dance congregation carefully rendered into English the Dakota spoken by the congregation's aged leader.

2.2

The origin of the Ghost Dance

Around 1890, there was a man by the name of Kicking Bear, who had a brother-in-law named Short Bull, with whom he was closely associated. Kicking Bear lost a daughter; she died; he roamed the plains, downhearted, unable to forget his loss. One night he saw a dream vision, stating that "all he worried about is known by Him Who gives power. There is a place where the dead souls gather." This he believed because it seemed to be *wakan*.[11]

He started off to find a spot where he could discover this, travelling through Montana to Nevada until he faced a mountain of rock. Halfway up was a house occupied by a human. Kicking Bear and Short Bull were welcomed by the occupants, all shaking hands. The occupant told them the purpose of their visit, saying, "You are looking for the soul of your deceased daughter; you firmly believe there is a place where souls gather. You are right."

This man was named Jack Wilson. He told them he could help them to see the deceased child among the souls. "You have to go further west, and there you will meet a bunch of people, a tribe, who have the power that they can enable you to see your child, a spirit in spirit-land. This group of people are overseers above the spirits, through the supervision of the Almighty Power. This tribe is the Thunderbirds, the mediators of the Almighty Power."

1.21   Jack Wilson had built a sweatlodge and placed in it sage. He laid Kicking Bear on the sage, covered him with a buffalo robe, and fanned him with an eagle fan. This put Kicking Bear into a trance, when he was able to go and see what Jack Wilson had promised him.

When, as he was in a trance, Kicking Bear approached the spirits' camp, he was walking on land. The camp was so big he couldn't see across it. He saw all his deceased relatives, father and mother, and among them his daughter. As far as he could see, the dwellings on both sides of him, left and right, had food (that is, meat), but none offered him food to eat. The dishes were wooden bowls like (a large, shallow wooden bowl said to have been used for feasts by the speaker's great-grandfather), no metal. He was satisfied, seeing his daughter and the tribe of spirits, and was about to return, when they said to him. "You've come this far, you might as well see the Creator, the Power that guides all things."

He was taken to see a Being, a Person Who was very magnificent. This Person gave him a pipe and sweetgrass, and told him to stand up-right and offer the pipe and grass to Him. He would then hear and an-swer them. The Creator thus confirmed the ancient way of praying to Him, and emphasized it was to be continued.

Another instruction Kicking Bear got was, "You thought your child had died and gone forever, but that's not the case. She had joined an-other tribe. When you rejoin your own tribe on earth, tell the people,

---

[11] Conventionally glossed as "sacred"; see Powers (1977:45–7).

'You are never happy when a person dies. You cut off your braids, you are downhearted. That's not pleasing to the One Who gave them life.' When you get back to earth, take a ball of earth, dampen it, put it into the fire, and take it out. You will see it has turned perfectly red. Powder it and mark your face with it, as a token of happiness, pleasing to the Power." He told him, "When one of the earthly beings—the humans— passes away, leave them where they pass away, so their bones turn into dust. You make a scaffold and lay them up there; this is not right. The birds can eat them. The body comes from the earth, and there is where it should return. You should bury in the earth."

Now, as he was descending, it seemed to him that he was very near the sun. As he was coming down, he sang a song:

"I've come on high.
"The Father enabled me to beat that height."

There was nothing holding him as he was coming down, but he was floating slowly down like the eagle feather on the pipe he had been given. He had been told that when he returned to his people, they should dance to that song, with an eagle feather tied to their hair. That's where wearing eagle feathers on their head began.

When he awakened from this sleep, he was in the same place where he had started, with all these instructions and visions clearly remembered. When he awakened, he told his companions what he had seen. He had left out some things, which Jack Wilson put in, straightening out his dream for him. Apparently Jack Wilson had seen where he traveled.

Before this, when a family lost a member, some men would shove a sharpened stick through their flesh and leave it there, some women would cut themselves to show they were in mourning, for a year. Since Kicking Bear told of his dream, this kind of self-cruelty was done away with. Since then, they turned it into a kind of religious dance: on the seventh day, they gathered on a high hill and sang songs pertaining to what Kicking Bear had seen. Men and women joined in happiness, wearing the eagle feathers and the paint Kicking Bear had prepared. . . .

Whether or not Sword's version (Mooney, 1896:796–8) correctly quoted the Teton delegates to Wilson, and whether or not the delegates correctly quoted Wilson, is not of concern here. What is important is that the Saskatchewan legend taught by Fred Robinson after 1902 reproduces the essence of Wilson's own vision recounted by him in 1892. By 1892, at least, Wilson was preaching an ethical life with fulfillment after death. . . .

The core of the Ghost Dance religion, acording to the Saskatchewan congregation, is the injunction to lead, as they phrase it, "a clean, honest life." Such a life will bring the believer reunion with his loved ones after death. The Saskatchewan congregation's leader insisted that the Ghost

Dance does not promise the return of the dead or the aboriginal way of life. He did admit that Kicking Bear had claimed that if all the Indians put their faith firmly in the Ghost Dance, they would gain great power, and with this power might hold out against the encroaching whites, eventually succeeding in restoring the old life. (Kehoe, 1968:298–300)

7

Consulting the Spirits at an Umbanda Center

Introduction

Umbanda, a spiritist religion, arose in the context of the "miserable" social and economic situation of blacks in Brazil. Spiritism, which was introduced into Brazil in 1863, underwent certain modifications when it passed from whites to the lower colored classes. In particular the spirits who incarnated themselves in participants in the ceremonies came to be identified with figures from the Indian and Negro traditions. However, because of strong color prejudice, mediums working with Indian or African spirits were called "low spiritists." Umbanda spiritism is an expression of Negro reaction to this state of affairs, and its success shows that it answered the "needs of the new mentality of the more highly developed black, socially on the rise," who saw that magic lowered him in whites' eyes, but was "reluctant to abandon his African tradition altogether" (Bastide, 1978:318). In recent decades whites have participated in Umbanda in large numbers. R. Bastide (1978:304–42) gives a detailed account of this social situation and of the nature of Umbanda's transformation of the older African traditions.

Umbanda is one of several religions found in modern-day Brazil in which "trance and spirit possession are practiced." According to Esther Pressel, it is "a religion that (a) has national, rather than regional, appeal; (b) is apparently linked with modern, rather than traditional, Brazilian culture; (c) is not limited to the African- and Indian-derived populations in Brazil, but has wide appeal to persons of European descent as well; and (d) is oriented more toward the middle, rather than lower, classes in Sao Paulo" (1974:115–6). While officially the population of Brazil is predominantly Roman Catholic, "dual religious commitment to Catholicism and Umbanda" is not unusual. Pressel traces this latter trait back to the sixteenth century and the cultural development of African slaves who were brought over to work New World plantations (1974:121–2). The strength of Umbanda is in the cities, and in the mid–1960's it was calculated that there were 4,000 Umbanda "centers" in Sao Paulo. These centers are "the real functioning units of structure in Umbanda," and because each is controlled by its own leader, they "are extremely varied in terms of their external forms, rituals, and beliefs." Still, there are some common features: "Everywhere the major ritual activity involves dissociation, or trance, which Umbandists interpret as possession by spirits of the dead. The spiritual entities diagnose and treat illnesses, and help solve a myriad of personal problems for the believers, who may come to the two weekly public sessions in search of spiritual assistance" (Pressel, 1974:132, 134). In addition Umbandists had a well worked-out classification of types of spirits which could possess a medium and a view of individual "behavior and well-being" which involved the notion of "supernatural fluids" (Pressel, 1974:134–41).

Pressel's study of Umbanda is part of a larger project on the "cross-cultural study of dissociational states," directed by Erika Bourguignon and others (cf. Bourguignon, 1965, 1968, 1976; Bourguignon & Pettay, 1964). Her last two chapters ("Trance and Spirit Possession at the Individual Level," and "Umbanda in the Brazilian Sociocultural Setting"; 193–221) will be of special interest to readers of this volume. There, among other things, she speaks of trance and possession behavior as learned and stereotypical, and of the benefits to both the individual and society of taking up the role of spirit medium. The selection which follows is the account of what transpires in a "typical" meeting at an Umbanda center.

Text (Pressel, 1974:142–7)

On the night of a public session one can observe the mediums entering the dressing rooms of a center from about 7:30 P.M. on. There they change from street clothing into their ritual garments. They have prepared for the session by avoiding heavy foods and alcohol during the day. Before coming to the center they took an ordinary bath followed by a ritual bath of seven herbs in their homes. As the rear half of the center fills up with those who have come to seek assistance, the mediums gradually begin to wander into the front part of the center. Men and women stand at opposite sides of the altar, women accounting for 60 to 75 percent of the total number of mediums.

2.12

2.1

2.12   The ritual garb of the mediums is nearly always white, but colored clothing may be seen in a few centers that are more African in cultural orientation. Women wear blouses with a simple round or square neckline and billowing skirts of midcalf length. Underneath are as many as five stiffly starched petticoats, which partially cover ankle-length pantalettes. A small triangular kerchief is tied behind the head. Yards of lace have been sewed through all the items. The men wear white trousers and shirts. Both sexes wear white tennis shoes, and everyone carries a white hand towel embroidered with the symbol of the center and edged with lace; it is used to wipe off perspiration and on occasion to help control a wild spirit that may appear. Some cult leaders require mediums in their centers to wear a ribbon diagonally across the chest or around the waist. It is usually the symbolic color of the leader's *orixa*.[1] The most important single items of the ritual costume are the *guias*, or strands of beads, which represent the spirits of each medium. The number of strings of beads is limited only by what the medium is able to afford and the number of spirits that possess him.

2.13   At about 8:30 P.M., when a sufficient number of mediums have assembled in front of the altar, the cult leader opens the *gira* (turn-around, i.e., the session). The drummers begin to beat the *atebaques* as the mediums sway or dance counterclockwise to the rhythm. The audience joins in the singing of songs, or *pontos*, to various *orixas* and to the other, lesser, spiritual entities. An assistant brings in a silver censer suspended from a long chain. It contains smoldering perfuming herbs and is used for the *defumacao* (perfuming and purification). The assistant carriers it to the altar, to the drums, to each of the mediums, and finally to the members of the audience. A wave of the hand brings the fumes closer to purify the body and to offer protection against evil fluids[2] brought to the center. Then each medium goes to *sarava* (salute, i.e., prostrate himself) the altar as the cult leader blesses him and extends a hand to be kissed. In some centers it is customary to pay homage to, then send away through songs, any *exus*[3] that may be lurking around.

2.13   After more drumming and singing, an assistant may take up a collec-

---

[1] The *orixas* are the most powerful of the spirit types in Umbanda. They are the result of a syncretism between West African Yoruba spirits and Catholic saints, and are considered to be so powerful that, if they should themselves possess a medium, he or she would "explode." Consequently, they "send spiritual envoys to possess Umbandists." They are important guardian spirits for Umbandists, and "in the larger Umbanda belief system" serve as the heads of "the seven major *linhas* (lines) of the spiritual hierarchy" (Pressel, 1974:137–8).

[2] Umbanda has a "theory of supernatural fluids," which are understood to be "spiritual emanations" from various sources (one's own spirit, the free-floating spirits of the dead, etc.) "that surround one's body and affect one's well-being" (cf. Pressel, 1974:138–42).

[3] "Spirits of people who led especially wicked lives" (Pressel, 1974:136).

tion from the audience. The cult leader or an assistant may then give a brief sermon in which the mediums are reminded of the Christian virtues of love and charity, and of the superiority of the works of Umbanda—small today, but grand tomorrow. The faults in the ritual behavior of the mediums may be called to attention. Prayers are offered to Ocala (Jesus Christ) and to other spiritual entities for the sick and troubled, and then permission is asked to open the *trabalho* (work, i.e., session of spirits who will "work" that night).

Without drum accompaniement, the mediums and the audience join together in singing

> I open my session,
> With God and Our Lady. . . .

When this song is ended, the drums are once more beaten furiously, and while everyone sings, the mediums begin to call their spirits. *Pontos* may be sung to call specific spirits, such as *Caboclo Sete Flechas* (Indian of Seven Arrows):

> When the Indian of Seven Arrows
> Comes, there from Heaven,
> Bringing a bow and arrows,
> To save, children of Umbanda,
> He is an Indian, he is an archer,
> He is the Indian who kills the black magician.

Some mediums begin to spin around rapidly, and as their heads and chests jerk back and forth in opposing directions, the spirits *baixam* (lower) themselves into their *cavalos* (horses, i.e., mediums). The hair of some female mediums becomes disarrayed. Since it is the night of the Indian spirits, the facial expressions of what had been smiling mediums are transformed into the stern countenance of the *caboclo* spirits.[4] Some of the Indians may move about as if they were shooting an imaginary arrow. They shout in the *lingua* (tongue) of their "nation." The spirits may dance for a few minutes, greeting each other by touching each other's right and then left forearms. When the drumming stops, they find their places and wait for members of the audience to come for the *consultas* (consultations) during which requests for help are made. The hands of the mediums rest behind their bodies, palms outward and fingers snapping impatiently.

An assistant known as a *cambono* watches over each spirit. He (or she) is frequently a medium still at the elementary levels of spiritual

2.13

---

[4] Spirits, said to be of "dead Brazilian Indians," who possess their mediums regularly on a particular night each week. The nights on which these spirits arrive are consistent for each Umbanda center, but differ among centers (Pressel, 1974:135).

development. In some instances, the *cambono* may be a developed medium who for one reason or another does not choose to participate by receiving spirits. The assistant makes certain that the spirit does not cause a medium to fall while in trance and sees to the general needs of the incorporated spirit. For example, he lights the cigar of an Indian spirit, or, when a spirit causes its medium to perspire heavily, he takes the embroidered towel from the medium's waist and wipes the face and neck.

1.41   Before the members of the audience can enter the front area of the center where the spirits stand, they must remove their shoes. Some Um-

2.2   bandists believe that this allows for better contact with the ground, thus permitting the "fluid charges" to become more activated; however, since most Umbanda centers have hardwood or concrete floors, this practice may simply be a retention of a similar one found in Candomble.[5] Others say that removing one's shoes is merely a sign of respect to the spirits. A more practical explanation lies in the fact that part of the ritual sometimes involves spinning an individual and that high heels could be dangerous.

On entering the sacred front area, a person is directed to one of the spirits by an assistant. If an individual wishes to speak with a specific spirit, he must wait his turn in line. The cult leader's spirit may be quite popular, and it may be necessary for a person to pick up a numbered tag at the entrance door. This encourages people to come early so they can get a low number and not need to wait until eleven or twelve o'clock for their consultation.

3.2   The *consulta* may cover any illness or personal problem that one could imagine—*qualquer coisa* (anything) as my informants put it. There are the usual aches and pains, nervous tension, fatigue, as well as "heart"

3.21   and "liver" ailment. When people wish to emphasize the spectacular, they cite cases of cancer cured by the spirits or refer to the several centers that specialize in spiritual "operations." There is always the problem of getting and/or keeping a job. However, it is not just the working people who bring their problems. Some businessmen also feel in need of some assistance from the "good" Umbanda *exus*, who can break a spell cast on them by some practitioner of black magic. Family quarrels, difficulties in love affairs, and even poor scholastic grades are brought to Umbanda centers.

Each personal problem or illness requires and receives individual attention from a spirit. In addition to giving advice for the specific difficulty, a spirit may tell one to purchase from an Umbanda store herbs for special baths at home or candles to burn while praying to an *orixa*. Be-

---

[5] A "traditional lower class Afro-Brazilian" cult (Pressel, 1974:115).

fore taking leave of a spirit, the person is rid of his bad fluids, which are giving him difficulty. This ritual is known as *passes*. The spirit passes his right hand over the person's body, pulling out the bad fluids. With each downward stroke the spirit flicks his wrist and with a snap of his fingers disposes of the fluids. Before sending the person away, the spirit may ritually blow smoke over him for added protection from evil fluids. After a final embrace from the spirit, the person returns to his seat.

Drumming and singing continue off and on during the consultation period. A spirit may occasionally possess a member of the audience, causing the individual to shriek and shake violently. The cult leader or an assistant will walk back to the possessed and gently quiet him. If the uninvited spirit should insist on remaining, he will be led to the front part of the *centro*. The cult leader tells the spirit that his *cavalo* needs to attend sessions regularly to develop his mediumistic capacities. After the spirit has left, the individual himself is told that he must return for further spiritual development.

As the crowd gradually begins to thin out, a few spirits not occupied with consultations begin to converse with each other. Others may dance a bit, as long as they do not disturb the session. Several *caboclos* may decide to leave early and hand their unfinished cigars to an assistant.   2.1

To avoid leaving his medium *carregado* (loaded, charged) with evil fluids accumulated during the "passes," the spirit shakes the clothing of his medium and makes passes with his hand over the body. Particular attention is paid to the head. As the spirit begins jerking the head and chest of its medium with opposing motions back and forth, a *cambono* steps near to assist the medium if necessary.   2.1

Some mediums fall backward into the arms of the assistant as the spirit leaves. They squint their eyes as if not accustomed to the bright light, wipe away perspiration, and may accept a glass of water. Disoriented, they may put a hand over their eyes.   2.1

As the lines shorten in front of some of the more respected and developed spirits, the assistants and those mediums whose spirits have already left may go to consult with a *caboclo*. The sessions usually last three hours. As the few who remain in the rear begin to yawn, an assistant moves among the spirits, quietly letting them know that the end of the session is near. The remaining spirits leave together as a special song is sung. The spirits may be dancing at this point. While everyone joins in singing the closing song, each medium again prostrates himself in front of the altar, and the cult leader gives him a final blessing.

The mediums return to the dressing rooms. After changing into street clothing, they leave with friends or relatives who have remained until the end. Later in the week the mediums return to the center for another night of spiritual "works." However, instead of the *caboclos*, it is the *pretos velhos*[6] who possess them. Usually, the *crianca*[7] spirits and the *exus* appear at an Umbanda center once a month.

In addition to the regular public sessions, cult leaders hold special *festas* for various *orixas* throughout the year. The most popular are those for Oxoce (St. Sebastian) and for Ogum (St. George). People bring special foods and frequently liquor to these festive occasions. There may also be a *festa* for the *pretos velhos* on May 13 to celebrate the liberation of Brazilian slaves. In December, the entire center may journey to the seashore in rented buses to honor the *orixa*, Iemanja, who is the goddess of the sea. There may be special Easter sessions, and at Christmas gifts are brought for the poor. A cult leader's spirit may baptize babies and perform marriage ceremonies, although these are not recognized as legally binding. All of these activities are highly idiosyncratic. The ritual is always changing with the fluctuating whims of a cult leader and/or his spirits.

2.3

[6] Aged and physically decrepit "spirits of dead Afro-Brazilian slaves" (Pressel, 1974:135).
[7] "Spirits of children who died between three and five years of age. . . . The playful and innocent child spirit is more accessible than the other spirits" (Pressel, 1974:135).

8
Siberian Shamanism

Introduction

Shamanism is widely acknowledged as an extremely ancient religious phenomenon, and Siberia has been a *locus classicus* for its study. There are, of course, differences among the various Siberian groups, but there are also common features which characterize the shamanism of that vast region. One way of formulating this commonality may be found in Grim (1983:33–55). Anyone interested in Siberian shamanism would want to consult Eliade's standard work (1964). In addition there are useful older surveys by Mikhailovski (1895) and Casanowicz (1925). Anisimov (1963b) and Vasilevich (1963) sketch the world view in the context of which this shamanism operated. Several other studies of specific topics may be mentioned: Hajdú (1968) and Basilov (1976) on the classification and distribution of various types of shamans; Lehtisalo (1937), Popov (1968), and Vasilevich (1968) on the "making" of a shaman; and Balázs (1968) on shamanic trance.

The texts which follow describe shamanism among the Tungus peoples of Southern and Central Siberia. A. Anisimov, from whose study of "the shaman's tent of the Evenks" the first two parts are taken, did his field work in the 1920's and 1930's, and he emphasizes that the materials he presents represent "the old ideology of the Evenks" (1963a:85). Because of his extensive work in the "history of Evenk clan society" and his broad and deep application of "the method of dialectical and historical materialism" to their religious history, Vdovin (1976:263–5) places Anisimov's studies of Evenk shamanism ahead of those of other ethnographers of his generation.

The last three parts of the text are excerpted from S. M. Shirokogoroff's massive study of the *Psychomental Complex of the Tungus* (1935). The texts themselves make it clear that Shirokogoroff had made lengthy and close observations of Tungus culture and shamanism (cf., for example, below pp. 168–71). The fact that he places shamanism in a broad socio-economic context and "deals with the shamanic practices of both the nomadic and the more sedentary division of the tribe," makes Shirokogoroff's work particularly important for understanding Tungus shamanism, though some would fault his tendency "to reduce the shaman to a psychopathic type" (Grim, 1983:20–1).

One notable feature of the following texts is the intensity of the audience's participation in both the selection and the continued functioning of the shaman. Additional introductory remarks will be found at the head of some of the subsections of the texts.

Texts

8.1 An Evenk shamanistic performance (Anisimov, 1963a:99–105)

> Traditionally, the Evenks conceived of their world as being divided into three spheres, situated along a "mythical shamanistic clan-river." The taiga where they lived their daily lives was the middle world. Above, at the upper reaches of the river, was the heavenly world, home of the immortal clan souls, while below, at the river's mouth, lay the underworld, the world of the dead (Anisimov, 1963a:112–3). During a performance, the shaman, in a state of ecstasy, communicates with various spirits, revealing to the gathered on-lookers the substance of what he has seen and heard. He or she may also, as here, undertake a journey to the lower world.
>
> Anisimov tells us that among the Evenks such performances are most frequently "connected with the expulsion of a disease-spirit" (1963a:99). When the sickness has proven resistant to other attempts at a cure, the clan shaman is summoned, and preparations are made by building a new tent, or making appropriate modifications in an already-existing one. The intensity of the clan members' participation in the ritual, from the physical preparations to the ecstasy of the performance, is noteworthy.

2.1

2.2

The construction of the shaman's tent and also the preparation of the shamanistic spirit-images were generally done by the whole camp, as a rule by the men. According to the character of the shamanistic spirit-images, their number and order of arrangement in the *darpe* and *onang*,[1] those present attempted to guess the shaman's intentions, the content of the impending performance, the significance for the clan of unexpected events. There arose among the clansmen lively conversations, creating that mood in the participants which, the shamans insisted, was absolutely essential to any important performance. It is essential to

---

[1] The entrance to the shaman's tent faced east. The *darpe* and *onang* are "'galleries'" that adjoined the tent, the former on the east and the latter on the west, and contained wooden representations of shamanic spirits. The *darpe* represents the upper world, the head of the shamanistic clan-river, and is constructed of young living larch trees. The tent itself represents the middle world, and the *onang* "the lower world, the river of the dead." The latter is made from "dead wood—a wind-fallen tree" (Anisimov, 1963a:86–7).

realize that in this preliminary stage, before the shamanistic activity proper, those present already felt the strong impact of the whole situation. In any case, when the ceremony began, many seriously maintained that they saw and sensed realistically everything that the shaman described by his actions.

With the coming of darkness, the shaman went into the shaman's tent, lit in it a small fire, and, imitating the cry of a loon, began to gather the clansmen for the fulfillment of the shamanistic activity. The members of the camp, one after the other, made their way along the *darpe* into the tent, wiggled past the huge images of salmon trout supposedly guarding the entrance from the upper world into the middle world (the tent), wiggled through the *ugdupka* (gate), and took seats in the pose characteristic of nomads (legs tucked under them) along the sides of the tent. When the last of them had wiggled through the *ugdupka*, small planks attached to it, representing spirit-watchmen, were lowered or placed across it and the entrance to the tent was considered closed. The journey which the participants in the ritual made was similar, in the shaman's words, to the movement of the souls (*omni*) out of the clan storehouse for souls (*omiruk*).

We shall describe the performance on the basis of our field notes, written from first-hand impressions during the 1931 expedition.

In the middle of the tent a small fire burned. The tent was in semidarkness. Along the sides sat the clansmen, talking softly. A pervasive feeling of expectation of something extraordinary heightened the nervous excitement, still more strengthening the mystical mood. Opposite the entrance the shaman sat. His pinched, nervous face pale; he, silent, alert, irritable, moved his shoulders, gently swaying from side to side. His face twitched, his hands trembled. To the right and left lay the images of spirits—the salmon trout, the *mayga*,[2] two pole-knives, fishspears, a splintered larchwood pole. The fire was surrounded on four sides by shamanistic spirit-images, salmon trout. At a sign given by the shaman, his assistant took from the *tursuk*[3] the shaman's ritual robes— the robe, the breastpiece, footwear, the cap (for minor shamans, a headband; for chief shamans of clans, besides the cap, an iron "crown" with a representation of reindeer horns), and mittens. The assistant then got the drum, warmed it over the fire for better sound, and quietly tested it to see that it was ready for action. Then he began to dress the shaman. The clothed shaman sat down on a small wooden platform which represented the shamanistic spirits of fish; he held the drum in his left hand, placed it on his left knee, held in his right hand the drumstick, and

2.2

2.13

2.12

---

[2] Trout.

[3] A birchwood pail or woven grass basket understood to be "a bundle of family guardian-spirits" (Anisimov, 1963a:99).

struck it against the outer side of the drum. The conversation broke off in mid-word. The shamanistic ceremony had actually begun.

The fire was damped. The drum sounded in the semi-darkness. The clansmen, pressing themselves against the sides of the tent, awaited the shaman's words with palpitating hearts. The most impressionable and those with the strongest imaginations looked with wide-open and protruding eyes at the grim figure of the shaman. Swaying slowly from side to side in time to the drum, the shaman began the invocatory song to the spirits in a quiet melodious voice full of inner feeling.

The invocatory shamanistic songs of the Evenks were always rhymed, rhythmic, full of clear and beautiful metaphors, and always accompanied by a rhythmical refrain. When the shaman had sung a verse of the song, those present repeated it in chorus. Then the shaman beat on the drum at regular intervals, accompanying the sound by the singing of a couplet, and led a rhythmical refrain, matching the note of the drum. Those present joined him. The drum again replaced the refrain. The second verse of the song followed; everything was repeated again in the same order.

In an improvised song of summons to the spirits, the shaman addressed his spirit-helpers, calling them to his aid in the struggle against the spirit of the disease. Addressing each of his spirits in turn, the shaman vividly described for the listeners its form, adorning it with all manner of comparisons, listing its services to the clan and the characteristics of its supernatural power. The shaman related in the song where the spirit was at the time, what it was doing, whether it obeyed the shaman's summons willingly or unwillingly, and, finally, how the spirit, submitting to the shaman's demands, left his clan territory and came to the shaman in the tent. At this moment, the song ceased and the sounds of the drum were gradually muffled, becoming a soft roll. The listeners with bated breath awaited the appearance of the spirit. The ensuing silence was broken by a sharp blow on the drum, changing into a short roll. In the silence following this, the voices of the spirits could be clearly heard: the snorting of beasts, birdcalls, the whirring of wings, or others, according to the spirit appearing before the shaman at the moment. Such conjuring tricks were not achieved by all shamans, however, but only by the virtuosi in this line—the *khogdy shaman* (great shaman). The sound of the drum was unexpectedly interrupted. The shaman yawned broadly, receiving into himself the spirit which had come, and again struck the drum. Well warmed over the fire, the drum sounded long, filling the half-darkness with sound. Those attending sat there under the impression of the appearance of the spirit, deafened by the incessant rolling of the drum. Then the drumming ceased. The shaman began the invocatory song to the next spirit. Rousing themselves from their torpor, the watchers picked up the shaman's words and everything began again in the same order, until all of the shaman's spirits were gathered.

Having gathered the spirits, the shaman distributed his orders among them in accordance with the order of the images of the *darpe* and the *onang*: some he ordered to guard the tent, others to be watchman on all the pathways of the shaman's activity, still others to remain with him to carry out his orders. Among the shaman's spirits, the *khargi* or animal-double of the shaman filled one of the first places. Under guard of the whole group of spirits the shaman sent the *khargi* to the lower   3.21
world to learn the cause of the clansman's illness. The sound of the drum became thunderous, the shaman's song more agitated. The *khargi*, accompanied by the other spirits, headed for the lower world by way of the shamanistic world-tree. There he found the *mangi*, the chief ancestor-spirit of the shaman, and learned from him everything of interest. In the less important cases it was sufficient for this purpose to turn to the nearest ancestor-spirit of the shaman, most often to the one whom the particular shaman had succeeded on earth. But cases were not rare in which the *mangi* proved incapable of establishing the cause of the disease, and the shaman was compelled to send the *khargi* for the same purpose to the upper world, to the supreme deity. . . .

The journey of the *khargi* to the other world is described in the   2.13
shaman's songs in such fantastic form, so deftly accompanied by motions, imitations of spirit-voices, comic and dramatic dialogues, wild screams, snorts, noises, and the like, that it startled and amazed even this far from superstitious onlooker. The tempo of the song became faster and faster, the shaman's voice more and more excited, the drum sounded ever more thunderously. The moment came when the song reached its highest intensity and feeling of anxiety. The drum moaned, dying out in peals and rolls in the swift, nervous hands of the shaman. One or two deafening beats were heard and the shaman leaped from his place. Swaying from side to side, bending in a half-circle to the ground and smoothly straightening up again, the shaman let loose such a torrent of sounds that it seemed everything hummed, beginning with the poles of the tent, and ending with the buttons on the clothing. Screaming the last parting words to the spirits, the shaman went further and further into a state of ecstasy, and finally, throwing the drum into the hands of his assistant, seized with his hands the thongs connected to the tent pole and began the shamanistic dance—a pantomime illustrating how the *khargi*, accompanied by the group of spirits, rushed on his dangerous journey fulfilling the shaman's commands. The drumstick in the skillful hands of the shaman's assistant beat out a furious roll. The accompaniment reached its highest point. The voices and snorts of beasts and the like were heard in the tent. Under the hypnotic influence of the shamanistic ecstasy,

those present often fell into a state of mystical hallucination, feeling themselves active participants in the shaman's performance. The shaman leaped into the air, whirled with (the help of) the tent thongs, imitating the running and flight of his spirits, reached the highest pitch of ecstasy, and fell foaming at the mouth on the rug which had been spread out in the meanwhile. The assistant fanned the fire and bent over the shaman's stiffened, lifeless body. The latter, representing at this moment his *khargi* in the land of the *khergu* (the world of the dead), was outside of this seeming corpse. The assistant, fearing that the shaman might not return to the land of *dulu* (the middle world), persuaded him to return as quickly as possible from the lower world, orienting himself by the light of the fire which he (the assistant) had kindled in the tent. The shaman began to show signs of life. A weak, half-understandable babble was heard—the barely audible voices of the spirits. This signified that the *khargi* and the spirits accompanying him were returning to the middle world. The shaman's assistant put his ear to the shaman's lips and in a whisper repeated to those present everything that the shaman said was happening at the time to the *khargi* and his spirits. The shaman's weak, barely audible whisper changed into a loud mutter, unconnected snatches of sentences, and wild cries. The helper took the drum, warmed it over the fire, and started to beat it, entreating the shaman (that is, his *khargi*) not to get lost on the road, to look more fixedly at the light of the tent fire, and to listen more closely for the sound of the drum. The drum sounded faster and louder in the hands of the assistant; the shaman's outcries became ever clearer and more distinct. The drum sounded still louder, calling the shaman, and finally became again the accompaniment of ecstasy. The shaman leapt up and began to dance the shamanistic pantomime dance symbolizing the return of the *khargi* and his attendant spirits to the middle world (*dulu*). The shaman's dance became more and more peaceful, its movements slow. Finally, its tempo slowed, the dance broke off. The shaman hung on the thongs, swaying from side to side in time with the drum. Then, in recitative, he told the onlookers about the *khargi's* journey to the other world and about the adventures that had happened. Freeing himself from the thongs, the shaman returned to his place. He was given the drum. The shaman's

3.21   song was again heard. The shaman transmitted the advice of the ancestor-spirits as to how the evil spirit of the disease should be fought, put the drum to one side, and paused. Someone from among the onlookers offered him a lit pipe. Pale and exhausted, the shaman began avidly to smoke pipe after pipe. With this the first part of the performance ended.

2.13   When he was rested, the shaman again took the drum and began to expel the spirit of the disease. At first he tried to persuade it to leave the
3.21   patient's body voluntarily. The spirit refused. The long-continued discus-

sion between the spirit and the shaman irritated the latter and turned into irrepressible outbursts of anger, cries, and threats. The sound of the drum again gathered strength. The shaman threw the drum to his assistant, leaped from his place, seized the thongs attached to the center-pole of the tent, and began to whirl around in a furious dance beside the patient, attempting to expel the spirit of the disease. Tired and powerless, the shaman returned again to his place, took the drum, and again struck up the song, asking his spirit-helpers what he should do next. On the advice of the *khargi* (the chief soul of the shaman, his animal-double), he began to expel the disease by fanning and rubbing the place of the illness with various parts of the bodies of animals and birds—hair from the neck of a reindeer, a piece of skin from the snout of a Siberian stag, a bear's forehead, the antler of a wild deer, skin from the forehead of a wolverine or a wolf, eagle feathers, and the like. But this also clearly showed itself to be insufficient. The irritated shaman denounced all manner of disease-spirits, sat down again, beat long and indignantly on the drum, and then, softening the blows, passed over to the usual melody and began to consult with his spirit-helpers on what he should do next. On the *khargi's* advice he proposed that the disease-spirit pass into a sacrificed reindeer. Between the shaman and the disease-spirit there began again a long dialogue; the shaman praised the flavor of the reindeer's meat, of the different parts of its body, and derogated the body of the patient as much as he could. The disease-spirit held to the opposite opinion. Finally, the shaman succeeded somehow in persuading the disease-spirit to accept the ransom. The sacrificial reindeer was brought into the tent. The sacrificial rope was fastened around the reindeer's neck and the loose end of it put into the patient's hand. To the sound of the drum, the patient, turning the end of the thong over in his hands, began to twist it. At the moment when the twisted rope pulled the reindeer's head, one of the men standing beside it killed the animal with a knife-blow. This meant that the disease-spirit ran across the twisted rope into the reindeer and struck it. The reindeer was skinned. The skin was hung up as a sacrifice to the supreme deity; the heart was given to the shaman, who seized on it and avidly bit into it. The shaman spat out a piece of reindeer heart into a hole made in one of his spirit-images, stoppered the hole with a wooden plug, and carried the image into the *onang*, ordering his spirit-helper to take the captured disease-spirit into the abyss of the lower world. But often the disease-spirit fooled the shaman and remained in the patient's body. Then the shaman spread out the skin of the killed reindeer under the patient, smeared the blood of the reindeer on the diseased part, and began to wheedle the disease-spirit out with the scent of blood. As soon as the spirit crawled out, wishing to taste the reindeer's blood, the shaman threw himself on the patient, licked off the smeared blood from the body, and spat it into the hole (cavity) in one of his spirit-idols, which took the disease-spirit into the abyss of the lower world. At other times, complicating the circumstances of the action, the shaman said that the disease-spirit would not come to this bait. Then the shaman, annoyed, once more threw himself on the drum. It sounded loudly in his hands, deafening the disease-spirit with abuse and threats. The shaman gathered all his spirit-helpers. These surrounded on all sides the disease-spirit residing in the person. The shaman began an account fascinating for its fantastic content, of the battle between the shaman's zoomorphic spirit-helpers and the disease-spirit. The latter hid itself in the contents of the stomach. Then, the most cunning of the shaman's spirits, the goose, pushed his beak into the patient's stomach and with it caught the cause of the disease. The shaman and his spirits cele-

2.2   brated. The joyful, deafening sound of the drum rang out. The clansmen attending the ceremony sighed with relief, but the joy showed itself to be premature. The disease-spirit tore itself from the goose's beak and threw itself in the direction of the onlookers. They were stunned with horror. However, another of the shaman's spirits, the splintered pole symbolizing the shamanistic tree, was in the runaway's path. The pole seized the disease-spirit, squeezed it into its wooden body, and under guard of two wooden watchmen (*koto*) came over to the shaman. The third and most fascinating part of the performance began.

2.13   The shaman's spirits, as followed from his songs and actions, were surrounding the captured disease-spirit in a dense ring, showering it with the most malicious jokes, ridicule, profanity, and threats. The spirits pinched it, nibbled at it, pulled at its legs, spat; the most irritated of them urinated and defecated on it, and so on. The tent rang with the sound of the drum, exclamations, the wild cries of the shaman imitating the voices of his spirit-helpers. The sound of the drum again reached a peak of intensity. The shaman tore himself from his place, seized the thongs attached to the tent pole, and threw himself into a dance frantic in its rhythm and intensity. Behind him two men held the thongs. The drum in the hands of the shaman's assistant groaned and died out in a thunder of beats. Wild screams, the snorting of beasts, bird voices rushed about the tent with the shaman. From under his feet flew brands, coals, hot ashes, but no one paid attention to this. With their cries the

2.2   onlookers tried to help the shaman. The ecstasy of the shaman and the onlookers reached its highest pitch; the captured disease-spirit was taken into the lower world by the shaman's spirits to be thrown into the abyss. On the brink of the lower world, the loon or another of the shaman's spirit-birds swallowed the disease, flew with it over the abyss, and there expelled it through the anal opening. After this the shaman and his spirits returned to the middle world, barricading as they went all the passages from the lower world. When they reached the middle earth (*dulu*), the shaman's dance ended. The shaman returned to his place. He was given the drum. To its sound he recounted to those present all the particulars of the expulsion of the disease-spirit into the abyss of the *buni* (world of the dead). A pause ensued and the shaman and his spirits rested.

The fourth part of the performance represented the clan vengeance   3.2
of the shaman and his spirits on the shaman of the hostile clan. The
shaman's *khargi* learned from his ancestor-spirits who had sent the evil   2.13
spirits to the clan. Exclamations of indignation and threats descended
from all sides onto the evil alien shaman. The shamanistic spirits of the
clan made up a group of zoomorphic monsters and under the leadership
of the shaman's *khargi* set out to avenge themselves on the clansmen of
the shaman who had sent the disease-spirit.

The following and concluding part of the performance was dedicated
to the gods of the above. A reindeer was offered them in sacrifice. The   2.13
skin of the sacrificed animal was hung on a long, thin larch at the altar
(*turu*)[4] and its meat was eaten by all of those present. In a special song
addressed to the gods, the shaman thanked the protectors of the clan for
the help received. He then performed a special dance symbolizing his
journey to the gods of the upper world. He climbed up, supposedly, by
the *turu* into the upper world and walked along the earth of the upper
world, passing the heavens one after the other, to the *Amaka sheveki*,
the supreme god. The shaman gave him for safekeeping the soul of the
patient—a small wooden image of a man attached to the top of the *turu*
larch. The *Amaka* entrusted the guarding of the patient's soul to the
spirit of the shaman. The shaman's return journey to the earth of the
dulu (middle world) was represented in the form of a strenuous, joyous,
noisy dance of ecstasy. Then the shaman went to the altar, stood beside
the spread-out skins of sacrificed reindeer, and pronounced a long *mol-
iurtyn*—an improvised prayer to the Christian deities.

Having arrived back in the tent, the shaman, at the request of those
present, began to divine by means of his rattle and a reindeer scapula.
The clansmen, in turn, set forth their desires. The shaman threw his
rattle up in the air and, from the way it fell, determined whether or not
the desire would be fulfilled. Then he took the shoulder blade of the
sacrificed reindeer, laid hot coals on it, blew on them, and predicted
according to the direction and character of the cracks in the bone what
awaited his clansmen in the future.

At the end of the performance the shaman's tent was abandoned. The

[4] "The shamanistic tree, *turu*, was an inseparable attribute in any shamanistic performance." A tall young larch with its top extending through the smoke hole of the tent, it
played a dual role: "guardian-spirit of the tent," and the shaman's "ladder for his journey
into the upper world." During intervals in the performance, "the shaman's spirit-helpers
rested on its branches and gathered strength. In the shamans' concepts, the *turu* larch
symbolized the shamanistic world-tree" (Anisimov, 1963a:85–6).

reindeer-skin covering (lap rug) was taken from it but everything else remained in place.

8.2 The place of the shaman in the Evenk world (Anisimov, 1963a: 111–6)

> The following account locates the shaman within the world as it is conceived by the Evenks. The shaman, it appears, has an essential role to play as defender of the clan territory against invasion by hostile, outside spirits. In this he serves a need recognized by other members of his society. At the same time, the shaman's performance of this function serves to enhance his or her status within the community. In the latter context Anisimov notes the tendency of the role to become hereditary, considered by him to be a relatively recent development, probably the result of "interclan warfare" and the accompanying deterioration of the old democratic clan structure (Anisimov, 1963:119). One can also recognize here two facets in the "making" of a shaman. On the one hand, he or she is designated by the clan spirits. On the other, it falls to the group to acknowledge this choice, and to persuade the chosen individual to undertake such an arduous task.

In order to understand, on a historical plane, the origin of the shamanistic rite, and shamanism as a peculiar form of priesthood, it is necessary to examine the special social position of the shamans and the evaluation of shamanism by the society.

3.2   From this point of view, the especially notable features are those concepts of the Evenks by which this special position of the shaman in the clan was maintained and reinforced as a norm of clan ideology. The most essential of these in this respect were, on the one hand, the idea of the clan *marylya* and, on the other, that of the mythical shamanistic clan-river. The concept of the *marylya* among the Evenks, as we have shown earlier, referred to the mythical shamanistic fence or stockade made out of spirits, with which the shaman supposedly fenced in the clan so as to protect its members from the designs of evil spirits. The shaman, carrying out the functions of this peculiar defender-leader of the clan, set up to this end the spirits subordinate to him around the clan lands, forming from the spirits a special shamanistic stockade-fence protecting the clan from as many misfortunes as possible. In the shamans' tales, such a *marylya* extended invisibly on the taiga as a long, impenetrable stockade from one ridge to another, from rivulet to rivulet, from one mountain to the next, enclosing everything in the clan lands in one isolated clan microcosm, the guarding of which was centered in the shamanistic spirits, that is, in the end it was thought to be in the hands of the shaman. Everything which was within this mythical clan stockage—the taiga, mountains, rivers, animals, fishes, tame reindeer, and man himself (the clansmen)—had to be considered as being secure, since day and night the shaman's spirit-watchmen guarded it by surrounding the clan lands. In the air various shamanistic bird-spirits guarded the clan lands; in the taiga there stood, for the same purpose, the shaman's animal-spirits, and in the water swam the shaman's fish-spirits, all protecting the clan territory. In this mythical clan isolation, which reflected the actual former clan separateness, the clan opposed all the rest of the world as a complete, special microcosm at the head of which stood the shaman.

However much the shaman and his spirits protected the clan, diseases and other misfortunes did not bypass the Evenks. However, this did not discountenance the shamans. In their opinion this was not astonishing. In the taiga, since it was the taiga, anything could be expected. The taiga is great, the earth mountainous, the rivers full of rapids. It is difficult for the shaman's spirit to guard all the passages and approaches to the clan lands. Besides, though the shaman's spirits were mighty, even they were not without deficiencies. They had their own characteristic weaknesses; the spirits might not be watchful and resourceful enough, they might tire and be inattentive, or, finally, they might prove to be less strong in an encounter with the foe. In all these cases, the result was that the disease-spirit penetrated unnoticed into the clan lands or broke through the shamanistic clan-fence by force, and began to destroy either people or tame reindeer or wild animals. If the evil spirit succeeded in slipping past or breaking through the shaman's *marylya*, the spirit-watchmen notified him of this and he began to expel the mythical enemies, that is, to shamanize. Having expelled the pernicious spirit and thus removed the cause of the misfortune, the shaman began to re-arrange his mythical collection of spirits, changing weak or careless spirit-watchmen for stronger and more industrious ones, strengthening the guard where he thought the passages and approaches were most vulnerable, and so on. Such activity (connected with the rearrangement) was carried out by the shaman during a mass performance at which his fellow clansmen were not only active participants but also an inspired audience, capable of seeing in waking hallucination everything that the shaman saw and said.

It is, of course, difficult for us not only to conceive of but even to understand the power and influence which this kind of *Weltanschauung* exerted in the psychology of the Evenks. If we could put ourselves in their place even for a brief moment and look at all this through the eyes of their clan ideology, we might be startled by the socio-ideological significance which the privileged position of the shaman would present to us. In attempting to interpret psychologically these norms of *Weltanschauung*, Suslov wrote:

3.2

1.31

The most terrifying moment in the life of the Tungus was that of the death of their shaman, who, with the help of his *etan* (shamanistic spirit-watchmen) protected the clan. According to the Tungus, a shaman was always murdered by another shaman, that is, an evil spirit sent by one shaman killed the other. And when the shaman dies, all of his *etan* also die, that is, abandoning hitherto living objects, they go with the shaman's souls into *khergu* (the lower world, the world, the world of the dead). Thus at the same time the *marylya* is destroyed. The evil spirits lying in wait for such an event throw themselves into the clan territory and may destroy it utterly. In such cases, another shaman, a kinsman of the deceased, appears on the scene, sets up a new *marylya*, and with the spirits who have made an appearance begins the shamanistic reprisal.

3.1

No doubt, beliefs about the mythical clan-fence, the *marylya*, not only maintained but also reinforced the position of the shaman, and further, not only reinforced but also established shamanism as a socially indispensable phenomenon, without which the clan could not exist. In this case, the shaman, having usurped from the clan the right to conduct the clan cult, and thus standing above the clan, represented not a usurper but a person who suffers in a special way in the interests of the clan; this idea was reflected in the prerevolutionary ethnographic literature, which was predominantly of a subjective- idealistic, populist tendency.

Even more significant in this connection were the ideas of the Evenks regarding the mythical shamanistic clan-river, the so-called *numengi khokto bira*, literally "watery river-road." According to ancient Evenk concepts, there was a special river-road for each clan, and also a large clan world, distinct from the *marylya*, one that embraced not only the middle earth, the taiga (i.e., the middle world), but also the upper (heavenly) and the lower (underground) worlds. All three worlds were thought of as situated along this river and were identified conceptually with it: the upper world with the upper reaches of the river, the middle world with its middle course, and the lower world with the mouth. Along this clan river-road, the Evenks supposed, the whole life of the clan in all its manifest forms proceeded. The latter were thought of as successive stages of reincarnation and were conceived in the form of a closed circle. On the upper part of the river live the immortal souls (*omi*) in one great tent, the so-called *omiruk*, literally "storehouse, receptacle of souls." On the middle course of the river is the middle world, the taiga where the Evenks and other peoples live; at the mouth of the river is located the land of the dead clansmen, who live in a great camp, headed by an old woman, the mistress. On the road to the world of the dead (the lower course of the river) lived old women, the mistresses of the clan river-road and the guardians of the path of clan life. When a man dies, his corporeal *been*[5] also dies. The shaman lays the corporeal soul of the deceased on a raft and takes it along the mythical clan-river to the world of the dead. On the road to the world of the dead, the shaman calls on the old women, the mistresses of the mythical clan-river, and with their help finally reaches the land of the dead. Having arrived at the shore, the shaman begins to shout across the cove, asking the mistress of the land of the dead to receive the dead clansman in her camp. When the shaman's voice reaches the opposite shore, activity begins there. At the shout, the mistress of the land of the dead comes out of the tent and orders one of the men to cross the river and take the deceased from the shaman. Having given over the raft (funeral dais), the shaman returns by the same road to the middle world, carefully barring the passages from one world to the other. Meanwhile, the dead man's shadow-soul (*khanyan*) has received a new substance, emphasized by its new name, *omi*, (from *o-mi*, meaning "to do," "to create," "to originate," "to initiate"), and has gone to the top of the mythical clan-river and settled in the clan *omiruk*. At the end of a definite period of time the *omi* return to the middle earth among men and supposedly give rise to a new generation.

This great clan world, embracing all three worlds of the universe, stood isolated from all others, being sealed within its clan boundaries. Other clan worlds, also conceived figuratively in the form of river-roads of life, were thought of as being located next to it as actually neighboring clans were. Like real clans, which might stand in a relationship of either kin or alien, friend or enemy, these mythical clan worlds were thought of as being either inimical or benevolent in their relationships. In case of hostility, alien spirits penetrated to the river-road of a given clan and caused death, disease, and other misfortunes. The Evenks supposed that hostile spirits penetrated to the clan by way of the lower world. In the lower world were the mouths of all the clan rivers of life. There, according to the shamans, were several lands; in each land lived special shamanistic spirits. If an alien shaman decided to cause harm to another clan, his spirit-helpers penetrated through the lower world to the mythical shamanistic river of (the selected) clan, made their way against the stream into its middle world, attacked the clansmen, causing disease and death. If alien hostile spirits succeeded in getting to the upper course of the river, a most dire threat hung over the clan; the hostile spirits could destroy the clan storehouse of souls and carry the immortal souls of the clan into the world of the dead; in this case, the Evenks believed that the clan would inevitably die out. In order that this should not happen,

---

[5] Human beings were thought to have two souls: the *khanyan*, or "shadow," which even during life could separate itself from the body for extended periods of time, and the *been*, or body-soul (Anisimov, 1963a:110).

the clan shaman barred all the approaches to the upper part of the clan river of life in a most careful way. At every tributary, ridge, and crevice, the shaman set up numerous gates of watchmen-spirits. In the air, at the head of the river, were the shaman's bird-spirits. The dry-land approaches to the clan storehouse of souls were guarded by a whole herd of shaman's animal-spirits. At the mouths of tributaries and on the river itself stood the shaman's fish-spirits in the form of a weir. The passage from the lower world into the middle world the shaman barred with an impassable weir resembling a fishing seine, in the middle of which he

3.2 placed an ingenious snare from which the pernicious spirit, he thought, could not escape once it had entered. Thus, from the point of view of shamanistic ideology, the fate of the clan was wholly in the shaman's hands, and, standing above the clan, the figure of the shaman was, for his fellow clansmen, not only full of social significance but also an actual force with which they could not fail to reckon in their personal and social life.

In the course of time a certain amount of material goods was accu-
3.11 mulated by the shamans. Shamanism as the primary archaic form of a developing religious organization, in order to keep these goods for itself and reinforce its high social position and privileges, had to justify ideologically both one and the other in the eyes of the clansmen. This function, it would seem, was fulfilled by the idea of the selection, "calling,"
1.2 so to speak, of the shaman by the spirits and the inheritance of shamanizing ability. In the first instance, it was asserted that the shaman was the
1.31 "chosen one" of the spirits, and that the functions fulfilled by him were sacred and inseparable from his person; in the second, that the transmission of these functions and the social positon and privileges connected with them could be perpetuated only hereditarily. According to the prevalent ideas on this matter, the spirits who (later) appeared in the role of the shaman's helpers went of their own accord to the future shaman, and forcibly chose him for service to the clan. In those cases where the young person chosen attempted to refuse, the spirits supposedly threatened him with death, and in order to back up their threat, condemned him to a long illness (a special form of Arctic hysteria and functional neurosis expressed by vertigo and giddiness). From the point of view of these ideas, the shaman was not a usurper seizing into his hands the sole right to carry out the ritual of the clan cult, but a clansman named by the clan's ancestor-spirits to defend his clan. Thus the shamans interpret, on the level of this social illusion created by them, the preparatory period preceding the official introduction of the shaman into the role of the cult-servant. The ancestor-spirits of the clan supposedly come to the future shaman and ask him to take on the duties of defender of the clan. The future shaman refuses. The spirits tease, threaten, and torment him, abduct him into the forest, drive him out of his mind, and so on. Noting

these signs of the shamanistic calling (initiated) by the spirits, the family   1.3
appeals for help to the old clan shaman. The latter shamanizes in the
presence of the clansmen'and reveals that the clan ancestor-spirits have
chosen the new shaman for service to the clan, but that he finds his
calling difficult, and that the spirits are taking revenge for his refusal.
Then the shaman and the clansmen begin to persuade the chosen one.
The matter ends by his agreeing with them, and, supposedly fearing his
own death and that of the clansmen (the spirits threaten not only him
but also the clan), he accepts the call of the spirits. The conclusion then
is that the shaman suffers for the clan and its interests.

These questions were treated in just this way in the time of populist
ethnography, represented by Shternberg, Bogoraz, and others, who, following this social illusion, were inclined to believe that the shamanistic
"gift" was not a privilege but a misfortune for the shaman. Connected
with this complex of concepts are views about the subsequent division of
the shaman's body among the spirits (they supposedly tear his body
apart, temper it in fire, forge it, anneal it, beat it for strength, and so
on), and also about the reincarnation of the shaman's soul into a spirit—
his animal-double—which represent the person of the shaman as sacred
and inviolable and the social position occupied by him as a logical result
of his supernatural qualities. On the strength of this, the shaman appears
to his fellow clansmen in the role of a person of most unusual qualities.   3.2
Although the shaman appears before the other members of the clan in
the usual anthropomorphic form, it is, nevertheless, not an ordinary one
but divided among the above-mentioned spirits. The soul of the shaman
is zoomorphic; his birth is connected with a mother-animal, his upbring-
ing with the shamanistic world-tree of life, wisdom, and sorcery, in which
the future shaman (or, more exactly, his soul) grew up, swinging in an
iron cradle. From this, naturally, the conclusion could be drawn that only
the shaman, endowed with these supernatural characteristics, could ful-
fill those social functions which were assigned to him by the society in
the course of socio-historical development. From this point of view, the
shaman's prerogative of carrying out the ritual of the religious cult is an
entirely natural phenomenon, conditioned in the first place by the fact
that such was the decision of the clan's ancestor-spirits, and in the second
by the fact that to this end the spirits had endowed the shaman with
special supernatural qualities which did not and could not belong to any
other member of the clan. From the point of view of the norms of clan
ideology, the shaman, to whom supernatural characteristics are thus ascribed, appears before the clan as a direct personification of its happiness, its welfare, and indeed its very life. Astonishing.testimony of this
is reflected in the Evenk concept according to which the shaman does   3.2
not cut his hair because, supposedly, it is the dwelling-place of the souls
of the clansmen. The custom of giving the shaman for safekeeping a lock

of hair, in which one of the souls of the person is supposed to reside, has the same significance. Thus, not only the welfare of the clan but its very life was thought to be connected with the shaman. Consequently, the tendency to guard this high social position and privilege within a single

1.31 family, for its descendants, become understandable. The ideas about the inheritability of shamanistic ability also reflects this social tendency. According to these views, not any clansman could be a shaman, but only a person among whose ancestors in the maternal or paternal line there had been a shaman. Such persons were considered of shamanistic descent and, by virtue of this, hereditary candidates for the receipt, from their ancestors, of the shamanistic "gift." In such cases, the descendants were thought to share the qualities of their ancestors and thereby to be distinguished from their fellow clansmen. If their ancestors had been chosen by the spirits, if they had been given by them special, supernatural characteristics, and served as the reflection of the will of the spirits, then the descendants also may and perhaps will be chosen by the spirits, since they potentially possess the qualities through inheritance of the shamanistic gift. Thus, the title of shaman, putting the shaman above the clan and granting him very real social privileges, had a clear tendency to be retained hereditarily within a family which was considered shamanistic in origin.

1.31   This tendency towards hereditary retention of the title of shaman by an individual family, hiding within itself the seeds of a priestly caste, is evidently a relatively late phenomenon. Its origin and consolidation in ideology and social life took place in the context of opposition from the old democratic tradition of the clan, which knew nothing of the hereditary choosing of shamans by the spirits and regarded the post of shaman as accessible to any clansman. A striking proof of this is the Evenk view of the so-called passive and active means of obtaining the shamanistic gift. That means of receiving it—the spirits themselves coming to the shaman and persuading him by force to agree to shamanistic service—is usually called "passive" in the literature. All of the features which we have mentioned above are characteristic of it: the coming of the spirits to the future shaman in the line of direct inheritance; persuasion and threats; the receipt of the shaman's agreement; and finally the dividing up of the shaman's body by the spirits and the subsequent reincarnation of one of his souls. All this in turn is possible only for people who are descendants of a shaman, since only descendants of shamans (people of shamanistic origin) are thought to possess the qualities of their shaman-

1.2 ancestors. Besides this there is also another means of receiving the title of shaman. For this, one had to go for several days into the forest, reproduce there all the features characteristic of the shamanistic choosing, acquire by long fasting and physical exhaustion an appropriate patron

1.21 spirit (the latter usually appeared in the dream) and then one could be considered capable of shamanistic service. The patron spirit who appeared in the dream (most frequently an animal or a bird) taught the person wishing to become a shaman all the particulars of the shamanistic ritual and provided the requisite number of spirit-helpers. After this the future shaman returned home and took the necessary instruction under   1.32 an experienced old shaman, mastering the rather complex procedures of the shamanistic performance. This form of receipt of the shamanistic gift shows strikingly that in the past the title of shaman and the conducting of cult ceremonies were not prerogatives of the shaman and could be filled by any member of the clan. However, the fact that in the recent past the "active" means of obtaining the shamanistic gift was considered by the Evenks not as effective and shamans of this type as weaker than, less valuable than, and, furthermore, unequal in rights to shamans of the first type (for they could not be chosen to the position of clan shaman), indicates clearly that under the conditions of the disruption of the clan structure, the ancient democratic principles of acquisition of the shaman's title did not prevail, but the new social tendency towards hereditary maintenance of this title in an individual family did. Just as the ancient primitive-communal relations yield place to those of private property, the democratic clan principle of performance of religious ceremonies yields place to a hereditary one, which later (in Polynesia, for example) develops into a class principle, and still later into a priesthood. (In support of this position Anisimov goes on to discuss "those ceremonies of the shamanistic cult connected with the receipt of the shaman's equipment.")

8.3 The Making of a Tungus Shaman

Transmission of shamanship among the Tungus (Shirokogoroff, 1935:344–6)

On different occasions I have already shown that, apart from the clan priests—*pogun saman*—of the Manchus, there are *two different kinds of shamans*, namely, the shamans depending on the clans and shamans independent of clans. Both groups are called *saman—saman*, but among some groups they are specified. So among the Manchus they are opposed to the *pogun saman* and both clan and independent shamans are called *amba* ("great") *saman*. . . .

Among the Tungus of Transbaikalia the term "shaman" is applied to all shamans, but there can not be several shamans in the same clan. Some of the shamans may be considered more or less powerful. These Tungus know shamans of neighbouring groups and naturally shamans of other clans. Among the Tungus of Manchuria there is a sharp distinction between the clan shamans, called *mokun saman* . . . and independent shamans, called *dona saman*—"the foreign (alien) shamans". Their

power does not depend on whether they are clan or independent shamans, but on their personal qualities. In reality, when the shaman is
connected with a clan, the conditions of assuming these functions are not
similar to those of an independent shaman. The difference will be clearer
when the process of formation of new shamans is discussed.

1.31   The shamanistic functions in a clan are naturally transmitted within
the clan, so that the transmission may assume a form of inheritance.
However, it may not always be so, as I shall now show.

1.31   Although among the Reindeer Tungus of Transbaikalia no formal prohibition of having two shamans exists, a coexistence of two shamans
never occurs. If there were two shamans, these Tungus say, one of them,
and more likely the older one, would die. The shamanship is transmitted
from a grandfather or his brothers to the grandchildren—males and females—from the grandmother (father's mother) to the grandchildren.
However, the shamanship may also be transmitted to other young members of the clan, usually missing one generation. The same practice exists
among the Khingan Tungus and other groups, but I have not observed it
among the Manchus. However, the missing of one generation may not
have the character of a regulation. In fact, the Tungus clans are not numerous, but one of the members must become (a) shaman; the shaman's
activity usually lasts more than a generation, for they become shamans
rather early and continue this function to their death or loss of efficiency,
i.e., on an average of more than thirty years; so by this time the son of
the shaman would be too old to become shaman. Moreover, there is

3.11   another reason, namely, the son is usually looking after his father-
shaman, because, as will be shown, the shaman cannot do two things—
the hunting and a regular carrying out of the shamanistic performances—so the shaman usually needs support of the junior groups, and
therefore both the father and the son cannot be shamans. It is thus evident that the existing practice is not of a legitimate form of inheritance.

Among the Manchus, who live in large families, the son may live in
1.3   the same way as his father, i.e., devoting his time and energy to the
shaman's function. The most common case is the transmission of shamanship from father to son. If there is no son, the shamanship may be transmitted to the son of a brother ("nephew"). A definite tendency to transmit shamanship to the males is observed. The son of a female shaman
has therefore more chance to become a shaman, although the daughter

1.1   may also become a shaman, if she has been sick because of spirits. Cases
when a daughter inherits her father's shamanship are even rarer. Moreover, among the Manchus, inheritance of shamanship by people from
other clans may occur, if during the shaman's life a connexion between
the spirits was formed and if the spirits consent to leave the clan.

The transmission of shamanship consists in a mastering of the spirits
left by the deceased shaman. Therefore the spirits are also interested in

the question as to who would be their master. In Manchu it is called "collected (gathered) spirits." If nobody in the clan were willing to take up the spirits, or there were no person who could do it, the spirits might be "collected" by an outsider. Such persons may be either members of two clans . . . which have the same shamanistic spirits, or by the family which often enjoyed the shaman's assistance during his life. Such a family (house) is called *jurumbo* and the shaman's spirits are supposed to be acquainted with the members of the family. If there is nobody who can master the spirits and if they cause harm, a shaman, familiar with the case, may accept them too. If the spirits can be carried away by an outsider—a new shaman—this may only satisfy the Manchus (and generally the Tungus), for in the mind of the people these spirits are a real burden. However, it is not always so—the spirits may return. If such is the case, the clansmen would call the shaman who "collected" the spirits, and he would perform the duties which are usually performed by the native shamans of the given clan. In such a case it would be likely that the next shaman would be again one of the clansmen. More precisely the candidate will be either the person who was affected by the spirits, or another member of the family that was attended by the shaman-outsider, this family in relation to this shaman being *jarumbo*. The spirits may gradually become common in both clans. In this way the shamanship may be shifted from clan to clan, because *the spirits of these clans are not fixed.*

The fact, observed in all groups, of the transmission of shamanship to females who are sooner or later married to members of other clans, might give the idea that the mastering and general dealing with the spirits is going on independently in the clans. This would not be exact. In fact, a female, being married, remains connected with her native clan— she has her own spirits, etc., she is protected by her native clan in case of necessity. . . . If she becomes a shaman, she attends all cases, when it is necessary to deal with the activity of spirits of her native clan; after her death her spirits (clan spirits mastered by her and other newly mastered spirits) will be "collected" by one of the members of her clan . . . and more likely by one of the grandsons of her father. However, there are some cases when a woman becomes shaman after being married, and yet she may master her native clan's spirits and those of her husband's clan, as an "outsider". . . .

The above indicated facts show the tendency of keeping shamanship in lines, where there already were some shamans, but practical considerations (no need of having two shamans), the system of organization (e.g. a dual clan organization), the clan specification of spirits, and the intrusion of new spirits do not leave much place for the elaboration of a rigid system of transmission of shamanship.

In case of shamanship, independent of the clan, its transmission is not regulated at all. Those who used to know the shaman personally and

those who are familiar with his spirits have more chance to become shamans. However, the transmission has also a tendency to confine itself to
the clan of the shaman.

Besides a formal side of the transmission of shamanship, so to say,
there is another side, namely, a transmission of the shaman's knowledge
to the candidate, which may take place prior to the formal installation of
1.3 the new shaman or after it. In the first case the old shaman may elect a
successor and work with him, in order to prepare him for further functions, to make of him a shaman. Such a "teaching" may last for years.
1.32 However, in the second case, the old shaman may happen to be forced
to teach a person who was not chosen by him. So if the candidate shows
inclination to become a shaman during the life of the old shaman and
proves himself to be an able man, he may become a shaman during the
life of the old shaman, and the latter would "teach" him. The "teaching",
as will be shown, may grow into a special complex with which I shall deal
further on. The transmission of knowledge may happen independently,
when the potential candidate is a clever person, a good observer, who
accumulates facts and forms of them a more or less accomplished system
of theory and practice. Such occurrences are common.

The woman who became a shaman (Shirokogoroff, 1935:346)

In 1915, in one of the Manchu villages near Aigun, a case, which
may be regarded as typical, was observed. (I give a translation) "A woman's grandfather and father were shamans. Both of them died and left
1.2 spirits. . . . The spirits entered the woman and she began 'to tremble'
(as the shamans do). A new shaman must be made (people said). However, the clansmen did not want it. Then they invited a shaman who
1.4 investigated the case, interviewed the spirits and declared that a trial
must be made, perhaps somebody else of her clan—a man or a woman—
may become a shaman too. The clansmen agreed to wait. In the meantime the spirit again entered the woman and carried her into the forest,
into the mountains. The clansmen rushed after her, but she quickly
climbed up a tree, and sat there on the very top of it. The men could not
get her down and returned home. Then she disappeared altogether, and
only after eight days of absence she returned home, and said: 'I was all
the time at home', while actually she had been absent. Then she refused
to eat and drink. Now she must become a shaman. In the course of a
year all which is needed—the costume, the wooden instruments, and a
spear—will be made for her. Then there will be a sacrifice to her spir-
1.32 its—a pig and some Chinese bread. During this year she will be attended by an old shaman who will teach her".

This case is very simple. The spirits persecuted the woman. She
2.1 wanted to become a shaman and acted according to the candidates'
model—she trembled, ran away, climbed a tree, refused food, "forgot"

everything. It looks much like a case of hysteria, in a heavy form. There were no other candidates and so she had to become shaman, after a special training. That served as a treatment for herself and relieved the clan of the spirits which might have done the same with other clansmen.

A contest for selecting a shaman (Shirokogoroff, 1935:347–8, 353–8)

I observed the case here given in all details during nearly two years. The Manchu clan *wujala* was in the Aigun district. The great grandmother had been a shaman. The "grandmother" had been a great and good shaman. She transmitted the shamanship to her son who died soon. Then her nephew became shaman. He held also the position of an official in the Manchu Bannermen organization. However, soon after becoming shaman, he was executed by order of the Governor General (in Tsitsihar), being accused of spying in favour of the Russians. According to my informers this accusation was groundless and was due to intrigues of the Chinese (not Bannerman!). The spirits were thus left without a master for twelve years. The error of the late shaman's son, whom I knew very intimately and whom I shall designate as A, was that in due time he did not burn the image of his father and did not make a sacrifice, so that his soul could not regularly proceed to the lower world, while it could not become *vocko* (spirit), for the shaman had been decapitated. In addition to the troubles done by the spirits, the soul of the shaman was also disturbing the clansmen. The shaman's wife, an old woman of over sixty years, and his two sons, A and B, both married, were worrying about the soul of their husband and father. The situation was complicated by the fact that the elder son's wife had been in intimate relations with the unfortunate shaman and had a son by him, while her husband was married to her, at the age of 11 or 12 years, when she had already been about twenty years old. For a long time no sexual intercourse between the young boy and the adult woman existed. The details as to the hysterical condition of this woman were already given. . . . Indeed, she not only lost the man whom she loved, but she could not settle her relations with her legal husband, and she was also a transgressor of social customs. . . . Her psychomental condition was thus exceptionally favourable for an extreme tension in this situation. Moreover, her grandfather and her father had also been shamans. The woman, whom I shall designate . . . by the letter C, had already quite suspicious fits in which she was visited (entered) by the soul of her lover, the deceased shaman, the father of her legal husband. She did everything which happens to the candidates; she ran away into the forest, climbed on trees, refused food, "trembled" etc. Being put in exceptionally favourable conditions . . . to observe her without being disturbed by the presence of other persons, I was witness of several fits, during which the most typical picture of hysterical character, with strong sexual excitement, was beyond any doubt: she was

1.2

2.1

lying on the stove-bed in a condition varying between great rigidity ("arch") and relaxation; she was hiding herself from light (the experiments were repeated); there was temporarily loss of sensitiveness to a needle (several experiments in different parts of the body at different moments); at times continuous movements with the legs and basin were indicative of a strong sexual excitement. Her cognition of reality was rather doubtful, for during her fits she did not recognize persons being around her. However, from time to time, or at least at the end of her fits, she was quite conscious of her surroundings and before a fit she looked for isolation and for a certain comfort for herself during the fit (choice of a stove bed).

The husband of this woman and a great number of influential clansmen were against her becoming a shaman. The chief reason was evidently her social position (her relations with the deceased shaman were naturally known) and the character of her fits, in the decipherings of 1.42 which the clansmen were not mistaken—she was not visited by the spirits (*vocko*) but by the shaman's soul. Her husband was very angry, when she pretended to have a spirit, and he even proposed to take it up himself. But she (the spirit) insisted A could not be a shaman. A's formal objection was that if she becomes a shaman, she would trouble the people, she would not stay at home, and it would be very costly to support her (which, by the way, he did not do!). But she wanted to become a shaman and the spirit—not only the shaman's soul—insisted upon a settlement of the situation; she had already experienced visits of the spirits for more than a year. The other clansmen rejected her, because they considered it shameful for the clan to have a woman-shaman, believing the male-shamans to be cleverer and to "know" more than women-shamans.

There was another candidate, the younger brother B. The clansmen 1.1 planned first to make him shaman. After a long sickness of B, about a year before the spirits (*vocko*) had entered him, about the same time as 1.2 they entered the woman C. Several times B visited an old grandfather (a senior of the shaman's clan) who knew *colo* and *kooli* (list and ritual) of 1.32 the spirits. After the execution of the shaman, there was nobody who saw performances, and many old men had already died. In fact, as will be shown, the grandfather knew everything about the clan shamanship. The candidate B was, seemingly, in all respects a normal person, but he was neither a worker, nor an honest man, according to some Manchus. In spite of this, the clansmen evidently wanted him to become shaman. Perhaps the entering of the spirit into him was a ritualistic performance.

Since the situation presented difficulties for a simple solution, it was decided to organize a trial of the two candidates, one of whom should be elected and the other rejected and cured.

This case shows candidate C with her disturbed sexual complex, per-

haps justified by hysteria, and candidate B who seemingly was an impos-   1.4
tor, urged on chiefly by "public opinion." This picture will be clearer
when the performance of the election is described. . . .

(In addition to the candidate and A) the other important participants
were: (1) the old shaman whom I knew rather well, and whom I observed
many times in performances; (2) the member of the jury, *Cuntin*, who
was not of the clan *wujala*, but who was one of the greatest authorities
on shamanism (he was a *pogun saman*) and for this quality was asked to
assist the case; (3) another member of the same jury called "an old man
of *wujala*" whose opinion counted; (4) a third member of the jury, whose
opinion was not of importance—the man was too old; (5) an influential
member of the community, E. The operation took place in January 1917,
in the village Kalunsan (*Oforo Tokso* in Manchu). As shown before, the
case was extremely difficult because of the hidden conditions of the female candidate C. The case was still more difficult, because the Chinese
authorities did not permit the carrying out of the performance—shamanism being formally forbidden. Being on very friendly terms with most of
the above indicated participants, A, *Cuntin*, the old shaman, E and D,
and having had under my observation, for a period over a year, both
candidates, I was not considered as a stranger. All these people were
convinced of my competence as to the conditions, ritual and spirits of
shamanism and the individuality of the candidates. In fact, on various
occasions I could give good advise concerning the persons who suffered
from the spirits, or who needed ordinary medical treatment (I used to
send them with my note to a professional physician). Moreover, being on
"friendly relations" with the local authorities, I was fortunate to obtain
the permission for carrying out this prohibited performance, which in its
turn created still closer relations with the people and even the clans
involved, and at last I was asked to join the jury as its fourth member.
This permitted me to be in close contact with all participants and at the
same time left me a certain freedom of action making me one of those
who did not disturb the actors. It should also be noted that, by that time,
I had already learnt the art of assistant shaman and, when necessary, I
did perform such duties.

A few days before the beginning, a complete set of pictures (*n'ur-
gan*), which represented all shamanistic spirits of the clan, was brought
from a village situated on the *sumbira* (the Sun River). Two shaman costumes were needed for the candidates, one of them for the female can-   2.12
didate was supplied from my ethnographical collection, and another was
found elsewhere. After spending a few days talking over the matter, I
found out that the participants, and generally the "public opinion", were   1.4
in favour of creating a new shaman. However, I found that some of these
people wished most to have an interesting performance and the concomitant feasts, and some were joking about the event. Continuous discus-

sions as to the nature of the spirits and their wishes were going on the whole time. Then a day for the performance was fixed and the people assembled. A, who was the husband of one of the candidates and the brother of another, was especially nervous about the coming event, so he always returned to discuss the matter with me, in general and in detail. The communications of A, who was supposed to be familiar with the spirits of his clan, were immediately communicated to the participants. . . . (During the performance, the pictures were hung on birch branches, and there were two tables with offerings of Chinese bread and a chicken. On one of these was a model of a Buddhist shrine, containing a Buddha figure, employed by the old shaman as a "placing"[6] for a mastered spirit. "Among the Manchu shamans the mastering of Buddha is a rare occurrence.")

By eight o'clock the jury and the old shaman had finished a copious dinner . . . with a moderate libation, so that the mood of these people was rather good. About one hundred, or perhaps more, were attending the performance and gradually occupied their places. The secretary took his place at the table of the *wujala* clan to keep the record; the members of the jury occupied places near the tables and the ground for action, in order to be ready to come to the aid of the candidates, if needed. A dozen, or thereabouts, of old men, very honourable persons, were sitting next to the jury. Nearer to the entrance, the places were occupied by the clansmen of a certain age in a number limited only by the size of the big room, perhaps twenty or thirty persons. Near to the entrance the ground was occupied by four permanent assistants. However, at critical moments of the performance, even members of the jury acted as assistants.

1.2 1. The old shaman, this time assisted by *Cuntin*, drummed and prayed to his spirits. The important spirit *xele mava* arrived and, through the shaman and in the interpretation of *Cuntin*, declared that it was necessary to produce a new shaman. The old shaman continued his praying to the spirits, asking them not to mingle with the spirits of *wujala* clan.

2. One man brought the news that a spirit had come into the candidate C. The old shaman and some other people went to her. Before the performance she had been in a state of great excitement. Now she was in the adjacent house, lying on the stove-bed and making "arch" from time to time; her pulse was 92, her breathing irregular and her eyes closed. Before our coming she had told her mother-in-law that the deceased

1.2 shaman . . . had come to her. The old woman, a sister of the candidate and the second candidate's wife, sat near her crying. The old shaman spoke to the candidate and wished first to establish friendly relations between the spirits, because the spirits of her native clan and those of

---

[6] I.e., a place of manifestation of some spirit.

his own clan used always to be friendly and were of common origin. Then he invited C to go to the other house and very carefully lead her forward repeating something rapidly and in a low voice. Candidate C was trembling violently all over. She was . . . put on the stove-bed under the pictures. . . . The "arch" continued and the eyes were closed showing distinct photophobia. The shaman sat by her side, calling the spirits and speaking to them. In the meantime I noticed among the persons present one who fell into extasy. Fiercely howling in rhythm with the assistants (he was almost speechless) he cried out incoherently (he had also some other physical defects). Suddenly the candidate C sat up on the stove-bed and firmly declared that the performance must be quickly carried out, that everything must be finished on the morrow, instead of in five days, as it was intended. Then a meeting of the jury and the old shaman was held. After a long deliberation, it was decided to ask *colo* and, if she could tell it, to make of her a shaman. While the preparations were made, it was possible to inquire as to the attitude of the audience.

The opinion was in favour of candidate C. Even a great friend, *Cuntin* whose daughter had a love affair with A . . . showed a favourable attitude towards C, in spite of the fact that A himself did not wish his legal wife to become a shaman. However, how sincere *Cuntin* was I do not know; he had occupied a small official position with the Manchu government for a long time, so he must have been familiar with cunning tricks. He now advanced the idea that it is easy to find out, whether a candidate really has a spirit, or is simply feigning; it is sufficient to prick the candidate with a needle, if a spirit is present, the candidate will not feel any pain; if she refuses to be pricked, it will be indicative that, either there is a "sickness", or the candidate is trying to fool the people. . . . 1.4

The authoritative man E, as well as the member of the jury D, were in favour of the candidate C. I naturally joined the opinion of these authorities, although A seemed to be discouraged and the candidate B looked gloomy. The hidden reason seemed to be that the brothers did not wish their father to become a *vocko*, which would happen if the candidate C became a shaman (and this possibility is even denied on theoretical grounds: the soul of a man, whose head was cut off, cannot become *vocko*), for the new spirit will not be favourable to the brothers who did not fulfil their duties of filial piety (Chinese complex!). 1.4

3. Since it had been decided by the jury to proceed with the trial of candidate C, she was prepared for the performance. The old shaman prayed to his spirits and to those of the *wujala* clan. The *wujala* clansmen fell on their knees in front of the picture, beat the ground with their foreheads, set up burning incense and prayed to the spirits. The same was done by the candidate C. She was evidently afraid of the coming trial and was trembling, although no signs of a hysterical fit were seen. The women arranged her hair, as it is done for girls, in two long plaits;

the skirt and belt with long conical trinkets . . . were put on. When she was dressed, she was almost unable to go out of the house to the spot where a kind of long table with a great number of burning sticks of incense had been prepared. She was helped by many people, including the old shaman, and was almost carried out on the arms of these people. Held up in a standing position by two men, her mouth wide open, she breathed the smoke of incense. The old shaman called the spirits. Then the spirit *mama saman* came. However, the man who was holding her

2.1 asserted that there was no spirit, the candidate was not trembling as much as she should be in the presence of a spirit like *mama saman*. The

1.4 old shaman was furiously jumping and dancing around her, urging her by his movements to come into the house. Hesitating and artlessly drumming, she entered. The old shaman, always in a rhythmic "dancing", began to push her from all sides with his sides and back. The impact was so strong that sometimes both of them fell back in opposite directions. The old shaman took the candidate in his arms and turned her

2.1 about in the middle of the room. One man held her by the belt. Still no extasy came and she could not fall down on the ground (which is required by the ritual); several times she tried to do it, but she could not fall, and at last dropped down on the rug in a semi-sitting position instead of falling backward "like a stick", being supported by a man. I surmised that perhaps the man who was helping her was not of those who wished to make her a shaman and intentionally did not give her his assistance to prevent her being hurt in falling. Therefore, I pushed away the man and occupied his place holding the candidate by the belt from behind. From this position I could much better follow her and could observe her reactions in the performance.

4. The old shaman asked her to start the *colo* (list of spirits) during

2.1 which the spirits are supposed to come, one by one. The candidate was trembling slightly, but in all parts of the body. However, for a very long time she could not start her reciting. As a matter of fact, the drum was

1.4 wet (not dry enough and barely dried), the husband A was continually interfering with his remarks and other persons were laughing at her. I noticed a man who was even pushing her and evidently provoking acts which are unforeseen by the ritual. I did my best to protect her and asked for a fresh drum. *Cuntin* was furious—he insulted and threatened her. Finally, after three hours from the beginning of her fit, she began to

1.2 introduce into herself, one by one, manifestations of the *mama saman* row. One after another the series of female *vocko* came. She could describe them; they declared that they had no master; the old shaman (her lover) had not used them for performances; they felt themselves offended by this attitude of the late shaman. Instead of going ahead with the other spirits, the deceased shaman was allowed to come again. He declared that his image must be made, that various inscriptions and "money" (in paper as used in the Chinese complex) must be burned on his tomb, for he was executed without being guilty; his soul could not find peace, but might attain it, if everything was done which he had required. In spite of this valuable information and steps later undertaken accordingly, the audience became furious that the candidate C could not go ahead with *colo*. She was immediately accused of making a joke out of a serious matter. *Cuntin* said that when a man is treated, some minor cheating is allowed, but if the question concerns clan spirits, one must be strict and careful, and perfectly honest and sincere, for the matter of clan spirits is the greatest matter which exists. A was desperate. He said that he had organized everything on his own responsibility, without formally consulting his clansmen (actually the clansmen had been privately consulted before the performance) therefore such a scandalous issue would not affect the clan, but only A alone and personally. The jury was called again, as well as the old shaman and other seniors. From the discussions it was clear that the general desire of the influential persons was that candidate C should not become a shaman. They said that the female spirits had refused to have a female shaman and that the male spirits did not want to have a male (sic) shaman, and furthermore, since the chief spirit *xele mafa* was a male, there must be a male shaman. However, there were voices in favour of candidate C. So the influential man E said that the candidate C was a sincere and good person, and that she had a spirit. In order to clear up some more details I maintained his opinion by bringing evidences of her having had spirits, of the unrealiability of the *colo* test, the fact that the drum had been bad, etc. This discussion helped to clear up some uncertain points. After the discussion, the husband A took me aside and told me all the details of his family tragedy which, in fact, I knew only in part and from other persons. The situation was clear; the candidate C was rejected and by her husband's frank declaration, in a state of great excitement, I could not longer maintain my position. The influential man E, being informed of the family affairs still maintained his former opinion.

At the beginning of the discussion the spirit was "called back" and she was left alone in another room, which permitted me to continue my observation: the nervous fit was not over. After one hour of rest she again dressed her hair, and returned to the room, where the performance was going on. She was exhausted, very sad and depressed, but she was memorizing every word of *colo*, at that moment already started by her competitor, candidate B. But it was too late to learn the *colo*, as had been done by the candidate B before the decisive day of trial.

5. During the discussion which continued a long time, while the old shaman was resting, it was decided that the candidate B should shamanize. I asked the candidate B, whether this time he would be successful or not, and he replied with a firm assurance: "there are spirits, and there

1.42

1.4

1.42

1.41

1.42

1.32

is *colo*". This reply made me understand that he *knew* the list of spirits. However, I was informed by many persons, that the "grandfather" (which means one of the superior to [sic] the father's generation-clan) who was a keeper of tradition and who, according to my information, had been visited for the purpose of *colo*, did not tell him the *colo*. Of course, one can learn *colo* not only from the "grandfather", and the candidate B could do the same from other people who had attended the periodical sacrifices of the late shamans. From all these doubtful statements and the general behavior of the participants it was evident that the clan leaders wanted candidate B to become shaman and they admitted as truth, perhaps sincerely believing in what they wished to be the truth. The candidate B with the air of an experienced man, smirking and behaving rather arrogantly, put on the skirt and belt (*sisa*) and was ready for action. The old shaman prayed to his own spirits and the spirits of the *wujala* clan. The *wujala* clansmen knelt in front of the picture, put up burning incense and heartily prayed to the spirits, as had been done with the candidate C. The old shaman and candidate B both remained standing in front of the tables. The old shaman called his spirits and *xele mora* entered him. Then there was repeated, in the same order and without variations what has been described above in section 3. The only difference was that the candidate B behaved as an experienced performer: he drummed well. (The drum was always prepared by A and other assiduous assistants and when needed changed). He made strong movements with his back (to produce *sisa* noise), he danced well, strongly pushed the old shaman and, when he "fell down like a stick" (actually he sat down!), he was trembling much more intensively than the candidate C had trembled and the trembling occurred exactly when it was required by the ritual, while this was not so with the candidate C who had been trembling the whole time. According to the man who was holding the belt, "he was trembling but not very intensively; anyhow the spirit was there". Then the old shaman proceeded with the *colo*. The candidate B successfully went on with nine spirits and suddenly stopped. Then it was found out that the *pogun cocko* had interfered with the performance. It was necessary to call them and pray them to allow the performance to continue. As soon as this difficulty was removed, the performance continued. Slowly and not without difficulties, the candidate recited, though in a very abbreviated manner, all of the spirits. The participants greatly enjoyed this achievement. I was told that the detailed enquiry would be made later. The spirit was allowed to leave and the candidate, half-unconscious, very tired, with limp limbs, and wet with perspiration was carried to the k'ang. A kind of deep satisfaction filled the participants. Everything was good—the new shaman knew *colo*; he could introduce spirits; he could drum and sing. The old shaman was proud. Then a ritual was carried out: thanksgiving to the spirits by the old shaman, while the new shaman was soundly sleeping under the pictures. It was already 5 A.M. The performance had lasted nine hours. After a meal (a very late supper) the audience dispersed, in order to take a rest.

(On the second day) A visited the tomb of his father (shaman), in a village situated a few kilometres away, where he burnt the image, etc., i.e. did all that had been required, as revealed through the candidate C the night before. A asked the "grandfather" mentioned before, an old man of seventy-eight, to come and participate in the performance. The old man was brought at 9 P.M., when the performance was already going on, and occupied a place by the side of the old shaman's table.

The performance began at 8 P.M. in the same disposition of the performers and audience. The same sacrifices were put on the tables and the same pictures were hung up. The performance began with a prayer to the spirits. The old shaman called the *xele mava* spirit which arrived. The old shaman was furiously drumming, while the candidate B, after having put on the skirt and *sisa*, danced in front of the pictures. Little by little he reached a great excitement and rushed out. Standing in front of the table with the incense, he breathed the smoke until the spirit *xele mava* (of the *wujala* clan) entered him. The old shaman tried to lead the candidate into the house, loudly drumming all the time, making a great noise with the belt and rhythmically stamping the ground with his feet. The candidate came into the hall and showed signs of his intention to go back into the yard. The old shaman barred the entrance with his body and sometimes beating the candidate with the heavy trinkets of *sisa*, compelled him to enter the room of the performance. Then the dancing of the two shamans was performed, so that after changing their respective positions they bumped each other with their backs with great force, which produced a loud noise from the *sisa*. The dancing is supposed to go on until the candidate attains the state of extasy and "falls down like a stick", aided by a man who supported him. (However, apparently this did not occur, for one leg was not "like a stick"; the candidate supported himself with the leg which was not rigid at all). This produced an impression, and the audience began to bring the performer to his senses, because he might have died, the soul being absent for too long a time.

Finally the candidate B sat down trembling. He made an attempt to run away, but a strong man caught him by the belt and kept him. The old shaman started his enquiry. At first the candidate replied inconsistently, but afterwards he began the enumeration of the spirits. The "grandfather" and jury were listening carefully to every word and the secretary was writing down what was said. An exchange of drinks was done; the spirit *xele mava* gave, on the drum, two small cups of Chinese wine to the grandfather who passed them to the candidate, who drank the wine without taking the cup into his hands. The candidate again made a mistake with the row of spirits. The spirit was sent off. Another

2.13

spirit was introduced outside of the house and the candidate was brought back on the arms of several people who put him on the stove-bed. He "slept".

1.4   A meeting of the jury was convoked. This time, with the participation of the "grandfather", a difficult problem was discussed, namely, what was to be done, since the candidate did not know the row of spirits just recited. The "grandfather" was very gloomy. Still more gloomy was A, who with a wry face and the corners of his mouth gone, was walking up and down the room. The "grandfather" was interviewed as to the points in which the candidate had failed. The old man explained that he thought the candidate could hear what was being talked about. The candidate was awakened and a new spirit was introduced. The candidate named, almost without an error, the spirits of the new row and went again to "sleep". In the meantime the "grandfather" was again interviewed as to other rows of spirits; some points were especially emphasized by A and his mother who was in the room, when no spirits were acting. Once more the candidate arose; this time the spirit *xele mava* came again and the candidate, glancing at the pictures, went on rather smoothly with the enumeration of the spirits, although he omitted the biographical details which were required. Once more the spirit was changed and *mama saman*, on which candidate C had failed, arrived. It was not easy to call in *mama saman*, which like all other great spirits, will not come at once. She was called in for three quarters of an hour. This time *Cuntin* was helping by correcting the names, and the candidate turned his eyes hopefully in *Cuntin's* direction.

1.4   I used this opportunity for making my inquiry as to the "public opinion". There were persons who said that such a hopeless performance was entirely A's fault. He and his mother did not want candidate C to become shaman, but A wanted someone else to remove the spirits forever. *Cuntin* thought that candidate B was a lazy and dishonest ("he does not pay his debts", he said) man who wanted to be shaman. It was clear that the candidate was helped by other people and he would never be a good shaman, the other people said. Others said that one of the causes of such a situation was that the methods with the trial by fire (a pit with charcoal), or with a stick covered with oxen intestines (the candidate must be able to hold the stick which is pulled by several strong men) and other good methods, implied by introducing group *buku* and *mani*, had been given up in the *wujala* clan. Some people were much dissatisfied and left the performance before its conclusion. However, A said that "although he (the candidate B) does not know all spirits, he still knows something". Some persons supposed that A's idea was to make his brother shaman and then to rid himself of the trouble of looking after his wife who was sick from spirits and needed a treatment by the new *amba saman* of their clan. A was greatly criticized for this attitude. The influential man E supported his own point of view by criticizing the method of the trial with *colo*. He himself and *Cuntin* knew *colo* by heart and they were practising assistant's functions, so that they might easily have become shamans, if tried on *colo*; as to the trembling, it can be produced after a short training, so it is not convincing, therefore there must be something else. He said that A's wife had a "straight heart" and she might be a good shaman. There was, however, another point of view, namely, since the performance was carried out and the spirits had been named, though with the help of other persons, and since there was trembling, the candidate could be admitted, for everything required by *colo* and *kooli* had been fulfilled. Such a formalization of shamanism is supported by the instances taken from the Mongol and Chinese complexes. In a somewhat depressed mood this day was finished with the usual thanksgivings to the spirits and the late supper after 5 A.M.

And so the performance continued for six nights. I shall not repeat the occurrences, but shall now point out some facts of interest. The spirit of the unfortunate father of the candidate B once entered him and expressed his great dissatisfaction with A, who did not show him any mark of esteem ("piety complex"), and declared that he had become a spirit (*vocko*) of the clan (even though as shown above this possibility was at first rejected). The wrong was left with A. The latter promised to give a good sacrifice of a large pig to the spirits of the new shaman; naturally his intention was to build up a bridge for the restoration of relations between himself and his father's soul which was now a spirit. Indeed, he had already spent much money (two pigs—$39.00, incense and straw for the stoves $15.00-altogether more than $55.00), but he hoped that other clansmen, even those of his wife, would help him. Although the new shaman did not know all of the spirits and could name only a part of them, he seemed to have reached extasy on the last day of the performance and fell down unconscious, "as white as paper, so that it was distressing to look at him", and the public opinion turned in his favour; he had "power" and for a long time there had not been such a good shaman. On the sixth night a sacrifice was offered to the spirits of the old shaman—a cock and Chinese bread, and two pigs were eaten by the participants, as a sacrifice to the spirits of the new shaman.

In my diary I find my conclusive impression from this performance: "It is the twilight of shamanism". But that was only my *impression*, perhaps formed after very tiresome observations. This opinion I am inclined not to repeat, but to modify as follows; an interesting case or readaptation of shamanism to the new cultural complex, in consequence of a partial disintegration of the clan and of the ethnical disintegration of the Manchus.

The shaman's dependence upon a supporting social unit (Shirokogoroff, 1935:350)

1.41   Along with the treatment of various elements which constitute shamanism as a complex, and along with the treatment of various conditions
which underlie or result from shamanism, we have seen that the part of
a community in defining whether the person, willing to be a shaman,
may actually become one or not, and the part of a community in maintaining this complex are always fundamental conditions of shamanism.
Without such a social approval, or consent, shamans cannot function. In
fact, we have seen that the shaman's chief function is a social function of
regulating the psychomental complex of the social unit, which may be a
clan where the clan organization is well established, a village where the
settled life has resulted in a strong territorial connexion, finally, even a
whole ethnical or regional unit, chiefly in the case when the clan organization is not fixed as a permanent system. Therefore the social unit
which forms a milieu for a shaman is not only a clan, as it is observed in
the greater part of instances, but there may be other units as well. So in
case the clan organization is destroyed, the social milieu for a shaman
may be shifted to any other existing unit. We have such instances even
among the Tungus and Manchus who settle in villages, in groups com-
posed of a few families of different clans. There are some shamans among
the Manchus who serve villages, and not clans, whence a new complex
of clients' families connected with a shaman has already originated.
There is another very important condition which may bring into life a
new grouping around an individual-shaman. This is the theory of spirits
which may remain outside of a clan. Since *dona* (Birareen and Kuma-
reen) spirits exist, the *dona* shamans may also exist. This is actually observed among the Birarcen and Kumarcen who are badly attacked by the
foreign spirits which, however, are not all included in the complexes of
clan spirits. The Khingan Tungus and Tungus of Transbaikalia have no
dona shamans; all of them are clan shamans, as it is also, at least formally,
among the Manchus. So long as the *dona* spirits are not incorporated
into the clan lists, the shamans mastering them are "foreign" shamans,
but, as stated, the *dona* spirits may also be mastered by the clan shamans, while *dona* spirits do not master clan spirits. However, when the
dona spirits are entered into the list of clan spirits, the *dona* shamans
cannot exist. It is thus evident that an influx of new spirits may produce
shamans independent of the clan. Still, these shamans will not remain
without a social milieu. The latter will be formed around them after a
series of successful cases of performances. Such shamans may easily become interclan shamans in settlements which consist of mixed clans. Finally, there are shamans who are not clan shamans and who may exist in
a special social milieu. There are cases of shamans who belong to distinct

ethnical units; for instance, several Chinese shamans practising among the Manchus; there are Dahur shamans practising among the Birareen; Buriat, Goldi, Manchu and Chinese shamans are occasionally invited by the Northern Tungus. Around them a group of clients will be formed who will function as their social milieu. Such cases may also occur without the interference of foreign ethnical groups, and even without *dona* spirits, namely, when there are different currents of centrifugal movement in a clan, which result in a loss of social unity in the clan. Since there are dissidents in the matter of treatment of spirits, shamans may appear approved by a part of the clan. Such an approval—a recognition—may lead even to the splitting of a clan. So that from time to time shamans may appear who are not recognized by a community as a whole, but only by a part of it. Anyhow these shamans will have their social milieu.

However, in exceptional cases, a person who has no social milieu, is   1.41 not recognized as a shaman, still tried to perform, either under a stimulus of practical calculation, or in consequence of a special psychomental condition. I have met a few cases of such persons among the Tungus and Manchus. Here, however, two different situations must be distinguished, namely, (1) when a person who pretends to be a shaman *is not yet formally recognized*, but is awaiting such a recognition, from time to time practises shamanizing without a milieu, and (2) when a person *is not and will not be recognized*. . . . These are not shamans, because they cannot produce a real extasy, especially without an audience, and they have no social functions, usually no paraphernalia, but they are either dishonest impostors or psychomentally affected people. By this I do not intend to say that they cannot become shamans, but I want only to indicate that they do not function as shamans, have no milieu and probably cannot assume the functions of shamans, because they are not recognized; this may be dependent, at least sometimes, on personal considerations.

Generally there are very few shamans who act outside of the clan and are recognized shamans. Their recognition by the social groups may take a shorter or longer time. If the shaman-outsider is successful, he will soon be recognized; if he is not successful, the recognition may be delayed. A great number of such shamans drop the practising of performances, when the recognition does not come soon. . . .

8.4 Shamanistic behavior among the Tungus

A performance which "failed" (Shirokogoroff, 1935:312–3)

(The performance took place among the Birarcen.) The purpose of the shamanizing was to ask for the help of a *seven* for curing a boy. There had been two shamanizings three days previously—one in the day time and the other at night—but no definite result had been obtained. The boy ws brought from the school where he was living (a boarding school established by the Chinese government) to the house of his relative who was performing (rather poorly) the function of the assistant. After the shamanizing the *arkaptun*[7] . . . was left above the boy's bed.

When the spirit was introduced, the shaman (a female) was helped by the assistant. The spirit declared that the child would perhaps die. This produced a reaction on the part of the assistant (he was a relative of the boy) who protested against the coming of the spirit if it could not help the boy. The spirits required a pig as sacrifice. The assistant replied that he was a poor man and could not afford it. However, after a long bargaining, it was decided that the sacrifice would be offered two weeks later, on the first day of the next month. After the shamanizing, a piece of yellow cloth was given to the spirit and hung up together with the *arkaptun*. The operation lasted until over one o'clock A.M.

About ten days later, i.e. before the term fixed at the shamanizing, another shamanizing was performed. In the meantime the boy had been cured and a pig had been bought. The shamanizing consisted of two parts performed at night, and on the next morning. As far as I could find out, the sacrifice was offered to the spirit of the shaman which had been helpful in the sickness of the boy.

This time the shamanizing was performed outside of the house. The shaman put on the costume and prepared herself for the extasy. The boy was sitting in the middle, while the shaman went round him with her drum. This time the shamanizing was not easy, for there was no assistant to help her. There were also present some people who interfered with her performance. The Chinese teacher, who was present, was a man of "modern style": he did not believe in shamanism and tried to disturb the shaman. Every time when she passed near him, he pushed or kicked her with his heavy leather shoes of European style. The shaman became nervous and could not concentrate. During the performance a spirit arrived who had nine female and nine male manifestations. Eighteen people were thus required to go rhythmically dancing around the boy, the shaman being in the centre. However, there were only seven women to perform and they were shy in the presence of the sceptically behaving Chinese teacher and the indifferent Tungus men who did not dare to join them in the presence of the teacher. The shaman became still more nervous, so that, when the women did not follow the increase of tempo in her movement, she slightly beat them with the drum stick. No effect was produced. Her spirits became angry and the shaman beat vigorously the women who ran away. Thus the performance failed. The second part was

2.2

[7] The *arkaptun* is "a large brass mirror" with "the symbol of a special shamanistic bird" which is attached to the back of the shaman's costume (Shirokogoroff, 1935:292).

performed in a very simple manner, as an ordinary sacrifice, with the usual incantations and prayers.

The shaman's costume (Shirokogoroff, 1935:287–9, 297, 301–3)   2.12

Among all Tungus groups and Manchus, as well as their neighbours, shamanistic performances require a certain number of special things used only for this purpose. These things may be called by the general term "shamanistic paraphernalia". Their number and forms vary greatly among the Tungus and the other groups. . . .

In the paraphernalia a great number of elements can be distinguished, the principal of which are (1) the costume which may consist of several elements: coat, apron, trousers, shoes, etc., or may be reduced to a single element, e.g. the coat, skirt, apron; (2) the head-dress; (3) the staffs; (4) the brass mirror-*toli*; (5) the drum with the drumming stick; (6) other musical instruments; (7) various placings for spirits, independent of other placings, and (8) various other implements. The complex of the paraphernalia may be rich or poor, for which there may be different reasons which will be discused later. Although theoretically a case might be imagined where there would be no paraphernalia needed for a shaman's activity, such an occurrence has not been observed. So, as a statement of fact, we must say that there is no shamanism without paraphernalia. It   2.1
can be supposed, and it will be shown when the performances are described, that the paraphernalia are needed for the performances and that without them the effectiveness of shamanism would decrease to such an extent that it would lose its functional "value" and would naturally be given up as a complex. In fact, the costumes and other paraphernalia are needed by most of the shamans for the production of self-excitement, self-hypnosis, and hypnotic influence over the audience. It should also   2.2
be noted that, together with the increase of the curative power of a shaman, there is usually an increase of paraphernalia. If a shaman has no paraphernalia, he or she is not a good shaman in the eyes of the people. The richer the paraphernalia, the more influential the shaman.

In looking at the geographical distribution of the elements it can be quite clearly seen that some coincidences are revealed with the ethnical group here discussed, and also with the geographical grouping of elements in the complexes. Both within the complexes abstracted, and within the ethnical units the combination of elements presents such a great variety that sometimes it is impossible to trace the lines of demarcation between two complexes connected with ethnical groups. However, there are no two absolutely similar complexes of paraphernalia observed in the individual cases of shamans, even within the same ethnical   2.3
unit and within the limits of the same (our theoretical construction) cultural type. The chief reason is that, as a rule, every shaman has his or her own complex of spirits, and with the change of fashions a great free-

dom in the choice of elements and their variations is left to the individual shaman. The choice of shamanistic paraphernalia is not a rigidly fixed, ceremonial complex. In this respect no comparison can be made with the Buddhistic paraphernalia, or with any other uniform complex ceremonial attributes. However, there is also an interesting exception, namely, the Manchus, among whom a tendency to uniformity is well expressed; but there are special reasons for this, which will be discussed later on.

. . . I shall give the description of various forms of costumes which may consist either of one or of several pieces which by themselves form a complex. . . .

THE COSTUME-DUCK consists of a coat, an apron, trousers, knee-protectors, and shoes (moccasins). The material used for the coat may be chamois, made either of deer (Cervus Elaphus) skin or of elk (Alces Alces) skin. The cut does differ from that of an ordinary coat, i.e. a coat resembling the modern European morning coat. The difference is that the back part is much longer and ends in a tail symbolizing the duck's tail. The sleeves are supplied with a fringed strip of chamois symbolizing the wings. The borders are also trimmed with a chamois fringe and hanging strips of chamois, all of them symbolizing feathers. The coat is usually ornamented with white reindeer hair from the neck, widely used by the Tungus as a material for ornamentation. Ornamental motives are various combinations of lines, strips and circles, much like those observed in the bone-carvings of the Chukchis, Eskimos, Samoyeds and other inhabitants of North Siberia and America. However, I have seen also a coat which was ornamented along the borders with applied coloured crosses of about 5 or 6 centimetres. According to the Tungus, the "cross" greatly helps in shamanizing—it may "have power".[8] The ornamented parts may also be coloured with the usual colours—black, red, brown, yellow, and blue. The coat may also have applied ornamentation symbolizing the bones of a duck. Instead of an ornamental symbolization of the skeleton, corresponding symbols of all bones made of iron may be used. Their number may be confined to only two bones of the wings, or all bones of the skeleton may be reproduced—it depends on the material facilities for procuring iron, which is not common among the Tungus. Usually the iron parts are not made by the Tungus, but are received in exchange from the Buriats and Yakuts.

In addition to the ornamentation of borders with the common "geometric" figures there exist ornaments made of white hair—stylized im-

---

[8] "I am not sure as to the origin of this cross-ornament, which might be a simple imitation of the Orthodox priests' chasuble. It is not in contradiction with the Tungus idea: since priests use this 'ornament', it may be useful for the shamans, too." (S.M.S.)

ages of domesticated reindeer, Cervus Elaphus, Alces Alces, bear, wild
boar, musk-deer, roe-deer, heath-cock, also ducks, and anthropomorphic
images. However, these images are not an indispensable element of the
"duck-costume".

Besides these, so to say permanent, elements there is a variable
number of pendants made of iron and brass which, however, are not
typical of the duck-costume.

The coat is usually supplied with two series of eight bells of two
forms: conical and spherical. The bells are real series for they form two
definite musical accords in the frontal and back parts of the coat needed
for the shamanistic performance and used by the shamans quite intentionally. The complex of bells and trinkets is called *arkalan*. . . .

THE COSTUME-REINDEER consists of the same elements, and is
made of the same material. The cut of the coat does not differ from that
of an ordinary coat. The ornaments may be lacking, but the coat must
have a set of iron bones symbolizing a complete skeleton of Cervus Elaphus. As compared with the "bones" of the duck-costume those of the
reindeer-costume can easily be distinguished, e.g. in representing sternum, rigs, and limbs. Animals and bells are attached to the coat as it is
with the duck-costume, but they are in a greater number and there are
special conical trinkets attached to other parts of the costume. In addition to the zoomorphic and anthropomorphic figures several other symbols are attached: e.g. a boat, a raft, a bow and an arrow, a semi-circle
("moon"), a circle ("sun"), a ring ("rain-bow"), a square hole ("heaven,"
the hole being the entrance into the upper world used by the shaman);
there may also be found: "stars", "thunder", "harpoons", as well as placings *bada*. These are symbols of phenomena with which the shaman has
to deal during his performance, when travelling into the lower and upper
worlds. The animals are manifestations of spirits which can be assumed
by the shaman during the performance.

"Snake". Both the duck and reindeer costumes have a certain number, not less than one, of chamois strips, about ten centimetres wide and
over a metre long. These represent *kulin*—the "snake", but they are
supplied with two heads, a tail, split into several parts, and four fringes
symbolizing the legs; the eyes are made of small glass beads. If there are
several "snakes", the largest "snake" is attached to the back, while two
small "snakes" are attached to the two sides. The big "snake" was styled
by the shamans as "the most important spirit who gives advice to the
shaman".

Mokil. On the back there are also attached images, known as *mokil*,
made of chamois dyed black. There may be only two pairs, but there
may also be four, as well as nine, or even 9x4, 9x8, 18x4 and so forth.
These combinations of two and nine are frequently met with in shaman-

istic paraphernalia and performances. Many series of nine are met with chiefly in the duck-costume, while that of two is found in the reindeer-costume.

The two types here distinguished are not always strictly followed. I have seen some costumes in which the elements of duck and reindeer were mixed up. The number of pendants and ornaments also greatly varies, depending on whether the shaman can afford to have two special costumes and how much they can be ornamented. *Lege artis*, the duck-costume, is supposed to be good for shamanizing in connexion with operations with the spirits of the upper world, while the reindeer-costume is supposed to be good for dealing with those of the lower world. I was even told that the reindeer-costume is "too heavy for going to the upper world". In fact, a good costume with all pendants, bells, etc., may weigh about forty kilograms, while an ordinary duck-costume will not be much heavier than a usual Tungus garment. It should be noted that the duck-costume *lege artis* possesses *mokil* in many series of nine, and has no symbols for boat, raft, etc., needed for travelling across the water for reaching the lower world. It must also be remembered that the travelling in the lower world . . . is much more difficult than the travelling in the upper world, so that the shaman-beginners usually have only the duck-costume. When they begin to go to the lower world, they attach more and more iron pieces so that by increasing the number a new, second costume, the reindeer-costume may be "constructed". When this is done all of the metallic pieces are taken off the duck-costume and transferred on the reindeer-costume. From that moment the shaman would alternatively use his two costumes for special forms of shamanizing.

From the above description of the two types of costumes it is evident that they are connected with two forms of shamanizing. . . .

THE APRON (*uruptun*) (Bar. Nere) is the most important part of the costume, for the shaman can perform, at least some acts, with the apron alone, but not the great shamanizing to the upper and lower worlds. In shape, the apron does not differ from the ordinary Tungus one, which is a piece of chamois with thongs for tying it around the waist, about seventy or eighty centimetres long and from twenty-five to forty centimetres wide, just enough for covering the chest and the abdomen, used by all Tungus as a supplement necessary to their open morning-coat-like dress in the Siberian and Manchurian climatic conditions. The apron is ornamented with strips of coloured chamois, or it is painted with the usual colours and ornamented with white reindeer hair. The whole apron is covered with a design symbolizing the world-universe—*turu*. In the middle there is a line, from which, at the height of two thirds, two other lines go up at a certain angle. This is the larch tree . . . above which the upper world . . . is situated. Two anthropomorphic symbols, representing "two great shamans who died long ago" and to whom the acting shaman must pray for helping to shamanize, are found in the upper part. There may be more than two symbols—four or eight. "If these shamans should fall down to the earth, the whole universe would collapse." The middle part of the design represents the Earth . . . (the middle world without the ocean). The lower part represents the lower world. The apron may be trimmed with a fringe and eight iron birds . . . , apparently "ducks".

A brass mirror *tolo* is attached to the apron. This is the most important element of the apron and of the whole costume. According to the shamans, such a mirror cannot be bought, but it must be found in the earth—it is sent by the *burkan*. (This is only a theory, for when the Tungus want one, they can have it from old costumes of deceased shamans. They get them from the Buriats as well. The Buriats can tell the Tungus that the mirror was found in the earth, although actually it came from China or Tibet with other buddhistic paraphernalia.) On the unpolished side the shamans distinguish in the centre a snake—*kulin*—which is naturally a dragon, and animals: a wolf, a cow, a roe-deer, a cow's head, a cock, a sheep, a horse, etc. which actually represent twelve cyclic animals. When the shaman looks at the polished side "he can see everything", i.e. it helps the shaman to hypnotize himself. . . .

Among the shamanistic paraphernalia, independent of the costume, the most important is the drum. Drums, regardless of their form and details, are used for shamanistic performances as a musical instrument for keeping the rhythm, for self-excitement of the shaman, and for influencing and regulating the psychic state of the audience. As to the musical character of this instrument, I shall leave it for a further treatment, and shall now confine myself to a description of the form of drums. . . .

Among the Transbaikalian Tungus the drum is found to be of two forms, namely, a regular oval and an egg-like, the greatest length being between sixty-five and seventy centimetres. The rim from six to eight centimetres wide, made of larch or birch wood, is covered on one side either with the skin of Cervus Elaphus, or with that of Alces Alces, so that the edges of the skin cover the rim and are fixed to its inside. The inside of the drum has a large ring placed approximately in the centre and held by thongs attached to the small rings fixed at the rim, so that they form a cross with a large ring in the middle. The thongs may be partly or totally replaced by the movable iron pieces with the thongs attached to the small rings of the rim and with the large iron ring. This construction is used for holding the drum in the left hand (for right-handed persons). Instead of a ring, a cross about fifteen centimetres long can be used.

At the internal side of the rim there are two iron braces with eight flat iron disks, with a hole in the centre, attached as trinkets. They are called *sekan*,—"the ear-ring". A variable number of conical trinkets may also be attached to the rim. Once, I saw four pairs, but there may be only two or eight pairs as well, but always by pairs. Other various placings and trinkets may be attached in the upper part of the drum on a special brace, e.g. I have observed a combination of a quadruped animal, a human face (*bada*), a bell and a conical trinket.

The external part, used for drumming, is covered with various designs, some of which I shall now describe as an illustration.

I. As a whole, the design represents *dunda*, the earth, as a firm part of the world; the shaman may use his drum as a canoe for crossing the sea. The design executed with double lines reproduces that found on the apron. . . . At a certain distance two lines corresponding to the actual form of the drum make a frame for the design, so that the internal lines are connected with the central design, while a double line runs near the border of the drum. Between the lower four pairs of lines eight lines connect the outer double lines. Two pairs of anthropomorphic images are placed on the left and right sides of the group of eight lines near to them. The part of the drum outside of the lines had in the upper section eight and at the lower part six pairs of anthropomorphic images. Between these two groups, on each side, the following animals are represented: the Alces Alces, the Cervus Elaphus, the roe-deer, the musk-deer, the cow, and the domesticated reindeer.

II. No design is placed in the middle of the drum. Between two lines there are two pairs of anthropomorphic images in the upper part and the same number in the lower part, and on both sides four animal images: Alces Alces, Cervus Elaphus, and two domesticated reindeer—a male and a female.

III. From a double lined circle in the middle eight double lines are brought to the border of the drum, representing eight legs on which the Earth is standing in the sea. . . .

Our description of the shaman costume would not be complete, if we do not give details as to the Tungus attitude regarding the costume. Unfortunately the early authors sometimes give quite a wrong picture. Remaining within the Tungus groups I have again to quote I. A. Lopatin who, by the way, reflects rather well the common attitude of ethnographers. In reference to the Goldi he speaks of the sacredness of the costume. . . . Such an approach is entirely erroneous as a formulation of facts and as a method. This is s simple transplanting of the European religious complex into a distinctly different one. I do not deny that is some cases there may be a complex approaching "sacredness", as opposed to the complex of profane things and persons, but no such facts are observed among the Tungus groups.

The Tungus attitude towards the costume is defined by the following conditions: the costume is a placing for the shaman's spirits; the costume may gather other spirits, and the latter may come into a conflict with the shaman's spirits; the women who have menstruations may frighten the spirits, for they have special spirits, or the other spirits are afraid of blood.

Since the making (sewing) of clothes is generally carried out by women, there is no exception for the shaman's costume. It is desirable that the costume be made by women who have no menstruations, i.e. by very young girls and old women, but if there is no such women, the sewing may be done by any other woman. However, when the work is finished, the costume must be "purified" with smoke of plants used for this purpose. Among the Manchus the work is done by girls and widows. The iron and brass parts are made by common smiths, usually Chinese.

The shaman's costume in the Manchu complex is considered as . . . "a dress of spirits". Therefore one must not use bad expressions when speaking about the costume, one must not do anything which might offend the spirits, e.g. spit, etc. Thus, the costume must be treated in absolutely the same manner as the other placings for spirits, e.g. the ribbons etc.

Since the shamans are acting on behalf of their clans, the making of a costume is a clan business, and the clansmen contribute to it. When the costume is worn out, or burnt (as a great number were during the Boxer Rebellion in Manchuria), a new one is made; but parts of a costume may also be renewed or repaired. The costume can be given up on various occasions.

1. If a clan cannot afford to have a shaman (e.g. when the clan is too small), the costume is brought to the forest, on a mountain, and hung up on a tree. After a certain time the spirits may leave the costume, and then it becomes simply an old, useless thing. If a new shaman appears, it will be necessary to make a new costume, and the spirits will enter into it.

2. If a clan wants to make a new costume, the old one is brought away as in the first case, but the spirits are asked to move to a new costume. Their entering is recognized by the fact that the shaman feels them and is able to shamanize in the new costume.

3. Somebody makes a present of a new garment to the shaman, and the old costume can be taken away.

No renewing of costumes is at present practised, the chief reason of which is the prohibition of shamanism by the Chinese authorities. Under this pretext the clansmen very often refuse to contribute their money. Such a condition could be created only in the present relative decline of shamanism and in the ethnical disintegration of the Manchus in general.

It is believed that when the shaman introduces into himself the spirit of fire . . . , the costume would not burn, even though the shaman should jump into a heap of burning charcoal; however, if there is no spirit, the costume would burn as any other thing, in spite of the fact

2.1   that it was being used as a placing for other spirits. Generally it is be-
      lieved that if there is no costume, the spirit (*vocko*) would not come, and
2.2   the shamanizing without costume is not regarded as a real shamanizing.
      There must be at least a *sisa* and *toli*.

     After the shaman's death, the costume may be handed over to *jar-
umbo*, i.e. to the house which used the shaman's assistance . . . , where
it will be preserved until a new shaman appears. Only some of the paraphernalia used for the secondary spirits, e.g. the trident, swords, axes,
etc. are buried together with the shaman. If one of the children of the
deceased shaman has been inclined, during his father's life, to become a
shaman, the costume would remain in the shaman's family. However, the
question as to whether the candidate would become a shaman or not, is
decided by the clan.

     The drum and other instruments have nothing sacred in them, but
there is a strict recommendation to avoid the production of sound, when
the shaman does not act, the reason being that the spirits may respond
on the drumming by coming and entering the people who cannot master
them. On the same ground the shaman's costume cannot be put on by
people who are not certain of being able to master the spirits. It is clearly
shown by the fact that the Manchus did not oppose my looking for details
and handling the costume as much as I wanted: in their opinion, my
attitude would not be offensive to the spirits. In this way the Manchus,
who are experienced and "strong in spirits", do touch the costume without harm to themselves and to the spirits. Some who are not afraid may
even put on the costume. Playing with the drum, when there is no danger of attracting the spirits, is very common. So one may see before and
after shamanizing "fearless" persons who touch the paraphernalia and
beat the drum. During the performance many people also touch the shaman's paraphernalia, especially the drums and special instruments.

     Certain precautions are used when the costume is carried from one
place to another, but these precautions are of the same character as those
of avoiding contact with other spirits, particularly the hostile spirits,
keeping off woman's blood, and abstaining from useless disturbance of
the spirits.

     The same attitude is characteristic of other Tungus groups. As among
the Manchus, the costume is a clan affair. The clan has to decide about it
and usually helps in making it. . . . As among the Manchus, the idea of
avoiding women's blood inspires certain precautions in the women's
coming into a contact with the costume. However, there are some parts,
as for instance *toli* in *arkaptun*, which may be left near a woman, when
she is attended by a shaman, and there is no danger for the spirits or the
shaman. Thus, there are spirits which are not afraid of woman's spirits,
and in this case the woman may touch some paraphernalia of a shaman.

Such ones are spirits of her own clan and those of her husband's with her. In fact, it must be so in principle, for female-shamans are common among both Manchus and Tungus. There is, however, a limitation, namely, when the female-shaman is menstruating, she does not touch the spirits' placing. Thus it is generally recommended to be careful with the shaman's costume. When the costume is carried on reindeer back or on horse back, it is put separately and is supplied with special thongs for packing. . . .

After the shaman's death the costume is put on a special scaffold, near his or her tomb. Among the Tungus who are settled in villages the costume is kept in the house. There are still some spirits which place themselves in the costume, so that the Tungus say: the costume may show signs of life—it trembles and makes a noise with its iron and brass parts. A candidate for shamanship would know exactly in his dreams where the costume is and would come to that spot. Then the costume might be bought (among the Birarcen), for a horse or so, from the relatives of the deceased shaman. However, the costume cannot leave the clan, and it will not be taken by a new shaman, if the spirits of the deceased shaman are hostile to him, or vice versa. The perishable parts may be renewed, so only the metallic parts are taken. In this way the costume may be transmitted from one to another generation, but always within the same clan.

However, the costume, even though carefully kept in the house or near the tomb, is a source of worry, for the spirits are in it. The costume cannot be thrown away, for there are spirits in it, and if they get free, they may bother the people. Therefore the Tungus always face the following problem: whether it is better to send off the spirits together with the costume, or to leave a permanent placing for them and thereby to avoid the creation of a new shaman. In case the spirits do not bother the people, it is very likely that the people who keep the costume would try to get rid of it without destroying it, i.e. to send the spirits off together with their placings. As a matter of fact, the spirits may leave the costume at any moment and again make trouble to the clansmen; it is therefore safer to send off the costume and the spirits. Naturally, in the taiga there are many costumes which are left untouched and finally are altogether forgotten.

Among the Tungus groups the shaman may gradually renew his or her costume, so that during the life-time all parts may gradually be replaced. We have already seen that there may even be made two costumes for different forms of shamanizing.

The same attitude is characteristic of the Tungus with reference to the drum. The Tungus attach to it no idea of sacredness. The drum is merely an instrument. I have seen among the Khingan Tungus a man who, wanting to shamanize, used an ordinary enamel basin ("made in Japan") as a drum. . . . What the shamans need is an *instrument*. However, some ideas ensuing from the complex "instrument" are also connectd with drum. As with the Manchus, the drumming without the intention of calling out the spirits is not practised, especially in the dark, for the spirits may arrive. For this reason the Tungus dislike idle drumming and used to stop it. However, when such a danger is out of question, one is allowed to joke and to beat the drum, provided that the drum is not damaged, e.g. by drunken people.

The drum may also be used in the treatment of certain diseases, but then it is used only as an instrument, e.g. for gathering swallowed things, as in the case of a swallowed and rejected needle, of the kidney of a sacrificial animal eaten by one of the persons who attended a sacrifice, etc.

8.5 The social functions of the Siberian shaman

3.0   The aims of shamanistic performances (Shirokogoroff, 1935:315)

From the instances of shamanizing shown in the previous chapter it can be seen that the aims of shamanizing may be different, but not all cases are seen in the above instances. When summarized, the aims of shamanizing may be classified into six groups, namely; (1) divination (discovery) of the causes of various troubles and of the future; (2) curing of persons; (3) transportation of the souls of dead people to the world of the dead and the governing of souls; (4) sacrifice to the spirits; (5) management of spirits and souls (including "mastering"); (6) various (e.g. new shaman). One and the same performance may have several aims, and it may have only one of the above indicated aims. (On the following pages the author discusses each of these aims in some detail.)

3.0   The social position and functions of the Tungus shaman (Shirokogoroff, 1935:376–8)

The social relations of a shaman are of two natures: firstly, relations established because of the spirits mastered by the shaman; and secondly, relations established by the shaman with his clients. As we have seen, the spirits are also of two natures—clan spirits and foreign spirits, according to which there may be two kinds of shamans: clan shamans and "out clan" shamans. However, both kinds of shamans need recognition, which may be either obtained by a complicated ceremony of election, with a real trial and a real discusssion of the candidates, or by the shaman himself owing to his successful practising of the shamanistic art.

3.2   There is a great difference between the formally recognized clan shamans and those recognized because of their personal ability; the shamans of the first group become an essential component of the clan functional organizations, while the shamans of the second group are out-clan shamans, whose influence extends over a limited group of "foreign" spirits and a very limited group of personal clients.

In fact, the shaman, after having mastered the clan spirits, relieves thereby all members of his clan from the worry of being badly affected by the clan spirits, and is ready to lend at once his assistance to any clansman. His assistance will be effective and not difficult, for the *spirits are mastered by him*—a small sacrifice, a prayer, and a conversation with a spirit will relieve the patient of his trouble. By this means a great number of cases of psychomental disturbances are almost automatically cured. Moreover, when the clan spirits, which are usually very powerful and well acquainted with the clansmen, are well looked after, they may assist the shaman in his fighting with the out-clan spirits, not to speak of the complex cases when the clansmen's souls cannot normally reach the world of the dead ("lower world") and when the shaman's assistance is simple and helpful, while that of an out-clan shaman may be even harmful, because of the mixing up of his spirits with those of the clan, which should always be avoided.

Thus from the functional point of view, the clan shaman acts as a *safety valve* and as a special clan officer in charge of the regulation of the psychic equilibrium among the clan members.

How close the connexion is between a clan and its shaman, can be seen from the fact of the formation of new clans, as it is observed among the Tungus of Manchuria . . . the division of a clan is conditioned by the need of a smoothly functioning marriage complex. If there is an unfavourable sex-ratio in the two clans, or there is an important increase or a decrease of one of the clans (especially in a dual organization), a splitting of a populous clan is very likely. There are certain regulations as to the time required, but even after a declaration about the division to the spirit *buga*, the conclusion of marriages is not assured, until the two clan shamans divide their spirits. So a new clan must be formed and the shaman for the "junior" (*nokun*) clan must be separated from the old one. It is done in view of avoiding the mixing up of the clan spirits which, *according to the theory, must be different*. When this operation is carried out the women may be interchanged. It is interesting that the division of spirits and the appearance of candidates, powerful enough for mastering them, which may occur before the formal declaration to *buga*, is interpreted in the sense that the division can be carried out even before the expiration of the term previously fixed, i.e. usually four or five generations. I have observed several combinations of different types of relations. This fact is very interesting, because here the social organization is reflected in the relations between spirits and shamans. But the divi-

3.2

sion of clans must not be regarded as an act of division of the spirits, and as a reflexion of the relations created by the shamans—the clan division is much older than shamanism.

The obligation to assist the clansmen in need results from the special position of the shaman recognized by the clan. As a matter of fact, this requirement may cause the change of the shamanistic art into a simple formalistic performance. This does occur among the clans which are very populous, and the shaman must attend too many persons. Since the shamanizing *lege artis* requires extasy and thus a great effort on the part of the shaman and since the latter cannot do it very often, the shamanizing changes into a ritualistic formality and as such does not satisfy the people. Among the Manchus a great number of shamans are tending to become mere performers of rituals. L. Sternberg relates that among the Goldi a shaman, very skilful in bringing souls to the lower world, was busy all the time with these performances and the Goldi were waiting for him for years before he could attend the people. Owing to this the clan shamans are sometimes superseded in their art by the *dona* (out-clan) shamans. There is moreover another condition in favour of the out-clan shamans, namely, in a great number of cases candidates for the clan-shamanship, who sometimes are not inclined to shamanship, are forcibly prepared by the senior clansmen, while all out-clan shamans assume their functions, because that is their vocation, and they usually have spent much energy before obtaining the position of a "recognized" shaman.

2.2   On the other hand, the attitude of the Tungus, and of the Manchus as well, towards the clan-shamans is always somewhat partial, the reason of which is the belief that such a person is needed for the clan (as I understand it, as a safety valve), and partiality of the clan is only one of the effects of a centripetal movement within the clan. The clansmen would always find an excuse if the shaman is not successful; so for instance, he might be said to be young, or too old, or the spirits might be suspected of being too lazy to work for their master, or some new unknown spirits might be suspected to be active. However, if the shaman shows no efficiency in his activity, which may be found out by the experienced elders, he may met with the general disapproval of his clan and in some cases may arouse all clansmen against himself, as a dangerous and pernicious person for the clan. This is the case when the shaman manifests his "bad heart". The clan may come to the decision to destroy him with the help of other shamans, or at least to cast him out, which practically means nearly the same as capital punishment. If the shaman is not appreciated by his clansmen, he also may give up his functions, but, as will be shown, this is not easy and almost impossible.

2.2   The Tungus (all groups, the Manchus included) recognize that the shamans are needed for the neutralization and the fighting of the clan spirits (other spirits as well!), and they believe that it would be much better to have no spirits, and consequently no shamans. So that if something were proposed which would eliminate the spirits, they would be ready to accept it. Together with it, the shamans would not be needed either. This attitude is not in favour of the shamans in general, but still it is far from creating a generally negative attitude towards the shamans. However, among all Tungus groups one may also meet with individuals who are hostile to the shamans in general, and according to them, the wrong emanates from the shamans themselves. Their voices become very strong, when the shaman is not supported by other clansmen.

The shaman must face these neutral and hostile attitudes. The young   2.2 shamans, are moreover bound by the social complex of junior-senior relations. In a great number of cases these relations put them in a difficult position for maintaining their own opinions which may not always be shared by the seniors. These difficulties are not so great when the shaman attains a certain age and the group of seniors becomes small. In this respect the shaman must adapt himself during all his life, for even being a senior he is bound by the will of the clan.

From the above remarks it is clear that the shaman does not become   2.2 an authority, as magicians and priests do, but throughout his life he remains a clansman whose steps are checked up by the opinion of critically behaving clansmen, the whole clan organization, and . . . alien ethnical groups which spread their influence over the Tungus.

A great role in the stabilization of the shaman's position is played by his personal success. If the shaman successfully attends some clansmen, he is invited again, so his position is strengthened. As we have seen, after the performances the shaman leaves his "roads" which are all the time used by his spirits. So that between the shaman and his clients a peculiar connexion, with the help of his spirits and a system of "roads", is firmly established. The influence of an out-clan shaman totally depends upon his personal connexions, while in the case of a clan shaman the same roads of clan spirits, though indirectly, connect the shaman with all other clansmen. A "road" left directly by a shaman greatly reinforces the personal connexion between the shaman and his clansmen.

In Manchu such connexion is expressed by a special term: the family . . . attended by the shaman is *jurun*; so it is called *jarumbo*, and the shaman is called *jarun saman*. These relations are usually established from the childhood of the shaman's clients, especially in the families which do not belong to the clan. If the shaman successfully treats a child of an age below ten years he leaves *targo*. The latter is a narrow strip of cloth (ribbons) attached to the shaman's head-dress. The usual colour for all shamans is red. In addition to a red strip, two more strips of different colours are given, e.g. yellow, blue, green, white, black, etc. These strips are supplied with two round *xoygo* (brass bells) and some fringes from the shamans head-dress. These are conventional placings for the shaman's spirits which are supposed to distinguish them according to the combination of colours, as it is with the *pogun vocko*. Such a placing is attached to the back of the child's coat (not always, for the parents become neglectful if the child is in good health) and worn so up to the age of ten years. Naturally the carrier of *targa* must not visit tabooed houses, *jatka bo* (after a childbirth) and *targa bo* (during the diseases produced by *ilxa mama*: smallpox, chicken-pox, measles, etc.), also those where people had recently died, for the shaman's spirit may "mix up" with these spirits. Besides *targa* the attended child may receive a brass mirror (*toli*), which must be preserved on . . . a shelf used for keeping placings for spirits—where the *targa* is also put after the age of ten years. . . . The person attended by a shaman must not seek assistance from other shamans, unless the shaman recommends it himself. (The girls usually do not receive targa and toli.) So that the shaman gradually forms around himself a group of permanent clients. Every first day and every fifteenth day of a new moon (month) the client must perform a ritual praying to the spirits of the shaman. Every year on the second day of the first moon (month) the client must attend (theoretically the client must come, even being at a distance of "one thousand li") the shaman's great annual sacrifice, . . . and bring with him some wine, Chinese bread, candy and incense (meat is not required!) for the sacrifice.

3.11   In November or December, after the harvest, the shaman during his visit to all houses in the village receives from every *jarumbo* some supply of grain (millet, wheat, and others). Rich families give him up to a ton of grain, the poor ones less. All other houses which are no *jarumbo* give him not less than about fifteen kilograms. The collected grain may suffice to support the shaman during a year. It should be noted that different shamans usually do not meet in the same houses, and a shaman would not go into a house where there is another *jarun saman*. If a shaman enters the house in which a *jarun saman* is acting, the latter would know it immediately and would tell it through his assistant. . . . The performance consists in a short prayer to the spirits and especially *apka enduri*.

3.1   The connexion which is formed between the shaman and his clients among the Tungus of Manchuria is still stronger when the attended person is a child. In a great number of cases, as shown, the shaman takes the soul of the child (male or female) and keeps it up to a certain age, sometimes up to thirteen or fourteen years. The shaman takes under his protection that component of the threefold soul which returns into other people and animals. If he would take all three components the child would die. The shaman leaves with the child a bell and brass mirror, or something else from his costume. These are placings for the shaman's spirits while the soul is kept by the shaman. The placings are always kept in a special birch-bark box near the sleeping place of the child, and they must not be lost. If loss should occur, it must be immediately reported to the shaman who will take special measures for recovering the control of the absent spirits, together with the placings. In this function the shaman's spirit is actually a guardian spirit of the child. After the above indicated age the soul is revoked by the shaman, and the above mentioned things are returned to the shaman. Some complications may arise when the shaman dies before the time of the restoration of the soul. However, it is supposed that all spirits, and naturally souls, become free after the shaman's death. If the soul of the shaman and his spirits, also the souls of children, are not captured by other spirits at the moment of the shaman's death, the child will not suffer any trouble. Therefore the Tungus abstain from having recourse to very old shamans, and naturally they do not ask for any help from "bad-hearted" shamans who during their fightings with other shamans may be destroyed at any moment. When the shaman collects the souls of children he makes them greatly dependent upon himself, and thus a very strong connexion between the shaman and his clients is formed. All of them want to preserve the shaman and to be on good terms with him. In case of trouble they form his own group of sympathizers, sometimes perhaps ever against their own will.

Naturally the more numerous are his permanent clients from their childhood, the more influential is the shaman.

Besides this special service rendered by the shaman to the children, he accumulates a great number of adult clients who were relieved by him of their troubles and thus became natural friends of the shaman. The adult clients who are known to a shaman usually address themselves to the same shaman, so that the latter, after getting more acquainted with the psychology of the client, becomes indispensable to the client. In fact, in all cases when a renewing of suggestion is needed, the client hardly can peacefully live without his shaman's assistance.

Indeed, if the shaman is at the same time a popular shaman and a clan-shaman, and if he does not "fight", his influence upon the clan may become very great. However, owing to the strictness of the system of social organization, he will not become "chief", or "head" of the clan. As a matter of fact, a quite special psychomental condition of the shaman, as was shown in the preceding chapter, would not permit him to become such a "leader", although he may be very influential, even with the military leader of the Tungus, as it was e.g. with Mukteokan and other shamans who defended with their art their people against foreign aggression.

From these instances we may see that the personal influence of a shaman may extend far beyond his own clan, and it will be a case of individual success.

Whether the shaman is liked or not, whether he is "bad-hearted" or "good-hearted", he always assumes, with his art and individuality, a special social position, which imposes a certain ceremonialism in dealing with him. The shamans are not called by their personal names, even by the seniors; joking and teasing, which are common amongst the Tungus, cannot be used with the shamans; the shaman is usually treated as a "senior". Among some groups the term "shaman" is not used in addressing the shamans. . . .

3.11 The economic situation of the Tungus shaman (Shirokogoroff, 1935:378–80)

In the discussion of the transmission of shamanism it has already been pointed out that the problem of maintaining shamans is of importance and may have an influence upon the election of a new shaman. Owing to the psychomental character of shamanism, most of the shamans are put in an exceptional position in reference to the chief industrial activity of the Tungus—the hunting. In fact, in Transbaikalia I have met with a shaman who could not kill big animals such as the elk, Cervus Elaphus, Cervus Tarandus—and therefore was chiefly hunting roe-deer. On his part it was a case of self-suggestion. Some shamans cannot hunt tigers and bears, for these are animals whose forms may be assumed (they become placings) by other shamans. A great number of shamans have no assurance in handling fire-arms. Dealing with the spirits and sometimes being attacked by them, as well as by other shamans, the shaman is usually not certain, when remaining alone, that this will not be used as a good opportunity for attacking him. It must be added that the shamans are sometimes kept busy with their duties of assisting clansmen and outsiders, so that they have no time for regular hunting. Owing to this, among the Northern Tungus, the shamans usually live together with other people who do the hunting for them, look after the domesticated animals, and, in general, take care of them. However, this care never takes the form of a complete control of the shaman's life, but is done within the limits of the usual Tungus relations, when a person partly invalid is assisted by other persons of the same clan.

The female shamans, whose economic activity is different from that of male shamans, may do their work better than the males. The only difference is that a female shaman, being busy with her duties, has no time for various handwork, such as sewing or ornamentation of costumes, reindeer harness, various boxes, etc., so that the equipment of her family is not as much ornamented as that of other females who have more leisure. Since the female shaman is often called from her home, she must also have somebody to look after her home, she must also have somebody to look after her children during her absence. Should she have a suckling babe, she would take it with her; but if the children could do without her, they would be looked after by other people. In the Tungus conditions of life this is not difficult—the Tungus usually stay in groups of no less than two wigwams and very often more than two. Being an honoured person, the female shaman may also expect that other females would do some indispensable work for her, such as the curing of skins, etc. The husbands of female shamans commonly do a part of the work usually done by the wives, which, generally speaking, is not rare among the Tungus: men very often help their wives in curing skins, particularly thick, heavy skins, e.g. elk skins, bearskins, etc., are often worked only by men.

Among the Reindeer Tungus of Transbaikalia the shaman receives for his service no remuneration, with the exception of some food taken after the sacrifice; but he may receive some fresh meat as a present, like any other guest. The shamans also receive kerchieves and sometimes additions to their paraphernalia, but neither have any importance in the material support of the shaman. The shaman never receives money. Thus the shamanship cannot become a profession which may permit the shamans to live only on what they may earn for this service to the clansmen and outsiders.

Among the Tungus of Manchuria the shamans never receive any remuneration, save fresh blood from the sacrificial animal, some drink, wine either bought from the foreigners (Chinese, Russians) or made by the Tungus themselves (berry wine produced by some Tungus groups), and some presents like kerchieves attached to the shaman's coat. The shamans cannot refuse to shamanize, even when there is no wine or kerchieves. They never accept money. All Tungus assert that a shaman cannot become rich. As a matter of fact, all shamans whom I knew personally were poorer than the average Tungus. Among the Birarcen there was a female-shaman with her husband who were so poor that they lived in a corner of a house belonging to other people. The husband was not a good hunter and had to stay with his wife to look after her and their babe. They had even no clothes in sufficient quantity for going to the mountains, and the child was usually half-naked. Another shaman, among the Reindeer Tungus of Barguzin, was the poorest man in reindeer, and when I knew him he had to go on foot, two reindeer being loaded with his belongings and children. After an accident in hunting he did not believe himself able to carry on hunting as he had done before.

It may thus be said that candidates to shamanship are not stimulated by any material interest, from the point of view of which they are in an inferior position that sometimes makes their lives a continuous suffering from poverty. But it should be noted that among the Northern Tungus the shaman, if he is not a "bad-hearted" person, will not be left to starve to death and will be supported by his clansmen and "clients". But it would be the same with any other Tungus.

The position of shamans is different among the Manchus. Among them, a shaman must shamanize without remuneration only for his clansmen, but clients outside of the clan must pay him. In the description of the sacrifice were mentioned a chicken, a dollar (rouble), a piece of cloth sufficient for a small dress, etc., taken by the shaman after the shamanizing. Small as it is, this remuneration alone may support the shaman, for he can carry out at least one shamanizing a day. With the custom of prayers after the harvest, when the shaman receives presents in grain from all houses of the village and in rather large quantities from *jarumbo*,[9] the position of the shaman may become even better than that of an average Manchu. In fact, it is quite common that a shaman has twenty or thirty *jarumbo*, some of which may be rich, and every year each of them supplies him with a ton of grain. The presents gathered by the shaman on the second day of the new year are also of importance. Presents of wine, incense, candies, bread etc. from a large number of *jarun* may be numerous enough for being used during a long time, and even being sold.

However, the clan shamans, as I have shown, may be kept quite busy by their functions within the clan, so that they cannot make of shamanship a profitable profession. But the *amba saman*, who are not bound by their clans, may reach a relative prosperity.

Among the Manchus I did not observe well-to-do shamans—most of whom were clan shamans—but among the Chinese shamanship was definitely changed into a profitable profession. During my work on the spot I knew several shamans, two of whom lived quite opulently, even in the city . . . and all of which were not tilling their fields, nor carrying on any other profession than shamanizing. It seems to be that among the Dahurs there was nearly the same situation, for I have met with shamans who lived by their profession.

The rather difficult economic situation of the shamans is not alone in making their life a kind of martyrdom: the hardships of shamanizing, the responsibility and hostility are associated with poverty; moreover, his movements are bound by a great number of restrictions; the future of his soul is not certain, and above all he cannot give up his shamanship. First of all, the functions, as shown before, keep the shamans in a state of great nervous and mental tension. The latter may personally be perceived as a pleasant condition; but since after every serious shamanizing the performers feel physically tired—it is a tiresome work—the shamans, after a few years of work, sometimes become half-exhausted. This exhaustion may be due to an uneconomical use of energy in the performances, which only sometimes may be based on pure ritualism and tricks, not requiring a special tension of the psychomental complex, and which usually are based upon a real extasy. If the shaman performs too often—I

[9] A family attended by a particular shaman.

have observed among the Reindeer Tungus of Transbaikalia some cases when three performances of little shamanizing were carried out in a day; a big shamanizing was carried out every night during great gatherings for weddings, etc.—he naturally becomes tired. We have seen that the shamans themselves sometimes want to perform, which may be understood as a sign of the shaman's personal psychic instability. In case the shaman himself should be susceptible to psychomental instability, he might become the prey of his own spirits, if he does not restrict himself in practising performances. So a shaman may gradually bring himself into a state when he would even be unable to carry out his work. If there is no other, very strong, shaman, there would be nobody to help him.

The shaman, being the safety valve of the clan and a clan officer, cannot refuse to assist his clansmen. Therefore, whether he feels himself strong or not, tired or not, he must attend. However, the shaman's psychic condition is not often noticed, perhaps it is not understood, and only when he becomes psychomentally "abnormal", his state is noticed, and then it is usually regarded as an evidence of new intrigues of spirits. Thus the shaman must not neglect his duties. He may be excused only   3.1 when he is very old and physically weak, or if the shaman is a female, when she is pregnant and generally *akipcu* (tabooed). If there is no such an excuse, the shaman may lose his position; however this happens very seldom. But since in a great number of cases a person becomes a shaman because of his own psychomental condition, which requires the "mastering of spirits", he, being deprived of his right of being a shaman, may lose his recognized ability of self-control and thus become the prey of his spirits. If after giving up this social functioning and after losing his right of shamanizing he should make an attempt to restore his positon, he would come into conflict with his clan and a new shaman. So he may become a "bad-hearted" man, with all the resultant consequences. The pressure of the clan is here much stronger than in the case of a common clansman—the shaman is connected with the spirits.

Since the shaman functions as a safety valve and as a regulator of the psychic life of the clan, he lives under the permanent feeling of bearing a great responsibility. In some cases it would not be cognized at all and would not be formulated, as I do it here, but this condition is a serious factor for the shaman, for it takes the form of a complex regulation of the relations existing between the spirits and the shaman himself. However, it is possible that in some rare cases old experienced shamans may come to a formulation of the situation in terms of psychic phenomena and to their regulation, which in turn would increase both the functions and the responsibility. The feeling of responsibility is probably a condition which implies the shaman's readiness to function when needed.

The shaman meets with another difficulty in his activity, namely—   2.2 hostility. A hostile attitude may come from a smaller or greater number of clansmen and outsiders. The shaman's failure to gain a general sympathy . . . may easily grow into a general hostility. In fact, if the shaman makes mistakes in his relations with the clansmen, he cannot be successful in attending them—he will be distrusted. If any trouble should occur, it would be attributed to the shaman; he might be reproached for causing the harm. Naturally, in defending himself, he might create a new hostility, to the extent of being regarded as a "bad-hearted" man who must be thrust out of the community. Such cases become especially frequent, when the shaman does not belong to the clan. As I have shown, among all groups there are always individuals hostile to shamanism in general, so the shaman, even a little known and little experienced beginner, must gain, if not their sympathy, then at least their neutrality.

2.2   From the analysis of the relations between the shaman and the spirits, his own spirits and those of other shamans, also his spirits and the complex of other spirits, we can see a great number of various prohibitions, avoidances, tabooes, binding every step of the shaman. Even in his family the shaman must be careful not to harm his wife, if he is a male shaman, or her husband, if she is a female, not to speak of the children. The shaman must avoid harming other people as well, e.g. at the time of childbirth and menstruation, in hunting, fishing and other forms of responsible activity. The shaman's spirits, which he carries with him, may always become involved with other spirits and a continuous trouble may originate from their conflict. Owing to this the shaman is always careful when finding himself among other people, traveling and carrying on his industrial activity. This implies a special attention of the shaman to his surroundings and allows him still less freedom than that which is usually enjoyed by the Tungus. The reaction of other people on the shaman responds to his cautious behavior, so that very often the shaman becomes more or less isolated.

Finally there is a special condition more, which deprives the shaman of the usual cheefulness of the Tungus, viz. the worry about the soul. As a matter of fact, for the shamans departing this life is not as easy as for other people. The soul may remain in this world, may be captured by spirits and afterwards mastered, so that the shaman's soul instead of a settled existence in the lower world will continue to say in the middle world. This becomes a new source of trouble during his life, and every shaman is constantly worried by this idea. . . .

9
Shamanism Among the North American Eskimo

Introduction

Knud Rasmussen, whom Campbell calls a "seasoned scholar and explorer" (1959:52) and Lessa and Vogt "one of the great authorities on the Eskimo" (1965:460), was leader of the Fifth Danish Thule Expedition, which during 1921–1924 crossed the North American Arctic from Greenland to Alaska. The numerous volumes of published expedition reports are still a major source of information about Eskimo culture. A more contemporary study of the Netsilik Eskimo[1] gives us an idea of the value of Rasmussen's contribution:

> . . .in 1923 came Knud Rasmussen, the Danish ethnographer and folklorist who traveled the entire Arctic coast of North America from Igloolik to western Alaska by dog team. In the eight months he spent with the Netsilik he amassed innumerable data about the subsistence techniques, migration patterns, social organization, and, most important, the intellectual culture of the tribe. Being partly of Greenlandic origin, Rasmussen spoke the Eskimo language fluently and was already well acquainted with Eskimo mentality. This allowed him to view Netsilik culture with considerable insight and interpret it with brilliance and ease. (Balikci, 1970: xxii-xxiii)

Balikci's own study of the Netsilik "draw(s) heavily on Rasmussen's classic *Reports of the Fifth Thule Expedition*" (1970:xiv).

The expedition reports themselves are difficult for the general reader to obtain, though excerpts may be found with relative ease. For example, two narratives about shamanic activity from *Intellectual Culture of the Iglulik Eskimos* (vol. 7 of the reports) are reprinted in Lessa and Vogt (1965:410–4, 460–4). In addition there is a one-volume account by Rasmussen (1927) which includes material on shamanism. Balikci's valuable study of Netsilik shamanism is also readily available (1963, reprinted in Middleton, 1967).

In the following selections from Rasmussen's account of the Copper Eskimo (1932) I have sometimes omitted Eskimo words, giving only the English translation. Introductory comments place each of the subsections in its appropriate social context.

---

[1] The Netsilik, also called the Seal Eskimos, live on the Canadian Arctic coast between Simpson Peninsula and King William Island (Balikci, 1970:xvii), to the east of the Copper Eskimo. Rasmussen's base for his study of the latter group was on Kent Peninsula (cf. 1932:12–6).

Texts

9.1 An Eskimo shaman's struggle with the Sea Woman (Rasmussen, 1932:24–7)

> Rasmussen's Cooper Eskimo informants told him of Arnakapsha-
> luk (Sea Woman), "the big, bad woman," who with her husband,
> Igpiarjuk, and a little child lives in a bubble at the bottom of the
> sea. Since she is "the origin of all taboo" and rules over the sea
> animals, she is the most feared of all the spirits, especially "in
> winter, when the ice comes and sealing begins." For should the
> people "break their taboo," she will shut up all the sea animals
> inside her dwelling. Hunting will suddenly fail, "and then the
> people can only be saved if a shaman forces Arnakapshaluk up to
> the top of the sea."

The manner of invoking her is this: all the people of the village
gather in a festival house out on the ice. When all are there, the shaman
comes in and makes a hole inside the hut with a snow-beater. This hole
must be to the right of the entrance opening. Over this small hole is laid
a caribou-skin jacket belonging to a man who is closely associated with
the shaman and a good friend of his. The shaman then gets on his kness
under the jacket, his elbows resting on the floor, and gazes fixedly into
the hole made by the snow-beater. This hole is just like a seal's breathing
hole, and the idea is that Sea Woman should come up through it. As soon
as the shaman's preparations get to this stage, all those in the festival
house (snow hut) join in the famous hymn that is to rise with irresistible
power from inside the people like a nivajalu't: a religious song of the
same kind as a magic song. It is sung in a monotonous, slow and very
solemn melody with the following words: . . .

> Great woman down there
> Will she, I wonder, feel a desire to move?
> Great woman down there
> Will she, I wonder, feel a desire to move?
> Will she, I wonder, feel a desire to move?
> Come out, you, down there,
> Come out, you, down there!
> Those who live above you, it is said,
> Call you
> To see you, savage and snappish,
> Come out, you, down there

The following is a description of what happened at such a seance:

They continued to repeat these words until at last the shaman an-
2.13   nounced that Sea Woman was approaching, and that all the men in the
festival house should hold on to him. They immediately threw themselves upon him, for now the Sea Woman had beset him, that is to say

her soul had taken up its residence in his body, and she now spoke in a deep voice through the shaman. As a rule she would tell them that the bad hunting was the result of some taboo having been broken, and that the constantly bad weather was due to people's indifference to the traditions of their ancestors. Scarcely had she launched these accusations when the women in their fear began to confess the breaches of taboo they had committed, the men meanwhile fighting desparately with Sea woman, who had quite taken possession of the shaman's body. He writhed in pain, struck out with his fists and moaned incessantly. They kept a firm hold on him and took care especially that he did not lift his head, as the spirit of the air is capricious and the houses of men only frail. They were afraid that the Sea Woman would level the festival house with the ice and let loose fierce storms, and this was certain to happen if the shaman merely raised his head a little. Then, as soon as women and men had confessed all, the shaman cried in a loud voice that Sea Woman's lamp was once more turned the right way up—indicating that as long as bad hunting lasted the lamp always stood bottom upwards, extinguished and dark. Shortly afterwards the shaman who was still fighting with the Sea Woman, shouted that now her hair was smooth and clean again: for as long as all sins are not confessed her hair is usually in the wildest disorder. Only when everything has been put in order again does Sea Woman return to her house by the same route as she has come. A little later the crying of a child was heard, and up through the same hole in the floor of the hut came the child from the bottom of the sea, entered the body of the shaman and spoke through his mouth. It cried, and said that Sea Woman had struck it on the head with a caribou antler because it had let the beasts get out to the people. The child spoke through the shaman with the same deep voice as its mother, for all those from the bottom of the sea speak with a deep voice. Then the child disappeared, and it was now Igpiarjuk's turn to appear in the same manner as the others had done. He, too, complained that he had been misused because he had helped to release the seals. Then he disappeared into the depths and the seance was over. The beasts had come back to be hunted by the people of the village.

It is said that Sea Woman comes riding up to the festival house on a seal; this opens a way up to the surface of the sea, and it remains open just like a tube, so that both her child and her husband can easily make the journey up to the surface alone.

For four days after Sea Woman has been called up to the festival house no woman must sew and no man must do any work whatever; no block of snow must be cut and no one must drive a sledge. If the men go out to the breathing holes they must walk, and, if they catch a seal, there must be no eating of its liver out on the ice as is the usual custom.

In answer to a question it is expressly averred that it has been forgotten how Sea Woman originally got to the bottom of the sea. All that is known is that she has always been there.

Sea Woman is also called a giver of strength, because she gives people sea beasts if only they do not break their taboo.

9.2 The shaman's "tricks" and their effect upon the audience (Rasmussen, 1932:29–31)

> Rasmussen tells us that in addition to their "public obligations" (curing the sick, subduing storms, destroying evil spirits, and obtaining a supply of animals for the hunt), "every shaman is fond of demonstrating his powers by doing tricks." One of the favorites is to allow a seal thong to be cut and then to appear to restore it to its original condition.

2.1   I have myself seen this trick performed on many occasions, and noticed that besides the whole thong, the shaman had a short line of just the same thickness and appearance. It was this line that he allowed someone in the festival house to cut, and, while working to make it whole again it was never difficult to conceal the severed piece in his clothing.

2.1   There are many ways of proving that one is in communication with helping spirits. It is a very common thing that when a thong is thrown from the inside of the festival house out through the passage, it is seized by one or more spirits outside. As soon as the line is taut the shaman gets people inside to haul on to the other end of it, and sometimes the spirits show that their strength is enormous.

2.1   Another favourite trick is to hold a mitten on the end of a snow beater out into the passage and, when the beater is withdrawn, the mitten is no longer there. If it is stuck out again, the mitten reappears on it.

During one of these demonstrations at which I was present, one of the members of my expedition came unexpectedly into the passage where the spirits were supposed to be, and there he saw two men—the shaman's assistants—hastily conceal themselves in an offshoot from the passage.

At Malerualik I had the opportunity of seeing a number of seances with shamans. They were all extremely naive and easily seen through if one watched at all critically. I was mostly impressed by the manner in which the shamans tried to get into touch with their helping spirits. Qag-

2.2   taq, for instance, often shamanized in a snow hut lying next door to ours. While people sat expectantly inside the hut, tense with the uncanniness of the scene and gripped by the mysteriousness of the unknown, Qagtaq was wandering about half naked in the snowstorm outside for the pur-

2.1   pose of getting inspiration; sometimes he would lie in a snow drift, and half naked as he was, he naturally soon got into a miserable condition.

After a little while he would go into the snow hut, shivering and wretched; he was then in a state of great excitement, looked round in a bewildered manner, and then started to tell about his visions out there in the snow-storm, speaking in riddles and often entirely incomprehensibly, in a high, shrill falsetto. All one could understand was that he had seen both dead and spirits. His sentences were interrupted by wild howls, and old women, stretching their imagination to the utmost, tried to reconstruct their meaning. The women, who had had much experience of shamanizing, drew upon a very lively fantasy, and all their suggested interpretations of Qagtaq's mystic oracular words finally built up so much material to work upon, that at last it was possible to construct an account of what it was the spirits had said through the shaman. Thus it was more a reconstruction based upon guesswork than an actual announcement.

2.11

One young woman, Taiphuina, who seemed to be very intelligent, had once been a shaman disciple but had given it up, as she "could not lie well enough". The shamans sought in vain to encourage her, saying "Once you start trying, and people are listening, you can almost always hit upon something." But it was all of no use.

Taiphuina's candid admission, given in answer to some questions I put to her, aroused great merriment among the people, where there were several shamans—in fact it was they who laughed heartiest; for they knew that people were so enthralled by all that is incomprehensible between earth and sky that nothing could shake the faith of their audience when a real seance was going on, no matter what was said.

2.2

All the seances I attended while with the Musk-Ox People were extremely naive in tendency and performance. It was only at Agiaq that, during the course of a protracted snow storm, I was present at a seance that was so well thought out and performed that it really made an impression upon me. Otherwise during all seances and demonstrations the audience is credited with almost fabulous faith in the truthworthiness of the shaman and the actual presence of the spirits; to those who did not share this faith it was impossible to retain the illusion that it was higher powers that were signifying their existence. In addition, their conjuring tricks were so childish and so perfectly easy to see through that the critical looker-on could only feel astonishment that they could be taken seriously at all. It is only the psyche of the shaman and his audience that prevent the whole show from being reduced to humbug and deceit. And of this there is no question. For the shamans themselves consider their various tricks to be means that bring them in touch with the spirits. The relationship between the natural and the supernatural is in itself so problematic that it is of no consequence if there is some "cheating" in the ritual during an invocation.

2.2

9.3 A shamanic performance to calm a storm (Rasmussen, 1932:52–61)

In mid-January of 1924 Rasmussen and his small party departed
the Hudson's Bay Co. post at Kent Peninsula on a 2200 kilometer
journey which would take them westward along the northern
mainland coastline of Canada opposite Victoria and Banks Islands
to Herschel Island in Mackenzie Bay, Yukon Territory. When
they left, the temperature was −42° C. and the blowing snow
was in their faces, so that they arrived at their first camp "wind-
torn and fairly exhausted." Forced by a snowstorm to remain
there an extra day, they then travelled on in "fine and pleasantly
mild" weather until, three days later, another snowstorm threatened: ". . . drifting mists lay over the terrain, and, just when it
was impossible to get our bearings, the dogs scented man. Off we
went at a sweeping gallop, and about three o'clock we came to a
village right out on the ice, where we received a tumultuous welcome. The village consisted of forty-six people—twenty-five
males and twenty-one females—and they told us the place was
called Agiaq . . ." The people helped them cut a snow hut out of
a drift "a little way from the village," and almost immediately the
storm descended. It continued for four days ". . . with unabated
violence, and all the folks who visited us had to carry snowknives
in case they lost their way; it was barely five minutes' walk, and
yet it was as much as one's life was worth to get lost. Nevertheless
the house was continually full of guests, men, women and children—in fact infants in their amaut, and once again I could not
but admire the ability of these people to adapt themselves to nature." While at Agiaq, Rasmussen witnessed the shamanistic performance referred to in Sec. 9.2

On the third evening of the storm we were solemnly invited to attend a shaman seance in one of the snow houses. The man who invited
us was a pronouncedly blond Eskimo, bald, and with a reddish beard, as
well as a slight tinge of blue in his eyes. His name was Kigiuna, "sharp
tooth".

The storm then seemed to have culminated. We had to walk three
together in order to keep upright, and there was no knowing when one
would have to build a snow house far from the place where the ceremony
was to be held. We were all armed with large snow-knives, and, with
heads bent almost down to the ice, we pushed our way towards the little
village. Kigiuna held me by one arm, and his partner for the night by
the other.

"It is the infant Narssuk that is crying, and there is a draught through
his napkin!" And they told me the ancient myth of the giant's son who
had revenged himself upon the people who had killed his parents by
flying to the skies and turning into bad weather. In the course of the
night they now intended to find out the cause of the child's anger and try

to subdue the storm. The wind took such a hold of us that sometimes we had to stand quite still and cling on to one another to prevent being blown into the pack ice that towered round about us. The tremendous gusts from the shore lashed us like whips, and after three or four strokes we were able to proceed until the next gust, followed by the screams of the stormboy, again stopped us and almost threw us down on the ice. I think that half kilometre took us a whole hour; how glad we were when at length we spied the warm beams of the blubber lamps in the shining ice window of the festival hall! Through layers of dogs that growled and snapped at us we crawled in through the long passage till we reached the hall, where all the seats on the platforms were already occupied by men and women.

The hall consisted of two snow huts built together, the entrance leading on to the middle of the floor, and the two snow-built platforms on which one slept were opposite one another. One of the hosts, Tamuanuaq: "the little mouthful", received me cordially and conducted me to a seat. The house, which was four metres wide and six metres long, had such a high roof that the builder had had to stay it with two pieces of driftwood, which looked like magnificent pillars in the white hall of snow. And there was so much room on the floor that all the neighbours' children were able to play "catch" round the pillars during the preliminary part of the festival.

The preparations consisted of a feast of dried salmon, blubber, and frozen, unflensed seal carcases. They hacked away at the frozen dinner with big axes, and, while the warmth of the house gradually brought a flush to all faces that had been lashed by the gale and the snow, they avidly swallowed the lumps of meat after having breathed upon them so that they should not freeze the skin off lips and tongue.

"Fond of food, hardy, and always ready to feast", whispered "Eider Duck" to me, his mouth full of frozen blood.

And truly, it was not only iron stomachs that were necessary for food like this; it required strong minds to make a festival out of a snowstorm.

The shaman of the evening was Horqarnaq: "baleen", a young man with intelligent eyes and swift movements. There was no deceit in his face, and perhaps for that reason it was long before he fell into a trance. He explained to me before commencing that he had few helpers. There was his dead father's spirit and its helping spirit, a troll from the legends, a giant with claws so long that they could cut a man right through simply by scratching him; and then there was a figure that he had created himself of soft snow, shaped like a man—a spirit who came when he called. A fourth and mysterious helping spirit was a red stone called Aupilalanguaq, a remarkable stone he had once found when hunting caribou; it had a lifelike resemblance to a head and neck, and when he shot a caribou near to it he gave it a head-band of the long hairs from the neck of the animal. In this way he made his own helping spirit into a shaman and increased its power twofold.

He was now about to summon these helpers, and began the seance with a good deal of modest talk to the effect that he could not bring them to us. All the women of the village stood in a circle round him and encouraged him with cheap prattle.

"You can, and you do it so easily because you are so strong" they said flatteringly, and incessantly he repeated:

"It is a hard thing to speak the truth. It is difficult to make hidden forces appear".

His gravity and almost defiant aloofness he maintained long, but the women around him continued to excite him, and at last he slowly became seized with frenzy. Then the men joined in, the circle round him became more and more dense, and all shouted inciting things about his powers and his strength.

"Baleen's" eyes become wild. He distends them and seems to be looking out over immeasurable distance; now and then he spins round on his heel, his breathing becomes agitated, and he no longer recognizes the people round him: "Who are you?" he cries.

"Your own folks!" they answer.

"Are you all here?"

"Yes, except those two who went east on a visit".

But he seems not to hear what is said, and repeats again and again: "Who are you? Are you all here? Are you all here?"

Suddenly his wild eyes turn toward "Eider Duck" and me, and he shouts:

"Who are those two, whose faces are strange?"

"Men who are travelling round the world. Men we are pleased with. Friends who also would like to hear what wisdom you can bring us."

Again Baleen goes round the circle, looks into the eyes of all, gazes ever more wildly about him, and at last repeats like a tired man who has walked far and at last gives up:

"I cannot. I cannot."

2.13 At that moment there is a gurgling sound, and a helping spirit enters his body. A force has taken possession of him and he is no longer master of himself or his words. He dances, jumps, throws himself over among the clusters of the audience and cries to his dead father, who has become an evil spirit. It is only a year since his father died, and his mother, the

2.2 widow, still sorrowing over the loss of her provider, groans deeply, breathes heavily and tries to calm her wild son; but all the others cry in a confusion of voices, urging him to go on, and to let the spirit speak.

Baleen names several spirits of dead folks that he sees in the house among the living. He describes their appearance, old men, old women, whom he has never met, and commands the others to tell him who they are.

Bewilderment, silence, and then a whispered consultation among the women. Hesitatingly they start guessing, naming some departed person who would fit in with what the shaman has said.

"No, no, no! Not them!"

The men stand silent, waiting, while the women scream loudly in shrill discord, no longer at a loss, but excited, trying to solve the riddle. Only the widow of the dead man who is said to be present sighs in despair and rocks her head to and fro, weeping. Then suddenly an old woman, who hitherto has remained silent up on the platform, jumps forward on to the floor and shouts the names of those whom the others had not dared to let pass their lips—a couple who have just died, a man and his wife from Nagjugtoq, whose graves are still fresh.

"qanorme!"

"qanorme!"

"That is just who it is!" cries Baleen in a grating voice, and an inexplicable, sinister feeling spreads over the company, because these two people were alive among them only a few days before.

Now they had turned into evil spirits, the very evil spirits that were causing the storm. Terror spreads in the house. Life the mysterious has allowed something uncanny to sink over them all; something that no one can explain is going on, throwing everything into confusion.

Outside howls the gale. A man cannot see his hand before him, and even the dogs, which otherwise are kicked out of the house, are allowed to seek warmth and shelter among the legs of these excited people.

Two visitors, man and wife, who live just next door but have lost their way, come in now, their mouths and eyes full of snow. This is the third day of the storm. There is no meat for tomorrow, nothing to eat, nothing to make them warm, and it seems as if this menace suddenly becomes alive. The storm-boy weeps, the women weep, the men murmur incomprehensible words.

The seance has lasted an hour, an hour of howling and invoking of   2.13
unknown forces, when something happens that terrifies us, who have never before seen the storm god tamed. Baleen leaps forward and seizes good-natured old Kigiuna, who is just singing a pious song to the Mother of the Sea Beasts, grips him swiftly by the throat and brutally flings him backwards and forwards, to and fro in the midst of the crowd. At first both utter wailing, throaty screams, but little by little Kigiuna is choked and can no longer utter a sound; but suddenly there is a hiss from his lips, and he, too, has been seized with ecstasy. He no longer resists, but follows Baleen, who still has him by the throat, and they tumble about, quite out of their minds. The men of the house have to stand in front of

the big blubber lamps to prevent their being broken or upset; the women have to help the children up on to the platform to save them from being knocked to pieces in the scrimmage, and so it goes on for a little while, until Baleen has squeezed all the life out of his opponent, who is now being dragged after him like a lifeless bundle. Only then does he release his hold, and Kigiuna falls heavily to the floor.

It was the storm that was being killed in effigy. The revolt in the air demands life, and Baleen seizes Kigiuna by the back of the neck in his teeth and shakes him with all the strength of his jaws, like a dog getting the better of another.

There is a deathly silence in the house. Baleen is the only one who continues his wild dance, until in some way or other his eyes become calm and he kneels in front of the dead and starts to rub and stroke his body to revive him. Slowly Kigiuna is brought back to life, very shakily he is put on his feet, but scarcely has he come to his senses again when the same thing is repeated—the same violent grip of the throat, the same wild dance in the house, the same gasping for breath, until the poor man is again flung to the snow floor like an inanimate bundle of skins. Three times he is "killed" in this manner! Man has to display his superiority over the storm. But when Kigiuna for the third time comes to life again it is he who falls into a trance, and Baleen who collapses. The old seer rises up in his curious, much too obese might, yet rules us by the wildness in his eyes and the horrible, reddish-blue sheen that has come over his face through all the ill-usage he has been subjected to. All feel that there is a man whom death has just touched, and they involuntarily step back when, with his foot on Baleen's chest, he turns to the audience and with astonishing eloquence announces the visions he sees. With a voice that trembles with emotion he cries out over the hall:

"The sky is full of naked beings rushing through the air. Naked people, naked men, naked women, rushing along and raising gales and blizzards.

"Don't you hear the noise? It swishes like the beats of the wings of great birds up in the air. It is the fear of naked people, it is the flight of naked people!

"The weather spirit is blowing the storm out, the weather spirit is driving the sweeping snow away over the earth, and the helpless storm-child Narsuk shakes the lungs of the air with his weeping.

"Don't you hear the weeping of the child in the howling of the wind?

"And look! Among all the naked crowds of fleeing ones there is one, one single man, whom the wind has made full of holes. His body is like a sieve, and the wind whistles through the holes: Tju, tju-u, Tju-u-u! Do you hear him? He is the mightiest of all the wind-travellers.

"But my helping spirit will stop him, will stop them all. I see him coming calmly, confident of victory, towards me. He will conquer, he will

2.11

conquer! Tju, tju-u! Do you hear the wind? Sst, sst, ssst! Do you see the spirits, the weather, the storm, sweeping over us with the swish of the beat of great birds' wings?"

At these words Baleen rises from the floor, and the two shamans, 2.13 whose faces are now transfigured after this tremendous storm-sermon, sing with simple, hoarse voices a song to the Mother of the Sea Beasts:

> Woman, great woman down there,
> Send it hence, send it away from us, that evil!
> Come, come, spirit of the deep!
> One of your earth-dwellers
> Calls to you,
> Asks you bite enemies to death.
> Come, come, spirit of the deep!

When the two had sung the hymn through, all the other voices joined in, a calling, wailing chorus of distressed people. No one knew for what he was calling, no one worshipped anything; but the ancient song of their forefathers put might into their minds. They had no food to give their children when next day came. They prayed for calm so that they could hunt, for food for their young ones.

And suddenly it seemed as if nature around us became alive. We saw the storm riding across the sky in the speed and thronging of naked spirits. We saw the crowd of fleeing dead ones come sweeping through the billows of the blizzard, and all visions and sounds centered in the wing-beats of the great birds for which Kigiuna had made us strain our ears.

With this ended the struggle of the two shamans against the storm, and, consoled and reassured, all could make their way to their snow huts and compose themselves to sleep. For next day they would have fine weather.

And it came. In dazzling sunshine and hardblown drifts we went on next day, arriving in the afternoon at Tree River, where both the Hudson's Bay Company and the famous Royal Canadian Mounted Police have posts.

On behalf of the company Mr. MacGregor gave us a heaty reception, and we were his guests for a day.

AFRICA

10
Two Nuer Prophets and their Pyramid

Introduction

The Nuer are a Nilotic people of the southern Sudan. Nuer culture, which has been extensively described by E. E. Evans-Pritchard (cf. especially 1940, 1956), is centered on the herding of cattle.

Among the Nuer there is no apparent rivalry between prophets and priests. Some of the best-known prophets were also priests (Evans-Pritchard, 1956:305), and because of their "special efficacy" based on "a special and intimate association with Spirit," prophets might be asked to perform sacrifices on behalf of the people. Indeed, the unusual earthen pyramid built by the followers of the prophet, Gwek (cf. the following text), became a "cult centre" where cattle were brought for sacrifice (Evans-Pritchard, 1956:306, 308). The fact that among the Nuer "prophetic powers tend to become hereditary" suggests another area of similarity with the priests, whose office is normally hereditary (Evans-Pritchard, 1956:309; 291–3).

Differences between the two kinds of functionaries reside mainly in the "spiritual powers" which derive from the prophet being possessed (individually inspired) by God "in one or other of his hypostases," with the result that in the prophet God speaks directly to humans. As a consequence, prophets function on an occasional basis in Nuer society, while priests have "an appointed sacrificial role in certain situations of the social life, particularly in homicide and blood-feud" (Evans-Pritchard, 1956:303–4).

On the whole, however, there seems to be a tendency for the distinction between priests and prophets to become blurred. T. O. Beidelman has shown that Nuer priests sometimes tried "to augment their power and influence through charisma both in terms of political manipulation as expressed by spokesmanship and leadership in raids, and through claims to more diffuse supernatural powers." For their part, "Nuer prophets may seek to routinize their charismatic power by converting this power into corporate, more stable authority," through the construction of shrines, the performance of ceremonies, and in some cases the assumption of a hereditary succession of power (1971:388, 399–400). Largely because of this blurring and because of beliefs about possession common in Nuer society, Beidelman casts doubt upon the view of Evans-Pritchard and others that prophecy is a late phenomenon among the Nuer, arising as the result of influences from the Dinka (a neighboring tribe) and the Muslim Mahdist movement in late 19th century Sudan (1971:377, 395–6; cf. Evans-Pritchard, 1956:304, 308–10 and Jackson, 1923:90–2).

Though reported instances of prophecy among the Nuer are not numerous, the role does appear to be in harmony with basic cultural patterns. For example, the Nuer attitude toward prophets is characterized by ambivalence, reverence, and fear (Evans-Pritchard, 1956:304, 307–8). These responses are predicated upon one of the underlying assumptions of the Nuer world view, viz., that Spirit in any form is dangerous, and is therefore something to be desired (for its potential benefits), but at the same time avoided. As Beidelman puts it (1981–82:153), "spirit itself, the ultimate source of life and order, also brings disorder, sterility and death, and the immanence of Spirit in persons and things relates to negation of vitality. The Nuer view Spirit as both foe and friend."

A second example of the social patterning of Nuer prophecy relates to the overriding importance of kinship structures in Nuer society (cf. Evans-Pritchard, 1940:*passim*). Evans-Pritchard makes it clear that a number of Nuer religious concepts draw upon notions of kinship, for example, ideas about God (1956:7–8, 115–22, 320), the *colwic* (spirits of persons killed by lightning; 1956:52–62), totems (1956:64), spears (1956:238–47), and initiation (1956:258). It is therefore no surprise when we find that among the Nuer priestly powers and office are generally inherited (it is possible for a "layman" to be invested with these powers by a person of a priestly lineage; Evans-Pritchard 1956:293), and that there is a tendency for prophecy to become hereditary (1956:309; Beidelman, 1971:400).

Again, it is generally accepted among the Nuer that spirits may enter into special relations with humans by possessing one of them. Sickness is the usual symptom of such possession. Though a prophet's symptoms may differ—the focus is on his unusual actions—the Nuer have no trouble recognizing and understanding the underlying state of possession. The fact that the prophets conform to certain social expectations with respect both to possession by various spirits and their behavior while possessed is thus a further indication of patterning (Evans-Pritchard, 1956:33–48, 305–7; Beidelman, 1971:389–95).

Finally, prophecy may have roots in another Nuer institution, which Evans-Pritchard fails to discuss, viz., the *ruic*, or "spokesman" (from *ruac*, "speech, talk"; cf. B. A. Lewis, 1951). The *ruic* emerged as leader when several sections of Nuer came together in a joint undertaking, most commonly war, and Lewis names and comments on over a dozen such men. The "influence" (*ruec*) of these men derived partially from clan membership, wealth, courage, and the like, but of greatest importance were matters of "character and personality," especially oratorical skill (B. A. Lewis, 1951:79–80). As it happens, great prophets like Ngundeng and Gwek, were also both leopard-skin priests[1] and "spokesmen," and Lewis is of the opinion that their performance of tribal functions depended upon their being the latter. For this reason "the emergence of the prophets led to no changes in the structure of Nuer society" (1951:83).

This last point prompts a further observation. Some of the activities of Nuer prophets, such as healing (cf. Willis, 1928:199, and the text printed below) and leading raids against enemies, had the effect of strengthening the fabric of the traditional culture. Similarly, the prophets were unique in their ability to symbolize the unity of a tribe and to extend their influence beyond the boundaries of a given tribe. They could thus become "pivots of federation between adjacent tribes (of Nuer)," and could personify "the structural principle of opposition in its widest expression, the unity and homogeneity of Nuer against foreigners" (Evans-Pritchard, 1940:189). Beidelman's final evaluation of these prophets is that they "are charismatic, but they are not peripheral to Nuer institutions in the manner suggested by Weber's description of a prophet as a revolutionary outside the normative, authoritative system" (1971:405).

The following text illustrates a number of these points. It differs from the other selections in this chapter in having been written by a colonial administrator, whose job was to control the native people, rather than by an anthropologist, whose task would have been to describe their culture. However, if we take this bias into account, Coriat (1939) provides us with our best picture of the operation of a Nuer prophet. The account is particularly interesting in its description of the interaction between the prophet and his followers and the colonial administration.

Text (Coriat, 1939:221–38)

In 1929, there took place in the Upper Nile Province military and police operations described in Government records as "Nuer Settlement". Pacification of the turbulent clans inhabiting that part of the country was the main purpose of the "Settlement" but its cause and the events which led to Patrol S. 8 which preceded it arose out of the machinations of the Lau[2] Nuer Witchdoctor Gwek Wundeng. It is with Gwek

[1] The most prominent group of ritual experts in Nuer society (cf. Beidelman, 1971:381–5).

[2] Or, Lou; one of the Nuer tribes.

and the Pyramid of Dengkur with which he was associated that this narrative is chiefly concerned but no account of either would be complete without mention of Gwek's father Wundeng and an endeavour must be made to shed some light on the latter's history before any clear picture can be given of the former.

Fiction and fact are inseparable from the welter of myth and fable in which is hidden the story of Wundeng Bung. The most notorious and possibly the first of the Nuer *Kujurs* or Witchdoctors, who until recently have been so much to the fore in our contacts with these tribes, a great part of his early life and time must be conjecture but this brief sketch for which I make no claim to accuracy has been drawn from some of the more generally known of the countless tales related from many sources.

The son of a tribesman with the euphonic name of Bung, Wundeng was born at Keij in the country of the Gatlek section of the Lau Nuer sometime between the years 1850 and 1860. His family belonged to a "Leopard Skin" clan and as such ranked as leaders in the Nuer hierarchy. By birth, therefore, his status was that of a full-blooded Nuer. There is, however, reason to believe that he was of partly Dinka extraction. Many of his relatives were Dinkas, he is known to have spoken the Dinka language fluently and he appears, throughout his life, to have been influenced by the manners and customs of that tribe. In character, if this can be judged by what we know of him, he was more typically Dinka than Nuer while the fact that his family held title to bear the "Leopard Skin" does not repudiate a Dinka orgin, as few of the Nuer clans were of pure descent and the admixture of Dinka was strong among the Lau.

Legend has it that the young Wundeng was "possessed of God" long before his initiation as an adult, so that we may assume also that his apprenticeship as a Wizard was served under a Dinka master, as at that period of Nuer history magic was the prerogative of the "Leopard Skin" or "Man of the Cattle" and was severely restricted in its use to the rituals and ceremonies of tribal custom, whereas in Dinka land, magicians and sooth-sayers were so to speak common property. At a time when his con-

1.2   temporaries were learning how to use a fish spear, Wundeng was mumbling incantations and making sacrifices of other people's goats much to the dismay of his family and the neighbours. One of the more common of his boyish pranks was temporarily to deprive of the power of speech anyone from whom he took offence and it is related that his mother alone was immune from his form of wizardry. For a boy, even one who would eventually wear the "Leopard Skin," such an unusual predilection for the black arts was regarded as some extraordinary manifestation of the "Spirits", to be treated with the respect it deserved. Matters reached such a pass it is said that many of the inhabitants of Keij moved for their greater comfort to more distant homes. It was as well for them they did so while the going was good, as in later years it was more than life was worth to offend the Wundeng dignity.

When of an age, Wundeng underwent the usual tribal initiation ceremony whereby he became a fully fledged warrior and assumed the privilege of his family by donning the "Leopard Skin". Thereafter for a year or two he carried out the normal duties of his office; hearing disputes concerning land and assisting in the settlement of blood-feuds. Then tiring of dull routine he reverted to his magic. "Leopard Skin" functions were relegated to the background while he added to his reputation as a worker of miracles. Before long he had become the most powerful individual in Lau and stories of his skill spread far beyond the confines of his own tribe. Many could testify to his cures of the sick and crippled, the potency of his spells and charms for procuring fertility in a barren woman or ridding one of a tiresome enemy, and the dire evil that befell anyone who so much as winked an eyelid at him. Fame brought wives and cattle in untold numbers but wealth alone did not satisfy him. It was by his success as a magician that he measured his ambition.

It is related that on the occasion of the birth of his eldest son Reth, he announced that the particular and potent Spirit by whom he was "possessed" and from whom he obtained his magical powers was one Dengkur. *Deng* is the Dinka name for the great spirit or Godhead. *Kur* in Nuer means War or Anger. Dengkur the God of War or the Wrathful God. A foreign sounding name to Nuer ears but adequate and awe-inspiring, and it was as the Dengkur that Wundeng became so widely known to the tribe of the Upper Nile.

It was soon after his *debut* as the Dengkur that Wundeng embarked on his greatest achievement, the construction of the huge earth work which became known as the Pyramid of Dengkur. How the idea of a Pyramid arose is a mystery but we may surmise that here again the conception was of Dinka origin.[3] The grave shrine, a mound of earth 3 ft. by 4 ft. high, adorned with beads and trinkets was a common sight in the Dinka country, but unknown to the Nuer. Perhaps it was the Dinka shrine that gave Wundeng his inspiration but whatever its origin the great pyramidal mound of earth far surpassed anything seen or heard of by either Nuer or Dinka.

There were three phases of the work before the Pyramid was finished. The first consisted in the building of huts at Keij. Until these were completed clients were compelled to pay for Wundeng's services in grass, timber or building labour. For the whole of one winter season, it is said work on the huts was unceasing. The second phase which lasted

[3] Alban (1940:201) suggests that the pyramid was built in order to counteract an epidemic of smallpox and rinderpest.

for two years concerned the food supply. During that period, no visitor or traveller, man, woman or child who did not wish to risk incurring the displeasure of the great Dengkur could visit or pass by the village of Keij without depositing in the store huts a handful of grain or a head of corn. When the granaries were full and an adequate food supply had been assured Wundeng entered upon the final stage. First, it is said, he shut himself up in his hut and refused to see or speak with anyone or to partake of food and drink for seven days. He then fell into a trance from which he did not awake until three days and three nights had passed. According to some accounts, he perched himself upon the roof of a cattle hut before falling into a state of insensibility, remaining on the top while vast crowds collected to see the performance. At the end of this period word was passed far and wide summoning all tribesmen of the Nuer clans to a gathering at Keij on the full moon of the month of the saving. Story has it that for days the plain of Keij was black with people. Blood feuds were forgotten. Not only from the Lau country but from the Garjak on the Abyssinian border, from the Gaweir of the Zeraf valley from the Nuong of the Jebel river and even from the Bul country north of the Bahr El Ghazal tribesmen foregathered at the behest of Wundeng. On the night of the full moon, in the light of a circle of fires Wundeng gave expression to the commands of the Spirit. Throughout the night he stood shouting exhortations to the assembled warriors. At dawn on the following morning he carried the first load of earth to the site he had chosen for his *Luak Kwoth* (House of God) and thus was begun the building of the Pyramid itself. From that hour until it was completed he supervised and controlled the work of thousands of Nuer. Mud was dug from adjacent pools and khors and carried in baskets to the ground where it was shaped and pounded to the required dimensions. As the mound rose in height, tiers of workers handed up the baskets to others above them. Bulls were brought from all over Nuer land and the meat was divided and eaten by the builders. When there was a shortage of bulls, corn was distributed from the granaries. Day after day the work continued. It is believed that four rain seasons passed before the *Bie Dengkur* (mound of Dengkur) was finished. A Pyramid of earth 60 feet high and of great breadth resembling a sugar loaf with a bulging base. On its apex and round the base were planted elephant tusks and in the heart of the earthwork, put there by Wundeng during the course of the building were embedded the horns of a white bull, the entrails of a goat and an assortment of bones.

Soon after the Pyramid was built the slave-raiders made themselves felt in Lau and Wundeng's power began to wane. Twice are the slave bands said to have attacked Dengkur carrying off all the people and ivory they could lay their hands on. Villages were laid waste, tribal organisation was broken up and the clans were scattered to the remotest parts of

the depredations of the Arabs. Nevertheless, although fear of the "Turk"   2.2
became greater than fear of Wundeng, the Pyramid was kept in good
repair and was a rallying ground for the warriors. In fact so prominent a
place had it taken in the life of the tribe that even in 1927 there were
many who believed that the new "Turk", small-pox, cattle disease and
other horrors were due to neglect of the *Bie Dengkur* and the wrath of
the Spirit.

Wundeng did not, so far as is known, try his hand against the Arabs,
and his spies kept him sufficiently well informed to enable him to show
a clean pair of heels when the "Turk" was in the vicinity. On occasions he
visited the Pyramid though he had deserted his village. Alarms and escapes and a scattered people gave him little opportunity for the display
of magic, but when he could he made encouraging prophecies and con-
cocted plausible excuses for his impotence to stem the ravages of the
foreigners.

It was during the Arab era that he had made for him by an old Anuak   2.3
friend a brass pipe. The pipe was made secretly and its existence was not
known until, during one of Wundeng's visits to the Pyramid when he
was accompanied by a large following, it was seen, to the astonishment
of the beholders, on the topmost point of the Pyramid with wreaths of
smoke issuing from the bowl. The Pipe of Dengkur though seen by few
became one of the greater of the Wundeng mysteries. Not only was its
possessor said to be invulnerable but it had peculiar properties as a
death-dealing instrument. At sacrifices and rites conducted by Wundeng
cattle were struck dead by a mere wave of the Pipe and it was whispered
that a few humans had also met their end in this way. Wundeng allowed
it to be known that the Pipe had been bestowed on him by the Great
Spirit and that it would, when the time arrived take its part in destroying
the enemies of the Nuer and ridding the country of the hated "Turk".

There is little of interest to recount, though many are the stories told
of the remaining years of Wundeng's life. He was still alive at the time of
the (British) occupation but took no part in the subsequent encounters
with the new "Turk" although the Pyramid was twice visited by Government troops. As affairs in Lau resumed a more or less normal state after
the departure of the Arabs, he again took up residence at Keij and continued to excel as a witchdoctor, but by that time other and smaller fry
had to begun to emulate his lead and he was too old or too weary to do
more than organise raids against the Dinka. He died at Keij in March
1906.

In about 1883 a son was born to Wundeng by one of his many wives.
He was named "Gwek" (the Frog) a fitting name for him in later years
with his misshapen arms and legs, squat body and short toad-like head.
The resemblance to a frog was enhanced by an unpleasant tendency to
slaver at the mouth. A morose sullen lad, Gwek had been an unlikely

person to succeed his father and after the latter's death it was believed
that the "Spirit" had taken possession of the eldest son Reth. It was soon
evident however that it was Gwek not Reth who had been adopted by
the Dengkur. This was apparent by Gwek's peculiar antics, balancing on
his head on the top of the Pyramid, yelling and chattering in an unknown
tongue during the small hours of the night, turning himself into a goat
and other habits of a similar nature. That there could be no mistake
about the matter was made clear when he was seen to spend several days
on the top of the Pyramid holding aloft the Pipe of Dengkur. Until then
the Pipe had only been seen with Wundeng and it was believed to have
returned to the 'Spirit' when the former died.

In his prime and when not in a trance Gwek had a stupid and rather
sheepish air about him. Although not in the same class as his father in
the magical line he inherited a good deal of the paternal cunning. He
was particularly successful in curing barrenness (possibly because it was
one of the more lucrative of his accomplishments) and an adept at falling
into a trance. It was almost a daily occurrrence to him to be "seized by
the Spirit" when he would appear to be overcome by something very
like an epileptic seizure. In these moods he would stand trembling and
shaking in every limb, foam at the mouth and utter blood-curdling cries.
Sometimes he would stand on the top of the Pyramid and yell to the full
extent of his lungs and usually on these occasions the performance would
conclude with an impassioned speech in which he would make vague
prophecies for the future. Although many had seen Gwek on the top of
the Pyramid, no one had been known to see him climb up or down.
Possibly, at such times it was thought proper to look the other way. On
the three occasions in 1923 and 1924 when I saw Gwek on the Pyramid
each time he went up during the night, spent the day on the top and
came down again the following night so I was unable to view either the
ascent or descent. Climbing the Pyramid was not easy. In 1928 at the
time of the S. 8 Patrol a trooper of the Cavalry and Mounted Rifles (now
Shendi Horse) succeeded in getting up in his bare feet without much ado
but when I followed suit after having discarded my boots, it was as much
as I could do to reach half way, as the smooth surface offered no holds.
To save an ignominious retreat I had to be hauled up the final pitch with
the aid of the soldier's cummerbund. The last part of the return journey
was accomplished by an involuntary and painful slide.

Two Patrols visited the Lau country in the early days of the administration but Gwek was not seen nor much heard of until 1918 when he
organized an attack on a company of the 9th Sudanese under a Native
Officer, which was on a reconnaissance from Duk Fadiat. The troops put
up a good fight but were outnumbered and all killed. This and other
incidents culminating in a series of raids on the Dinkas led to the Lau
Patrol of 1918. Government forces were concentrated at Nyerol just

south of the Dinka border and from there advanced into the country. Within a few miles of the Pyramid at Nyownyow the column was attacked by a body of Nuer led by Gwek in person. A white bull was driven in front of the advancing tribesmen but a burst of machine gun fire made short work of the bovine advance guard and the beast fell with its hear towards the Nuer. Such an unpropitious omen was the signal for immediate retreat and Gwek escaped in the rout, his followers suffering heavy casualties. There was no further resistance to the Government. The troops continued the march to the Pyramid and other parts of the country were visited before they returned home. At the conclusion of operations an attempt was made to administer the Lau by more frequent visits and a post was established at Nyerol but Gwek, like his father, kept at a distance.

In 1921 rumours of an impending raid by the Lau against the Dinka of Duk Fadiat (then a Government Station) caused a commotion on the Dinka border and produced a stream of complaints real and imaginary against the Neur. To allay Dinka anxiety, Mr. H. C. Jackson then Deputy Governor of the Upper Nile Province made a tour of the Lau country, during the course of which he visited the Pyramid. He was accompanied by the Senior Medical Inspector, Mr. H. C. Footner, and travelled with a small escort of Police. On their arrival at the Pyramid, they were, contrary to expectation, met by Gwek in person but the moment Mr. Jackson dismounted from his horse Gwek became "possessed" and yelled solidly for half an hour. At the end of this exhibition, however, he behaved as the perfect host and during the ensuing long and useful discussion he denied any ill will towards the Dinka, gave assurances that he would be friendly to the Government and agreed to pay a yearly tribute of one bull. His one request which was acceded to was that a half brother of his, Bul Wundeng, a stupid and furtive looking youth should *Kab Bieni* (take the cloth) and act as his representative in any further dealings with the Government.

Nothing more was heard of Gwek until the April of 1923 at which time I was stationed at Ayod Post in the Gaweir Nuer country. Owing to disturbing reports which were circulating of a tribal raid which Gwek intended to lead against the Dinka on his southern border, I thought it necessary to make an unannounced call at the Pyramid. Accordingly I set off and after a three days' march arrived shortly after sunset one evening. A very cold welcome awaited me. Bul and several of the elders of the village came out to meet me but it was clear that I was not wanted. I was told that Gwek was at home but was engaged and unable to see me. There was a good deal of demur when I said I proposed to make a stay but after some discussion camp was pitched close by the Pyramid on the far side from the village and my party settled down for the night. The following morning just before dawn I was awakened by loud shouts and   2.1

cries which seemed to emanate from some point high up on the Pyramid. The incessant noise prevented further sleep and the morning light disclosed Gwek standing erect on the top and still shouting raucously. For the whole of that day he remained in more or less the same attitude, shouting most of the time. A curious spectacle and a remarkable exhibition of endurance. Later in the morning Bul and other members of the family came to see me and suggested that I should call again in a year's time but I explained that I quite understood that Gwek was unable to confer to the best advantage when "possessed" and that I should wait in camp until the "Spirit" had retired. There was no sign of Gwek the next day nor on the three very long days which followed but on the fourth morning he appeared by my police lines leading an emaciated and hungry looking bull and followed by what appeared to be the entire population of Keij. After suitable introduction had been made the bull was presented as a gift, was accepted and carried off to its fate by the Police and Gwek and I moved to my tent where we settled down to talk to each other. Except for a slightly peeved air Gwek seemed quite ready to talk and by the evening we were almost affable together.

Further visits followed during the course of the next few years and on one occasion in 1925 Gwek visited District Headquarters which had by that time been moved to Abwong. He arrived with a small army of followers and laden with gifts. Much friendly talk ensued and many protestations of good will to the Government were made before the conclusion of the visit. During this tranquil period there were few clashes with authority although some uneasiness was caused at times by minor raids against the Dinka and in 1926 relations became a little strained as a result of a habit Gwek had begun to acquire of making frequent tours in the neighbouring Jekaing Nuer country accompanied by tax evaders and other ne'er-do-wells.

Early in 1927 as an outcome of the policy of Devolution, Chiefs' Courts were set up among the Lau and a band of Chiefs' Police was formed to assist the Courts. The Police differed from the habitual nude state of the tribesmen only in that they wore an embossed white metal armlet. Whether it was the uniform or some other attraction the force became universally popular with the young warriors who found the work a new outlet for their energies. The success of the Police as a Government institution gave an impetus to the Courts which rapidly became the centre of tribal life. Hours could be spent arguing over the ownership of a prize cow or discussing tribal politics and a good audience was always assured. The fairness of the decisions given and the promptness with which they were enforced by the Chief's Police did not impress
3.11 Gwek who began to find his income adversely affected. Many of those who would normally have turned to him in the hope of obtaining justice

by payment of a small reward went instead to the Courts. Others who desired to effect some knavery by presenting him with a suitable gift found their efforts frustrated by these same Courts whose members were versed in all the wiles of the Witchdoctor.

Gwek bore for a while and then prepared to strike. Alarming rumours began to spread and gather weight. The courts were a ruse of the "Turk" to destroy tribal custom. Chiefs' Police would be absorbed into the ranks of the"Turk's" soldiers. These and similar stories were freely discussed. Within a month there was a perceptible change. Chiefs evaded attendance at the Courts, Chiefs' Police were absent when their services were needed and an atmosphere of general uneasiness prevailed until the end of the dry season when Gwek showed his hand for the first time. A new road had be then been cleared from the Sobat river at the mouth of the Khor Fulus to Kan on the southern edge of the Dinka border. It had been proposed to carry the road through the Lau country to the Duk Fadiat Dinka border and thus to open communications between Bor and the Sobat. In order to broach the subject of roads which I knew was not likely to be a popular one, I summoned a meeting of Chiefs and Elders to meet me at Nyerol. Gwek was also invited. I had expected a half hearted response but all the Chiefs and many of the Elders appeared. Gwek however, was not present. Disregarding his absence I set about the purpose of the meeting and explained the objects of a road and roads to the tribesmen but my attempts to raise an interest met with no response. There was a sullen and apathetic air about the meeting quite unlike the hearty gatherings common to the Nuer. It was while I was labouring heavily on the benefits conferred by easy communications that the sound of singing was heard. From the trees at the fringe of the camp emerged a group of Nuer 40 to 50 strong all singing heartily and led by an individual whom I soon recognized as Gwek. Advancing to the group of Chiefs who were seated in a semi-circle faicng me, Gwek held up his hand for the chorus to cease and stepping past the men in front of him squatted down beside the senior Chiefs present. There was no surprise evinced at his arrival and as there was much ostentatious movement to the side to make way for him it was obvious that he had been expected. Gwek spoke no word and made no signal of any kind but sat staring at the ground in front of him. I retorted by ignoring the interruption and continuing my discourse on roads but I had not spoken for more than ten minutes before Gwek rose to his feet. "The Lau know not how to make roads. Drive your Dinkas. Let the road be for such as the Dinkas" and with that he stalked off accompanied by his chorus who again broke into song as they vanished from sight into the trees. I felt prompted to do several things but chose the alternative I liked least by assuming an air of indifference to the episode. A desultory

3.2

and uncomfortable quarter-hour followed after which, expressing the hope that the coming dry season would see the road well on its way to the south, I left the meeting.

Leave followed shortly after this but just before my departure, two Chief's Police came to see me. With some hesitance they explained that they were anxious for my safety and had come to tell me not to venture into the Lau without an escort of soldiers. They told a long story the gist of which was that Gwek intended to make war, that the opening of a road to the Dinka border had caused much alarm among the Nuer and that any continuation of the highway into the Lau country would be the signal for a general rising. They described how Gwek had reminded the people of a forgotten prophecy of Wundeng's that the Turk would many times defeat the Nuer in battle but that a time would come when the Turk would make a great white path through the Dinka country. When that path reached the Nuer border, a plant would sprout on the peak of the Dengkur pyramid. The plant would grow till it reached the height of a man. The Nuer would then rise and drive out the "Turk" for ever. The plant, my informants said, had been seen by all who visited the Pyramid. These two youths accompanied me to Malakal where they remained during my absence on leave and were with me subsequently throughout the operations of the S. 8 Patrol and the Nuer Settlement in the year following.

Nearly four months later I arrived in Khartoum on return from leave to hear that the District was in a state of revolt and that punitive measures were contemplated. Continuing my journey to Abwong by air I arrived at the Station within a day and there learned the full account of events during my absence. Gwek had sent his emissaries to all parts of Lau and to neighbouring Nuer tribes exhorting the warriors to prepare for a war against the "Turk." War drums had been beaten and hundreds of bulls slaughtered as sacrifices at the Pyramid. Dinkas on the Nuer border had evacuated their homes and gone for protection to the Government Posts at Abwong and Duk Fayuil. Other reports alleged that two well known lesser Witchdoctors, Char Koryom and Pok Keirjok, had marched to the Pyramid with several hundred tribesmen to await Gwek's orders. As is usual at such times it was difficult to sift the grain from the chaff and in an endeavour to discover how far the state of excitement had spread I left for Nyerol with a troop of mounted Police as escort. I had hoped to make contact with some of the Chiefs whose sections were alleged to be disaffected but it was obvious before I reached the Dinka border that the trouble was real. Owing to the difficulty of ensuring protection at night I was compelled to turn back at Nyerol. Punitive action was unavoidable and Patrol S. 8 of 1928 was the outcome.

It is unnecessary to describe the operations which followed. Suffice it that a large body of show-moving troops had the effect of frightening

Gwek and dispersing his warriors. The young men went for their health to the territory of neighbouring tribes leaving the aged, the women and the children to greet the troops. There was no fighting and by the time the force had reached the Pyramid most of the Chiefs had submitted. Surprise raids on villages reported to be harbouring the Witchdoctors ceased to be a surprise by the time the objective was reached. The only diverting incident in a series of long and ineffective marches was the surrender of the Witchdoctor Char Koryom who gave himself up with his entire clan 200 strong after seeing a Royal Air Force aircraft fly over his camp. He was arrested, marched as a prisoner to the base camp at Nyerol and securely fastened with head ropes to a log of wood. He escaped the night of his arrival, by freeing himself of his shackles and leaping over a line of sleeping men, a sentry with rifle and fixed bayonet and a stout 5 feet thorn zariba.

To round off the operations and impress the Nuer the Pyramid was demolished or partly demolished by the Engineer troops. After a week's hard work a charge of high explosive was lodged in the far end of a tunnel dug into the base of the Pyramid. Chiefs and their followers were then assembled to watch it go off. They were told to keep their eyes on the Pyramid which would vanish with a reverberating bang when I droppeed my handkerchief. The result was something of an anti-climax. A puff of white smoke and a few lumps of earth tumbling down the side was all they saw but fortunately, if one could judge from their expressions, the effect was adequate. Excavation into the bowels of the Pyramid produced nothing but the horns of a bull.

After the withdrawal of the troops affairs resumed their normal course but nothing was heard of Gwek and an undercurrent of uneasiness was apparent. It was not however until the rains that unrest broke out again. During the absence on leave of the District Commissioner, the Nuer attacked the station at Duk Fayuil after a large tribal raid into the Dinka country during which they carried off cattle and slaves in great numbers. Fortunately the Police Sergeant at Duk Fayuil, one "Kalam Sakit", belied his name to good effect as the Nuer were repelled with heavy casualties. The raiders were led by the Gaweir Nuer chief Dwal Diu who until then had taken no part in the earlier disturbances but there was clear proof that Gwek had been the influence behind Dwal's fall from grace.

It was evident that until Gwek could be arrested there could be no peaceful administration in the Nuer country and that unless a decisive lesson could be applied to the affected areas, the trouble was likely to be contagious. The difficulty was how to do so. The effect of past Patrols had not been lasting. The movements of large bodies of troops disturbed the country without giving the young tribesman a taste of the corrective medicine he needed. A display of force dispersed warrior bands but did not lessen their desire for plunder or war on tip-and-run lines. the Nuer Settlement supplied the answer.

The Nuer Settlement was the name given to a plan of operations whose purpose briefly was to effect the capture of Gwek and other Witchdoctors, to disperse rebellious elements, to prevent so far as possible a disruption in the normal life of the tribe and to ensure that all peacefull minded tribespeople should not be drawn into such active operations as might be necessary to secure the submission or defeat of Gwek and his followers. To carry out the plan three conditions were essential. The first was that only small bodies of the most mobile troops should be used under the guise of police rather than military operations. The second was that the military and political officers should act so far as possible on local initiative and guided by local conditions, free from any centralised plan of operations. The third was that certain defined areas in which there was ample water and grazing for cattle should be allocated under the control and supervision of political officers for the settlement of peaceful elements. A carefuly worked out plan enabled all these conditions to be fulfilled. Two large areas were reserved for settlement. The one was on the Khor Fulus for the Gun section of the tribe and the other on the Sobat river for the Mor clans. Explicit instructions were issued by verbal explanation to all Chiefs and others whom it was possible to summon and by message to all parts of the Lau countrty. Directions were given for the movement of all able-bodied men, women and children with their cattle and chattels to camps within the two settlement areas. Ample time was allowed for the thousands of people and vast herds of cattle involved. It is as well to point out here that this forcible movement of population on such a large scale is not as horrifying as it sounds. All the Lau clans are semi-nomadic and a general exodus from rain season villages to distant dry season summer camping grounds is a normal part of tribal life. The tribesmen were warned that after the expiration of a time limit all men found outside the settlements were liable to arrest. It was hoped by such means to induce Gwek and his followers either to submit or to fight. At suitable places adjacent to each one of the areas a perimeter camp was constructed and garrisoned by a company of the Equatorial Corps. These were to afford protection to the occupants of the areas and to serve as bases of operations for the mobile troops. At each base a mobile column was formed of troops of Calvary and Mounted Rifles and Mounted Police. Guncol column was to operate within the territory inhabited by Gun section of the tribe in which was situated the Dengkur Pyramid. The Morcol column for patrol of the Mor section country. The period of time allowed for the transfer of the clans to the settlement areas expired on February lst, 1929. By that time nearly two thirds of the tribe had concentrated within these areas.

On the evening of the 31st January the Guncol force consisting of two troops of Cavalry and Mounted Rifles and one troop of Mounted Police moved out from the base camp on a night march to the Pyramid. The column was commanded by Captain G. Eastwood with Captain F. Goring-Johnstone as his second in command. Major Wyld and myself acted as political officers. From information that had been obtained it was believed that Gwek with a large following was at the Pyramid but it was not known whether he intended to offer resistance or would escape as he had done during Patrol S. 8. Owing to the uncertainty of Gwek's line of action it had been decided to march during the night but not to arrive at the Pyramid before daylight. In order that there should be no ineffectives all transport was left at the base. By midnight the force was within 5 miles of Dengkur and a halt was called until an hour before the dawn. Two Nuer walked in during the night with the information that large bodies of men had been converging on the Pyramid and that Gwek was preparing to attack the Government force whose arrival was expected. This was cheeful news and shortly after the march was resumed the sound of drums being beaten was heard in the distance. When the dawn came and the light grew clearer the peak of Dengkur Pyramid was visible in the far distance and before long our scouts could be seen signalling "enemy in sight in large numbers." Shortly they were galloping back to report large concentrations of Nuer. By 5.30 A.M. the Pyramid was in full view. Clustered at the base and massed in groups between the Government force and the Pyramid were large numbers of tribesmen. The din of war drums was incessant and several individuals were seen rushing to and fro between the larger groups brandishing spears. When within 400 yards of the Nuer the troops were halted and the order given to dismount and form square. The Nuer by this time were clearly visible. Dancing round war drums, rushing to and fro violently flourishing their spears and uttering raucous war cries. There was no attempt to impede the troops so a further advance was made without altering formation, each man leading his horse. About 50 yards on a small bull was discovered lying trussed to a stake driven into the ground and its head directed to the advancing troops. The bull was released and the advance continued but the Nuer still forbore to attack. Within 250 yards of the Pyramid, Major Wyld and I cantered our horses out in an endeavour to draw the warriors but this had no effect on the dancing hordes and the column was again halted. Two shots were then fired over the heads of the mass. This produced an immediate result and with amazing rapidity the Nuer attack was launched. Two long lines of men rushed out to either flank in an attempt to surround the troops while the main body of Nuer in the centre advanced more slowly but singing lustily and driving ahead of them a solitary white bull. The order to fire was given. The leading men and the bull reached to within 120 yards of the square before they fell and within a few minutes the whole mass of Nuer were fleeing in all directions. A long pursuit over rough and broken ground followed. Gwek, arrayed in a leather skirt with an iron skewer clutched tight in his hand and a brass pipe, the pipe of Dengkur, lying beside him, was picked up dead beside the white bull.

There was little more work for the troops and within a month there was complete submission of the remaining clans. By the end of that dry season the Lau had forgotten Gwek and the Pyramid of Dengkur.

One of Gwek's chief songsters was wounded and captured at the battle of the Pyramid. From him it was learned that Gwek had told his followers that the bullets from the Government rifles would be as water and drop to the ground. On being questioned as to whether he believed in Gwek's magic power he scoffed at the idea. He was then asked why he had supported Gwek. "Would you" he said "if you have a master, turn on him in his hour of need?" Which is typical of the Nuer character.

11
Spirit Mediums Among the Shona

Introduction

Among the Bantu-speaking peoples of what are today Zimbabwe and Zambia, prophecy occurs in a well-defined system of spirit mediumship and in connection with the centralized cult of the high-god, Mwari. Although the literature tends to refer to these functionaries as mediums, I am choosing to treat them as prophet-like intermediaries, since their entrance into their roles is predicated on a "call" involving dreams and strange behavior (Garbett, 1966:146; 1969:115; Colson, 1969:73–4). In addition they are subject to possession, and "when 'possessed' they speak as long-dead spirits" (Garbett, 1969:106). Ranger gives two instances which occurred during the rebellions of 1896 and 1897 of such messages causing the natives to take up arms and kill whites (1966:109–10, 128–9; cf. also Fry, 1976:27, 30; Daneel, 1970:42, 44, 50, 80; Colson, 1969:71). It should be noted that possession in itself is not sufficient for the assumption of this role, since among the Shona, spirit possession is rather common, but spirit mediumship is "comparatively rare" (Garbett, 1969:105; Colson, 1969:90, 94; cf. Daneel, 1970:55). Among the Korekore a candidate for mediumship should be sponsored by an acting medium, and must undergo rigorous tests before being accepted into the office (Garbett, 1969:115–6). This leads Fry to describe Korekore spirit mediumship as a "bureaucratic structure" characterized by "ossified charisma" rather than "personal charisma" (1976:56–62), though it should be remembered that there are variations among the different groups of the region.

Social patterning of the organizational features of Shona spirit mediumship is everywhere evident. In one of its aspects this patterning is territorial, the entire land being conceived of as divided into a series of units of increasing size and comprehensiveness: land shrine neighborhoods, spirit provinces, spirit realms, and (in situations like the rebellion of 1896) linkages of spirit realms (Garbett, 1966:141–4). These units have a mythico-historical base, insofar as each "is associated with, and often named after, one of the original Karanga invaders, or a descendant of one of the invaders, or occasionally an autochthon" (Garbett, 1966:141). It is possible that there is some connection between "the extensive organization associated with the cult of the spirit mediums" and the ancient Monomotapa kingdom (Garbett, 1966:139).

These territorial units also have a kinship base. The spirits of these original men are the guardians of their respective spirit provinces, and "are believed to protect the fertility of the earth and control rainfall." Further, the various spirit guardians are genealogically related to each other, and the mediums hierarchically ranked according to the genealogical seniority of the spirit guardian each represents (Garbett, 1966:141). Garbett notes that the lineal descendants of the Karanga invaders are prone to consider themselves the only "true" Korekore, though they are only part of a larger group of people that speak the Korekore language and follow Korekore customs (1966:138–9).

The territorial aspect is independent from the political organization of chiefdoms. Spirit province boundaries may overlap several chiefdoms, or they may be ancient chiefdoms that have lost their political function and acquired a ritual one (Garbett, 1966:144). Regardless, when the focus is on matters connected with territory, one consults the spirit medium of the area in which one's garden is located.

The patterning also has a lineal aspect. There is a direct link between chiefs and the cult of the spirit mediums. Some of the spirit guardians are, in fact, "royal ancestors, who have living patrilineal descendants, and . . . are represented by mediums" (Garbett, 1966:145). A kinship base is in evidence here: living rulers are aided by their ancestors (cf. Kopytoff, 1971), and considerable attention is paid to the genealogical hierarchy of the mediums themselves. This results in a change in procedure from that just described: to consult a medium as the representative of an ancestor, one comes to him from wherever one resides.

One other aspect of patterning may be mentioned, viz., the apparent conformity of the message of these mediums itself to the expectations of the society. The clue here is that, when asked a question, the medium often does not reply at once, but "may order beer to be brewed and say that 'he' (i.e., the spirit guardian/ancestor) will go away and consult with the 'other spirits' and deliver his answer at some future time" (Garbett, 1966:147–8, 155; 1969:119). Such delays are a common enough feature of the operation of mediums that observers are led to suspect their function is to allow public opinion on the matter to solidify and be discerned by the medium. A similar concern is probable even when there is no delay in rendering the decision. Fry has described the grounds for success of one medium in this way: "(his) divinatory technique was based to a large extent on his empirical awareness of the regularities of Zezuru social structure. Due to the great number of divinations which he had carried out he was aware of the structural tensions in Zezuru society and on the basis of this knowledge he was able to predict tensions in particular situations which appeared to his clients as miraculous insight." In a word, his "socio-psychological insights were perceived as divine revelations" by his audience. Fry also suggests the possibility that while in trance the diviners' "intuition" may provide them with "insights which would escape them in more 'ordinary' states of mind" (1976:35).

Returning to the matter of differences among the various groups of this region, Colson informs us that, in contrast to the territorial and lineal patterning of Korekore spirit mediumship described above, Tonga prophets operate independently and have not developed an elaborate cult. Mediums are treated like ordinary members of the community, which corresponds to the traditional culture's lack of rank or elaborate social organization. Among the Tonga, households are expected to be independent and leadership "situational," and men turn to the basangu spirits (spirits particularly concerned with "community welfare") "only in emergencies." Thus, despite apparent borrowing of ideas about spirit mediumship from the Shona (especially the Korekore and Zezuru), the organization of Tonga mediums has conformed to established social patterns (1969:74–8).

As to the difference between Korekore and Zezuru mentioned in passing earlier, Fry argues that "the Korekore are much more concerned with *controlling* spirit-mediumship than are the Zezuru," and connects that fact with the relatively greater amount of control the Korekore are able to exercise over their "social experience" in general.

> While the Zezuru experience rapid change, and unpredictable future, rapid economic or political success on the basis of personal charisma, and diminishing control in terms of grid and group, so their religious life features dynamic charismatic spirit-mediums and highly fluid and little-controlled pantheon of spirits. The Korekore, on the other hand, represent a much more static state of affairs, where the old groups and categories continue to control social experience. This fact is reflected in the emphasis they place on their centralised past, and on their religious belief in a hier-

archy of spirits coupled to a constant striving to control spirit-mediumship (1976:66–7).

It is not that the Zezuru group studied by Fry lacked the conceptual means to organize their mediums more rigidly. Indeed, he tells us that "the people of Chiota[1] think of their religious organisation in the same way as their political organisation. When describing the relationships between spirit-mediums they draw the parallel with the political structure, noting that just as the village headman refers unsolved cases to his subchief who in his turn refers them to the chief, so the junior ancestors give way to more senior ones, who in their turn recognise the superiority of the heroes." It is just that in practice neither the public nor the mediums feel compelled by this "cut-and-dried ordering of ritual authority" (1976:44). It seems safe to generalize that while existing social patterns always exert some control over manifestations of prophecy, the degree of that control can differ widely depending upon other variables.

The Shona spirit mediums' role as upholders of social institutions is evident in four ways. First, they are called upon to designate and install a dead chief's successor, a task of some importance, since the peculiar rules of succession insure competition among "a number of candidates, all with more or less equal claims" (Garbett, 1966:137, 145, 152–70). Related to this function, the mediums also give advice regarding the "inheritance of wives and family titles." Abraham goes so far as to suggest that the royal spirit-cults "operated primarily as a conservative pressure-group in defence of the political *status quo* . . ." (1966:38).

Secondly, the spirit guardians and their mediums were associated with protecting the earth's fertility and guaranteeing adequate rainfall. In connection with this function they promote harmony among the people and faithfulness to the traditional culture, a third aspect of their role as "central" intermediaries. Garbett tells us that each spirit province has one or more land-shrines named for the spirit guardian at which offerings are made for rain and the crops. At the dance following these offerings the spirit medium goes into a trance, during which he receives gifts from the people and, speaking as the spirit guardian, exhorts them "to uphold the laws of the forefathers." It is considered very important that everyone contribute grain for the beer used in the annual land-shrine ritual, and that everyone come together in amity (1969:120).

The same concern with the preservation of tradition is evident in the cult of the high-god, Mwari, who speaks through a possessed spirit medium from a cave shrine at Matonjeni, and whose words are carried by messengers (*vanyai*) to out-lying spirit provinces. Normally, the *vanyai* make two visits to Matonjeni each year, the second after the harvest,

---

[1] A "tribal trust land" in the former Southern Rhodesia.

when the people are eating the "crops ripened by Mwari's rain." On that occasion the messengers must report to Mwari on whether enough beer is being brewed for the annual land-shrine rituals. Daneel remarks that "this type of visit clearly illustrates the co-ordination of traditional religious activities in remote areas, with a centralized agency" (1970:58; cf. 54). Mwari was also consulted at Matonjeni on matters of chiefdom succession. An account of one such consultation, which Daneel himself was permitted to witness, is reproduced in the first of the following texts.

Finally, there is the matter of political centralization. In the absence of a strong central government the spirit mediums were able on occasion to unite the people along ethnic lines against foreigners. The objects of their opposition could be either white (Ranger, 1966; Daneel, 1970:30–5) or native. As an example of the latter, Daneel reports an oracle against a monarch whose kingdom was the result of his people having over-run the southern portion of Shona territory in 1830:

> When the pioneer settlers of the British South Africa Company started moving across the Limpopo in 1890, the voice of Mwari is reported to have said to Logengula: 'You who are so busy killing people. You are a little man. Climb on top of a high hill and see these people who are coming up. See their dust rising in the south. My white sons whose ears are shining in the sun are coming here.' To the Shona the arrival of Mwari's 'white sons' meant a radical curb in the tyrannical power of the Ndebele invaders (1970:29–30).

It seems probable that during the period of the Rozvi confederacy (ca. 1693–1830) the Mwari cult functioned as a "centralizing religious authority" (Daneel, 1970:22–6).

Texts

11.1 Consulting the god, Mwari (Daneel, 1970:41–5, 76–81)

> The Southern Shona tribes of Zimbabwe have an "elaborate cult for worshipping and consulting the Supreme Being," Mwari. To them Mwari is not considered a remote god, but one who gives rain in times of drought and advice in times of political crisis. Since, however, he is "beyond and above the hierarchies of ancestral spirits," he does not answer private prayers, but is accessible only through special spirit mediums. Popularly designated as *Mwari vaMatonjeni* ("the God of the Matopo Hills"), M. L. Daneel found that this "Shona oracular deity" was still being consulted in the mid–1960's (cf. 1970:15–9). In the excerpts which follow Daneel describes first the officials and procedures at an important oracle shrine and then an occasion on which he was permitted to accompany a messenger who had come to consult the god.

. . . the Voice (of Mwari) has never ceased to speak at Matonjeni. . . . The priest colony at Chokoto's village, popularly referred to as Wirirani, no doubt represents the major present day cult complex at Matonjeni. In the mountains surrounding Chokoto's village there are no less than three shrines where the Voice can be heard regularly. . . .

The officials of the Matonjeni shrine complex (Wirirani, Nejelele, Mazwawe and Maguhu) keep in regular touch with each other through jointly attending the annual rain feasts, as well as by the interchange of *hossanah's*[2] and spirit-mediums. Thus the messages of Mwari can be partly controlled over a wide area. During my visit to Chokoto's village, Makomana, the son of Hobo, was resident there. His mother was an *mbonga*[3] and his father the paternal uncle of Chokoto's father. An *hossanah* (male dedicated to Mwari) from Plumtree district, he first lived at the Njelele shrine since 1940, before he moved to Wirirani in recent years. Makomana is only one of several relatives of Chokoto's who have lived or are still living in the distant shrine communities. In this way Chokoto gained access to inside information about the continuous ritual procedures within the total network of shrines, and could thus exercise a certain amount of control.

Chokoto's own colony of priests comprises four adjacent villages. The headmen are: Simon Chokoto, who had recently inherited his deceased father's position; Usingaperi Peura, a muVenda and Simon's uterine 'grandchild'; Machonda, Simon's brother-in-law; and one of his maternal uncles. All four are interrelated. As uterine 'grandchild' and brother-in-law, both Peura and Machonda belong to the 'wife-receiving lineages' in relation to Chokoto's, which places Chokoto in a senior position as far as kinship relations are concerned. On the other hand, the 'joking relationship' between him and his maternal uncle would render any threat to his authority by the latter harmless. Each of the four men has a ritual office in the Mwari cult. Simon is the high priest (*mupiinzi vebasa*: lit. the one who controls the work), and Peura the keeper of Matonjeni. The other two belong to the junior cult ranks of *hossanah* and *jukwa dancer*,[4] whose privilege it is to dance in honour of Mwari during ritual ceremonies.

Next to Simon and Peura, the other important ritual officers at the apex of the cult hierarchy are the following: Simon's younger brother, Adamu, the 'second priest' who, as the high priest's representative is sent on errands further afield; Kombo, their oldest sister, who acts as

---

[2] Male "cultists dedicated to Mwari in their youth" (Daneel, 1970:20).

[3] Females dedicated to Mwari in their youth.

[4] Dancers who have been possessed by *jukwa*, spirits "believed to have emanated directly from Mwari" (in contrast to the *midzimu*, which are spirits of dead humans; Daneel, 1970:50).

high priestess; MaMoyo the second wife of the deceased Chokoto who, as spirit-medium (*svikiro*[5]) represents Mwari's Voice in the cave; and Simon's wife, who attends consultations at the cave as the spirit-medium's 'understudy' and future representative of the Voice.

Adamu, his sister Kombo, their families and MaMoyo live at the homestead of the deceased Chokoto near the main shrines at Mt. SaShe. This is where visiting *vanyai*[6] are housed. When delegations from the outlying districts arrive with their gifts for Mwari, the two leading kraal-heads, Simon and Peura, are summoned to Chokoto's homestead, where discussions with the *munyai* take place in the presence of the above-mentioned officials (junior cult officials do not attend these meetings). Peura, as oldest male officer and keeper of Matonjeni, presides over such meetings, while Mamoyo (the 'Voice'), the priests and priestesses listen attentatively to what the *munyai* has to say about the conditions in his own *nyika* (chiefdom or country).

When the *munyai* is taken to the shrine after sunset or in the early morning before sunrise, the women have already taken their places at the cave. One is not supposed to know that MaMoyo is in the cave, and she is well hidden. Kombo, the priestess and main interpreter of Mwari's messages, is seated together with Simon's wife within view at the mouth of the cave when the men arrive. After taking off their shoes the men approach the cave in single file. Simon leads the way, followed by Peura and the visiting *munyai*, with Adamu in the wake. They sit down in order of their authority near to Kombo, with their backs to the cave, facing in an easterly direction; the direction from which Mwari came to install Tandaudze, His son as first Priest. On these occasions the name Mwari is never uttered, but God is addressed by His praise-names: *Dziva! Mbedzi! Shoko!* Once Mwari has acknowledged the arrival of the cult officers and the *munyai*, by greeting the delegation from the cave, the *munyai* is asked to present his gifts. These are passed from hand to hand to the mouth of the cave where Kombo is seated. Communications can now start in all earnest. Mwari's high-pitched voice, coming from the cave, speaks in ChiRozvi, the old dialect of the Rozvi kings. Kombo then interprets the message into Sindebele; Simon, with the aid of Peura, further translates it into Chikaranga if the *munyai* happens to be a MuKaranga. During the whole ceremony Kombo is regarded as the closest to Mwari in her capacity as high-priestess. She is called 'grandmother of the country' and is imputed to be 'the mother of all the people', because in her ritual role she is somehow looked upon as the 'wife of

---

[5] Officially recognized spirit-medium through whom the *mhondoro* (senior tribal ancestors) are approached.

[6] Sg. *munyai*; local messengers of Mwari.

Mwari'. Simon, as *mupinzi vebasa*, respects Kombo in this capacity. Once the Voice is heard, he allows her to speak first before he takes the initiative. The whole flow of the conversation sometimes stalls at this juncture, because Simon and Peura must decide which parts of the *munyai's* speech and replies are essential enough to relay to Mwari. Simon's wife and Adamu are observant onlookers.

There is no doubt that Simon, Kombo and to a lesser extent Peura, hold the positions of power in the cult. I have not heard Blake and Thompson's distinction of Eye, Ear and Mouth being applied to their functions, but it is possible that the Voice in the cave is actually the Mouth, Kombo and Simon the Ear, and Peura the Eye. If so, the main authority would lie with the Ear, since this is the office traditionally inherited in the priestly Mbire lineage. Of great significance is the fact that Peura, the keeper, is a muVenda and MaMoyo the Voice, a muRozvi.

Here we find the links with and continuation of the historical past, because even before they migrated to the southern parts of Rhodesia and northern Transvaal, the Venda had been closely associated with the Mbire tribe and regularly sent delegations to the Matonjeni shrines. Though their messengers now visit Matonjeni less frequently than before, we see that some of their kinsmen are still actively involved at the cult shrines.

MaMoyo's position raises the question whether the Rozvi are still exerting much influence over the Mwari cult. One might even ask if hers is not the key position at Matonjeni because, being the Voice, she impersonates Mwari, being identified with Him in her ritual capacity. In the same way as the ordinary spirit-medium of an ancestral or tribal spirit 'become' the spirit when he or she is possessed, so MaMoyo 'becomes' Mwari when she speaks with Mwari's Voice in the cave. Her position, however, is not quite the same as that of the ordinary *svikiro*. In the first place her role is a secretive one, which is never publicly mentioned and indeed is actually supposed not to exist, for the people are told that it is Mwari Himself who speaks from the cave. In the second place, she is promoted to her position as the voice because of her status as the wife of the high priest, and not because the Spirit had proclaimed her as his 'mouthpiece' in the manner ancestral or *mhondoro* spirits 'call' their mediums. In the third place, she falls under the jurisdiction of her 'acolytes'—Simon and Kombo—as situation unlike that of the ordinary *svikiro-nechombo* (spirit medium-acolyte) relationship in which the *svikiro* wields the power. On the other hand, the authority of the Mbire priest and priestess is not absolute. They hold MaMoyo in high esteem, because as a member of the royal Rozvi lineage she represents the age-old association between the Mbire and Rozvi tribes. The Rozvi dominance of the past is therefore not completely lost. *Mbonga* women, sent

2.1

to live at Matonjeni, are still predominantly Rozvi. These women become the wives of the priests, keepers and sometimes of the messengers. This on the one hand guarantees Rozvi continuity in the important office of *mbonga-svikiro* at the shrines and on the other perpetuates the ancient kinship group-pattern of mutual obligation and privilege between the priestly Mbire and royal Rozvi. It also preserves the slight 'subordination' of the wife receiving (Mbire) lineage over the wife-providing (Rozvi) lineage in the basic Shona pattern of affinal kinship relations. . . .

*   *   *

We should now turn to Mwari's 'verdict' on the situation in Gutu, as I witnessed it at the cult shrines. In January, 1967, I accompanied Vondo to Matonjeni. Machingura at that stage had not yet been officially installed as the new chief, and Vondo on this occasion therefore still carried the gifts on behalf of acting Chief Munyonga. This trip did not, in the first place, concern an 'emergency request' for rain, as one may have expected to take place at this time of the year, but Mwari was to be
3.2   consulted on a matter more important to the Gutu inhabitants, that is, the chieftain succession. Several days of deliberation passed in the priest's colony before I was allowed to accompany the priests to the cult cave. The responsibility for a final decision on my eventual presence or absence at the ceremony was placed on the spirit of the recently deceased Mai vaDuwe, the previous 'Voice of Mwari', whom I had met in
2.13 1965. She consented, and on a bleak moonlit night Simon Chokoto led us up the slopes of Mt. SaShe in single file. Fifty yards from the cave we took off our shoes and then approached the place where High Priestess Kombo and Simon's wife were already seated, facing the east. We followed suit and sat down with our backs to the cave.

After we had greeted Mwari with the clapping of hands and loud exclamations of his praise names: Mbedzi! Dziva! Shoko!, Vondo opened the discussion in Chikaranga:

"I am well, Shoko, and I have come on behalf of Chief Gutu. But these days we have no real Gutu (no real chief), Shoko! The acting chief says: 'Where I rule I try my best, but there is no true chieftainship at the moment. So what will I do in such a position?' The chief said: 'Go to Shoko where you worship, and give him these £4!' Then there is another matter your *mbonga* (referring to the deceased *Mai* va Duwe) knows of, namely the European who has come with us. She had allowed him to come here, so we brought him along. He has his gift here. It is a black blanket, a black cloth and £3, Shoko. He said that he only wants to see how we worship and also how we settle chieftainship problems (lit.:arrange the chieftainship of the land). That is why I came with him, Shoko. Those are the matters I have brought before you. About the attitudes and behaviour of the Gutu *vachinda*[7] I will tell you later on."

High Priest Simon briefly interpreted Vondo's words to Mwari before our presents were passed to the mouth of the cave.

The Voice from behind us (high pitched as if in a trance): "Who is the successor in Gutu?"

Vondo: "It is Gadzingo, Shoko. Gadzingo says: 'I am the elder but they don't want to make me chief in my chiefdom. When I (Vondo now speaking as Chief Munyonga) collect the gifts of Matonjeni, the people refuse and say, 'Munyonga, we do not want you to rule us! You are an orphan now and you have had your chance at ruling the country.' This is the *'muromo'* (lit: mouth, i.e. message) given to me by Munyonga, Shoko."

The Voice now entered into a lively discussion with Simon, Peura and Kombo in Sindebele and ChiRozvi. To its further enquiry about the legitimacy of Gadzingo's claim, Vondo reassuringly replied: "Gadzingo is the elder who must become chief, but the people have said that they want a young one. We have refused on the grounds that Ghikaranga laws make no provision for a young one to become a chief. I have to come and ask you if a young one can be appointed as long as an elder can still be found."

The Voice: "*These young ones who have been educated, they disobey the Karanga laws!* They change the Karanga customs because they insert our laws into the European customs. *They mix the old with the new!* The children are supposed to build the country, but they are the ones who run to the beer-pots and cause trouble when they come from there. *They ruin the country!* (lit: they kill the country). Gutu actually wants Gadzingo, because it has been arranged long ago that the reign should be in his hands. Go and tell this to Chief Munyonga! Everyone wants the chieftainship, even if they are too young and that is wrong!"

The whole delegation: "Yes, so it is, Shoko!"—with the clapping of hands and the calling out of Mwari's praise names.

The Voice continued: "Tell the *changamire* (this word is usually used when dignitaries are addressed; in this case it referred to the European visitor) that the law of this place speaks as follows: 'What has happened at Gutu is wrong.' I am now tired of the long drawn out dispute in Gutu. Their affairs never come to an end. People of other chiefdoms come here and have their problems settled, but Gutu carries on without end. It is because this matter is handled by (African) youngsters who make use of European customs. They have thrown away the African customs. Europeanism does not mend the country! (or, We cannot govern the country according to European ways!).

---

[7] Subchief or ward headman.

"I (Mwari) do not want to speak to these Europeanized Africans. *The Europeans are the children of my sister.* I love them, but with regard to this law, I have no need for them. I do not want them to approach this place where I live, because they do not act properly. They always fight with the country. Do you hear what I have said?"

Vondo and myself: "Eye! Yes!"

Vondo: "Well, as you say yourself, Shoko, matters are complicated in Gutu. The chief sits down like somebody who forgets. He even forgets to send gifts to Matonjeni. Therefore I (now speaking as Chief Munyonga) have decided that it would be a good thing if this European were to visit Matonjeni. So I told my messenger, 'Go with this European so that he may see for himself what happens at Motonjeni!' I thought that, perhaps, things will turn out well because I trust the European. What he says happens. So I said to myself, 'Let me send these two men, Vondo and the European, because I must honour what customs have been left me by my fathers.'"

The Voice: "I have allowed you, European, to come here today, because of Gutu's wish, but I do not want any other European to come here again. From today on, No! My eyes do not want to see another European approaching this place. I have allowed you to come here. You are the first European to have come and speak to me and that is enough! One of your 'relatives' (referring to the Native Commissioner of Essexvale) once sent me some beer and an ox. A feast was arranged and the ox killed for me. I granted him his request for rain. But I do not want to sit down and speak to him. This I do not want! These things disturb me. I have allowed only you. If there is anything you want to know in the future you may come again, but you must come with Gutu!"

Myself: "I am very grateful Shoko that you have allowed me to reach this place. I have heard what you have said, so I will go back relieved and with joy. I have heard what you have said about your law, and I shall remember."

Vondo 'interprets' my message: "This European says he is most thankful for your kindness, and if trouble arises he will tell Gutu: 'Don't kill the people! Go with your complaints to Shoko, where you have requested rain and have received it.' We thank you, Shoko, that you have started giving us rain on the day we came."

The Voice: "What Gutu has done is good and I am satisfied. I have allowed it once, but if I see another European coming here to see this place I will fight you, Gutu."

Vondo (after deliberating with Simon): "We shall take your message to the District Commissioner at Gutu and we shall tell him that this thing he plans to do together with the young ones, is wrong. It would break up the country and matters will not progress well. We will go as your witnesses to testify before the District Commissioner what has been said at Matonjeni about Gadzingo."

The Voice: "It is laid down by Karanga law that the chieftainship should be in the hands of the elders. The lawful elder is the one who can keep the chiefdom well. The young only cause disunity. They destroy!"

Myself: "Once again I have heard you, Shoko. I know that the chieftainship should be taken by an elder. I do not know what the District Commissioner and the Gutu people will ultimately decide, but I will carry your message to them and urge them to follow the old law."

The Voice: "I greet you! Travel well."

We arose and left the cave in single file amidst the ululations, of the women, profuse handclapping and resounding Dzivas! and Shokos!

Half an hour later we were all sitting round a fire listening to Vondo's detailed account of what had happened at the cave. At the request of   2.1 MaMoyo, who had walked into the village a little while after our arrival from the cave, he recounted all that Mwari had said. Nobody showed any surprise at MaMoyo's questions. They all pretended as a matter of course that she had really been absent during the whole ceremony and nobody ever hinted at her presence in the cave during the discourse with Mwari. Like a true *svikiro*, who is supposed to be ignorant of the message the spirit speaks through his possessed medium, she correctly acted her role as an attentive listener, as if Vondo's narrative was completely new to her. Both of them played their roles exceptionally well, Vondo as informant and MaMoyo as inquisitive questioner. MaMoyo was in fact finding out whether the *munyai* had correctly memorized the essentials of Mwari's message.

11.2 A Zezuru Spirit-Medium (Fry, 1976:34–5, 38–42)

Peter Fry began his field work in the Chiota Tribal Trust Land of Southern Rhodesia in the mid–1960's, a time of political and social unrest in that country. Over the previous seven years a series of Black African nationalist parties had been formed and banned, and the movement itself was fragmented. In 1965 Ian Smith declared Rhodesia's independence from Britain, and hopes that the country would soon be governed by majority rule were dashed. It was, as he describes it, not an easy situation in which to carry out anthropological research (cf. Fry, 1976:1–4, 107–23).

From the beginning Fry had determined "not to be preoccupied with studying religion and ritual," partly because his interests lay elsewhere, but also because he "had been led to believe that 'traditional' beliefs and practices were dying out and were of little significance to the contemporary situation." He gradually became aware, however, that just the opposite was the case. Native beliefs and practices were on the increase, and since they "were related to the rise of African nationalism," they were "of considerable relevance to the social life of the people of Chiota" (1976:3).

Fry determined to undertake a study of spirit-mediumship. For a time he had great difficulty gaining access to mediums and ceremonies, but his fortunes took a turn for the better when his native assistant, a school teacher named Thomas Mutero, began to display the symptoms of spirit-mediumship and was subsequently initiated as a high-level medium. *Spirits of Protest,* which delves in detail into the sociological and political ramifications of Zezuru mediums, is the result.

Fry's study goes into detail about matters that have been of interest to us throughout: trance and spirit possession, the "making" of an intermediary (with special emphasis in this case on the need for the new medium to be accredited by an important, established spirit-medium), the critical relationship between the medium and his audience (which is the basis of the former's status), the medium's function as upholder of the community's welfare, and the like.

The text which follows gives a characterization of one important high-level spirit-medium, David Mudiwa, who figures prominently in Fry's narrative account of a two-year period of social conflict in the village of Tatenda (cf. 1976:68–106).

2.12
Spirit-mediums fall into two broad categories, the high-level and the low-level mediums. The former are hosts to either hero spirits or very senior ancestor spirits, while the latter act as hosts to junior ancestors. This difference is apparent from the different cloths which they wear during trance. The high-level mediums wear wholly black cloths and the low-level ones half black, half white. The present of white in the low-level mediums' cloths was interpreted by one informant as symbolising their having lived since the arrival of the whites in Rhodesia.

3.1
High-level mediums differ from low-level ones in style and scale. The former, if they are popular and successful, carry out their seances in large seance houses (*banya*), are surrounded by an administrative staff to take care of operations and to look after those who come to consult. They

3.11
may reach the stage when they have to abandon all other activities and are then able to maintain themselves and their followers on the income derived from the fees which the clients are charged. The more popular the medium, the more well-known and powerful his spirit, the higher the fees and the larger is the scale of operations.

Low-level mediums, on the other hand, do not have seance houses and only fall into trance from time to time or at the occasional formal rituals which are held by their lineage groups for their ancestor spirits. They do not generally receive clients from beyond the confines of village or lineage and do not charge fees.

Although the high-level mediums are credited with greater powers than the low-level ones (only the former are able to make rain and to prophesy) the basic function of all mediums is that of divination. On the strength of the belief that all spirits are omniscient and in contact with one another, mediums in trance are supposed to be able to know the reasons for all misfortune. At divinatory seances they are expected to reveal the causes of affliction to their clients. **3.0**

But because people go to a medium for divination with some idea of what they expect to hear, the medium is obliged to find out what this is and to present the 'truth' to his clients as divine revelation. If he fails, then the disappointed clients can ignore the 'wrong' pronouncement by claiming that the medium was not in trance, or—and this was very common—that the witchcraft involved in the misfortune was so powerful that it had affected the divining powers of the medium. In either case a 'wrong' pronouncement is a blow to a medium's prestige; reputation being won and lost on the ability to divine 'correctly.' **2.2** **3.1**

Divination, like many of the spirit-mediums' functions is half way between art and science. The spirit-medium has to size up the situation and produce, *ex cathedra* an explanation of his clients' misfortune which is acceptable to them.

David/*Kafudzi*,[8] as a high-level medium, had a sizeable administrative staff, one of whose duties was to receive and care for clients as they arrived. Undoubtedly a certain amount of relevant information that emerged from these prior contacts with the clients was passed on to the medium and he entered the seance with this and other information that he might have gleaned from ordinary gossip or prior consultations. By and large, however, he had to start the divination from scratch and produce his analysis of the situation without appearing to use non-mystical techniques.

David/*Kafudzi's* divinatory technique was based to a large extent on his empirical awareness of the regularities of Zezuru social structure. Due to the great number of divinations which he had carried out he was aware of the structural tensions in Zezuru society and on the basis of this knowledge he was able to predict tensions in particular situations which appeared to his clients as miraculous insight. This interpretation is supported by the way in which seances were conducted. Clients were instructed to sit facing the spirit-medium according to their genealogical relationships. Men sat to his right as fathers, brothers, . . . while the women sat to his left as sisters, mothers and wives. . . .

The eldest man present was asked to explain why they had come to divine and his reasons were translated by an acolyte into the language **2.13**

[8] David Mudiwa is a person, and Kafudzi the name of a water spirit. The convention, "David/*Kafudzi*," is used by Fry to refer to David Mudiwa, possessed by Kafudzi.

which David/*Kafudzi* spoke (see below). David/*Kafudzi* would then suggest a relationship of tension between two of the people before him, say a woman and her sister-in-law or a pair of brothers. If he succeeded in exposing a tension that really existed and was relevant to the situation, then the reaction of his clients was usually sufficiently obvious for him to be able to pursue this particular line of enquiry. It sometimes happened that such preliminary questions produced no results, in which case he generally resorted to asking the women one by one which had been using love potions (*mufuwhira*). This exploitation of inter-sexual tensions nearly always evinced enthusiasm amongst the men and frequently led to elaborate confessions on the part of those women who were forced by the general consensus into making them. David/*Kafudzi* surely realised either that all women use *mufuwhira* or that even if they don't they can

2.2   be forced into confessing to it when sufficiently cajoled. From the point of view of the clients, however, David/*Kafudzi's* socio-psychological insights were perceived as divine revelations. Impressed by the medium's divinatory powers, clients were generally maneouvred into giving away more than they realised about themselves and about what they had been thinking in relation to their problems, so that the medium was able to reach the kind of explanation that they had previously had in mind.

David/*Kafudzi* and other mediums, then, exploited what they knew about social tension and the symbolic meaning of dress and gesture to explain misfortune. Contented clients left the seance convinced of the truth of what they had heard, willing and ready to carry out the ritual injunctions prescribed as necessary for the alleviation of their misfortunes. . . .

David Mudiwa was born in a village in Chiota in 1930. After being
2.2   educated up to Standard III at a Methodist primary school, he became interested in religion and after a brief flirtation with the Vapostore sect,[9] entered the Methodist Church as an evangelist. He was so successful as a preacher that his congregation was able to raise sufficient funds to build a small chapel on the outskirts of his village.

Towards the end of 1963 he began to suffer from chronic stomach pains and to go into wild frenzies while preaching; so wild, in fact, that the congregation had to chain him down. His condition worsened and
1.21   through dreams he was led to visit a spirit-medium in Zwimba Reserve. There he was told that he was being troubled by a spirit which wished to make him its medium. Rituals were held in Zwimba and David became possessed by three spirits, *Kafudzi* which was described as a water spirit (*nzuzu*); an obscure hero spirit related to the clan of hero spirits belonging to the Nyandoro clan; and the ancestor of David's father's father's

---

[9] "The Vapostore (Apostles) are a Zionist sect operating throughout Southern Rhodesia. Their presence in Chiota is not very marked." (P. F.)

father. He returned to his village where he built a small seance house on the top of a slight hill overlooking the Methodist chapel.

It is at this stage in David's career as a medium that I first met him in April of 1965. He no longer held any church services and the chapel was being used as a guest house for the clients who had begun to consult him as a spirit-medium. Apparently people had at first been rather confused by his change of status from Methodist evangelist to spirit-medium, but after a short time the quality of his divination and his reputation as a healer brought him ever more consultants.   1.41

Soon business was so brisk that he was obliged to build a bigger and better seance house and was able to increase his fee from 5s to 10s and upwards depending on the nature of the problem. There gathered in David's village a small administrative nucleus made up for the most part of people who had been indicated as new spirit-mediums and who were undergoing ritual treatment. This staff looked after clients as they arrived and took care of the premises. David bought a car in order to be able to visit sick people and paid two excellent thumb-piano players to provide the music for his seances.   3.11

David/*Kafudzi* soon became especially noted for his ability to detect witches and sorcerers, for exorcising witching spirits (*shave ro uroyi*) and for his skill in 'bringing out' new spirits in those he had identified as potential spirit-mediums. The village was now full of sick people seeking cures, young men and women undergoing ritual treatment as neophyte mediums and women waiting to be possessed by their witching spirits that they might later have them exorcised. At weekends, the village was inundated with people from Salisbury who came by bus and car to consult on all manner of problems, ranging from money and employment difficulties to impotency, from severe sickness to the loss of relatives. As satisfied clients returned to their villages or to the towns, David's reputation increased and his sphere of influence expanded. Those who had come in order to become spirit-mediums returned to their vilages and set up their own practices, but they maintained contact with David, and spread his fame even further.   3.21   2.2

By the end of 1966 David's reputation was almost as high as, if not higher than the mediums of well-established hero spirits in Chiota like *Biri na Ganiri* and *Chitswachegore*, and *Kafudzi's* status as a water spirit had also improved. It would be difficult to pin-point this change in status, but imperceptibly *Kafudzi* became a hero with a complex history and a wealth of detail about his previous mediums. David/*Kafudzi* enjoyed telling this history; of how *Kafudzi* had been a member of the Vatemani clan which had lived before the formation of Shona society at a place called Guruuswa to the north of the river Zambesi; of how he had possessed mediums in other parts of the world, one in Dar-es-Salaam and another, a 'Hindu' who had lived in the Himalayas. Visitors to the   3.1

seance house were treated to more elaborate details and descriptions of the geography of the Himalaya mountains.

By the time that I left the field in 1966 the followers of David did not remember that *Kafudzi* had ever been a mere water spirit. History had been made.

2.2   Of course there remained pockets of opposition in Chiota, notably amongst the followers of other mediums and, as will be seen from the extended case history in chapter 5, there were those who were able to regard him as a mere upstart and to ignore his pronouncements. But in spite of such opposition his success was remarkable.

In trying to understand David's success, it is possible to discern elements which have a purely personal nature and lie beyond the scope of sociology and others which are more technical and which might indicate a number of generalisations about the way in which spirit-mediums acquire popularity. It is with the latter that I am immediately concerned.

David Mudiwa, in common with most of the spirit-mediums of Chiota, was riding on the crest of a wave of cultural nationalism which was sweeping that region of Rhodesia at the time. There is no doubt that the mood of the people was propitious for his particular brand of spirit-mediumship; his ritual emphasis on witchcraft and the induction of new spirit-mediums, his constant appeals to 'traditional' values and his subtle use of certain African nationalist symbols were an important aspect of his success. This aspect of spirit-mediumship in Chiota will be examined in greater detail in chapter 6, but it is sufficient to note at this stage that David had been a Methodist evangelist and his move over to spirit-mediumship reflected the general religious trends of the time.

More particularly, David was a good diviner, he knew how to use the
3.1   income that he earned from his seances to increase his popularity, and he was able to augment his sphere of influence noticeably due to the emphasis he laid on 'training' new spirit-mediums.

I have already described his divinatory technique, so on this there is
2.2   little to add. He succeeded in offering the kinds of analysis that his clients wanted and which they were able to accept. As far as cash income
3.11   was concerned, he was particularly astute. At first all the money (and on some weekends he earned upwards of £400) was put to specifically communal use. The seance house was built, food was provided for visitors from long distances, thumb-piano players were paid and houses and shelters were built for the neophyte spirit-mediums and administrative staff. Very poor clients were not always charged while those who could afford to pay more were expected to do so. The money was not used for personal grandisement and the more money that was used for other people the more David's popularity increased, for he was soon surrounded by a number of people who could only repay him with loyalty.

Latterly he began to use his cash to start a retail business and to build a luxurious house for his two wives. There were hints of criticism of this behaviour, which never became really serious because he employed his friends and relatives as workers and continued to be generous to others.

His policy on new spirit-mediums was particularly important. Young 1.32 men and women who had been told they were to be mediums stayed in his village upwards of a year. They enjoyed his hospitality and attended his seances, contributing with any help they could give. Bit by bit, as their spirits began to 'come out', they absorbed the ritual techniques and learned their calling. Even though there is no place for learning in Zezuru belief (for the spirits are believed to be all-knowing), the neophyte mediums saw David's village as a school. When the time came to return to their home villages, the new mediums kept in touch with David, who would be invited to preside over any important rituals they might enact. They built their own seance houses and began to do as their master had done, even 'bringing out' their own disciple mediums. By this process, David, who remained at the centre of the network, acquired steadily 3.1 more and more faithful adherents.

In a sense, all these techniques could be learned and applied by any spirit-medium. But they are all difficult and few are the spirit-mediums who have achieved David's success. The personal element is much more difficult to pin down.

Zezuru spirit-mediums are dramatic figures, and much of their fame is derived from the way in which they conduct themselves both in the ritual context and outside. David, even when out of the ritual context, left no doubt of his spirit-medium status. Apart from using a black shirt, 2.12 he generally travelled with his musicians and an imposing sword stick (*bakatwa*). He carried an air of authority and importance.

But it was his ritual performance which earned him his greatest fame. The seance house was of exaggerated proportions and its dark in- 2.13 terior was awesome. On entering it was possible to discern little, but as one's eyes became accustomed to the gloom it was possible to perceive the designs of lions and other animals picked out on the mud walls, and the many large black cloths which festooned the rafters. Opposite the main door was a pile of black cloths and animals' skins, on which would be seated a few neophyte mediums all in black. To their left were the musicians. Behind them a small door led to a sort of antechamber from which David emerged. As he entered the music became more energetic and he and his disciples rose to dance. In essence, the dance was not so different from modern western pop dancing; it was highly expressive and individualistic, allowing for extemporisation on a basic foot-pounding rhythm. During the dance *Kafudzi* would 'arrive' and, with the cessation of the music, the seance proper would begin.

David/*Kafudzi* did not speak ChiShona, but a language which, it was believed, had been the language of the Vatemani clan. This language was based on a simplified Shona grammar with a changed vocabulary whose words tended to have a wider semantic field than ChiShona ones. The medium's disciples all had a competence in this language, but clients did not. The latter could only talk with David/*Kafudzi* through an interpreter, which created an even greater respect for the powers of the medium. This language had a further important function in accentuating the mutual solidarity of those who could understand it.

All these aspects of David/*Kafudzi's* performance, and others which it is not necessary to list here, served to emphasise his divine powers and to differentiate him from other spirit-mediums.

The successful medium, then, relies on his capacity as a diviner, his ability to foster a wide circle of adherents, his ability as a showman, and a certain amount of luck. David/*Kafudzi's* phenomenal rise was exceptional in its scale and rapidity, but it was also normal. Spirit-mediums rise and fall in popularity and their success or failure in capturing and manipulating public opinion affects not only the relative standing of the mediums themselves, but also that of the spirits which they present. David/*Kafudzi's* position is therefore precarious. As we shall see later, not all the people of Chiota believed in his powers and even those who do may one day become disillusioned. Should this occur, they may easily bring about his downfall. Spirit-mediums are continuously subject to being discredited . . .

INDIA

12

Spirit Possession and Its Mythic Prototype
Introduction

The Baiga are a native tribe of Central India, which in the 1930's occupied a territory around and extending westward from Bilaspur in the present State of Madhya Pradesh. For the six years prior to writing *The Baiga* (1939) Verrier Elwin lived and travelled in their country. During that time, he tells us, he "talked freely with hundreds of Baiga in their own language, made many intimate friends, overheard a great volume of village gossip, settled a host of quarrels and disputes, and assisted at nearly all the ceremonies described in this book." His permanent residence was in the village of Dindori, Mandla District, and since his "nearest English neighbors were a hundred miles away," he was "compelled not only to work but to relax in tribal company." In addition he had "the advantage of being neither an official who might seem too alarming, nor a missionary who might seem too respectable," and as a result was "simply regarded as an amiable and eccentric person who was interested in everybody and everything, and to whom people could say anything that came into their heads" (1939:xxviii-xxix).

Elwin found that although their material culture had "almost disappeared before the highly organized and efficient trades-unionism of the Hindu caste-system," neither Christian missionary propaganda nor "the prevailing Hindu civilization" had had much effect "upon the Baiga's mind" (1939:xxvii). Thus at the beginning of his discusion of Baiga mythology he says, "I have put this chapter in the middle of the book as a sort of symbol. For the mythology of the Baiga is the central power-house of the life and energy of the tribe. Those institutions that have a legend to vitalize and control them are living; those that have not are slowly dying out. . . . These myths then are no mere fairy stories, nor just primitive attempts at a scientific explanation of things. At every point there is the closest contact between them and the daily life of the tribe. To the Baiga they are the records of veritable happenings which set the social order on its course, instituted tribal law, and established him in his unique position as Bhumia Raja, lord of the earth" (1939:305,

307–8). In the text that follows we will be able to see both the mythological prototype for spirit possession and examples of its modern manifestations.

Before turning to the texts, some words should be said about the Baiga deities. Elwin found the pantheon to be "exceedingly varied and elastic," differing to some extent "from village to village." The people, he said, tended to worship everything they could, "in order to be on the safe side. When the new Satpura Railway first made its way into the hills, a Baiga was found offering coconuts and chickens to the engine. . . . Baiga theology is directed, not to knowing more about God, but to knowing about more gods" (1939:54–5). It is also important to note that "the Baiga have lost their own language, and can thus only describe their deities by Sanskrit or Hindi words. This gives their pantheon a spurious air of civilized theology and Hindu respectability. Bhagavan is worshipped by Hindus, but he is a very different being from the Bhagavan of the Baiga lengends. The Baiga Mahadeo, deceitful and cowardly, bears no resemblance to the mighty being of Hindu theosophy . . ." (1939:55).

In the Baiga creation myth there was at the beginning nothing but water, upon which floated Bhagavan, sitting on a lotus leaf. Using dirt rubbed from his arm, the god created his daughter, Karicag (the crow) and sent her to find "some earth" from which he could "make a world." With the aid of Kekramal Chhatri (the great tortoise) she accomplished this mission. Bhagavan spread the earth on the waters, where it expanded until it covered them. But even after its slippery, muddy surface had been dried by Pawan Daseri (wind) and had received mountains, valleys, and trees from Bhimsen (a giant), "it still wobbled." There follows in the story the creation of Nanga Baiga and Nanga Baigin, the male and female ancestors of the Baiga, who eventually performed the actions necessary to stabilize the earth: "From the Agaria (a sub-tribe of the neighboring Gond), who was born on the same day as the Baiga, they got four great nails. Nanga Baigin made herself naked, and drove the nails into the four corners of the world. . . . At last the world was steady. Then the two Baiga, being weary, lay down, the man in one corner of the world, his girl in the other. Their feet met in the middle" (1939:36; cf. 308–16). Subsequently, the Baiga were given the jungle as their special home, and, as the following text describes, Nanga Baiga became the first spirit medium.

Texts (Elwin, 1939)

It is now that we make the acquaintance of a new and somewhat different cycle of legends concerned with two mysterious beings whom, for want of better names, the latter-day Baiga have called Mahadeo and Parvati. But they bear no resemblance to the august and splendid deities of Hindu theology. Mahadeo is not a Baiga deity. "Mahadeo comes from afar, he is a stranger," said Thuggur the Dewar[1] to me. In the legends, Mahadeo and Parvati are simply a typical couple who get the better of the Baiga at every opportunity. They might almost symbolize a conflict of the Baiga with civilization.

Mahadeo was the son of Amardevi who lived in a lotus that floated on the surface of the ocean. When he grew up he desired his mother, and married her, changing her name to Parvati. Mahadeo took his wife to Nanga Baiga's jungle, and there they lived on roots—it was while they were searching for roots that they came to know Nanga Baiga.

They used to play hide-and-seek together in the jungle. Mahadeo would hide something and they all had to find it. Then Parvati would hide something. Nanga Baiga would call out the name of a tree, and they had to try to find it. Nanga Baiga and his wife always won the game, because their eyes were white and they could see everything. So Mahadeo and Parvati said, "We must put an end to this!" Parvati said to Nanga Baiga, "Why not get some bhilwa fruit? If you put its juice in your eyes, it will make you very beautiful." So Nanga Baigin went and got some of the fruit and put it in her eyes, and some also in her husband's eyes, but it only burnt them and that is why the Baiga's eyes to-day are so black and they can see no more than other people.

Then Mahadeo and Parvati made birds and animals out of mud and they gave life to them. Nanga Baiga and his wife gave them their names. They all decided that the Baiga should not eat tigers, jackals or hyenas. They also made the exogamous septs which are to stop brothers and sisters living together.

After a time Parvati became pregnant, and went away to her own house. For twelve years Mahadeo lived alone in the jungle and worked as a carpenter. Parvati felt very lonely: every day she used to ask, "When will he come?" At last she made a tiger from the dirt she rubbed from her breast and sent it to frighten Mahadeo, hoping that he would then run home to her. When he heard the tiger roaring, Mahadeo said, "For twelve years not even a bird has dared to twitter near me and now what is this?" He threw wood-shavings all over the tiger, and turned him into a jungledog. The tiger-dog ran home and sat in Parvati's lap. She put fire in a stick and thrust it into his mouth, and he ran back to Mahadeo, turning into a tiger again as he went.

Then Mahadeo called Nanga Baiga and Nanga Baiga said, "What's the matter now, Mahadeo?" Mahadeo fell at his feet and said, "Do go and kill this tiger for me." Nanga Baiga picked up his axe, he went into the jungle, and threw his axe at the tiger and killed him.

There was a banyan tree forty-eight miles long. Nanga Baiga buried

[1] The "highest grade of medicine-man"; the term probably derives from that for lamp-lighter, referring to "the practice of divination by a lamp"; Elwin, 1939:343).

the tiger under the tree. But as he was digging, he cut one of the roots, and the tiger drank milk from the root and returned to life. He went again to trouble Mahadeo. Mahadeo called Nanga Baiga and was very angry. They had a quarrel. Nanga Baiga at last went back to the jungle to kill the tiger a second time. He raised his axe to hit him, but the tiger lifted up his paw, and said, "Wait, listen to my story." So Nanga Baiga sat down on the stump of a tree and began to smoke his pipe.

The tiger said, "Whenever I catch men, goats, cattle, chickens in a village, all the people will call on you to help them. You won't get gold or silver—that is for the Hindus. But wherever you do your magic in a village or forest, there I will never come, and the people will trust you and will give you enough for your livelihood."

When Nanga Baiga heard this, he thought, "What has this Mahadeo done for me? If I make a pact with the tiger I will always have enough to drink at least. For food I can get roots. I will do what the tiger desires." So he let him go.

One day soon after this the tiger killed a Gond, and the headman of the village sent for Nanga Baiga to protect the village. They agreed to give Nanga Baiga a goat and one rupee's worth of liquor and two coconuts. So all night he sat 'looking' in his winnowing fan and gourd and in the morning he went to the Agaria[2] and had four nails made. He called everyone to the place where the man had been killed. The ground was red with his blood. Nanga Baiga made two little images, one of the sin that had killed the man, the other of the (magic herbs of the forest).

Then Nanga Baiga called on all the tigers in the world by name—the white Shet-bagh, the horned Singh-bagh, Lataria-bagh the hyena, Jalaria-bagh, the cattle-eating Dhor-bagh, Kowachi-bagh the leopard, Bundia-bagh, Gul-bagh, the small Lorcha-bagh, the tiny dog-like Bhusur-bagh, Dandhia-bagh, the tailless Buchi-bagh, the small-eared Tajia-bagh, the magic, wooden Khunta-bagh, Tendua-bagh the panther, Chita-bagh and Son-chitti-bagh.

The *barua*[3] entered into him and he trembled all over. He leapt in the air and caught hold of the Sin-Image. Then they understood that that man had broken a law of the tribe; perhaps he had been to (i.e., had sexual intercourse with) someone in his own sept—no one could say— and so he had been standing on sinful earth, and the tiger had been able to kill him. Then Nanga Baiga drove a nail into a tree, and they all shouted, "Be off, be off, Buchi-bagh!" Then he went to another tree and drove a nail into that and they all shouted, "Be off, be off, Bundia-bagh!" He went again to a third tree, and now they all shouted, "Be off, be off,

[2] A Gond sub-tribe.

[3] This term, usually used of the person whom a god "rides" (i.e., possesses), here seems to refer to the possessing spirit itself.

Jalaria-bagh!" At the fourth tree, after he had driven in the nail that should close the tiger's jaws in that place, Nanga Baiga himself said, "O Dharti Mata, O Banaspati, to-day I Nanga Baiga have fixed the boundary of this village. I Nanga Baiga, make it free from every kind of tiger!"

From that day Nanga Baiga has been lord of all wild animals. (Elwin, 1939:325–7)

*   *   *

In modern times when a person was killed by a tiger, the Mati Uthana ceremony was performed. Elwin supplies the following description of one such ceremony.

When we reached the field of the tragedy, the whole party of about two hundred men and, curiously enough, two little girls who were unrelated to the dead man, sat down under the tree where the tiger's pawmarks could still be quite clearly seen. The headman showed everybody the marks on the ground which revealed the course of the man's struggle with the tiger, and we saw the cloth and tobacco-pouch and axe lying where they had been left, all that now remained.

There followed a long discussion. It was amusing to see the bovine, placid Gond sitting quietly pulling at their pipes, their faces completely void of intelligence,[4] while the Baiga shouted and gesticulated, arguing with the utmost acrimony the difficult question of what was to be done next. Rawan (a famous old Dewar) had not come and there was no Dewar present of sufficient dignity to carry on the proceedings. It was interesting to note that throughout the whole course of the ceremony these discussions continued; the Baiga spectators were continually shouting advice and directions to the main actors in the rite.

At last a council was formed of the five chief Dewar of Bohi and neighbouring villages, but it remained to be decided in whose name the ceremony was to be conducted. The spectators shouted that the council should summon Thakur Deo[5] and ask him about this. So the elders moved away a little to one side of the crowd, but they discovered that no one had brought any fire. This led to another violent altercation, and after a long wait some smouldering cow-dung was brought, and gum from a sarai tree dropped upon it. The Dewar called on Thakur Deo. Suddenly, after about five minutes, the god came upon one of the bystanders who threw himself on the ground, and began to tremble and shake his head in the conventional manner. A few minutes later, the god also caught young Charka who was standing with a group of boys higher up the hill. I shall never forget the dramatic and beautiful sight that this

2.1

---

[4] One of the two persons killed by the tiger had been a Gond.
[5] A god considered to be lord and headman of the village.

boy made rushing down the hill with his hair flowing about his head and his arms outstretched. He flung himself on the ground with the greatest violence, and after rolling over and over went and squatted before the council, gently trembling in all his limbs.

2.13   Then the Dewar began to talk, very gently and familiarly to Thakur Deo in the two men. "Rawan hasn't come. You see our difficulty. We are all in terror of this tiger. What are we to do?" The two *barua* kept on trembling and shaking their heads. At last the older man said, "Bodan Dewar's sons can do this." Bodan Dewar had been a very great Dewar in the old days, but neither of his sons were magicians or knew anything about the business in hand. The elders were rather disconcerted, and they said, "But everything may go wrong, these boys know nothing." "That is my responsibility," answered Thakur Deo. "That is my order." The elders again said, still in that curious familiar style, "Please don't let there be any mistake." Then Thakur Deo saw an axe in someone's hand, and he said, "Whose axe is that?" The owner said, "Mine." Thakur Deo said, "If I take it away, what can you do to me?" The elders said, "He can do nothing." Thakur Deo answered, "Then just so, as I've ordered Bodan Dewar's sons to do this, it will be accomplished through them." Then the council asked Charka the same questions and he confirmed what the other man had said. Thakur Deo left the two *barua*, and they got up and went away. Charka's face was strained and tired. His loin-cloth had become disarranged and his companions greeted him with loud and ribald remarks about his appearance. He had only been possessed by the god once before. Neither he nor the other man nor Bodan Dewar's sons were in any way related to either of the dead.

Then the council followed by most of the company, went across the field to where a scrap of rag and the blood-stained earth marked the place where the tiger's victim had met his death. The elders sat down in a semi-circle with the two dull and heavy-looking sons of Bodan Dewar, both thoroughly alarmed, sitting in front of them. The rest of the company stood in two long lines between the council and the big tree where we had been sitting. Someone went round with an axe removing any stumps of trees in this space. Then there was another long wait. They had forgotten to bring any chickens. The childen came, and then it was found that there was no millet. So there was another long wait. At last everything was ready. The Baiga among the spectators had of course been constantly shouting instructions and encouragement to the council.

2.13   When the millet came, the leading guru, who was Jethu of Bohi, put a few drops of sarai gum on the fire in the name of all the *devata* and the sons of Bodan Dewar. He began to tell the legend of Nanga Baiga and Nanga Baigin who had driven nails into the earth and had become lords of all wild animals. He recalled the first time this rite had ever been performed, when Nanga Baiga had been called in to repair the broken boundaries of a village and had bound the mouth of the tiger. Then a man beat the ground violently with his axe and cried, "Get up, stand up!" Jethu made a little cone of mud to represent a man and set it on the ground. He put some millet into the hands of the two sons of Bodan Dewar, and they waited for a few minutes, but the tiger did not come upon them, and presently they were allowed to get up and go away. Then Baghesur Pat "recognized with delight the body of Deriya", the father of the boy who had been killed, and to the astonishment of every-   2.1 one, he came upon him, and Deriya was possessed with the spirit of the tiger.

It was an exciting, almost an awe-inspiring sight. Deriya is a slim, rather sinister-looking man, and now with his long hair hanging over his eyes, and his lithe body half bent to walk, he fully looked the part. He began to roar, and run very swiftly all round the field, wherever the tiger had gone. Then he suddenly turned towards the hill and ran into the jungle. A lot of people chased him, they made a regular beat and drove him back. He came creeping through the long grass and then suddenly leapt roaring into the space left by the crowd in front of the elders. He leapt to and fro, dashed himself on the ground, but could not take hold of the little image of the man. For a witch had bound him. He cried out, "I've eaten one, now I'll eat another." Hearing this, Jethu hurriedly made another little image. After that all the elders took tobacco and had a quiet smoke.

Then Thakur Deo and the Mata[6] came on other men, and they too shouted and threw themselves on the ground. For a time nothing happened. Then Deriya jumped to his feet again, and again ran to the forest and returned. But this time when he came he rushed straight to the two little images and caught them both in his mouth. The people seized him and squeezed his throat so that he could not swallow, and one of the Dewar very carefully took the mud out of his mouth and washed it twice with bitter water from a gourd and then with liquor. Jethu took the images and put them in a little gourd and buried it, placing a big stone above it. Then Deriya ran back about twenty yards, and Bodan Dewar's elder son took a chicken and threw it towards him. The first time a man put up his hand and caught the chicken, and Deriya turned on him with such a ferocious snarl that the man ran back to the village. The second time Deriya caught it and tore off its neck. He ran away towards the jungle drinking its blood as he went and chased by many of the people. They caught him and he threw the chick's body away and a Dewar picked it up and buried it with the mud images.

Then Deriya caught a Dewar by the hand and dragged him at a great pace for about half a mile to a rock that overlooked all the valley below.

---

[6] "Mothers of disease."

There the Dewar drove a nail into the rock, and Deriya shouted at the top of his voice:

> "*Aji-bagh, taji-bagh*, break a twig, break the leaves! *Ataria-bagh, lataria-bagh*, tiger of the nail, tiger of the rocks, tiger with the horns, this is the order of guru Nanga Baiga.
> "O tiger, come out, and go away to the thick jungle. Come out, for here there is nothing to eat or drink. You will get nothing here. Away with you to the thick forest! This is the order of Guru Nanga Baiga. Away with you to the thick forest!"

2.1 Then we all shouted as loudly as we could, a great shout that echoed through the forest, and then kept silence listening whether earth would answer or not. For if a peacock cries or monkey chatters or deer calls in answer to that shout, the Baiga know that their magic has been successful. But on this day there was no response from the earth. After that Deriya was given liquor and he spat it out on to the nails. The Dewar laid his axe on the top of the nail and muttered a mantra. Then we went round and repeated the ceremony in two other places. Once they drove the nail high up into the tree under which the dead man had been caught. Every time we shouted and listened, but not once did earth reply.

All this time the relatives of the dead man, who hitherto had played no part in the proceedings, had been preparing a great feast down by the bank of the stream. . . .

When the food was ready, the relatives of the dead man, both men and women together, sat down and were served by a relation by marriage. . . .

2.1 After this the Baiga Dewar, the same Dewar who had gone with Deriya to drive the nails, a young and energetic Dewar who seemed to act as a sort of agent for the rest, performed the ceremony known as Bel Todna. This is for the special protection of the dead man's family, and for the reward of the magician. The close relatives gathered in the middle of the stream, the dead man's father stood in front and behind him his brother, his widow, his daughter and his relation by marriage. The dead man's brother had brought a long thread, and he carefully tied this three times round the little group. The Dewar put a little rice in the father's hand, and brought a chicken and made it eat a little of it. Then the Dewar walked round the group and splashed water over them. When he came back to the front he took the chicken and the thread together in his hand, and with one sharp movement broke the chicken's neck and the thread. He gathered up the thread in his hand and holding it under the water walked down stream for a few yards and there buried them under a big stone.

3.11 There was then a pause while some vigorous bargaining followed about the fees payable to the Dewar for their services throughout the day. When this was agreed, the Dewar went and lay flat down in the bed of the stream, while someone covered him completely with a cloth. Then each of the dead man's relatives stepped over him one by one, putting a little money on the cloth, and they went down stream without looking back. Somehow they were to find their way home. When they had all passed, the Dewar sat up and counted the gifts that had been made. On this occasion he seemed well satisfied. By this time everybody else had sat for food and so we went as quickly as possible to join them. (Elwin, 1939:300–04)

*   *   *

> Such possession can also be an important means for divining, or diagnosing, a disease.

But there is another very important type of divination where the god   2.1
speaks directly, through the mouth of a man or woman who has passed into a state of dissociation. In every village thre are a number of people known as *barua*, those on whom 'the god can ride'. During most ceremonies, and indeed at any time of quickened religious excitement, these persons are liable to fall into a sort of frenzy—they throw themselves on the ground, their limbs twitch spasmodically, they wag their heads desperately to and fro, . . . they beat themselves with iron scourges, they thrust iron spikes through tongue or cheeks. The god is riding upon them. At such moments, he often reveals secrets that have not been discovered by the ordinary methods of the gunia.

Some magicians, in fact, trust to this as their usual method of divination. They fix a day when their clients are to visit them—every Mon   2.1
day is a common choice—and regularly fall into trances and prophecy. This is known as *dham*.[7] The *dham* requires a certain amount of apparatus. The magician builds a little shrine for himself, and erects a couple of poles before it. He may furnish it with a wooden ladder; with a swing; with a rope studded with iron spikes; an iron chain, spiked, having a knob at the end; a flat board studded with spikes; and a pair of shoes also covered with spikes. When the god rides upon the magician, he may rush up the ladder—not touching it with his hands, he may beat himself with the chains, sit on the spike-studded board, swing violently in his swing, or walk about on the spiked shoes. He may tie branches of thorns round his body. He does undoubtedly achieve a certain degree of anaesthesia. Then from the top of the ladder, or from the spiked seat, he utters his oracle with great authority.

---

[7] A form of divination.

Phulmat has a shrine of this kind, and people go to her for *dham* every Monday. (Elwin, 1939:381–2)

*   *   *

The possessed person may perform the functions of a healer, as
the following description of a *jagar* ceremony shows.

This is the classical treatment for snake-bite. A number of men gather round the victim and begin to sing mantra. As they continue, the
2.1   rhythm of the music affects the more sensitive among them and Nag Deo climbs on one of the *barua* who falls on the ground, and contorts himself
2.13   in the usual manner. Presently he goes to the victim, sucks blood and poison from the wound and spits it out into a pot of milk. Then he throws himself on the ground and counts very quickly, "One, two, three . . ." up to twenty and cries, "This is the bidding of Daugan Guru! Arise! Attend! Beware!" Then he jumps up and sucks the blood again, repeating the whole process three or four times. While he is going so, the onlookers sing with increased vigour and play on the drums. . . .

> May the poison come out and his body grow cool as water!
> May the aches in every part of his body,
> And the pain in his belly be stilled!
> May he once more bathe his body!
> May he once more take his food!
> May he once more walk in his courtyard!
> May he once more walk in the forest and the open field!
> There may the tiger and the bear
> Turn into stones before him!
> May every snake become a stick!
> May thorns and stubble melt like wax!
> When he walks by night, let him not go as an ant,
> Stumbling on his way!
> May light dawn on him! (Elwin, 1939:394–5)

*   *   *

Finally, Elwin gives us two brief autobiographical accounts of the making of a *barua*, first a woman, Phulmat, referred to above, then a man, Jethu, a Dewar who took part in the Mati Uthana ceremony already described.

Pulmat

When I was twenty or twenty-one years old, I saw in a dream all the twenty-one Mata and all the *devata* coming to visit me. They wore
1.21   golden ornaments, and a Mata took the form of a Chamarin. They said to

me: "We have come to you. You are to be our servant. You must obey
us." I said: "I am only a poor woman and I have to work daily for my
living. What can I do for you?" They said: "If you don't obey us, we will
beat you and carry you away." Then they disappeared and I awoke.

Another day, not long afterwards, they came again and said the same   1.1
things. After I fell very ill. All the magicians came, but they could do
nothing. Then my father-in-law came and he said: "I cannot save her.
Take her to her father." So they carried me to my father, and when I saw
him I fainted. Everyone began to weep. But when I recovered, my father looked in his winnowing-fan and he said: "You are ill because you
didn't obey the gods when they came to you in your dream." So then I   1.11
decided I would do whatever the gods told me, and I recovered.

After that, every Monday the god came to me. At the time of my
second son's wedding, the god rode on me, but he told me nothing.

Then Hagru took me to Karadih. We lived happily there. A man in
Karadih fell ill and the magicians went to him. The god came to ride on   2.1
his brother, and came on me also. From that day I have been a magician.
Every Monday the god rides upon me.

Since then I have cured two men, three women and three children   3.21
of their diseases.

When he first came the god spoke very clearly to me. But then one
day my husband's brother's wife went to the *deosthan* during her period
and since then the god has been dim.

At that time I had two dreams. In the first my soul went flying up   2.11
into the sky to catch the sun. I had nearly reached it, and was stretching
out my hand to grasp it and pull it down when I fell down, down, down
into a lot of mud. I stuck in the mud and couldn't get out. But an Ahir
boy came and pulled me out, and brought a lot of water and washed me.
Then he sent me home. When I got there my husband took his sickle
and made it red-hot in the fire and burnt my vagina with it so that I
awoke.

Another day I dreamt that I fell very ill and died. I met many gods   2.11
and they treated me with great honour and put me in a chariot and took
me to Bhagavan's house. The chariot stopped on top of a tree. Then the
tree caught fire and the chariot flew up into the air. I caught hold of one
of the wheels, but my hand slipped and I fell down, and so awoke.

Once a man was very ill. They called five magicians to save him, but
they could do nothing and he died. Then the god rode on me, and I
brought that dead man back to life.

So nowadays in Kotalwahi, whenever anyone is ill, they bring coconuts and some liquor to me on a Monday, and the god comes upon me,
or I 'look' in the measuring straws or my winnowing-fan and tell them
what is the matter, and the sick person gets well again. . . .

Jethu

While I was still a boy I became a magician. My grandfather was very fond of me and taught me everything. At first he made me sit with the winnowing-fan and gourd, and he himself sat beside me to see if there were any mistakes. From my boyhood I have been a *barua*. When the god comes, all men look very small to you, about three feet high. You don't know what you are doing. When the god comes violently, you don't recognize anybody. You feel as if you were drunk. Afterwards you feel very tired and your head and shoulders ache all night. (Elwin, 1939:137–8, 169)

13
Hill Saora Shamans and Their Tutelaries

Introduction

The Hill Saora are one of the native tribes of east-central India. Living in villages distributed on either side of the border between Ganjam and Koraput Districts of Orissa, west and a little south of the coastal city of Puri, their numbers in the early 1950's were estimated to be approximately 100,000. Their main source of livelihood is agriculture; they grow rice in hill-side terraces, millet and maize on cleared plots in the forest, and tobacco and various vegetables in small gardens near their houses. In Elwin's eyes they are a people "remarkable for their independence of spirit, and for the manner in which they have preserved traditions that must be very old" (1959:lii; cf. 1955:311–5).

According to Elwin, "Hill Saora religion is extremely elaborate and occupies a major part of the attention of the people, priests and laity alike." The pantheon contains many deities, though "the inspirations of a thousand shamans import into both doctrine and myth a great deal of variety, with the result that there is considerable confusion in the Saora mind even over so fundamental a matter as precedence among the gods." Shamans and priests play an imporant role in the society. Their myths are concerned with virtually every aspect of their lives, and being "comparatively free from external influence, many of them are strikingly original" (1954:liii-lv).

Between his volumes on the Baiga (1939; see above) and the Hill Saora (1955), Verrier Elwin wrote approximately a dozen books on the cultures of various central Indian tribes. During part of this period he was employed as an anthropologist by the government of the state of

Orissa and by the national government, but much of his work was carried on in a "private capacity," with the assistance of various grants and individuals (1955:xix). He began his fieldwork among the Hill Saora in 1944, and during the next seven years visited all their important villages. He witnessed many ceremonies, some often enough that he was able to assist in their performance. Where the latter was possible, he tells us, "I was able on the first occasion to give my attention to observing and recording what the shamans were doing; on subsequent occasions to overhear and to record what they were saying. I took down the incantations, prayers and trance-dialogues directly, usually squatting on the floor as near as possible to the officiating shaman, who invariably ignored my presence" (1955:xvii). He recorded autobiographical narratives of shamans and other religious leaders, and studied myths, ikons, and ritual paraphernalia. During this time he was able to gain some facility in the difficult Saora language, and also employed three local residents whose services as interpreters he judged to be "quite first-rate" (1955:xvii-xix).

Elwin seems to have been genuinely interested in and sympathetic toward the people among whom he worked. His reporting is thorough and non-judgmental, and one has the impression that the Saora, like the Baiga, came to accept him as a routine, if somewhat eccentric, presence. One can perhaps judge something of the character of the man by the nature of the praise he has for his chief assistant, Sundarlal Narmada Prasad: "His tact, his affection and his knowledge made a great appeal to the Saoras, and it was widely believed that he was a Saora boy whom I had adopted many years ago and who had now returned to visit his old tribe. Sunderlal's remarkable versatility may be gathered from the fact that similar legends have made him in turn a Muria, a Gadaba and a Bondo" (1955:xviii).

Elwin's study of the Saora has been criticized by V. Turner, essentially because he "does not write as a social anthropologist, but as an eclectic ethnographer, and where he interprets, he uses the language of a theologian" (1967:181). In a word Elwin does not examine systematically "the relationship between ritual and social structure," and as a result one is unable to arrive at definitive answers to questions which arise from Elwin's material. What, for example, was the social status of individuals prior to their becoming shamans, or the "structural role" of shamans in "the day-to-day adjustment or adaptation of Saora society" (1967:184)? Turner's essay repays study, both for its clear methodological statement and its suggestions for interpreting certain of Elwin's data. For all its limitations, however, Elwin's material remains a rich resource for someone interested in prophet-like intermediaries.

The Religion of an Indian Tribe has many native autobiographies and descriptions of ceremonies which Elwin himself witnessed. The focus of our concern in the texts which follow will be on male and female intermediaries whom he calls "shamans" and "shamanins," respectively. These are present in every village, with the shamanins sometimes out-numbering their male counterparts (1955:145). Other religious function-aries, like priests and several types of helpers at shamanic performances and funerals, are present as well. The Hill Saora make a distinction in both name and function between the priest (Buyya; offers sacrifice on behalf of the whole village, assists the Chief in village governance, etc.) and the shaman (Kuranmaran, or in the case of the shamanin, Kuranboi; "diviner, medicine-man and celebrant at every kind of sacrifice"), but the distinction between the two roles sometimes blurs. Priests can become shamans, and shamans often officiate at important ceremonies (1955:128–9).

As to the relative status of these two functionaries, Elwin comments that "for practical purposes the Kuranmaran, the shaman, is the most important religious figure in a Saora village." He is a diagnostician, a healer, and a "repository of tradition." He has a divine "tutelary-wife" who guides and helps him, and once this marriage is effected, "he is continually in touch with the gods and ancestors of the other world, and if he is adept he may develop a wide practice, for he is not confined to his own village, but may go wherever he is summoned. He is regarded with respect and often with affection, as a man given to the public ser-vice, a true friend in time of affliction" (1955:130–1). Shamanins are held in similar high regard, though sometimes their ability to function is un-dermined by jealous this-worldly husbands (1955:167, 171).

The texts printed below contain five life-stories and several general-ized descriptions of shamanic activity. Anyone who reads them all (pref-erably at a single sitting) will be impressed by the stereotypical concep-tion of how one comes to be a shaman (proposal of marriage by a tutelary god, initial resistance and then acceptance by the candidate) and rather strictly patterned trance behavior of the shamans. Additional data on shamanism in this general region of India may be found in Rahmann (1959) and D.M. Spencer (1970–71).

Texts

13.1 Life-stories of Hill Saora shamans

Kintara, an elderly shaman from Hatibadi (Elwin, 1955:135–7)

I was born in Jaltal, an ailing child with a great head that caused my mother much pain. While I was still in the womb, my father mistook a snake for a bit of wood and struck it with his axe. This snake was really the god Ajorasum[1], and when I was born he made me very ill. But my

---

[1] "A snake-god who lives in streams," and "troubles pregnant women and babies" (1955:96).

father called a shaman, who sacrificed a fowl to the angry god and dedicated a pot with many promises and I recovered. Later, when I was old enough to play with other children and take the cattle out to graze, my father sacrificed a buffalo to Ajorasum on the bank of a stream.

When I was about twelve years old, a tutelary girl called Jangmai   1.21
came to me in a dream and said, 'I am pleased with you; I love you; I love you so much that you must marry me.' But I refused, and for a whole year she used to come making love to me and trying to win me. But I always rejected her until at last she got angry and sent her dog (a tiger) to bite me. That frightened me and I agreed to marry her. But almost at once another tutelary came and begged me to marry her instead. When the first girl heard about it she said, 'I was the first to love you, and I look on you as my husband. Now your heart is on another woman, but   2.1
I'll not allow it.' So I said 'No' to the second girl. But the first in her rage and jealousy made me mad and drove me out into the jungle and robbed me of my memory. For a whole year she drove me.

Then my parents called a shaman from another village and in his trance my tutelary came upon him and spoke through his mouth. She   2.1
said to my parents, 'Don't be afraid. I am going to marry him. There is nothing in all this; don't worry, I will help the boy in all his troubles.' My father was pleased and bought a she-goat, and two cloths, bangles, a ring and a comb and arranged the wedding. The shaman sat down in the house, put the gifts and a new pot in front of him, tethered the goat near by and, singing, singing, fell into a trance. My tutelary's mother, father   2.1
and sisters brought her to me, and I fell to the ground unconscious. Jangmai asked for her cloth and the shaman dressed me in it. Then she demanded the other things, gift by gift, and they put the ring on my finger and gave me the bangles and necklace, and did my hair with the comb. They gave the second bit of cloth to my tutelary's elder sister. They killed the goat for Jangmai's father, mother and brother. Then the others went away and only Jangmai remained. She said to the shaman, 'Tie up a pot in my name and put rice for me in a cooking-pot. I have married this boy in order to protect him and care for him.' The shaman then made me sit with rice in a winnowing-fan[2] and my hand moved over it of its own accord, and I danced for a long time. Then I put some rice in a new pot for my tutelary and tied up all the things we had bought for her in a bundle and hung it from the roof.

Jangmai's possessions are always there, hanging from the roof, and   2.1
when she asks for them I take them down and show them to her. Often

---

[2] These are flat, woven, squarish implements shaped rather like the blade of a scoop shovel and used for a variety of tasks. "All over India it is regarded as sacred," and Saora shamans use it in divination. "To rub rice in a fan is perhaps the most usual method of inducing trance" (1955:204).

at the Harvest Festivals she comes for her coloured cloth; I put it on and dance in her name. Whenever I go on a journey I put a little palm wine by her pot and say, 'Now I am going on a journey. If a god meets me on the way he may catch hold of me, but I am going to wear your cloth so that the spirits will recognize me and leave me alone.' Then I put the coloured cloth over my shoulder or tie it round my head as a turban, and when gods see me they say to themselves, 'This is a tutelary's husband; we had better leave him alone.'

2.1 Four years after I became a shaman I married a (human) wife, Dasuni. Before we were married, my wife and I lived in the same village and I tried to seduce her. The first time I tried I failed, and my tutelary said, 'If you do this sin, your eyes will burst open,' so I left the girl alone till we were married. After the wedding, Jangmai came upon me and spoke through my mouth to my wife Dasuni saying, 'Now you are going to live with my husband. You will fetch his water, husk his rice, cook his food: you will do everything, I can do nothing. I must live below. All I can do is to help when trouble comes. Tell me, will you honour me or no, or are you going to quarrel with me?' Dasuni answered, 'Why should I quarrel with you? You are a god-wife and I will give you everything you need.' Jangmai was pleased at that and said, 'that is well. You and I will live together as sisters.' Then she said to me, 'Look! Keep this woman as you have kept me. Do not beat her. Do not abuse her.' So saying, she went away.

2.1 Every year, when I give Dasuni a new cloth, I also get one for Jangmai. When her clothes get old I ask her permission to let Dasuni or her children wear them. For now I have a son and three daughters from Dansuni; the boy is twenty-four years old. And from Jangmai I have a son and two daughters in the Under World.[3] The boy is now about twenty and his name is Darsana. One of the girls—Sundri—is fifteen, and the youngest—Sugmi—is ten. When Darsana was born his mother brought him to me and told me his name; she put him in my lap and asked me to make arrangements for his food. When I said I would, she took him down again to the Under World. I sacrificed a goat for the child and dedicated a pot. But I did not dedicate pots when the girls were born, for a boy stays at home but a girl goes to a stranger's house. At the Harvest Festivals these children bother me a lot, for they come crying, 'O father, give us rice and a fowl, give us some liquor, for we're awfully hungry.' This is a nuisance, for it means I have to make sacrifices for them as well as for their mother.

When my tutelary is in her period she does not visit me, and I cannot do the work of divination at that time. When she washes her head

---

[3] The ancestral dead and the tutelaries are thought to live in this world, which is characterized by its dim light and unhappy living conditions (1955:68–71).

she tells Dasuni, 'Now I am clean; wash the clothes and clean the house.'
So Dasuni washes all our clothes and cleans the house. My tutelary's
periods last three days.

In the year I became a shaman, my mother died in child-birth. A
year later my father planted a stone for her. We didn't get enough to eat,
so we moved to Lugurmundi and it was there I married Dasuni. I have
never been to any woman except my wife. A year after my marriage, my
father died, for my mother's ghost came to him and said, 'You are an old
man now, and you don't get enough to eat. Come and join me.' When he
heard this, my father died peacefully the following day. At one time I
often used to see him in dreams, but a few years ago he died a second
time in the Under World, and they burnt his body with castor wood.
Now I see him no more.

In Lugurmundi I was always sick and hungry, and my tutelary said,
'You will never be happy in this village. Don't stay here. Go and build a
house in Hatibadi.' That was twelve years ago. At first when I asked
Kittung[4] for a place to live in, he would not give it to me. But I sacrificed
a pig to him, and he relented; he gave me a site for a house, and now we
live there happily.

Samiya, a fifty-five-year-old shaman from Sogeda (Elwin, 1955:138–9)

My mother was a shamanin. When she fell ill for the last time, she
said to me, 'Now I am going to die. My tutelary will come to you; whatever he tells you, follow it exactly.' The old lady died and as she had
foretold, her tutelaries—she had two of them, one named Lausa, the
other Sarker—came to me in a dream. They said to me, 'Son, your   1.21
mother is dead; now who will serve us? You must look after us; if you do,
we will arrange your marriage.' So I began by serving my mother's tutelaries and at every festival I used to give them rice and wine.

Then one night they came to me with two young girls. One was a
Paik, the other a Dom by caste. They both wanted to marry me, but I
didn't want a Dom girl and refused to have her. My mother's tutelaries
were very angry and beat me with thorn bushes until I agreed to do what
they wanted. At the wedding I sacrificed a goat and three fowls, and I
dedicated four pots, for my mother's two tutelaries and my own two, and
I drew a separate ikon for each of them.

From my Dom tutelary I have had one daughter, Ilianti, who is now
ten years old. Every now and then all four tutelaries come and take me
to the Under World. Since I fly with them I get there very quickly. The
ancestors there are miserable enough, some lame, some blind, some
with only one side to the face, many with great wounds. But the gods fly

---

[4] The term means "god," and Elwin notes that there is a great deal of confusion in "Saora
theology" about the number and identity of Kittung(s) (1955:111–3).

about like birds; they are small as little birds. They have large and splendid houses and keep every kind of animal as pet.

3.21   As a shaman I cure so many people that the gods and the dead dislike me. They say, 'When we come to fetch the sick, you stop us and drive us away with your goats and cocks.' Once the ancestors were so annoyed that they sent Dorisum[5] to attack me and I fell very ill with pneumonia and nearly died. I consulted two other shamans, but they could not do anything, and in the end I had to cure myself.

3.21   One of my most difficult patients was a man named Antanu. He was driven mad by the shade of his dead brother, whose widow Antanu had beaten and driven from his house. 'Look at this good-for-nothing creature,' said the shade to me. 'He shares none of his things with his unhappy brother. He refuses to arrange the Guar[6] for me, and just sits about in my house drinking and enjoying himself, while I have to wander in the woods, cold and hungry and thirsty. Well, now I am going to make him wander with me.' So he drove Antanu out of his wits and made him roam about in the jungle, sleeping at night under trees, without proper food. At last he came home, haggard and raving, and we thought he was going to die. I stayed five days by him; I ate my food where I was, I never left his side. All those days the shade took no notice of me whatever, then at last he said, 'I will only let him alone when he does the Guar for me.' Antanu promised to do it at once, but directly he got better, he forgot all about it, and the shade was so annoyed that this time he attacked me for deceiving him, as he put it, and I had to sacrifice a buffalo at my own expense.

Tarendu, about fifty; the son of a shaman and himself a shaman at Pattili (Elwin, 1955:139)

My father at first refused to marry his tutelary, so she took the form of a wild boar and attacked him. I too had a lot of trouble before I was married, for several tutelary girls were after me. First a potter woman came to my house. I hid inside and she put a pot on the veranda and went away. When she had gone I came out and smashed the pot. Then a Pano girl came with skins and again I hid inside. She put the skins on the veranda. When she was gone, I came out and threw the skins away. Then came two Saora tutelaries, sisters, the elder was cross-eyed, the younger lame and fat. When they arrived I was up a sago palm. They called to me, 'Give us some wine too: we are both going to marry you.' I looked at them and said, 'O no you aren't.' At last came a Paik girl, a

---

[5] "A god of cattle graziers. He gives fever and makes people thin" (1955:101).

[6] An important ceremony for admitting the "shade" of a dead person "to the company of the ancestral dead." It is performed "at any time from a few weeks to several years after death," and has as a prominant feature the planting of a stone, or "menhir" (1955:358–78).

lovely girl in fine clothes; she smiled at me from a distance. She said, 'I am a Paik girl, and you are only a Saora, but I am going to marry you.' I said no, but she caught hold of me and took me to the Under World, where she shut me up in a stone house and gave me nothing to eat. I grew thin as a tamarind leaf, and then she took me to the top of a high date palm and shook it until I was so terrified of falling that I promised to marry her after all. Her name was Sirpanti.

But I forgot all about it, and the result was that I went crazy and   2.1 wandered about the fields like a lunatic until after several months I suddenly remembered what I had promised. At once I arranged for the wedding, sacrificed a goat, dedicated a pot, drew her an ikon, and in no time I was quite well again and began my work as a shaman.

Sirpanti always says to me, 'If you do any sin, you will die.' Every   2.1 year I give her a new cloth and a bangle. One day she gave her cloth to my human wife, for Sirpanti likes her and looks after her.

One year Labosum[7] was angry because I had not sacrificed to him for three seasons. I am always forgetting things like that. He wanted to carry off my wife, but Sirpanti quarrelled with him and drove him away. Another time Galbesum came from Boramsingi and told me in a dream, 'You are a great shaman. I like you. Keep me in your house and I will help me in every way.' Of course I forgot all about this too, and Galbesum sent a tiger which killed two of my cows. Then I sacrificed a pig, and made a pot and an ikon for her, and now Galbesum too lives in my house.

Sondan, a shamanin from Bungding (Elwin, 1955:149)

When I was a little girl of about ten years, some tutelaries came from below to betroth me with pots of wine. One of them took me by force at night, and gave me a lot to drink. They were very pleased with me. When I told my parents they knew that the gods would be pleased with us and would help us. As I grew older, I used occasionally to lose consciousness, but generally only for a few minutes at a time. My father called a shaman and he said, 'A tutelary wants to marry her. That is why   1.3 he gave her wine to drink. Now give her a winnowing-fan.'

I had no one to teach me, no guide or instructor. But I took the fan and poured rice into it. Soon a tutelary came. My father asked him, 'Why   2.1 do you keep on troubling this girl? She may die if you don't leave her alone.' But the tutelary said, 'No, I am pleased with your daughter. I have given her a lot of wine to drink and I am going to marry her. Then if anyone falls ill and she sends for me, I will tell her what is the matter, and help her to cure her patient. I insist on marrying her. Give me a

---

[7] An earth-god "worshipped at most agricultural ceremonies for the fertility of the soil" (1955:114).

she-goat and I will come into the house.' At that my father killed a she-goat, filled a pot with rice and hung it to the roof and the tutelary came into the house.

2.1   So now I was married and five years ago I had a child from my tute-lary. I knew it was born, for my tutelary used to bring him at night for my milk. He came when everyone was asleep and cried and drank my milk. People in the village heard him, but my own family slept as if they were dead. Later I married a man in this world, but because I have had a child in the other world I don't think I will ever have one here.[8]

Ikam, a medicine-man and shaman (Elwin, 1955:258–62)

My father's tutelary was called Sundri and he had four children by her, two boys—India and Behera—and two girls—Goi and Ajari. India has married a shamanin at Gunduruba; Goi is the wife of Karana, the shaman of Jirango; and Behera and Ajari are not yet married.

When I was about sixteen, Sundri came to my father with a young tutelary girl called Tinrai and said to him, 'Find me a husband for this 2.1   girl.' My father thought, 'I have a son. If he marries this girl, he too will be a shaman and will continue my work.' After this, whenever my father offered sacrifice he used to make me sit beside him, though I used to beg him not to force me to this work, of which I was much afraid.

Then one day Tinrai came to me in a dream and said, 'Your father 1.32   promised to marry you to me; that is why he has been teaching you all these things. Now I have come for the wedding.' I said, 'But I don't want to marry you,' and jumped out of bed.

My father was now very old, so old that he could only hobble about on a stick, and his father's ghost came to take him away. But when a goat was sacrificed he let him alone. Then Dorisum tried to take him, but Sundri said, 'He is mine and when the time comes I shall take him. In the meantime no one else is to touch him.' Then again my father fell ill and sent for another shaman to treat him, but Sundri came upon him and said, 'The old man is now very old and sick. If he stays longer in the world, there will be no end to the gods and ghosts who will come for him. It is better that he should go with me now.' So she took him and he died. Since he was taken by his tutelary, he joined the other tutelaries in the Under World, and now he himself has become a tutelary.

Four months after this, my mother was taken away by Ratusum,[9] and she herself became Ratusum, and in that form came soon afterwards and took away my eldest sister Jaggi, for she said, 'I am old, and there is no one to bring me water and give me food.' We tried to persuade her by

---

[8] Subsequent to her conversation with Elwin, however, Sondan gave birth to a son.

[9] "A singularly malignant deity, a cannibal, the god of night" (1955:121).

sacrificing a pig to her at night, but it was no use. Then Kukkusum[10] took my second sister Joman, and Rugaboi[11] took the youngest. But my brothers are alive, and both are married and have children.

One night, while my father was living, I had a dream of many spirits dancing and shouting. I was frightened and ran down the street dancing and shouting too. My father offered sacrifice and cured me. But he said, 'It was a tutelary. You will have to become a shaman.' I replied, 'Give them anything you like, but don't make me a shaman.' So my father offered a hen to the tutelary to let me go. But when the hen was offered rice, it refused to eat. All the same my father had it killed.

2.11

2.1

The next night the young tutelary girl Tinrai came with her whole family on horses and elephants. She left the party to dance on Borong Hill, and she herself with her mother Sindrai, wearing white clothes and with her hair hanging down, came to me. She did not speak a word, but tied my hands and feet, picked me up and took me to Borong Hill. I said, 'What have I done to make you tie me up like this?' Tinrai said, 'I desire to marry you. I will make you a medicine-man and teach you every kind of medicine. But if you refuse I shall take you, tied up as you are, to the Under World.'

1.21

Tinrai left me alone on the slope of the hill. A tiger came by. I screamed with fear and tried to climb a tree. Tinrai and her mother stood a little distance away roaring with laughter. Then I sat on a rock and presently the ogre Kambutung[12] came out of a cave and growled at me. In my terror I fell off the rock and Tinrai picked me up. She said, 'You see the dangers that threaten you because you refuse me. Now tell me, will you marry me or not?' By now I was so frightened that I was ready to do anything and I said I would. I awoke and wandered through the village crying loudly.

My father was very disturbed about this, but before he could do anything about it he died. I was very busy then for several months seeing to the affairs of the family and preparing for the Guar, but soon after the Guar had been concluded, Sundri came with Tinrai and said, 'Son,[13] your father promised to marry you to this girl. I am old woman now and will not marry again. I will live with my daughter-in-law, and whenever you are in any difficulty I too will come and help you.' When she said that, I agreed.

2.11

The next morning when I woke up I remembered what had hap-

---

[10] Perhaps an alternative spelling of "Kukkusumoi," whose name derives from the Saora word for "cough" and who gives people coughs and pneumonia (editor; cf. 1955:114).

[11] "One of the names of the smallpox goddess" (1955:122).

[12] A very dangerous god identified with the bear and the whirlwind (1955:109).

[13] "Ikam counted as the son of his father's tutelary, and his wife was thus her daughter-in-law" (1955:260).

2.1   pened and I made arrangements for the wedding. The following Monday
        I fasted and made an ikon[14] for my tutelary as I remembered my father
        had done, and dedicated a new pot. I sacrificed two fowls and offered a
        man's cloth and a woman's cloth. There was another shaman with me.
        Sundri's father came upon this shaman and said to me, 'I have come to
        give you my daughter.' Then Tinrai's brother came and said, 'I have come
        to give you my sister. Look after her well. If you get into trouble over
        anything, send for me.'
            My sister-in-law came and said the same thing. Then my mother-in-
2.11   law came and said, 'Look, my daughter loves you. That is why she is
        marrying you. Care for her well. Give her food and clothing. Do what-
        ever she tells you; never try to do anything on your own.' Finally my
        own Tinrai came, not on the other but on me myself and cried, 'I am
        pleased with you. Because of my pleasure in you I have married you. If
        there is ever any trouble I will help you. Prepare a pot for me. Give me
        cloth and bangles.' So I put rice in a new pot and hung it up, and gave a
        white cock for Tinrai's relatives, and a cloth for my brother-in-law. They
        were all pleased and went home happily.
            After this I married a wife in this world. One day I beat her and
        Tinrai came and said, 'I am your god-wife and this other has to live with
        you. She does all your house-work and gives you good food. I do no work
        for you and come and go as I please. Yet you do not trouble me; do not
        trouble her either.'

2.11   From Tinrai I have one daughter. She is now four years old and her
        name is Sitrai. When she was born her mother brought her to me, and
        put her beside me and lay down herself on the other side of me. When
        little Sitrai groped for my breasts and didn't find any she began to cry. I
        jumped up and looked everywhere, but there was nothing. Sometimes
        Tinrai visits me every night, sometimes not for eight or fifteen days.
        When I offer sacrifice or go to help the sick, I call her and she comes
        with old Sundri to help her.

3.21   Gradually more and more people came to me and I was kept very
        busy. Then one day I began the work of a medicine-man. I had been
        called to Mannemgolu to perform the Doripur ceremony.[15] Soon after I
        got home, I began to have sharp pains in the stomach. I called another
        shaman and he had a pig sacrificed for me, but it was no use. That night,

---

[14] "Ikons" refers to drawings made "on the walls of houses in honour of the dead, to avert
disease, to promote fertility and on the occasion of certain festivals. . . . The routine procedure, which is almost standardized, is for the shaman to recommend the painting of an
ikon as one of the means of satisfying a god or ancestor who has brought trouble on a
home" (1955:401; cf. 401–44, which contain many illustrations of such ikons; also, section
13.2, below).

[15] A curing ceremony which involves the sacrifice of a buffalo to the god Dorisum (cf.
note 5 and 1955:267–71).

Tinrai came and said, 'So long as I am with you, do not run about con- 2.11
sulting shamans and wasting your money. I myself will tell you what to
do. It was the people of Tammegorjang, an evil village, who did magic
against you.' Then in my dream she showed me a certain hill and a sago
palm growing there. 'There is the medicine you need against sorcery,'
she said. 'Take it; you will find it bitter; but if you drink it, you will
recover.'

Next morning I went to the hill, and there was the tree just as I had
seen it in my dream. I offered wine and rice at its foot, and dug in the
ground. I found the root of which Tinrai had told me and took it home. I
pounded some of it up and mixed it with water and drank it. It was
indeed very bitter, so bitter that I vomited. But that was a good thing,
for I brought up two little worms which had been sent into my body by
the Tammegorjang magicians. After this I gave the sorcery-medicine to
many people.

Another medicine I learnt was the tiger-medicine. A man called
Tinpa of my own village was caught and killed by a tiger. We were all
very frightened and the women did not dare to go out for wood or leaves.
We sent for a shaman from Abada who was supposed to know what to do,
but he was no use. That night my tutelary came to me in a dream and 2.11
showed me a great rock on the Barong Hill, and an *abba* tree growing
beside it. She told me to get the medicine which I would find at the root
of the tree and give it to the people.

So next morning I bathed and went fasting to the rock with four
other men. I made them sit down some distance away so that they should
not see what I was doing. I offered rice and wine to the tree and then
dug up the root. As I dug it up a thrill of fear went through the men who
were with me, as if a tiger was approaching, and they shouted and fired
their guns. I took the medicine home, and after we had burned the
bones of the dead man, I gave some of the root to everybody, and there
was no more fear of danger.

Pararegaman is the medicine to be used after a murder or if someone hangs himself. A boy called Mursui, the only son of his parents,
hanged himself in his house while the family ws out in the hills. We
never knew why he did it. That very night I had dreamt that the boy had 2.11
hanged himself. I was very frightened and did not go to the village for
two days, but slept outside in my forest-hut. Then my tutelary came in a
dream and showed me a place on the Laso Hill above Gailunga, where a
sargiya tree was growing. There was a rock beneath it and on the rock 2.1
something that looked like an onion, which was the medicine we
needed. I went to the rock and sacrificed and brought the medicine
home. The people were on the point of sending to Rajintalu for a shaman
who was said to know what to do, but I told them that I had the medicine
and could attend to the matter myself. I sacrificed a pig and mixed the

medicine in water and gave it to the people to drink. It was very strong, they behaved like drunken men after taking it, and many of them vomited.

In the same way I learnt the *ajoraregaman* and the *doriregaman* to be used at the Ajorapur and the Doripur, and that is why I can perform these sacrifices as well as the others.

I have given the *tonairegaman* to many people. There was a man in Gunduruba who was a very evil sorcerer. He died and turned into a sorcerer-shade. In this form he attacked Agari, the wife of Jamno, in Gailunga. They sent for me and I found her suffering from very bad pains in her legs and body. I sacrificed and brushed her with a feather, and

3.21 when she had taken the medicine I brought two hairy caterpillars and some blood from her chest.

In Sogeda, a man brought some powerful magic with him from Assam. He called a Mannesum and sent him with it against one Bopna.

3.21 When I went there I found poor Bopna with such severe pains in the back that he could not sit up. After I had given the medicine I brought two fishbones out of his body, and after that he was all right.

Benu and Siap, two men of Mannemgolu, quarrelled over a field and

3.21 Siap put magic in Benu's wine. When Benu drank it, he fell ill and his body swelled up alarmingly. From his belly I brought out two date-palm grubs and a small bit of pig's bone.

When I am called to administer the sorcery-medicine, I never go

2.11 that very day. I wait, because for one thing I have to get the medicine fresh and for another I must have the right kind of dream. Some years ago the Chief of Rajintalu was attacked by a sorcerer and four men came to call me. I said I would come the following day. I went to find the medicine, but it took me a long time, for there was none in the usual

2.11 place. That night I had a dream. I dreamt that as I was going to Rajintalu, I met a bear. That was all right, for I frightened it away. A little later I met a tiger, and I frightened that away too. But as I was approaching the village, while I was crossing a field, Kambutung came out of a stream and attacked me. I jumped into the water and shouted myself awake. After this dream I decided that it was taboo for me to go to Rajintalu and the Chief had to get someone else who was no good at all.

2.11   I have learnt everything from dreams, but when I am in trance I have no idea of what I am doing or saying, and afterwards I do not remember anything.

2.2   I am usually called about twice a month to give the sorcery-medicine and perhaps twice in the year to give the *pararegaman*.

13.2 An account of a shaminin's marriage (Elwin, 1955:156–8)

On 20 April 1946, I assisted at Sogeda at the dedication of a young shamanin named Sarpoli, a girl of about fifteen years who had recently passed the menarche. Two years later she was forcibly married to the Chief of her village as his fourth wife. The ceremony was conducted by the talented shamanin Sinaki and was lengthy and confused, for there were many irrelevant features.

Sarpoli had contracted to marry her tutelary, who was named Naianto, some months before and she had told her friends that he was young and handsome. She had several dreams in which he came to her and said, 'I have travelled everywhere, but I have never seen anyone who attracts me so much as you do.' After some persuasion she agreed to marry him. But she then changed her mind, and this led to another dream of a less pleasant kind; now Naianto carried her down to the Under World and shut her up in his house. But she managed to make a little hole in the wall and her soul slipped through and escaped. Naianto was very angry and followed her home and made her unconscious. Through the shaman he threatened that if she did not agree to marry him, he would keep her tied up in his house—thus suggesting that she would remain out of her wits for a long time. Her family promised that the marriage would be celebrated as soon as possible and a fowl was sacrificed, after which the girl recovered.

On the day of the dedication ceremony, the first task was to paint a suitable ikon on the wall of Sarpoli's house, and the official artist, the Ittalmaran, was summoned. He painted a large picture representing the tutelary's house and his many servants and friends in the Under World. Sinaki then made an altar beneath the ikon with little mounds of rice, a lamp and cups of wine. She sat before it, and presently her own tutelary came upon her, closely followed by Naianto. She rose to her feet and carefully examined the painting with her lamp, and Naianto said, 'It is good, but there should be drawings of my mirror and a comb.' For he had asked Sarpoli to give him these things as a wedding present. The artist completed the picture, and then Sinaki and Sarpoli's mother made the girl sit between them and washed her hands and feet with palm wine, saying, 'Today you are married; today you will become great.' Then Naianto again possessed Sinaki and said, 'I am well pleased with this girl and I will marry her and take her to the Under World, where she will see all her new relations.' Sarpoli's mother was distressed at this and cried, 'We have made you a beautiful house on the wall and have prepared the marriage feast; if you take the girl below she will die.' This annoyed the tutelary and he said, 'Don't talk to me like that; if you won't do what I want, I'll have nothing more to do with you,' and he went away. Then Sarpoli herself got frightened and ran away and hid behind a grain-bin. When she did this, the tutelary returned, very annoyed, and demanded to know where his future wife was hiding.

Members of the family quickly brought the girl back, made her sit down and her mother and the shamanin Sinaki held her by the hands

1.21

1.1

1.11

2.1

2.13

and began to chant the usual incantations. A cock had been dedicated for sacrifice to the tutelary, and it was persuaded to perch on Sarpoli's head: it remained there for a considerable time. A very large company had assembled by now, and two other shamanins took swords in their hands and began to dance. Sinaki picked up two new earthen pots and tossed them in the air, throwing them up and catching them again and again. This was a test—if the pots did not break it would be a happy marriage. When she had finished and the pots were undamaged, Sinaki began to

1.32 instruct the younger girl in her duties, saying, 'This is the day of your marriage; from today you will be great, and from today you are to work in such and such a way.' She told her the names of the gods, and how to divine, and how to offer sacrifice, and though none of the information can have been new to her, the instruction took over an hour.

2.13 Sarpoli seems to have been rather alarmed at the multiplicity of the duties that were falling to her, or it may have been just a natural modesty, for she again ran away to hide. The tutelary repeated his protests, and the girl's mother pleaded with him. 'Don't be angry; she is still very young and does not know how to do things properly yet. You yourself must teach her what to do, and then she will know how to behave.' They again brought Sarpoli back and made her sit down in front of the altar. Then Sinaki prepared to dedicate the two pots with which she had already tested the omens; she cleaned and husked some rice and put it with a ring and some turmeric into one; tied a thread with a brass bangle round the other, and hung them both up in front of the new ikon. Then she sat down and made the dedicated cock perch on her shoulder. She fed it with rice and wine, and gave it a little bit of mango, after which mangoes were distributed to everyone present. Somebody killed the cock and it was taken into the kitchen to be cooked. Then Sinaki took Sarpoli in her arms and called on the tutelary to visit them. He came and Sarpoli fell into a trance for the first time. The two girls lay down together, and Sinaki put one of her legs across Sarpoli's body as a symbol of the physical aspect of the marriage. Some of the people laughed at this and Sinaki rebuked them. 'We are gods; we do what we will. Do not laugh and do not interefere.' Then Sinaki addressed Naianto: 'Now you are married to this girl, don't trouble her, don't desert her, but always come willingly to help her.'

2.1 After this the whole party went round the village, and wherever there was a house of shaman or shamanin, they showed Sarpoli the ikons on the wall and the sacred implements of divination. They returned, and once again Sinaki held the young bride in her arms; she rubbed her body with turmeric and again explained her duties, taught her and nursed her as if she were a little child.

The ceremonies continued throughout the day. There was dancing and many shamanins came from neighbouring villages and fell into trance and prophesied. The proceedings concluded with a feast to which the members of Sarpoli's family group and a number of important people were invited.

13.3 The shaman's wages and perquisites (Elwin, 1955:449–52)   3.11

But can a shaman make a decent living? In answering this question, we must remember first that the shamans and shamanins live for a large part of their time the ordinary lives of Indian peasants. A shaman has his property, his fields and his herds, he may engage in trade, he may work for Government. A shamanin is generally married, she performs the ordinary duties of the home; she works in the family fields and clearings, plies the spinning-wheel, takes her produce to market and earns her living like any other woman.

But on the other hand, a shaman or shamanin, especially a popular one, has to spend a great deal of time away from the ordinary business of life, and this is one reason why young people are so reluctant to obey the dreams that summon them to a dedicated life: the constant interference in the work of the fields or house does involve an economic loss; after an exacting ceremony a shaman may be too exhausted or too fuddled with wine to do any work that day; and his attention too is diverted—the dream world in which he lives is not the best setting for agricultural success.

Yet the profession of shaman is not unprofitable. He receives, in kind, a small but useful income which compensates for the considerable loss of time and energy involved in his work, and this income—it must be remembered—is additional to the regular annual profit which comes to him from his fields and clearings, his herds and palm trees.

As in other professions, there is a very wide diversity in the shaman's receipts. A shaman who is qualified to act over the whole range of ceremonial, is known to be favoured by the spirits, and has a practice extending over a number of villages, will naturally have a larger income than one who can, for example, officiate only at the Ajorapur,[16] or who has no tutelary and thus cannot enter into trance, or who is restricted by custom or competition to his own village.

An important aspect of a shaman's life is the fact that for much of his time he lives free of cost. Since every Saora ceremonial ends with a feast, and since it is essential that the shaman should share it, he gets a very large number of free meals. Some shamans get at least one such meal every day, some get even more. And these meals are good square meals—plenty of rice, vegetables, perhaps crabs and fish, and nearly always a generous share of meat. And of course as much palm wine or

[16] A sacrifice for the protection of small children, especially from snakes (cf. note 1 and 1955:271–82).

liquor as one can hold. It is not easy to estimate the value of such a meal in cash. In a town it might well cost two or three rupees; on Saora standards it is probably worth about a rupee.

I will now examine the actual incomes of some shamans and shaman-ins, and try to assess what they really come to. The Saoras share to the full a common human frailty, a reluctance to reveal the truth about their incomes, but I found that though a shaman was very unwilling to say what he received from agriculture, he was much more forthcoming about his ritual profits. For, in the first place, these are known to everybody; they are on a more or less fixed scale; and they are not taxed. In the second place, the shamans felt that they grew in dignity as they counted 3.1 up their takings. I do not think, however, that they exaggerated: there wre too many friends and neighbours present during my inquiries, and every figure was publicly checked.

Ikam, the medicine-man of Kamalasingi, is an adept and famous practitioner, and since he is the only medicine-man in his part of the country, he is summoned to vilages over a wide area. The following is his own estimate of his income for the year 1950.

There are first a number of ceremonies, for which it is taboo for a shaman or medicine-man to receive payment. On these occasions he shares in the feast, but he cannot take anything away with him. Ikam said that during 1950 he performed the following ceremonies:

> Parapur Twice
> Ratupur 4 times a month
> Lambapur 10 times in the year
> Kurrualpur 10 times in the year
> Jammolpur 6 times in the year

The last three ceremonies are for the dedication of seed, for the protection of the hill-clearings before sowing and for the profit of the pulse harvest. Ikam goes each year to ten different places for these and, at each, feasts with the people, but can take nothing away. At other rites there are definite perquisites, and I give their approximate value at 1950 prices in the Saora country.

Ikam said that he celebrated the Tonaipur and Doripur on an average twice a month, and the Uyungpur, for the Sun-god, three times a month. He was even more in demand for the Ratupur, which he estimated at four timas a month. Obviously these figures are approximate, but they may not be so far out, for they are the sacrifices which are most generally offered. Ikam, therefore, on his own estimate, received in 1950[17] a total of Rs 24 in cash and Rs 254–2–0 in kind. But in addition to this he had

---

[17] "In 1950, in this part of the Saora hills, rice was selling at Rs 2 a measure, a fowl cost from Rs 2 to Rs 4, and buffaloes were from Rs 25 to Rs 35 without the skin" (1955:451).

no fewer than 187 good meals, which I have suggested were probably worth a rupee a time. We may, therefore, to be on the safe side, estimate Ikam's annual income as a medicine-man at about Rs 450.

There was no death from tiger during the year, but even if there had been it would hardly have affected the total; for at this and the Parapur which is celebrated in cases of suicide and murder, the shaman may not accept anything but his food.

13.4 Shamanic trance (Elwin, 1955:469–77, 483)

The trance occurs, or may occur, as a feature of any ceremony at which the spirits are invited to be present, provided there is a shaman qualified to accommodate them.

But if the ceremony is being conducted by an ordinary priest, or by an Idaimaran,[18] or by a shaman not fully qualified, then it proceeds to its conclusion more expeditiously, but without the excitement and interest that a shaman in trance invariably provides. Shamans may also fall into trance on occasions at which they are performing no official function; I have often seen shamanins fall to the ground in a state of spirit-possession at entirely secular dances or during the processions of a Harvest Festival. On more than one occasion I have been somewhat embarrassed by a shamanin going into trance as a result of listening to my gramophone. 2.1

Once a shaman passes into a state of dissociation anything may happen. The belief is that he is possessed by a spirit, or more usually, a succession of spirits who speak and act through him. He is supposed to be completely under their control and to have no knowledge of what he is saying and doing. Yet although there is no programme, and there is endless diversity in detail, there is a remarkable general similarity throughout the whole Saora country in the way the shamans talk and behave at these times. 2.1

There is generally great confusion and, as I say, anything may happen. There may be revelations and discussions about matters entirely unrelated to the sacrifice or festival at which the trance occurs. The dead are always breaking in, for—it is said—'at the least sign of love the dead approach'. A ghost may take the opportunity to give instructions about the disposal of his property or to demand a quite different sacrifice later on; a god may give warning of an epidemic or threaten ruin to the crops. The regular course of the proceedings may also be interrupted by visitors who drop in for a consultation. For once it is known that a shaman is in trance, it is economical to consult him, for it is supposed that now the door to the other world is open, the spirits are there thronging to get 2.1

[18] The Idaimaran functions only at funerals, and usually only at the family level (1955:141–4).

through, and it is a good time to consult them about one's personal affairs, however irrelevant they may be to the matter in hand.

2.1   There is a fairly definite routine of entering on an officially-induced trance (as distinct from those which occur spontaneously), and there are several ways of preparing for it. It is generally preceded by a period of invocation when the shaman[19] squats on his heels before the altar or ikon, makes offerings of rice and wine, and calls on the spirits to attend. When he feels that 'they are on the way', he changes his posture, sitting upright on the ground with his legs stretched out straight in front of him. He takes a fan of rice in his left hand and lights a little lamp which he waves above the rice and places by the altar. Then he begins to rub his right hand round and round in the rice, calling as he does so on his tutelary to come upon him. He continues doing this for as long as perhaps five minutes, and his voice grows fainter until suddenly he gives a start, his whole body stiffens, his arms extend straight before him and both his hands clench themselves tightly over his fan. His attendants at once catch hold of his arms and legs and bend them and unclench his fingers; this sometimes involves a regular struggle to break down the rigor which the trance induces.

2.1   Then there is a pause. The shaman sits with head bent, legs straight forward, his arms stretched along them. And then all at once he begins to speak in a high-pitched unfamiliar voice, sometimes using a few Kui or Oriya words; this is the voice of the spirit who has come upon him.

2.1   After this there is no programme, no routine. The shaman *becomes* whatever spirit has possessed him for the time being, and within an hour he may play a dozen different parts. He appears to be entirely out of his own control. He weeps, laughs, jokes, curses. Now he is a woman and pretends to give suck to a child; he puts anything given him on his head as a woman does. Now he is an old man, wears a big hat and hobbles round driving imaginary herds before him with a stick. Now he is a tutelary's horse and demands water and drinks it with great noisy gulps. A bawdy ghost comes upon him, and he demands a woman, catches hold of one, and makes a token attempt at intercourse. As an old man he coughs and spits; as an old woman he sheds tears, pats his shrunken breasts and combs his hair. When the ghost of old Jigri came one day at Boramsingi, the shamanin tottered about on a stick complaining of her sore foot just as Jigri used to do in life.

2.2   Although a shaman engaged in sacrifice or incantation may be left severely alone, there is always a crowd when he goes into trance. For here is pathos and humour, bargaining and gossip; a good shaman provides first-class entertainment. And there is nearly always a hot discussion, the congregation remonstrating, pleading, arguing; the spirit com-

[19] "All this will apply equally to a shamanin" (1955:470).

plaining, abusing, threatening at first, then gradually softening in the face of promise and persuasion.

Normally a shaman's own tutelary comes upon him first, and after 2.1 that a succession of gods and ghosts. The sign that one is going and another coming is that the shaman's voice falters and dies away; his body jerks convulsively and his hands slide down his legs to his feet; sometimes he scratches his armpits. There is a pause and then he begins to speak in a different voice.

When everything is over, the shaman relaxes; he spits into his hands, rubs them together, rubs them over his face, yawns, stretches himself; he is like someone waking up.

Although the most common way of inducing trance is by the aid of 2.1 rice in a winnowing-fan, there are several other methods.

A new earthen pot, which will later be dedicated to a spirit, may be used to induce a sort of auto-hypnotism. The wife of Somra, at Taraba, who was a well-known shamanin, affected the use of the pot in preference to any other method. I once watched her in trance for two whole hours as she talked with her tutelary and his relatives. After hanging up two coloured cloths for her daughters in the Under World, she dedicated a pot to the tutelary and began to speak into it, holding it close to her mouth, first to one cheek and then to the other. She threw it up and down, catching it in both hands and all the time calling on her tutelary husband to come to her. For a time he did not come and she wept. Her attendants sat behind her ready to catch her when he did come. Suddenly she stiffened and fell back into their arms. The tutelary refused wine and demanded a little rice-beer; the shamanin had to mix some rice-flour with water and drink it. Then one by one all her relatives in the Under World came upon her and she talked to them in turn, singing into the pot which she held caressingly to her mouth. Sometimes she held the pot with one hand and rubbed rice in a fan with the other. When all was over she hung the pot up before an ikon.

The *kuranrajan*[20] and the hide-gong are also used to induce the 2.1 proper rhythmic atmosphere for trance. The shaman accompanies his invocations on the fiddle, and soon the quiet rhythmic music accomplishes the desired result. The steady beating of a hide-gong serves the same purpose, and so may a dance. The shamans are very sensitive to any kind of rhythmic music or movement.

I can best give some idea of what happens in trance by describing an actual case, one of scores which I have attended. On 22 December 1950, Iswaro the young Chief of Boramsingi, and nephew of old Jigri, fell ill, 3.21 and an old shamanin, by name Sahadri, was summoned to discover why.

[20] A two-stringed musical instrument made from a bamboo stick and a large gourd (1955:211–2).

The actual period of trance lasted from 2.30 to 3.45 in the afternoon.

2.13   Sahadri sat with two Idaibois to assist her before a small altar consisting of a basket of rice and a pot of wine, beneath an ikon for her tutelary. Her patient, Iswaro, sat just behind her. She began in a squatting posture and, taking a pinch of rice between her thumb and forefinger, passed it over the boy's back as she chanted, calling on the ancestors:

'Was it one of you who threw a bit of wood at him or sent a worm into his belly or hit him on the head with a stone? Why has he got this pain? Come and make him well. I call you with rice. Whether you be Rajas, whether you be servants, come all of you. Come Jigri, come Jigri's mother, call the other ancestors. Do not come by a roundabout way, come by the straight road. Do not rest in caves or under trees or on the banks of streams, but come straight here.'

She threw away the rice and, turning to the ikon, offered wine before it. Then she stretched out her legs and took a fan in her lap. One of the Idaibois[21] handed her a small basket of rice. Sahadri lighted her sacred lamp and waved it round and round above the basket; she examined it carefully, smelt it, took out some of the rice and peered at it, passed her hand through the flame of the lamp and then threw a few grains towards the ikon. She poured the rest of the rice into her fan, and began to rub her right hand round and round in it, calling on her tutelary as she did so.

'There is a good road. Come quickly and help me discover what is wrong here. Whether it is a big matter or a small matter, it is for you to see to it. Is this boy's pain due to sorcery? Is it the work of a god? Is it a god of this world or of the Under World? Is it Uyungsum? Is it the god who lives in aeroplanes? Gogoji Rajaji, take this matter into your ears and attend to it. Goiyaraji Kararaji (famous old shamans who had become tutelaries), come and help. Whether it be tough or tender, soft or hard, come to us and help. Look in your books and come. Do not trip or stumble on the way; do not stub your toes against stones in the path. You who live with Kittung, come. If there is a rock in the way, break it open; if there is a tree in the way, knock it down; if you are in an aeroplane, descend.'

The shamanin continued in this strain for about fifteen minutes, calling on every god, ancestor and tutelary she could remember, and then gradually her voice began to die away; she herself seemed to grow weaker; you could almost see her passing out of normal consciousness. She spoke slowly, then more slowly, until she was silent but for little gasps and cries. She gave a sudden start, her body tensed and stiffened, her hands gripped the sides of her fan.

The Idaibois at once caught her arms and legs, and after a little

---

[21] The "female counterpart of the Idaimaran" (1955:143 and note 18, above).

struggle relaxed them; it was harder to force open the clenched hands. There was then a pause of about a minute of complete silence, and for once there was not so much as a whisper among the onlookers. Then Sahadri jerked her body sharply and picked up some rice, smelt it, threw it up into he air and began to rub the rice in her fan. Suddenly she gave a loud scream, which indicated that her tutelary had come. Through her he cried, 'What are you bothering me for? What is it you want now?' The Idaibois and the others in the room at once began to explain, all speaking at once with a tremendous chatter. 'Tell us,' they said, 'was it a god of the forest or a god of the path?' 'Why,' asked the tutelary, 'had the boy been somewhere?' 'Yes, he'd been to Jampapur.' 'then I'll go and find the god who did it and bring him here. But it might have been a plot of your enemies in Boramsingi and Kittim. Personally, that's what I think it was, but I'll go and find out.'

The shamanin jerked forward, her hands slid down her legs, and she remained silent with bent head for a couple of minutes. This was supposed to allow the tutelary time for his inquiries. Another violent jerk announced his return. The shamanin put her lamp beside her and began to rub her rice again. Once more everybody began to shout questions. The tutelary refused to answer till he had a drink. The shamanin took a long draught of wine, but the tutelary (speaking through her own lips) abused her. 'This is water. Get me some proper wine, and in a tumbler. There is a sahib here. That shows that this is an important occasion; I must be treated right.' There was another pause while someone went off to my camp to get a tumbler. When it came, it was filled with wine and the shamanin took a long drink. 'That's better,' said the tutelary. 'Now tell me again, what is it you want?' More screaming voices answered him.

'There was a banyan tree', said the tutelary at last, 'on the path to Jampapur, and the tutelaries of Singjangring and Jampapur had put their pots of gruel in its shade while they had a chat with some ancestors from Ladde who were returning home after a sacrificial feast. The boy kicked one of the pots over as he went by. You must give a pig in compensation at once.'

After another drink, the shamanin gave another jerk as a sign that her tutelary had departed. She was then visited by a procession of ancestors. One of them, Iswaro's paternal uncle, admitted that he had been there under the banyan tree, but disclaimed any share in the incident. Then the ghost of the shamanin's own dead husband came and discussed family matters with her sister who was sitting near by. Rather late, for owing to the sore on her foot she could only hobble along, the ghost of Iswaro's formidable aunt Jigri arrived. She demanded to see the pig proposed for sacrifice. She now showed that she had taken with her to the Under World those sound financial gifts which had made her so prosperous in life. The shamanin (in her character as Jigri) took the pig in her lap and carefully examined it. 'It is not very fat,' she complained. 'You paid far too much for it. Couldn't you get some of the money back? In any case, it's too small. When we have important visitors in the village, we ought to do better than this. Why don't you sacrifice a buffalo?' The spectators explained volubly, stressing their poverty, their debts, the failure of the crops that year, the endless demands upon them. Jigri laughed derisively. 'I've been watching you ever since I died. You may trick others, but you can't trick me. You can't see me, but I can see you. I know just how well off you really are.'

Then an old man with an obvious hangover, who was not even related to Iswaro, came in and insisted on the shamanin inquiring into the cause of his bad head. Sahadri passed her hands over his body, removed something from it and placed it in the fold of her cloth, then pulled at his fingers and toes. The ghost of a man who had been murdered some years previously came upon her, saying that he was now Uyungsum and that the old toper must give him a buffalo. This was rather more than he had bargained for, and he hastily put some rice in the shamanin's hands and clasped them in his, saying, 'Look, you and I are old friends; we used to go drinking together; you wouldn't want to bother an old friend.' But the ghost swore with an oath that unless he had a buffalo he would take his old friend away.

This interesting discussion was interrupted by the return of Jigri's ghost; she was not satisfied about certain matters concerning the disposal of her extensive property, and in particular insisted that he niece Arari, who had let her down by marrying before her dedication as a Guarkumboi had been completed, should not be given the keys of any of the storerooms.

The proceedings continued with a score of irrelevancies. Young Iswaro was completely forgotten. Sometimes the talk was homely and good-natured; the spirits laughed and made the people laugh with them. But sometimes they discussed the scandals of this and the other world, and a ghost would be angry and abusive.

At last, when it was approaching four o'clock, the shamanin's tutelary returned and showed an interest in the patient of the day. He made the shamanin blow violently in his nose and ears, feel his ribs, blow on his stomach, stroke his legs and thighs, squeeze his arms. Then he said, 'He's going to be all right. Sacrifice that pig at once, and there will be no more trouble. Give me something to drink and I'll be off.'

The shamanin took a long drink out of the tutelary's special tumbler, jerked violently to show that the spirit had gone, and then relaxed completely as a sign that she was coming out of her trance. She spat on her hands and rubbed them over her face, yawned and sat up. Then without any pause she turned to me with a beaming smile and asked for some medicine for itch!

What are the shaman's own sensations while he is in trance? Some   2.1
say that they feel intoxicated, as they well may in view of the amount they drink on behalf of their spirit-guests. One shaman compared the trance to his first experience of sexual intercourse: 'Everything went black before my eyes.' Another also compared it to a first intercourse, but more poetically: 'It was as if the sky and the earth were made one.' A shamanin at Baijalo rubbed her eyes on coming out of trance because, she said, 'Owing to the god everything was dark'. Yet another said, 'My throat is parched and I feel very thirsty. I feel like someone lost on a lonely road.'

All shamans agree that they know of what goes on during the trance,   2.11
the details of the conversations, which spirits came to them, how they themselves behaved. But some of them say that their inner experiences of a sort of dream world vary according to the kind of spirit that possesses them. The dead, for example, are far more exhausting than other spirits. A shaman at Tumulu described his experience like this:

When a god comes on me, everything is dark: people look very small and of many colours; sometimes I see a bazaar, a river, hills and many animals—horses, elephants and monkeys. When everything is over, two lovely young girls come to me and catch me by the hand and cry, 'Come with us to our world'. I resist them and it is the act of pushing them away that wakes me up.

Another shaman, Samiya of Sogeda, had similar experiences of the   2.11
Under World while he was in trance.

When a tutelary comes upon me, I see a great white house and a broad straight road with elephants, horses and soldiers, just as they might be here, but all very small. There is an office with clerks writing at tables, and the police bring in people naked with their hands tied behind them. I see a banyan with many monkeys and gods sitting in talk below. When the tutelary is on the point of going away, two pretty girls catch me by one hand and two other girls catch me by the other and they say, 'Come, come!' I wrench my hands free, and the tutelary departs.

It is bright when a tutelary is with me, but when the ancestors come everything is dark. I do not know where I am or what I am doing. I see nothing but mountains and a winding road. There are houses in rows, very small, and their doors are as small as windows. Many tigers prowl round the villages. The women are dressed like Saora women and their babies are usually crying for food. There are great rocks and people sitting on them; they are silent as if they were thinking about something. When the ancestors depart, I feel as if I am falling into a pit, and after they have gone I am completely exhausted.

This seems to be the general opinion, for Sondan the shamanin also said that 'When a god comes, everything looks beautiful to me, and when he leaves me I do not feel at all tired. But when an ancestor comes, everything is dark and when he goes my body is worn out and aches in every bone.'

2.1 These experiences compare, of course, with the dreams of the Under World which every shaman has and the general picture compares with those of the ikon paintings. But the sense of exhaustion, and the motif of the pretty girls who would keep the shaman for ever in the world of dream are peculiar to the trance-state.

2.1 But whether the shamans know what they are talking about or not, they do in effect give a dramatic exhibition of what the spirits are supposed to be like. The records of these trance-sessions, therefore, throw much light on Saora theology, on the relations of the living and dead, of human and divine, and above all on the character of the gods. . . .

2.1 It is impossible to watch one of the greater Saora shamans or shamanins in trance without being impressed by their extraordinary quality. For his work a shaman must not only have a good grasp of theological principles, but a considerable knowledge of local geography, history and economics; he must be acquainted with the circumstances and genealogies of every family in his circuit; and he must also be well aware of village gossip. In the state of dissociation, all his varied knowledge and experience comes to the fore and is expressed in a dramatic performance which often has a genuinely healing effect.

THE PACIFIC

14
Kamoai, "Canoe" of the Goddess Jari
Introduction

In this section and the next we turn our attention to New Guinea, where a variety of millenarian movements known collectively as "cargo cults" has attracted considerable scholarly attention (cf. section 15, below). Leaders of cargo cults are not the only intermediaries to be found in New Guinea, however, as a recent collection of essays entitled *Prophets of Melanesia* demonstrates. As the editor of that volume, Garry Trompf, remarks, "Without denying that figures happily described as prophets have arisen in connection with (cargo cult) activities, it bears emphasis that Melanesian prophetism is a phenomenon in its own right and ought not to be confined within the ambit of cargo cultism" (Trompf 1977a:13–4).

The text printed below represents a substantial portion of one of the studies included in Trompf's volume, "Kamoai of Darapap and the Legend of Jari." Its author, Matthew Tamoane, is a native Melanesian who, at the time of publication, was employed in the Curriculum Division, Education Department, Papua New Guinea Government. His account shows that he had first-hand knowledge of the situation about which he wrote. A number of the people, including Kamoai, Jari's intermediary, were in fact his relatives.

Prophets of Melanesia contains several additional detailed accounts of intermediaries (Trompf, 1977b; Jojoga, 1977), several of whom manifest considerable Christian influence (Fergie, 1977; Tuza, 1977).

Text (Tamoane, 1977:174–8, 198–211)

The people of Darapap (Murik Lakes, East Sepik Province), like many other groups of people in Papua New Guinea, are strong believers in the existence of controlling supernatural powers. Such beliefs have been passed down from generation to generation, and even today, with the introduction of Christianity, older people still believe in powers which are regarded as Satanic by some Christians.

Before Christianity was introduced to Papua New Guinea, and in particular to the people of Darapap, our forebears believed that powers existed which were much superior to human powers. These supernatural powers included those regarded and worshipped in the Sepik as gods and goddesses, as well as the ancestral spirits, and people depended on them for their well-being. The people's daily life was closely connected with the supernatural world, in fact religious beliefs were part of the economy of the community.

In Darapap today the village elders still maintain such beliefs. Each clan or sub-clan has its own 'family' god or goddess, while the spirits of dead relatives are regarded as mediators between living humans and the deities. Sometimes people convey their needs and requests to the gods through their ancestral spirits, although most times requests are made directly to the deities. The family (or clan) gods[1] are consulted for direction and guidance on matters concerned with day-to-day living. If a clan member wants to go hunting for wild pig, for instance, he calls some fellow members to his house and tells them both of his plans and his reasons for going hunting. After talking, the members will dedicate some food to their family god, and the huntsman will make his request to that god before the other members. All members must agree together or else the god will not fulfil the request. The request may be as follows: 'Our family god (the name is then inserted), tomorrow I am going to hunt pigs and will take the dogs with me. I want you to give me two pigs. You must direct the dogs to the pigs and help the dogs to kill them. Make the pigs weak when the dogs start fighting with them'. To end his request, the man calls the name of the god again and says: 'This is all I have to tell you. Come now and eat with us'. The other clan members will support the request by repeating the god's name, and adding, 'This is true, we all agree that you provide his request'. The food is then eaten in the name of the god[2]

Most family gods have a *ga'in* (= 'canoe' in Murik, the language of the Darapap people), and this is a particular member of the clan who is possessed by the given deity on special occasions. He or she is the medium through which the family god communicates with the people. The *ga'in* becomes possessed whenever the clan members wish to request something special from their deity, when the members want to know the cause of a sickness, for example, or whether they will be successful in a hunt. The god is supposed to speak through the *ga'in* and foretell what is going to happen with regard to their requests. It is as if one is setting

---

[1] "There are deities recognized by one whole clan in particular. Family deities are those specially attended to by a smaller group within the clan." (M.T.)

[2] "Consensus is important. If someone who should be at the gathering is not present—because he is disgruntled in some way, for example, then the family god will not act." (M.T.)

out in a canoe; one has to get into it. And so the deity 'gets into' the
ga'in—to tell about future events and exploits.

Along with these minor family or clan deities, the Darapap people
have their high god known as *kakar*, the superior deity for the whole
community. He is understood to be a god of war and is 'kept' at the main
fire-place of the cult house. He is placed on a small ark-like platform
some seven square metres in size, and this platform is placed beneath
the roof above the main fire-place, being supported by four poles. The
high god is taken as the composite of a number of war clubs. These clubs
carry carved faces and were used by former Darapap warriors, who were
said to have originated from Wagiromoa (near Moim, Angoram Sub-
Province), floated down the Sepik River, settled first on Walis Island and
then at Saure (near Wewak), and eventually found it more peaceful in
the place where they stay presently. All through their journeyings, the
ancestors used these clubs to fight and kill those who engaged them in
war. Tradition has it that the great ancestral warriors clubbed their enemies to death with these weapons, and that the carved heads were not
fashioned by human hands but 'conceived' by the famous ancestral
woman named Areke. Each club denotes a god, but when considered
altogether they are taken as one—as *kakar*—in much the same way as
the three Persons of God are taken as one in the Christian religion.[3]

Whenever the people wish to consult *kakar* they must make an offering of food and *galip* nut in the name of *kakar*. The *gapar* or the elder
priests are the only persons qualified to handle the *kakar*; women, children and indeed anyone who has not been initiated into the *gapar* priesthood are not allowed to see or handle the *kakar* nor even participate in
the discussions about it. Whenever the *kakar* is consulted the leading
member of the *gapar* will announce: 'Kakar will come down tomorrow',
although he is not consulted as often as the *brag* (the family or clan gods).
He is so sacred that consultation with him involves much initiatory preparation. The *kakar* speaks through an older priest who is a special *ga'in*
called *gapanor*, which means '*kakar*-possessed'.

The Prophetess and the Myth of Jari

This article is about Kamoai of Darapap. Kamoai, a grandmother of
mine who died in 1964 in her mid-sixties, was considered a special per-
sonage by the villagers of the whole Murik Lakes area because she was
possessed from time to time by the goddess known as Jari. Before discussing the career of this remarkable woman, it is necessary to present
and analyse the long and complex myth of Jari as it has been pased on

[3] "For further information, see M. Somare, *Sana; an autobiography*, Port Moresby,
1975, pp. 15–6, 30–1." (M.T.)

from elders to initiates. This long, strange legend, here published for the first time, is interesting for its own sake as well as for the light it throws on Sepik oral history and the specific role of Kamoai.

At this point Tamoane recounts the myth of Jari (1977:178–98), a summary of which follows. The villages mentioned are located along the northeast coast of New Guinea on both sides of the Sepik River, between Bogia and Wewak.

Jari was born in the village of Karoam from an adder who lived in a pile of coconut husks and was impregnated by the urine of villagers. When she reached womanhood, she would play on the beach each evening with the village youths, but would always disappear early and return home. Eventually, her companions became suspicious, and one evening they successfully carried out a plot to capture her. She married one of her captors, and in time gave birth to a son.

One day Jari placed her son in a reed basket, asked her mother-in-law to watch him, and went off on an errand. In her absence her mother, the snake, came and slid into the basket to play with her grandson. When the child cried, the father snatched him out of the basket and burned the snake in a fire. Jari immediately sensed her mother's death, and when she returned, it was confirmed. She continued to live with her husband, but one day when he was out hunting with the other men, she set a pot of water on the fire, put in some bananas, and cut up her child into the boiling water. She then sabotaged the village canoes and made her escape.

Jari travelled to a series of a dozen villages, where she either created a tidal river (". . . by drawing a line on the sand with her broken paddle. Standing over the line she urinated, and the river came about. 'You go in and out', she told the water. What she meant was that, at high tide, the ocean water could go into the lake and mangrove swamps, but during low tide the water could go out to the ocean.") or brought medicine for aiding in difficult childbirths ("'We are helping a woman to delivery', they replied, 'We are going to cut her open, get out the man-child, and then bury the mother.' . . . The women said to Jari, 'You should have come here a long time ago. We have destroyed many a good woman this way.'").

Next, Jari married Kamandong, and changed for the better his unsatisfactory, from her point of view, mode of existence. She provided him with "proper" betel nuts, pepper, and lime (which he agreed were "better than mine"), as well as tobacco and a penis. Kamandong was eventually captured by "fish-woman," but with the aid of a magician made his escape and returned home safely. Jari was waiting for him, but as soon as he arrived, she left for another village, Manumbwamot, and married another man, Arekendamot. Soon she ran away to Manam Island with Areken-

damot's trading partner, Divadiva, and married him. After Arekendamot's death, Divadiva took her back to the mainland, "but
Arekendamot's younger brothers fought with him, and they cut
Jari into two halves. They took one half of her and Divadiva took
the other. . . . This is the end of her legend."

This long story is a subject of interest in its own right. It explained
many different facets of life to the coastal peoples who told and retold
it—how fire was created, for example, why the rivers are tidal, and how
it is that most births, despite their pain, are successful. If there was once
a time when fires and rivers were lacking, when people's eating habits
were unrefined, when mothers died in childbirth, Jari brought about a
better situation and new skills. Thus the legend explains why things now
are as they are. Above all, however, it is the story of a powerful goddess,
whose origins were special, whose life also suggests her special relationship with women or those who seek love and marriage, and whose influence is understood to live on.

When Jari was severed in two, it is said, one half was taken back to
Manam Island (where she is remembered in stories and called up as a
helpful spirit), and the other half lived in the bush, inland from Manumbwamot, in spirit form and as a hidden power. This power eventually
shifted to a point between Bogia and Angoram, to the villages of Sanai
and Gapun. Although she had bestowed gifts and skills on the people
while she was among them, her hidden powers now came to be relied
on, especially at Sanai and Gapun, for healing and for effective sorcery
against enemies. These two villages paid much attention to her, certainly
by the beginning of this century, though how long before that is difficult
to tell.

Now stories about Jari currently circulate between the Murik Lakes
and the Bogia area, including Manam Island. As the legend should not
be taken as a story of coastal Sepik migrations, but is specifically about
the journeyings of a supernatural being, we may well ask why so many
villages from different cultural groups possess their versions,[4] and more
importantly, how Kamoai of Darapap came to be Jari's agent. The legend,
it appears, given that Jari was supposed to have been cut in two at Manumbwamot, near Bogia, has moved in a westerly direction, and it has
played a significant part in coastal trading relations. Stories of Jari
reached the Murik people in pre-contact times, and women have called
on her name at female initiations for a long time, but Jari's possession of
Kamoai (and possibly the specific version of the legend given above)
made their appearance in Darapap under very particular and more recent circumstances. When the Murik people were establishing them-

---

[4] "The groups include the Nor, Gapun, Ottilien, Manumbo, Sepa, Lilau (as well as
Manam) speaking peoples." (M.T.)

selves in the territory they presently occupy, their effort to beat back enemies led them as far east as Sanai. Attempting to wipe out previous inhabitants who had stood in their way, they used to cross the Sepik and make incursions on enemy groups further afield. Young men and women from Sanai were frequently captured, brought back to Darapap, and put to death before all the villagers. On one occasion, however, when two small children, a girl and a boy named Bang, were brought as captives, an old man stopped them from being killed, insisting that they were too young and ought to be brought up at Darapap. This special adoption, best dated to the 1920's,[5] resulted in freer access to the world of Sanai beliefs.

Exchanges of gifts and beliefs with the Sanai followed upon the marriage of the two newcomers within Darapap village. It happened that an old, rotten carving of Jari was brought as a gift to Bang, who was now a young man, and its reception indicated that her power was available to the Darapap people as never before. Aprawa, my grandfather's brother, a skilled wood-carver, had close familial ties with the man who had adopted Bang, and he fashioned a new image of Jari, a one foot high female figurine with large breasts and a *rami* round her waist. Thus Jari became a family goddess at Darapap, and Kamoai, Aprawa's sister-in-law, 1.2 belonged to the relevant family. Kamoai knew of Jari's power, but a *ga'in* must be marked out by the supernatural being, gods taking control of men, goddesses of women. Kamoai is understood to have been marked out by Jari, and the first sign of this was after the birth of her fifth and last child. By then she was at least thirty and the year was about 1930–1. The first possession came as a surprise. She felt as if she were intoxicated—it was not unlike the way one sweats and talks nonsense after chewing certain betel nuts—and the sensation of being taken over by Jari was not complete. An image used by my uncle Bosai Namanus to describe this incident (and the image was probably Kamoai's own) was one of a fish which has only been half-speared and which 'half escapes'.[6] It was not long afterwards, however, before Kamoai could no longer escape.

Kamoai as diviner, prophetess and clairvoyant

Kamoai was certainly not the first woman to have been possessed at Darapap; other goddesses, Usim and Kambam who had their own legends and also their own cults at Sanai, have (supposedly) marked out 2.2 women from different Murik Lakes villages. In the Murik area, however,

---

[5] "In arriving at this date I have taken into account that the girl, who married my father's younger brother, is still alive." (M.T.)

[6] "Bosai remembers this episode because he was present." (M.T.)

Kamoai alone had been taken by Jari, and Kamoai is famed for having been possessed more often than any other female *ga'in* in the area and for being an outstanding personality.

In many respects Kamoai appears to belong to the category of diviner. Because she was a *ga'in* she was frequently consulted by people who wished to know if sorcery was being worked against them, or the reasons why relatives were sick. On other occasions people sought advice about the best time to go hunting or fishing, or the best means to stop sickness. Those coming to consult would be required to offer food to Jari, and bringing betel nut and tobacco with the food, they would address their questions to the goddess. Sometimes the answer came quickly, other times they went away to wait. Kamoai used to take the food and place it before the figurine, which stood on a carved wooden bowl but was later placed in a box. The figurine stood in her house and was fenced within a small sanctuary. Having laid down the food, Kamoai would put the person's request to the goddess. On most occasions she was possessed, but not always immediately. She would then got to the questioners or proceed to their house under possession and delivery the answer. If she was not possessed, Jari was supposed to make her appearance in the questioners' dreams, so that subsequent conversations with Kamoai would confirm what actions were necessary, or whether a given trouble was caused by sorcery, by displeased family gods or by ancestors. My cousin Kem Saope has vouched for the accuracy of Kamoai's hunting forecasts; time and again he, and his uncle before him, consulted Jari before hunting with dogs and received exact instructions as to the best places for a catch. They always found a prey.

On numerous occasions, however, Jari spoke through Kamoai without warning or consultation. She would descend from her house and walk straight to the big man, to an elder or *gapar*, or any particular person connected with her message, and deliver the oracle. Under normal conditions, Kamoai was never very outgoing; she was shy and reserved. But when possessed she appeared most excited, words flowed from her mouth evenly and quickly, and she would walk backwards and forwards in front of her listener(s) with rather formal gesturing and in a detached manner. When possessed, too, she spoke as Jari. Jari referred to Kamoai as her mother, so that in reply to a question she often replied, 'You asked mother to let you know the cause of this sickness. . . . ', or such like. When Kamoai was controlled by Jari, in fact, she spoke to her husband as 'mother's husband', and to her sons as 'uncles'. Even though possession usually followed when she was consulted, it is her unexpected, unsolicited outbursts which suggest that she could be described as a prophetess.

Some of her unexpected messages are more outstanding than others.

(margin annotations: 3.0, 3.21, 2.13, 2.1)

We can begin by considering what could have been Kamoai's first pronouncements under possession, at a time we can date to about 1930–1.[7]
As young ten year old boy, Bosai Namanus disobeyed his father's orders
to go with him to cut mangrove sticks for their house. Instead he went
playing in the lake with other boys, only to find himself attacked by a
crocodile which lay waiting for him under a log. When his father, Mar-
imb, came home, he found his son lying badly gashed in the centre of
2.1 the village. Two utterances reassured him, however, that the boy would
survive. One came from his brother, who, possessed by the god Moar-
enor, said 'He will live. Because he disobeyed his father I have taught
him a lesson', and the other was from Kamoai, who, under possession
also, said something similar. At this stage Kamoai was hardly a prominent
person in the village, but her message was in support of a leading ga'in.
It is interesting that ga'in, even if they are mediums for different deities,
do not compete with each other by making opposite or contradictory
statements. If there is any competition at all, it only takes the form of
slight modifications. Kamoai, for example, was often vague about who in
particular was going to die, or who performed what sorcery, but other
ga'in would follow her lead by attempting to be more specific. Again, if
a prediction by a ga'in was not not realized on a certain day, other ga'in
would spend time explaining why it would happen on another day, and
not the first one specified. Kamoai probably began, then, as one who
supported or modified other, better known ga'in, until she herself rose
to prominence through her frequent possessions.

2.1   Kamoai's warnings and predictive oracles, especially those which
came without consultation, and which were often delivered in picture
language or with the literal meaning kept veiled, remind us of classical
or Old Testament prophecy more than anything else in her career. Taken
over by Jari, she was outspoken against sorcery. Using the image of the
changing tides—which relates back to the legend of Jari—she would
declare if there was going to be a 'low tide' in the village or a 'high tide'.
A low tide meant that things could be seen clearly, so that trouble could
be found and removed; a high tide meant plenty of trouble, but it could
not be seen clearly in the turbulence. Such picture language was used
when she realized sorcerers were present, or people who could take
news away to them. It was common for Kamoai to admit that 'the roots
of the coconut (or the betel nut) have already gone into the soil', or in
other words, that the sorcery had gone too far or had done its work too
well in any one particular case. Only when suspected people were absent
would she be more specific.

On one occasion in 1953, for instance, she came to my father as he

---

[7] "Bosai told this story and he is now in his mid-fifties." (M.T.)

was building the policeman's house at the edge of the village. He was on   2.1
the roof-top when she came up and cried,

> 'Uncle, I am coming to you to ask what measures you are taking
> concerning my aunt, Kiso, who will die very soon! You listen to
> me! She is not sick from sickness but from sorcery, and if you do
> not take quick action, she will shortly die! I know the village to
> which the sorcery can be traced. It is Moasan. Go to Moasan, and
> when you beach your canoe and face the village, you will find the
> source of the sorcery in fried sago in the fifth house on the left!'

Sauma, the husband of the sick woman, rowed with his brothers to
Moasan when he heard of this oracle. Sword fish flew up before the
canoe and stood on their tails in the water, and mullet floated close to
the surface as they neared the village. These were both recognizable
signs of recovery. They arrived at the village, and stated their cause. The
people, as was the agreed practice, came down from their houses so that
the sorcery could be traced. Following Kamoai's instructions, Sauma
found the fried sago in a box in the fifth house. He took it out and placed
it in cold water, and it is understood that sorcerers keep their chosen
items very hot. Not long after Sauma's wife recovered. Kamoai had combined her warning oracle against sorcery with clairvoyance and a knowledge of healing methods.[8]

In her warnings against sorcery Kamoai also coupled prediction with   3.2
a concern for the social and moral cohesion of Darapap. When a person
died, for example, she would sometimes exclaim, 'He is not the only one
to die, but others will die after him, unless we clean up this village!' The
elders understood her allusions to sorcery and usually ordered a house
to house investigation if Kamoai hinted at sorcery within Darapap.
Again, she predicted the arrival of people to the village, but not ordinary,
innocent visitors or newcomers, only those culpable of sorcery or who
were known companions to sorcerers. In her efforts to fight sorcery,
therefore, she defended the cause of peace, justice and order within her
area, a feature characteristic of prophetism in ancient Israel and other
contexts.

One famous oracle is closer to the style we normally associate with   2.1
prophets. In 1943 the people of Darapap accepted the invading Japanese, and allowed soldiers to live in their village. Americans who escaped from Japanese hands in the area reported which villages were col-
laborating, and in 1944 Darapap was bombed by the Allies. Kamoai
foresaw this event. People close to her heard her warning to 'Flee from
the village to the lakes! Things with wings will be coming!' and most

---

[8] "Various informants confirmed this story, including my cousin Kem Saope." (M.T.)

people took this advice before the bombing took place. Kamoai is naturally famed for this oracle. Her last child, however, a young teenage mother, was killed during the bombing, and her tiny baby boy was covered with shrapnel. Jari, with Kamoai as her mouthpiece, reassured the family: 'We do not have to be afraid, I will make sure he does not die.' Despite the fact that you could virtually see into his body through various holes, and the fact that he suffered from recurrent fits, the boy lived until 1972, when he fell off a canoe and drowned.

2.2   Although she made these various predictions and acted as a controlling factor in the moral life of Darapap, Kamoai fulfilled a purely traditional role and no Christian influences were involved in her work.[9] At one point in 1961 I refused to allow her to repeat magic words over my foot, which had been infected by a sting-ray, and I reminded her I had become a Christian. As I lay in agony I remember her complaining as she went off; 'You can go on with your pain and in the end die, because this religion has come and mixed you up'. Kamoai was marked out as

3.2   Jari's ga'in, and the way her actions were rooted in tradition is clearly illustrated by her dealings with the women of the area, and her concern for female affairs. Jari was the goddess of love and marriage; she had once worn koskos to seduce her various husbands. At female initiations it was Kamoai's task to pass on Jari's powers of attraction to the young women. On the occasions these initiations took place, she often seemed to become possessed out of sheer merriment, and on the following day was very embarrassed about her overexcited behaviour.

Kamoai's (or Jari's) interest in romance can be exemplified by a story belonging to the year 1956. Some young people went fishing. They stripped off, caught the fish and then returned to the beach to cook it on the mangroves. They were naked because they had been in the water. Back at the village Kamoai was possessed and saw the whole scene, and she commented about it to the members of the family with her. As usual, she laughed about love, and the size of the sex organs of those in the party. 'So I see them', she concluded, 'and they are naked'. When the young people came home and heard what had happened, they were amazed, and admitted she was right.[10]

Jari, then, can be described as diviner, prophetess and clairvoyant. Her work was specifically connected with the powers of a goddess, however, and thus prescribed by the traditional spheres of that sambamarogo. She did not predict the outcome of wars, for example, because this was something left for the high-god kakar, who was called on by the

---

[9] "The Catholic (Divine Word) missionaries did not get established in the Murik Lakes area until 1920, and the Seventh Day Adventist Mission, strong in Darapap, was founded in 1952." (M.T.)

[10] "My main informant for this story is Kem Saope." (M.T.)

people of Darapap as recently as 1957, when they went to war against neighbouring Karau.[11] Thus Kamoai was the prophetess of Jari in particular. Now that she is dead no one is Jari's mouthpiece. My uncle keeps the image ready for a new *ga'in*, but at present prayers are uttered to the goddess with no certainty as to the outcome of requests. What will happen? Will a new *ga'in* arise? Papua New Guinea is changing. . . . .[12]

15
The Community Designates a "Cargo Prophet"

Introduction

World-wide, there have been a great many movements whose participants expected and made active preparation for a new and, from their point of view, more satisfactory world order. Often referred to as "millenarian movements," they are frequently encountered among native populations whose traditional culture has been threatened by the presence of a colonial power, usually European. In Melanesia many of these movements take the form of "cargo cults," and, according to Burridge, are directly comparable "with the Ghost-dance cults of North America, and the 'prophetist' movements among African peoples" (1960:xv).

The term, "cargo cult," has been used to designate a type of movement occurring in Melanesia at least since the late eighteenth century. Though a specific movement is likely to be short-lived and display local idiosyncrasies, there is a certain recognizable similarity among them. In all of them the natives recognize the fundamental inequity of their situation: a relatively small number of light-skinned outsiders has access to apparently inexhaustible supplies of valuable manufactured goods ("cargo"), which for the most part they selfishly withhold from the dark-skinned natives. In this situation the hope arises, often promulgated by an inspired leader, that there will soon be an upheaval resulting in the dramatic regeneration of the world order. Religious ceremonies are instituted for the purpose of helping effect this anticipated acquisition of European cargo (cf. Burridge, 1960:xv-xxiii).

The "flavor" of these movements can be conveyed by citing several examples. In 1893 Tokeriu, the leader of the "Milne Bay movement,"

---

[11] "This is Michael Somare's village, and my people won in the fight that day. Michael Somare, however, was not in his village on that occasion." (M.T.)

[12] Tamoane's account ends with this ellipsis (editor).

was "inspired by a spirit which resided in a traditionally sacred tree." He prophesied the imminent destruction of coastal settlements by a tidal wave, which believers, however, would survive. This would be followed by ideal weather conditions, resulting in an abundance of garden produce, and "the coming of a huge ship with the spirits of the dead on board," who would be united with their living kinsmen. Meanwhile, European material goods were to be abandoned, and the faithful were to move inland and construct a new village, out of reach of the impending storm. And since in the new order food would be so abundant, stores of garden crops were to be consumed and all pigs killed and eaten. Tokeriu's adherents followed his bidding, among other things slaughtering 300–400 pigs, but became disillusioned when the promised disaster failed to occur (Worsley, 1968:51–54). A similar hope for the millennium existed among the Baining of New Britain around 1930: "there were rumours of the imminent resurrection of the dead. The mountains would collapse into the valleys to form a great plain covered with fertile gardens and fruit trees which would require no cultivation. Dead pigs and dogs would come back to life, but native sceptics and Europeans were to die in the earthquake" (Worsley, 1968:90). Sometimes it was held that the material goods currently being enjoyed by the Europeans had in fact been manufactured by the ancestors for their descendants, but had been hijacked by the Whites before it could reach them (Worsley, 1968:105).

The so-called "Vailala Madness" arose in the Gulf Division of Papua in 1919. The movement was characterized by group possession, and during its life had several inspired leaders, the first a man named Evara. The latter "prophesied the coming of a steamer, carrying the spirits of dead ancestors on board, who would bring with them the 'Cargo'. . . . Later teachings stated that the Cargo was to be allotted to villages by the signs of identity on the crates. The spirits had revealed that all the flour, rice, tobacco and other 'trade' belonged to the Papuans, not the Whites. The latter would be driven away, and the Cargo would pass into the hands of its rightful owners, the natives." Traditional rites for worshiping the dead were altered by burning the ancient costumes and paraphernalia and introducing European elements like tables, chairs, "special cult temples" called "offices," and flagpoles (Worsley, 1968:75–90; Williams, 1923, 1934).

Finally, let me mention the John Frum (Jonfrum) movement, which arose on Tanna, an island in the southern New Hebrides, in 1940. In the new order prophesied by this leader "the natives would get back their youth, and there would be no sickness; there would be no need to care for gardens, trees or pigs. The Whites would go," and mission schools would be replaced by native instruction. John Frum would provide all the money needed to buy the desired European goods, and believers were encouraged to dispose of their "long-hoarded savings" (some threw their European money into the sea). Great feasts were also held to use up stores of food. Attempts were made by officials to repress the movement, but additional prophets emerged, and along with them a "new theme: John Frum was King of America." One of these prophets commanded his followers to construct a landing strip in anticipation of the arrival of airplanes bearing cargo (Worsley, 1968:152–60; cf. Barrow, 1951; Guiart, 1951, 1956; O'Reilly, 1950).

There have been literally hundreds of cargo cults, occurring virtually to the present time. The best over-all survey is Worsley (1968), though briefer surveys of several movements may be found in Chinnery and Haddon (1916–17) and Eckert (1937). On an early movement in Fiji see Thomson (1895, 1908), Sutherland (1910), and Brewster (1922, chapters 23 and 26). Two of the finest and most detailed studies, setting specific cargo cults within a native social and conceptual context, are Lawrence (1964), to which we will shortly turn, and Burridge (1969; cf. also 1953–54, 1957, 1960). Another recent and fairly detailed study of a specific cult is Meggitt (1973–74). There is abundant literature on these movements, and those interested in delving into it many consult the bibliographies in Worsley (1968), as well as the earlier compilation by Leeson (1952) and volume indexes of the journal, *Oceania*.

In his *Road Belong Cargo* (1964) Peter Lawrence has described one particular cargo movement that occurred in the southern Madang District of New Guinea. His study has considerable historical depth, covering five successive "cargo beliefs" that emerged during the period 1871–1950. From our point of view perhaps the most informative aspect of this development is the way in which, despite the continual presence of colonial regimes, "the traditional value- and epistemological systems" persisted and shaped each of the cargo beliefs. Indeed, so powerful was this native world view that in the "fifth cargo belief" (1948–1950) it caused the people to declare one leader, Yali, to be an intermediary, though he himself made no explicit claims to have been specially designated by the cargo deity. In what follows, then, our concern will be less with the actions of the intermediary than with the strong ideological stereotypes which shaped both the actions and the perception of them. Since Lawrence's description is both lengthy and rich in detail, the best approach seems to be to provide a summary statement relating to the history and ideology of the beliefs, followed by a brief text dealing specifically with the "cargo leaders."

There has been a long-standing debate over the nature and causes of millenarian movements, or "crisis cults," a class to which the various cargo cults are often taken to belong.[1] As in the case of the Iroquois and

---

[1] The literature in this area is vast, and I can do no more than offer the reader some suggestions for approaching it. LaBarre (1971) is a lengthy summary and evaluation of

the Ghost Dance (see above, Sections 5 and 6), it is clear that such move-ments often arise in situations where a native culture finds itself in con-tact with and pressured by another culture, more powerful and techno-logically more advanced. Lawrence is at pains to point out, however, that "total social or cultural disintegration is not a necessary condition for cargo cult" (1964:223). For while it is true that colonial occupation pre-cipitated the Cargo Movement in southern Madang, it was the native culture itself which provided the "enabling conditions" for the move-ment. Great changes in the natives' way of life did occur, but at base these were "purely superficial. In the economic and social field, the loss of some institutions and addition of others did not seriously affect the basic principles of traditional behaviour and relationships, and the values associated with them. In the intellectual field, the epistemological sys-tem, although given new content, preserved its original form. From this point of view, therefore, the Cargo Movement was conservative rather than revolutionary" (1964:223).

---

research on crisis cults, ending with a review of various theories of causality. Since none of the latter appear to exhaust the data of a given movement, his assessment is that "re-ductionism is rampant in crisis cult studies" (1971:26). Another critical assessment of ear-lier studies may be found in Lanternari (1974). Because they discuss so many views and provide a rich bibliography, these two articles are a good introduction to millenarian movements and the promises and pitfalls of studying them.

From the numerous studies discussed by LaBarre and Lanternari, several are worthy of special comment. Wallace (1956) is a widely-known and frequently-cited essay. According to Wallace, "a revitalization movement is . . . a deliberate, organized, conscious effort by members of a society to construct a more satisfying culture." Such movements have a common "processual structure," proceeding from a steady social state through stages of stress and revitalization to a new steady state. The much more elaborate theory of Bur-ridge (1969) runs along similar lines: millenarian movements are redemptive processes which arise when cultural integrity is threatened, and aim toward the creation of a "new man" defined by new rules of morality and assumptions about power. That is to say, such movements arise when people find themselves unable to participate in or control "that power whose ordering connotes a higher or more satisfactory redemption," and begin to regard themselves (or feel that they are regarded by others) as "just rubbish." In this intolerable situation, they try to order power and render it intelligible, pointing toward a new integrity" (1969:107). While such circumstances frequently occur in the "colonial" situation of contact between widely-differing cultures, they are not exclusive to that situ-ation (cf. 1969:86–96, on the Jains of India). Both Wallace and Burridge stress the impor-tance of "prophets" in this process. Finally, we should note the classic study of Lanternari himself (1963: critically reviewed in 1965; cf. also 1962–63), which takes a "sociohistorical approach" and views such movements within the context of the contact between Western and native cultures. His final assessment is that they signal the "exhaustion . . . (of) tra-ditional religion in its effort to procure salvation," and provide for the masses new religious impulses which eventually "pave the way for reform in the cultural, political, and social structure of secular society" (1963:254).

A good deal has been written specifically on the interpretation of cargo cults; cf. Belshaw (1950), Inglis (1957), Stanner (1958), Jarvie (1963), and C. Long (1974).

The people of coastal Madang inhabited small, primarily agricultural villages. There was little division of labor and no idea of production for profit, with the result that "the economy had no strong internalized forces of change and tended to be stationary" (Lawrence, 1964:11). Over this whole region "the content of social relationships and hence the values they expressed were everywhere the same: the bestowal of reciprocal advantages or the exchange of goods and services on the basis of equivalence, guaranteed by the approximate equality of access to economic resources enjoyed by all members of the society" (1964:225). Material goods were useful not only in the practical affairs of daily life, but also as "the symbol of all important relationship and social status" (1964:225).

Neither the presence of European goods, nor the plantation system, nor indentured servitude undermined the traditional economic system and values. European artifacts did make important changes in the people's lives (steel axes and bushknives, for example, made work much easier), but they merely took the place of some native artifacts in the exchange economy. "Indentured labourers remained essentially subsistence wage earners," who had little idea of the commercial value of the commodities they helped produce. Nor "did they appreciate that the Europeans did anything to earn their livings. White men did no physical labour—certainly little to produce the luxury foods, goods, and machinery they enjoyed in such abundance. At most they carried out minor repairs on ships, aircraft, and motor-cars, but machinery needing serious overhaul had to be sent to Australia. Otherwise, they directed the work of native employees, sat in offices and wrote on bits of paper and, when they wanted fresh supplies of goods, sent their servants with chits to the stores" (1964:228). As a consequence, there were no native entrepreneurs.

The close relationship between the "value- and epistemological systems" is evident. "Traditionally, the natives regarded their cosmos as a finite and almost exclusively physical realm, in which man was the focal point of two systems of relationships: actual relationships between human beings (social structure); and putative relationships between human beings, deities, spirits of the dead, and totems (religion). . . . The keynotes of social and religious life were materialism and anthropocentricism, and knowledge was ascribed to divine revelation rather than the human intellect" (1964:9). Though the people had considerable secular knowledge (agriculture, communication via slit-gongs, seamanship, and the like), this was not considered to be a human intellectual achievement. "Except in minor matters, they dismissed the principle of human intellectual discovery. They accepted myths as the sole and unquestionable source of all important truth" (1964:39). Thus, while "Western religious teaching had its direct counterpart in the native intellectual tradition" and could be "at once assimilated," Western secular education had little impact, for the opposite reason (1964:230–1).

At the very beginning of his study Lawrence announces his intention to ask "three obvious questions, which immediately puzzle newcomers to a cargo cult situation." The first is about the motivation for the cult: Why was European wealth considered so important and of such high social value that natives "spent decades of patently fruitless effort to discover its source?" (1964:5). On the basis of what has already been said, there appear to have been two reasons. "First, it became an economic necessity: it had obvious advantages over their own goods, which it swiftly replaced as the area was brought under control. Second, it became an index of their self-respect. Because their demand for it always exceeded the supply, the problem of its availability caused considerable anxiety. Hence they attributed to it the same kind of social importance as they had done to their traditional material culture: they came to regard it as the symbol of their status in the new colonial society" (1964:232).

The second question concerns the means employed: Why, ignoring secular activities, "did they believe that this wealth could be obtained almost entirely by ritual activity?" (1964:5). The answer to this problem is to be found in the assumptions of the native epistemological system, in which "the total cosmic order was still regarded as finite and anthropocentric—with few if any supernatural attributes—and the relationships between its human and superhuman personnel as specified and predictable. It existed solely for the benefit of man. Its origins could be accounted for only by myth. It could not have come into being except for the activities of a deity or deities, who then surrendered, subject to certain conditions, to human direction." Thus, the cargo had to be regarded as "the crowning achievement" of the deities, and not as "the product of human endeavour and skill," and the "means devised to solve the technical problems of explaining its source and exploiting it to the natives' advantage were of exactly the same kind as those used in the case of the traditional material culture." That is to say, the "relationships between human beings, cargo deity, and ancestors were so defined as to establish the natives' inalienable rights to the cargo as a concomitant of living" (1964:235). Ritual was, therefore, the culturally sanctioned way to affect these relationships and obtain cargo (cf. 1964:17–9, 29–33, 243–9).

The third question has to do with the effects of the Cargo Movement: What is its "general importance?", and "what sort of situation has it contributed to or created?" (1964:5). Here Lawrence describes the developing movement as a complex mixture of "reformist ('non-nationalist')" and "nationalist" tendencies (1964:256–71). But despite this variegated character of its expression, "cargo ideology has now become an intrinsic part of the culture of the southern Madang District. It is no longer just grafted on to but virtually represents the natives' whole way of life. It provides . . . a tremendous feeling of self-respect under European domination. As an intellectual system, it explains European economic superiority with much greater logic in native eyes than any description of Western financial transactions, industrial research, and factory organization with all their complexities and seeming contradictions can ever hope to offer" (1964:269).

In the following text Lawrence comments in general on the cargo leaders, and at length specifically on Yali. Since the latter is the focus of our interest, some additional information about him seems in order. Yali was born in a village in the bush about 1912. He left home early to work for the Europeans, acquiring a command of Pidgin English. In the mid–1930's he joined the Police Force, and during World War II, fought with the Australians. He was deeply impressed by what he saw in Brisbane and Cairns in 1942–43, and embraced what he understood to be a promise by the Australians to develop New Guinea after the war along the lines of Australia. Yali impressed Europeans "as an exceptional native" (1964:126). He had a sense of personal responsibility, a liking for Whites, and the appearance of Western-style rationality. Yet he was illiterate, and below the surface had only a "very shallow" understanding of Western culture (1964:117–27).

After the war, Yali came to prominence in the southern Madang District, advocating a secular "rehabilitation scheme" based on cooperation with the Australians which made the Cargo Movement unnecessary. Even at this stage, however, many natives understood him to be a cargo leader. But after the government took him and nine others to Port Moresby (August-December, 1947) for indoctrination about its long-range plans for native development, Yali became disillusioned. As he told Lawrence, "'I realized now that the talk of the officers in Brisbane was bullshit—that was done with now—we just wouldn't get anything—the white men had lied to us and didn't want to help us. We just wouldn't get anything to give us a better life'" (1964:170). Initially, his conviction was that the best road for the people to follow was away from both Christianity and cargo doctrine and toward a revival of traditional religion. Eventually, however, he came under the influence of a "new cargo prophet," Gurek. As a result of illegal activities, he was arrested and imprisoned for five years (1950–55), and the movement faded away (1964:171–221).

Nevertheless, cargo activity in southern Madang did not come to a complete end. Since 1950, the cults "have been small and lacking in central direction in that they have been pagan and quasi-Christian at random" (1964:266). In 1951 and 1953 two cults arose which expected

Yali's return "to Madang with warships and merchantmen laden with cargo to take over the reins of government. The horizon was scanned for his arrival, and pagan ritual revived to speed it up" (1964:266). There were other indications as well that "many people continued to regard Yali as their leader" (1964:268). Yet in the "making" of Yali as a cargo intermediary it was not supernatural designation, but societal beliefs, that played the crucial role, as we shall now see.

Text (Lawrence, 1964:249–56)

The conclusions drawn so far apply also to the leaders in the Cargo Movement. Admittedly, they often had qualities which they did not necessarily derive from the original culture. Kaut, Kaum, Yali, and Tagarab all had outstanding, even dominant, personalities, although this was not an absolutely essential qualification for leadership. For instance, Polelesi of Igurue, when I met her between 1949 and 1953, seemed little different from other Garia women. Again, individual leaders often showed considerable political intuition and skill. Kaut and Tagarab exploited the Japanese Occupation to their own advantage, and Yali was particularly adroit in his dealings with Europeans.

The political importance of the cargo leaders' careers is considered in a later context. Here we are concerned only with the basic principles that governed their conduct. From this point of view, we may regard them as the catalysts of the Movement, around which its different cults crystallized and grew, precisely because in most of their activities they operated within the limits imposed by traditional values and assumptions, which they accepted as automatically as did their followers. The only possible exception was Yali between 1945 and 1947.

2.1   In this field, there were two relevant features of traditional leadership. First, the leaders' most important duties were to initiate and organize annually recurrent undertakings, especially in economic life. The mainspring of these undertakings was the people's recognition of their importance (as, for instance, in agriculture) and desire that they be carried out. The leaders' roles as policy-makers were extremely limited: they rarely, if ever, originated entirely new schemes but only acted in ways that their followers had already intended. Second, the acknowledged intellectual basis of leadership was the mastery of ritual which would guarantee the completion of the enterprises discussed. The leaders were believed to possess the esoteric formulae and other information originally taught human beings by the deities during the age of antiquity in the course of personal association with them or in dreams. Occasionally they could have similar experiences themselves. But although their knowledge was sanctioned by divine origination, the real test was personal success. When a leader failed or was overshadowed, his followers might transfer their allegiance to others.

With the possible exception already mentioned, the cargo leaders who emerged after 1914 where the direct successors of these men. Their careers, although normally shorter because of the nature of external conditions, depended on the same sort of considerations. Their roles as policy-makers were still governed by the demands of their followers. They might initiate new doctrines but had to suit them to the people's current aspirations and intellectual assumptions. Although they claimed their knowledge from a divine source they had to demonstrate success or fade into obscurity. They may be divided into three groups: the renegade mission helpers; the prophets of the Fourth Cargo Belief and the period after the Second World War; and Yali.

2.2

During the Third Cargo Belief, the renegade mission helpers almost entirely replaced the traditional leaders and eclipsed the official headmen. As they exercised *de facto* control over Christian teaching within their congregations, they easily convinced the people that they alone could provide the new wealth for which, with the opening up of the country, there was a growing demand. They were thought to have learnt the cargo secret from the missionaries, who had either inherited it from their predecessors in the period of the Christian Creation or even themselves been taught it in the course of personal meetings with God and Jesus Christ.[2]

After 1933, with the rise of the Fourth Cargo Belief, the mission helpers lost their influence. As they could not satisfy the demands of their followers, they had to give way to a new group of prophets or, as is illustrated by the case of Dabus in the Bagasin Rebellion, attach themselves to new cults as 'technical advisers'. The laity had no compunction about deserting them for other leaders who not only offered better hopes of success but also matched their own growing sense of hostility to the Europeans by promising them weapons for waging war. These new prophets—Kaut, Tagarab, Kaum, and, after the war, Pales and Polelesi—still claimed to derive their authority from the same kind of source as the mission helpers. But, in keeping with the current native mood, they no longer acknowledged dependence on white men. They did not rely on second-hand instruction from the missionaries (from whom they deliberately dissociated themselves on the grounds that they were false teachers) but claimed to have acquired their special knowledge on their own account. They had established the close personal association with

---

[2] "The Garia, for instance, believed that Europeans could actually meet and talk with God and Jesus Christ on the streets of Sydney. 'Photographs' in Bibles proved the point." (P.L.)

the cargo deity and spirits in visions; they had died and gone to Heaven; or, like Kaut in the late 1930's, they impersonated important biblical figures and claimed to have contacted the cargo deity by mechanical means.

Yali was far more complex as a person than the other cargo leaders, partly because of his more varied personal experiences and partly because he had continually to satisfy the demands of two distinct groups— Europeans and natives. Yet ultimately even he cannot be excluded from the general category. On the one hand, his Rehabilitation Scheme can be described at first sight in almost rational terms. It appeared to be a definite break with both the traditional past and the Cargo Movement: a secular programme based on the expectation of Administration aid in return for the wartime loyalty of native troops, which was designed to satisfy the people's economic aspirations. That the District Office at this time saw it in this light is clear from its consistent support: it sanctioned Yali's appointment of secretaries and 'boss boys', if not 'policemen', and it employed him in the Department of Native Affairs. The ideas he himself expressed at the outset were far in advance of those of his predecessors in the Movement. Although he expected a free hand-out of goods at Port Moresby, it was to include primarily building materials and machinery with which the people were to re-equip themselves. An improved standard of living would not be instantaneous but would be achieved only by some physical effort and village reorganization. Yali had at times considerable social and political intuition. He appreciated early on that the natives needed the missionaries for reasons of education. After his return from Bogia, he worked for the definition of the missions' authority in relation to his own, especially *vis-a-vis* property rights, marriage, and religion. Because the Administrations had so far chosen to remain neutral on this issue, he had no defence against the meddling of native mission helpers. He rectified this in Port Moresby by drawing up his 'Laws' and having them sanctioned by the Administration.[3] He was a born manipulator- his usurpation of the authority of the O.C. Saidor and deluding of the District Office about his activities after 1948 showed the greatest shrewdness.[4]

On the other hand, to judge Yali purely at this level and see him as a primarily secular leader would be to misunderstand him. The task he had undertaken was sufficiently Herculean to daunt even the most

---

[3] These "laws" are a set of documents, drafted in Pidgin English by Yali and some literate members of his party in Port Moresby (1947), which attempt to combine the "best features" of the European and native cultures. Lawrence describes them as "the first written statement of the aims of the Rehabilitation Scheme" (1964:173; cf. 166–78).

[4] The reference is to Yali's effectively taking over the administration of law among the natives that was the responsibility of the Officer-in-Charge at the Administrative Station in Saidor; cf. Lawrence (1964:210–21).

skilled and best-trained administrator of the day, but he was barely fitted for it. In spite of his experience of, and fellowship with, Europeans and his adoption of their personal living habits, he had never really rejected the values and assumptions of his own society. Although he had not been fully trained in traditional ritual, he accepted the native interpretation of the nature and dynamics of the cosmic order without question. He never divorced its secular from its religious aspects. He saw the involvement of gods and ancestors in human affairs not as remote and indirect but as immediate and instrumental. He was convinced that he had been saved after the Hollandia debacle by his respect for the local deities.[5] He subscribed to the general principles of the Cargo Movement. He believed the prophecies from Karkar in 1941–1.[6] He was quite satisfied that the money and 'flags' brought to him in 1946 could have been sent by God and the spirits, and he was fully persuaded that he had himself witnessed similar phenomena at Kurog nearly two years later. He never really saw beyond the exterior of Western culture and was not aware that it was based on entirely different principles from those underlying his own. He understood the Brisbane promises, on which his Rehabilitation Scheme ultimately rested, merely as a means of evading the issue of cargo cult, which aroused antagonism among Europeans only because it was an attempt to steal their property. Although actual dealings between natives and Europeans would be secular, the goods to be made available were still derived, directly or indirectly, from a cargo deity, who would remain under exclusive European direction. He saw the future relationship between Europeans and natives as being very like those between groups linked by trade in the past, when finished goods (clay pots and wooden bowls) could move freely from one area to another, although the ritual secrets involved in their production were jealously guarded by their owners. Although he recognized that the people would have to work to raise their standard of living, beyond modernizing their villages with new building materials, he was never very clear about the form such work would take. He certainly did not believe in an instantaneous transformation of native society, but he thought that it would be achieved in relatively few years. He could not see that it would require the re-education of a whole new generation.

Thus Yali did not turn to religion to solve his problems after the collapse of the Brisbane promises solely for reasons of convenience. Admittedly, under the terrible pressures of the moment, he saw it as the

2.2

[5] After an abortive wartime mission in 1944, Yali accomplished a dramatic overland escape from the Japanese which won him personal acclaim among both European troops and natives; cf. Lawrence (1964:124–6 and, with respect to his view about the role of a local deity in the escape, 130–4).

[6] A native mission worker, whom Yali had helped to arrest, had accurately predicted the bombing of Madang by the Japanese (Lawrence 1964:122).

best means of saving his reputation, and of revenging himself for the personal humiliation and betrayal he had suffered. But, at the same time, there was nothing in his own mind to inhibit the decision. It is significant that his spontaneous reaction, after Tarosi's disclosures about Evolution, was to try to regain control of the situation through the pagan revival.[7] When Gurek's genius transformed the pagan revival into the Fifth Cargo Belief, he immediately found the new doctrine intellectually acceptable, his one misgiving being fear of administrative reprisal and his own disgrace. Thereafter there was little in his behaviour to distinguish him from the cargo prophets who had preceded him. He impressed on the people that he had special knowledge of, and power from, the new cargo source—the pagan deities. After 1948, he glossed over in public the secular propaganda for hygienic and orderly living he had stressed between 1945 and 1947, although it still remained his personal standard. Of all the 'laws' he brought back from Port Moresby, the only one he consistently expounded was that authorizing the Kabu Ceremony.[8] The strength of his personal commitment to the new cargo doctrine was shown by his disregard of the District Officer's indirect warning at Saidor in October 1948 and participation in the ritual until a new months before his arrest in 1950. Only after two years of persistent trial was he finally disillusioned.

2.2   This endorsement of traditional values and intellectual assumptions was vital for the position of the leaders of the cults described. Burridge has written of their counterparts in the northern Madang District as the 'new men' of native society: they would restore dignity to their followers and win them the respect of Europeans. This description fits also the cargo leaders of the southern Madang District. Yet it must not be taken to mean that these southern leaders were idolized as a completely different type of human being, qualitatively apart from ordinary natives, as Burridge (1960) seems to imply for the Bogia area. They were 'new men' only in that, as ordinary natives, they would achieve the success their followers desired. They would vindicate before the world the values for

[7] The discovery while in Port Moresby (cf. note 3) that some of the European administrative officers were apparently indifferent to Christianity and that, while the missions had taught that all humans were descended from Adam and Eve, some Europeans believed in descent from "the monki" (Yali linked these ideas with native totemic conceptions), increased Yali's anger against the missions. The latter, he believed, had "deliberately deceived the people" hiding the "truth about human origins." Since they could not be trusted in so simple a matter as this, they could not be relied upon to "reveal the really important secret they possessed—the ultimate source of the cargo" (Lawrence, 1964:176; cf. 173–8). Tarosi was a native and an "Administration teacher trainee," who had been selected to be the "mentor and guide" to Yali's party in Port Moresby (Lawrence, 1964:168).

[8] One of the ceremonies through which the ancestor spirits were honored and their good will sought.

which ordinary natives had always stood, and the assumptions which ordinary natives had always held. Even the honour accorded Yali—his
large houses at Sor and Yabalol, the 'station' at Sangpat, and his *de facto*
recognition as 'District Officer of the Rai Coast'—was intended to mean
not that he himself belonged to a new social class but that he had at last
forced the white masters to accept the people as a whole on their own
terms.[9]

From a severely practical point of view, had the cargo leaders of the   2.2
southern Madang District attempted to expound doctrines based on
ideas entirely foreign to their people, they would not have got the automatic following they did. Before they could have inaugurated their
schemes they would have had to expend a great deal of time, energy,
and patience in explaining them in order to get a hearing at all. In fact,
however, as they kept close to the concepts of their culture, they could
win rapid acceptance merely by announcing a programme of ritual and
taboos that purported to satisfy the people's economic demands and current socio-political aspirations, and by substantiating it by some plausible
claim of having been in contact with the cargo deity and spirits of the
dead. As long as both doctrine and ritual stayed within these limits, the
cult would gather its own momentum and need very little reiteration of
the specific beliefs underlying it, especially among the mass of its devotees. We have seen several cases where, just as in the traditional situation, outlying peoples were prepared to adopt a particular form of ritual
without inquiring carefully into the teachings associated with it, on the
grounds that it was perfectly consistent with their ideas about the work-
ings of the cosmic order and that there were others nearer the source
who knew the myth of origin. Thus, whereas the Third Cargo Belief was
widespread because of the general misinterpretation of Christianity, in
the Fourth Cargo Belief many inland peoples, who supported the Letub,
Tyagarab, or Kaum, knew very little about the Kilibob-Manup myth.
Inland Letub villages appear to have retained Christian beliefs with
slight modification. A few of Tagarab's less attentive followers assumed
that the cargo deity was God rather than God-Kilibob. This was even
truer of ther majority of Kaum's supporters, who were never given a
crystal-clear account of Tagarab's doctrine. In the Fifth Cargo Belief, although the natives of the inland Rai Coast were all aware that the pagan
gods were now claimed to be the cargo source, they knew very little of
the theological argument which had linked God and Jesus to Dodo (Anut)
and Manup, and Jesus-Manup to the other 'satans' in 'Rome'. In all these
cases, Kaut, Tagarab, Kaum, Gurek, and Yali were able to carry all before

---

[9] "Yali, of course, claimed publicly to be superior to ordinary natives. But the masses
regarded him implicitly as a more powerful version of the traditional big man—essentially
as *primus inter pares*." (P.L.)

them by force of personality and demonstration of personal conviction. The rank and file were confident that their leaders were in full possession of all doctrinal details, although they themselves were at best only partially informed.

1.4   The only occasion when a leader did not address himself to his followers in this way was the inception of the Rehabilitation Scheme in 1945, when Yali tried to introduce a programme that did not include
1.41   ritual activity. The project got out of control almost at once. As Yali promised everything the people wanted, he got as quick and favourable a response as had his forerunners. Yet, because he did not take sufficient pains in explaining the scheme, was careless in his choice of words when relating his experiences in Australia, and did not clearly dissociate himself from general cargo ideology, the people distorted his propaganda by the end of the year. It had to be made consistent not only with their economic and socio-political aspirations but also with their intellectual assumptions. They could not understand that Yali intended to achieve his aims by means which were at least an attempt to evade cargo cult, even though he never denied its validity. They had to interpret him as a conventional cargo prophet before he and his teachings could be intelligible. Like his predecessors, he had to have received the charter for his programme from the cargo deity during some special experience. He had been killed at Hollandia in 1944 and had visited God in Heaven as a spirit of the dead. He had seen the Hand of God, and the Light of God shone on his body.

CHAPTER III
THE SOCIOLOGY OF STORYTELLING AND THE TRANSMISSION AND PRESERVATION OF THE INTERMEDIARY'S WORDS

The functioning of an intermediary necessarily involves both actions and words, though not always in the same proportion. In the conjuring ceremony of the shaking tent, for example, speaking takes the form of a conversation with the spirits through whom the hearers derive information of a specific and temporally-limited nature. In Arctic shamanism the words and actions of a performance establish contact with and mastery over the spirits, and their main outcome is a successful cure, placation of the spirits to get a boon, or the like (cf. Balikci, 1963). Words can, however, become the focal point of attention, especially when an intermediary provides instructions for daily living, or stories about him or her begin to circulate. Such a circumstance is especially likely in the case of millenarian movements, the dynamics of which Burridge has described in terms of a transition from a period of "old rules," through a time of "no rules," and to an era governed by "new rules" (1969:165–70). Where teachings and stories persist, the manner of their preservation and transmission becomes a matter for investigation.

The persistence of traditions depends upon a variety of circumstances, some of them fortuitous. Such factors as the duration of the movement, the literacy of its adherents, the institutionalizing of an oral tradition, the preservation of documents, and the presence of reporters are all relevant. For the Ghost Dance we have informal correspondence and interviews with a few participants, as well as the observations of some outside reporters, the most notable of whom was James Mooney. Though at first glance the available material looks adequate, a closer examination reveals that it is difficult to be entirely certain about the original content of Wovoka's message (Overholt, 1974:41,47). For Handsome Lake the situation is somewhat better. Besides considerable contemporary reportage in Quaker missionaries' journals, we know that the religious community which survived Handsome Lake took conscious steps to preserve his teachings. And as the years passed, the figure of Handsome Lake himself was transformed, with the result that his name became a standard element in prayers unconnected with the recitation of his words.

Questions about the persistence of traditions have been of considerable interest to students of the Old Testament prophets. Reconstructing the historical development which culminated in our written texts has proven difficult, however, because the prophetic traditions of the Old Testament are rich in words, but poor in specific information about the social context(s) in which they originated and were preserved. This chapter will explore some of the sociological complexity involved in the transmission of prophetic traditions.

Oral Tradition and the Old Testament Prophets

Interest of Old Testament scholars (in the social dynamics of the prophetic traditions) is evident especially in the period around World War II.

In "Prophecy and Tradition" (1946) S. Mowinckel focused on two topics which proved to be central to the subsequent discussion, viz. the form in which the prophetic traditions were preserved and the manner in which they were transmitted to subsequent generations. He acknowledged cases in which a prophet himself was responsible for having some of his own words committed to writing (cf. Isa 8:1,2, 30:7–8; Jer 29:1, 36, 51:60), but argued that the oral preservation of the tradition in a circle of disciples was of great importance.

As to transmission, one issue Mowinckel addressed was the fixity of the tradition. He considered transmission to be a creative process in which the contents of the tradition were likely to be altered as the people's circumstances changed. He thought of the prophet's disciples as potentially a living spiritual and productive entity, borne by the consciousness that at least some of its members were themselves charismatically inspired prophets. The activity of such a circle would, therefore, be characterized by an interaction between creative personalities and the body of tradition which the group had accumulated and retained (cf. 1946:66–71; also, Ackroyd, 1962:15–8). Mowinckel was thus critical of the inclination of H. S. Nyberg and I. Engnell to view oral transmission as relatively changeless (1946:26–36; also, Widengren, 1948:8, 92–3). As we shall see, modern studies have confirmed Mowinckel's skepticism.

Though he acknowledged flexibility and creativity, Mowinckel focused on a literary product and not the dynamics of oral performance situations which presumably were so important in the early decades, if not centuries, of the tradition's existence. Thus, changes in the tradition were viewed by him as responses to broad historical situations, and not as the result of interaction with specific audiences. As a result, his interpretation suffers from a certain lack of sociological concreteness. (For a recent attempt to be more specific about the social location of "the fellowship behind the book" of Isaiah, cf. Eaton, 1982.)

A second issue with respect to transmission is the relationship between oral tradition and any existing written text. The important point here has already been implied, viz. that there was in all likelihood a constant interaction between oral and written transmission. Thus Mowinckel could say, "The joining by tradition of the originally independent sayings to 'tradition complexes' of varying length is both an oral and a written process" (1946:66). The probability of such interaction has also been stressed by Widengren (1948) and Ringgren (1950), the latter on the basis of a study of doublets within the prophetic books and the psalms.

In a subsequent essay (1962) Mowinckel made an important addition to his views on these matters when he acknowledged the necessity of an appreciative audience for the survival of any tradition.

But what is to be said about those who transmit the tradition in either its oral or written form? E. Nielsen cautioned against imagining oral tradition as a phenomenon of popular, lower class culture, and written texts as characteristic of the upper classes. In the Ancient Near East writing was a skill possessed by a relative few specialists. Similarly, the "active preservation of (the oral) tradition" was also in the hands of "specialists, whether narrators or rhapsodists, or saga-tellers, or singers and poets, or reciters of law" (1954:30–1; cf. 23–31). It is presumably to such groups of specialists that Mowinckel referred when he spoke of "a circle of prophet disciples" (e.g., 1946:68), and Gunneweg when he wrote of "circles of tradents" or of "disciples" (1959:50, 48). Yet one does not have a very clear idea of just what is involved in being a member of such a "circle." Who were these persons, and how were they selected and trained? How did they maintain and transmit the tradition to others, and on what occasions? Such questions probe the nature of a social reality which we must presume underlay the transmission of the prophetic traditions.

Like Mowinckel, Nielsen and Gunneweg argued that in the transmission of the prophetic materials oral and written traditions coexisted, sometimes from the days of the prophet himself. Gunneweg considered the oral mode to have been "normal" (1959:48), and Nielsen suggested that the written form of the tradition could have functioned as "an aid or support of the oral one" (1954:34–5). At any stage of the process the idea that the word of God was authoritative, powerful, and effective in situations beyond those in which it had originally been uttered could have motivated a commitment of a portion of the tradition to writing (Gunneweg, 1959:71–76), as could some cultural crisis, such as syncretism within or political events without (Nielsen, 1954:60–62). However, citing the case of the Talmud, Nielsen pointed out that committing the tradition to writing does not necessarily bring oral transmission to an end.

Nielsen also referred to the role of the audience as a "control" in the process of oral transmission:

> Especially in those cases where tradition is flourishing, i.e.,
> where there are many traditionists of the same text, the individ-
> ual traditionist has a very small chance of carrying through a cor-
> rupt recension. His guild brothers, but first of all his listeners,
> have been of immeasurable importance in upholding the tradi-
> tion, whether these listeners were teachers who were to examine
> the scholars in the canonical texts (cf. late Judaism, Parseeism,
> Islam), private members of the tribe who heard the exploits of
> their tribe celebrated in the odes of the tribal poets (as the Bed-
> ouin do to this day), or those taking part in the annual national
> and religious festivals (e.g., Israel). (1954:37)

One notices that Nielsen couched his discussion in terms of "text," and
assigned the audience something of a proofreading function. There is
little sense of oral transmission as a dynamic process in which audience
and specific situation produce novelty.

G. Ahlström addressed some of these same issues. Like others he
noted the Old Testament evidence that both oral and written transmission can begin with the prophet himself; indeed, Jer 36 not only shows
that the prophet caused his utterances to be written down, but also that
he had memorized them. In some cases disciples may have "carefully
transmitted and also studied" the "words of the prophet master"
(1966:78). This would have been appropriate behavior, since the prophet
was considered to be a spokesman of the deity, and "the divine word
should be remembered" (1966:73, 76). And though these disciples sometimes acted as prophets themselves, they "would not have allowed other
utterances into the prophetic tradition which were not in accordance
with the mind and the intentions of their master" (1966:81).

As we shall see, anthropological studies suggest that traditions are
almost certain to be altered in the process of oral transmission. Thus,
even if we accept as accurate the report that on one occasion Jeremiah
dictated his own past utterances to his disciple (Jer 36), we are not required to think that he had accurately memorized the "original" version
of these words. Indeed, v. 32 seems to imply otherwise. It does in fact
seem reasonable to assume that the disciples' utterances were broadly
"in accordance with the mind and intentions of their master" (Ahlström,
1966:81). Still, we will do well to allow for innovation and creativity, even
the possibility that messages of hope for the nation were on some occasion seen as appropriate in the traditions of pre-exilic prophets. Furthermore, the case of Handsome Lake, to be dealt with in detail below,
shows that the presence of a written text at an early stage in the transmission of the tradition neither guarantees the survival of the "original"
form of the message nor suppresses creativity in oral transmission.

With respect to Old Testament prophecy, it is also probable that creative written reinterpretations of tradition lie behind our present texts.

One may mention here the many discussions of "Deuteronomistic" elements in the Book of Jeremiah and "priestly" elements in the Book of Ezekiel (on the latter cf. Clements, 1982; McBride, 1983).

Meanwhile, R. Culley (1963) advanced the discussion by bringing modern studies of literature and folklore to bear on the problem of oral tradition. Cully identified two modes of oral transmission. On the one hand, there is strict memorization, often found in conjunction with a written text like the Vedas, Hebrew Bible, Talmud, or Quran. In such cases the text can serve as "insurance against change or error" (1963:118). On the other hand, there is a freer form of transmission, without a fixed text. The latter requires a well-trained artist, who utilizes traditional elements, and whose every performance involves a certain amount of improvization, or "re-composition" (1963:118–21).

There are several points here that deserve emphasis. First, oral transmission normally takes place before an audience and entails some degree of improvisation. In many of the cases cited ". . . composition and transmission are so closely related that transmission is accomplished by continual recomposition." There is, therefore, no "original text"; the "work exists only in its various performances" (1963:118,121). Second, in such a situation the audience has something of the role of a censor: it will only listen to what it pleases, and oral literature depends on acceptance for its very existence (1963:121).

In 1976 Culley edited a special issue of *Semeia* on "Oral Tradition and Old Testament Studies" in which he updated his earlier studies and suggested ways in which studies of oral tradition could be applied to the analysis of Old Testament texts (1976:15–20). Essays in the same volume by Coote, Gunn, and Van Seters also have this latter focus (in addition, cf. Coote, 1976b).

Finally, B. Long (1976a) utilizes anthropological field studies to suggest a more sociologically realistic context for the discussion of a particular problem of Old Testament study, viz. the "question of *Sitz im Leben*." By defining *Sitz im Leben* in terms of the dynamics of performance, Long attempted to 'loosen up' the usual understanding of that concept in Old Testament scholarship. Field studies show that it is precarious to assume an essential and definitive setting for every genre, and to imagine an audience as simply a watchdog over tradition. Rather, the performer and audience interact in a particular cultural and historical situation in which the tradition is creatively manifested (cf. also 1976b, and along somewhat different lines the discussion of Isaiah's rhetorical situation by Gitay, 1983).

It would, I believe, be generally agreed that there are two phases to be studied in the transmission of any prophetic tradition: 1. the prophet himself, whose activities take a certain form and evoke a certain reaction from his audience(s), and 2. the subsequent tradition. The latter will in some sense continue what the prophet began. But there will also be alterations as situations and audiences change, disciples take up the role of prophet, and traditions *about* the prophet take their place beside those portions of the tradition which purport to be *from* him. What is in dispute is the dynamics of this process of transmission.

The initiation and transmission of tradition should be viewed as a sociological process, involving real people in real situations, and an analysis of traditions from this point of view raises, as we shall see, a whole series of questions. If Old Testament scholars have slighted some of these questions or have given their treatments of the problems a a literary slant, it is because they study primarily a written text, rich in religious statement but poor in sociological data. Yet we may safely assume that in Israel, as elsewhere, the transmission of tradition was a complex social process. We may hope that familiarity with the details of such processes in other cultures will make students of the Bible sensitive to the kinds of social realities that most probably were involved in the transmission of its prophetic traditions, and will suggest some new lines of interpretation for various texts. Certainly the now-famous Parry-Lord studies of oral composition have had such an effect on the study of poetic portions of the Old Testament (cf. Culley, 1976). The remainder of this chapter will, therefore, be devoted to two tasks: a discussion of some questions which might be asked as part of a sociological analysis of the oral transmission of tradition, and a case study of the development of one specific tradition.

The Sociology of Storytelling

Within the past several decades there have been a considerable number of studies by anthropologists and folklorists of oral literature and its transmission. In what follows I intend not so much to undertake a comprehensive review of this literature as to discuss some of the questions that it raises about the transmission of tradition. While there is a certain amount of over-lapping in this series of organizing questions, each refers to matters that can profitably be dealt with separately and helps to illustrate the complex social reality that underlies the transmission of tradition.

Let me say a word about my use of the terms "story," "storyteller," and the like. They are, frankly, terms of convenience. Up to now I have spoken mostly of "traditions" and the "circles" or "disciples" that are presumed to have been responsible for their transmission. But in reality oral literature comprises many genres, which in turn are transmitted by a variety of speakers. I have, therefore, chosen "story" and its derivatives as comprehensive, convenient, and neutral terms by which to refer to both the traditions themselves and the agents of their transmission.

How are the stories preserved?

The first thing one wants to know about stories is, who preserves them? The answer differs from case to case. The legends about Sheikh Hussein, a late 17th century Muslim missionary who is venerated as a saint among Galla-speaking peoples of Ethiopia (for historical background cf. A. D. Smith, 1897:53–60, and J. S. Trimingham, 1952:253–6), are told by both "men of religion" and "ordinary laymen" (Andrzejewski, 1972b:467). In some American Indian groups the formal telling of stories was the domain of competent elders (e.g., Darnell, 1975; Toelken, 1969), while among the Evenks of Siberia shamans were the principal storytellers (Vasilevich, 1963:47). In Dahomey clan-histories (*hwenoho*) were told by elder men to other members of the clan, while the king had a "professional minstrel-rhapsodist" who daily recited "the names and praise names of the king's predecessors" and who was subject to severe penalties if the recitation was not "letter-perfect" (Herskovits, 1958:15, 21).

Even when many other members of the group are more or less familiar with the stories, the difference between an authoritative "performance" of the story and a translation, interpretation, or paraphrase of it is often recognized and may be signalled by changes in oratorical style (cf. Darnell, 1975:318). D. Hymes distinguishes between knowing a tradition ("knowledge what") and assuming responsibility for performance ("knowledge how"; 1975:69). We may also note that *who* preserves a tradition, and under what circumstances, has implications for *what* is preserved. Hymes, for example, shows that the particular version of a Clackamas Chinook myth he studied had been affected both quantitatively and qualitatively because "it has reached us through a line of women" (1971:76).

Secondly, one should ask about the form in which the stories are preserved. With respect to genre, answers will vary. The Galla distinguish between oral legends and prayer-poems (Andrzejewski, 1972b), the Cree between sacred stories and stories about the past (Darnell, 1975:319), and the Dahomeans between clan-histories and tales (Herskovits, 1958:14–6). With respect to mode, we can say that the stories we are discussing are in the main passed on in oral form, a fact which to some extent at least is related to the overall literacy of the group (Andrzejewski, 1972a:1–2).

Hymes points out that in situations where the preservation of stories is primarily oral traditions slip away when not used: "continued performance has been a condition of survival" (1975:70). He found that among the Chinook Indians whom he studied much was already gone, while what had survived was mostly material which continued to be of relevance to the ethos of the community (1975:70–1).

Who tells the stories?

We have already begun to answer this question, but now further distinctions need to be made. One might ask, for example, whether a given group of stories is genuinely a part of the popular culture, such that anyone can tell them, or whether their telling is restricted by custom or rule to certain individuals. If the latter is the case, are these individuals specially trained? Are they rewarded for their performance? As one would expect, the answers to these and similar questions differ depending upon the culture and specific situations within it. Let me give some examples.

Often one finds a special class of storytellers. Sometimes, as in the case of the Cree Indians, this appears to be a customary role informally assumed (Darnell, 1975). At other times the selection and training is more formal. R. Finnegan reports that the role of royal poet in Rwanda "has tended over the last few generations to become a hereditary one" (1970:86–7). D. Ben-Amos tells of a one- to three-year period of training undertaken by would-be storytellers in Benin (1975:37–40). In Dahomey recitation of *hwenoho* is restricted to adult males of the clan (Herskovits 1958:17).

Many societies reward the storyteller. In some instances a person's whole livelihood might be derived from such activity (cf. Finnegan, who observes that the need to make a living can have an effect upon the storyteller's subject matter: 1970:86–7, 92–7). Mostly, however, one cannot make a living at it (cf. Ben-Amos, 1975:36, 41–5). But the storyteller may receive food, lodging, money, small gifts, or special treatment on the job or in the group (e.g., Dégh, 1958:105–19), not to mention such non-material rewards as the respect of other members of the community (Dégh, 1958; Darnell, 1975:321–4).

Frequently, storytelling is not restricted, and Finnegan notes that the Limba of northern Sierra Leone have no word for expert storyteller (1967:69–71). But even in such cases "gifted raconteur(s)" are apt to be recognized and sought out (Dégh, 1958:125, 116, 118–9, 126–7; cf. also Willis, 1970:249).

How are the stories told?

We now turn our attention to "performance," in particular to the relationships that exist between performer and tradition (oral or textual) on the one hand, and performer and audience on the other. It is important to note at the outset the dynamic character of performance. Hymes (1975:18) defines performance as ". . . cultural behavior for which a person assumes responsibility to an audience," and calls it "a key to much of the difference in the meaning of life as between communities." Or consider the following statement by Finnegan (1977:28–9):

The skill and personality of the performer, the nature and reaction of the audience, the context, the purpose—these are essential aspects of the artistry and meaning of an oral poem. Even when there is little or no change of actual wording in a given poem between performances, the context still adds its own weight and meaning to the delivery, so that the whole occasion is unique. And in many cases . . . there is considerable variation between performances, so that the literate model of a fixed correct version—*the* text of a given poem—does not necessarily apply.

In this respect, oral literature differs from our implicit model of written literature: the mode of communication to a silent reader, through the eye alone, from a definitive written text. Oral literature is more flexible and more dependent on its social context. For this reason, no discussion of oral poetry can afford to concentrate on the text alone, but must take account of the nature of the audience, the context of performance, the personality of the poet-performer, and the details of the performance itself.

First, to the matter of text. Even where some members of the society are literate, there is often no authoritative written text from which a performer may be said to be working (cf. Andrzejewski, 1972a; Darnell, 1975). The Galla legends about Sheikh Hussein are made up of "short self-contained episodes," which the storyteller links together in varying sequences (Andrzejewski, 1972b:467), and Herskovits (1958:23–4) observed a similar method of composition among tellers of Dahomean *heho*, or "tales." Similarly, there is great flexibility of content in Benin narratives, the shortest of which may last two to three hours and the longest twelve to eighteen; the important features of good narration are precise details in whatever episodes are included in a given performance and a storyteller's ability to unify all the episodes (Ben-Amos, 1975: 52–3).

There is, then, an "emergent quality" to performance. R. Bauman notes the uniqueness of individual performances (he cites A. Lord's studies of composition in performance in his discussion), commenting that ". . . completely novel and completely fixed texts represent the poles of an ideal continuum" between which "lies the range of emergent text structures to be found in empirical performance" (1975:303). Toelken found that his Navajo informant, Yellowman, "recompose(d) with each performance" of a story. Indeed, tapes revealed that when he told his stories without an audience, Yellowman's narrative style lacked the special intonations, dramatic pauses, etc., which characterized a performance. This led Toelken to conclude that ". . . the narrative drama, far from being memorized, emerge(d) in response to the bona fide storytelling context" (1969:221). The implication is that changes, including elaborations, from one performance to the next are valued, and not characterized as "incorrect" or "secondary" renditions of the story (cf. Finnegan, 1967:97–8, 101–2; 1970:10).

The actual performance is always in some sense stylized. According to R. Abrahams, a pattern emerges which is "describable in terms of redundancies (style), decorum (expectations), and rhetoric (the uses by the performer of these patterns to entertain and persuade)." This pattern provides the performance with a latent order or continuity, while at the same time allowing "a certain freedom of action" (1972:76). As Bauman puts it, a performer's "competence rests on the knowledge and ability to speak in socially appropriate ways." This means in effect that performance is governed by a certain set of "ground rules," i.e., by "the set of cultural themes and social-interactional organizing principles that govern (its) conduct" (1975:293, 299; cf. Hymes, 1972:53–6, 63–4; 1975:18). Toelken's discussion of the "textural elements" in Yellowman's telling of the story would serve as one illustration of this (1969:224–7), and Darnell's description of a traditional performance by a 97-year-old Cree man another (1975:221–36).

This stylization affects both the form and content of performance, and rests, of course, on cultural knowledge shared by the performer and his or her audience. The extremely "allusive diction" of Galla hymns praising Sheikh Hussein, which has the effect of making them incomprehensible to outsiders, is predicated upon the devotees' thorough familiarity with the oral legends about the saint (Andrzejewski, 1972a:3–6, 29). P. Amoss' study of secrecy among the Coast Salish Indians offers a particularly striking example of how cultural knowledge allows inferences to be drawn from stylized behavior (in this case "entranced" dancing), even in the absence of direct verbal communication (1977:134–9).

Audiences differ in such respects as size, the amount of direct involvement in the performance, and the purpose for which they are assembled (cf. Finnegan, 1977:214–31). Generally speaking, their reaction to the performer is of critical importance. Sometimes these reactions are themselves stylized, with members of the audience participating in an opening dialogue, "answering" the storyteller, singing a chorus, or the like (cf. Finnegan, 1967:67–9, 1970:10; Herskovits, 1936:142; Seitel, 1980:27; Shack and Marcos, 1974:24). In any case the effectiveness of a performance depends upon the performer's ability to communicate with the audience and excite it to participation. "The idea that lies behind performance is a remarkably simple one: to set up rhythms and expectancies which will permit—indeed, insist upon—a synchronized audience reaction" (Abrahams, 1972:78; cf. Dégh, 1958:132–3; Finnegan, 1970:92–7; Seitel, 1980:26).

The reaction of the audience may serve to validate the performer (cf. Amoss, 1977, and Darnell's observations about the social significance of the spatial location of participants in the performance she witnessed,

1975:321–4). Indeed, performance is likely to be avoided where the audience would be unsympathetic (Darnell, 1975:317). This also suggests that the storyteller is likely to consider the make-up and disposition of the audience as s/he composes the "text" delivered in a particular performance (cf. Finnegan, 1977:231–41).

Lest anyone doubt the importance of such "socially appropriate" patterns of communicative interaction, B. Bernstein demonstrates the existence in modern British society of communications codes characteristic of and promoted by social classes. Such codes have the effect of acting "selectively upon what is said, when it is said, and how it is said" (1972:473).

On what occasions are stories told?

As to the occasions for performance, one might in principle expect an important distinction between religious and secular traditions, and examples can indeed be cited of stories with religious content being used within a ceremonial context. However, as our own experience suggests, religious ceremonies are not the only valid locations for telling such stories. Andrzejewski reports that hymns or prayer-poems uttered in praise of Sheikh Hussein are utilized on pilgrimages and in prayer meetings, and are thus an important part of the saint's cult. Yet these same hymns may be heard at private parties or in tape-recorded versions on public buses (1972a:3; 1972b:469). Similarly, Shack and Marcos found that all three types of "religious" poems of the Western Gurage people of Ethiopia were sung both in the context of religious ceremonies and in secular settings, such as work parties (1974:2–5, 24, 29, 38).

Perhaps it is sufficient to observe that in many societies specific events and situations are recognized as being appropriate for the telling of certain kinds of stories. Some of these occasions are more formal than others, and all imply a certain set of expectations on the part of the participants (cf. Ben-Amos, 1975:21–35; Dégh, 1958; Finnegan, 1967:64–6; Overholt and Callicott, 1982:24–9).

Why are the stories told?

There are many reasons for telling these stories, of which I will mention only a few. Andrzejewski found that the "express purpose" of telling the legends about Sheikh Hussein was "to show one's devotion to the saint by remembering him and spreading knowledge about him" (1972b:467). Sometimes performances are intended to have an effect on some aspect of the social structure. "Official" poets, attached, for example, to a court, may have the function of upholding the status quo (Finnegan, 1977:188–91; Herskovits, 1958:20–1). Among the Anang of Nigeria proverbs were regularly used in certain judicial proceedings to sway the opinions of the audience and justices (Messenger, 1959). On the other hand, Bauman speaks of the performer's "potential for subverting and transforming the status quo," offering as an example the youthful Dick Gregory's use of joking to defend himself from neighborhood bullies (1975:305).

Teaching cultural values has often been an important reason for the transmission of tradition. Yellowman explained to Toelken that he told his stories so that his children would "grow up to be good people" (1969:221), and over a century earlier George Copway, a Christianized Ojibwa Indian, wrote that his people had "a great fund of legends, stories, and historical tales, the relating and hearing of which, form a vast fund of winter evening instruction and amusement." After describing his own youthful reaction to these stories, he commented, "These legends have an important bearing on the character of the children of our nation" (1860:95–7). Similarly, Herskovits comments that while most Negro children in Paramaribo, the capital city of Suriname, attended school, "they still listen after dusk to Anansi-stories, and they are encouraged by the older women in the yard to recount them to one another . . . and to end with the proper moral, or the proper explanatory sentence" (1936:141). One is reminded of Deuteronomy 7:20–25.

Sometimes the telling of stories served the very mundane purpose of making monotonous work easier (cf. Dégh, 1958:106–9, 114–5). Nor should one overlook the entertainment value of stories (cf. Dégh, 1958:105, 109, 111–2; Seitel, 1980:29; Overholt and Callicott, 1982:24–9). Of course, more than one of these purposes (for example, in the case of Ojibwa winter evening storytelling, education and entertainment) could operate simultaneously.

What is the relationship of the stories to the wider life of the community?

A few further observations can be made on the social setting of the traditions. Perhaps the most important thing to be said is that the stories sometimes do directly affect the lives of people in a given society. This may be true at a quite general level. Ben Amos, for example, found that the Benin tales contribute to "ethnic identity" and pride, and thereby help "sustain traditional culture" in the face of pressures inherent in contact with Europeans (1975:15, 21; cf. also Darnell, 1975).

Stories can also relate in a more direct way to practical matters of everyday life. This is illustrated particularly well by Herskovits' observation about the Dahomean *hwenoho*, a category of stories encompassing myths, clan chronicles, and related materials:

> What is of significance for us here is that these *hwenoho* are in the fullest sense living spoken documents, important psychologically as affording a sense of time depth in cultural experience.

> But they are even more important in day-to-day intertribal and
> intratribal economic, social and political dealings, where they are
> productive of a whole superstructure of claims and counter-
> claims, and constitute a record of infringements of prerogatives
> and rights that only await an opportune moment for redress.
> (1958:22)

Among the Galla, the telling of stories is central to piety and the religious
life (Andrzejewski, 1972b:467). Ben-Amos notes that the introduction of
a certain kind of narration (*akpata*) "elevates an occasion to a high social
status" (1975:36).

Stories can also reflect tensions within a community. Among some
Somalis, a genre of "oral anti-legends" has arisen attacking the credulity
of believers in Sufi saints like Sheikh Hussein, and there is also a kind of
oral drama which seeks to expose "imposters who exploit the belief in
the miraculous powers of the saints" (Andrzejewski, 1974:26–30).

The stories of a society will certainly reflect the wider life of that
society, a premise which underlays Overholt and Callicott's treatment of
Ojibwa Indian tales (1982). It is good, however, to heed Finnegan's warning that it may do so in a way which is selective and indirect. In a given
instance stories may "express the views of minority or divergent groups
within the society at large, or convey ideas pleasing in a literary context
but not necessarily acceptable in everyday life." "Literature," she says,
"is essentially people acting," and one of the things they are doing is
creating the world around them (1977:265, 273). The same social context
can, after all, give rise to several genres of tradition, which may sometimes be antagonistic, as witnessed by the existence among the Somalis
of pious oral legends, as well as oral "anti-legends" and drama, the latter
expressing an entirely different view of saints and intermediaries (Andrzejewski, 1974).

The Development of the Handsome Lake Tradition: A Case Study

At this point we turn again to the Seneca intermediary, Handsome
Lake, this time using the "New Religion" that he inaugurated as a case
study in the persistence of traditions from and about a prophet. In the
years following Handsome Lake's death (1815) the pressures of evangel-
ical Christian missionary activity and land negotiations caused the Seneca to split into two factions, the "pagan" and "Christian" parties.
Though not all its adherents were actually baptized, Wallace estimates
that by 1830 the latter group comprised perhaps half of the total population (1972:324). Against the "trusting identification with white men"
characteristic of the Christian party, "most of the leaders of the pagan
group . . . clung to the fact that they were Indians and sought for the
most part to find in the memory of Handsome Lake a figure with whom

they could identify." Beginning in 1820 Chief Cornplanter, Handsome
Lake's brother, experienced a series of visions, the gist of which was that
he should "have nothing further to do with white people or with war"
and which in specific contents were often reminiscent of the teachings of
Handsome Lake. Yet by the time of Cornplanter's death in 1835 the
unity of the group of Handsome Lake's fifteen original associates on the
Allegany Reservation was fragmented: some had died, others moved
away, and still others converted to Christianity (Wallace, 1972:326–30).

The tensions generated by this factionalism reached a peak in the
period 1818–1822. The missionaries were demanding an abandonment
of Indian identity and calling those who refused this course "pagans." As
a result, "some of those who chose to retain pride in being Iroquois felt
forced to oppose everything any missionary proposed," turning even
against the Quakers, who had a long history of beneficial work among
them, who had been supporters of Handsome Lake, and who themselves
had opposed the evangelists. As Wallace describes it, "bizarre antiwhite
prophecies began to circulate, which violated both the word and the
spirit of Handsome Lake's preaching." Witchcraft accusations and exe-
cutions increased in number and caused additional conflict between the
two parties. But this "panicky retreat into nativism" was opposed by "the
responsible leaders" of the nonChristian group, who wanted both "to
retain the loyalty of the people to the old way" and to accept those white
customs which seemed to them most useful. Thus,

> beginning in 1818 . . . leaders of the pagan party undertook to
> define the form and spirit of the old religion. In order to do so,
> they called upon the memory of the great prophet, Handsome
> Lake, whose position with regard to religion had been firmly tra-
> ditional but who had also been in favor of education, of economic
> progress, and of social harmony, and who had refused to condemn
> Christianity, hoping for mutual tolerance and respect among
> people of different faiths. Their effort to consolidate the old reli-
> gion by appealing to the well-remembered teachings of the
> prophet gradually produced between 1818 and 1845 a new reli-
> gious institution—a church—devoted to the preservation and
> propagation of the prophet's message. (Wallace, 1972:331–2)

This process began in the summer of 1818 with a religious council at
Tonawanda, which location was to become the "head fire" in the annual
circuit of meetings at which the Gaiwiio is preached in the Longhouses
of the various Iroquois reservations (cf. Shimony, 1961:35–6). At this
meeting "many speakers repeated the lessons of the prophet and urged
their importance upon the listeners," and a "minor prophet" recounted a
vision confirming the teachings of Handsome Lake (Wallace, 1972:332–
3). Over the next twenty years his sayings were "cherished and repeated"
by his followers, some of whom "harangued the people" at various Iro-

quois ceremonials "with recitals of the prophet's moral commands." During this period, two more prophets confirmed the validity of Handsome Lake's visions (Wallace, 1972:333–4).

In this manner the tradition lived on and grew, and "by the 1840's the constant recitation of the prophet's teachings and the accumulation of confirming dreams and visions by minor prophets had produced a large body of legend and text, more or less accurately recounting events in the prophet's life and his various visions and moral lessons" (Wallace, 1972:334). Several versions of the Code emerged, notably those of Blacksnake at Allegany and Jimmy Johnson (Handsome Lake's grandson) at Tonawanda. Eventually, the latter became "the standard by which other speakers' versions were judged, and it was this version that was carried from village to village in the fall of each year in the Six Nations Meetings" (Wallace, 1972:335; cf. Shimony, 1961:191–203). During this period, the architecture of the meeting house (modeled on the traditional longhouse) and the ceremonialism of the Longhouse Religion were also taking shape. In the words of Wallace (1972:336),

> The forms of the Handsome Lake Church were set about 1850 and have changed little since then. The dream-guessing rites and the white dog sacrifices, which aroused the indignation of white people, were gradually left out of the annual ceremonies and were no longer performed by the early part of the twentieth century. But these are not essential to the institution. Now the adherents of the Old Way are sometimes called conservatives or old-time people. What was revolutionary in the prophet's day is now, one hundred and fifty years later, the extreme of traditionalism.

The central rite of the Longhouse Religion is the periodic recitation of the Code of Handsome Lake and the "personal confessions and moral exhortations to lead a 'good' life" which are associated with that act (cf. Shimony, 1961:191–203). What, then, can be said about the accuracy with which Handsome Lake's words were preserved? During his lifetime, the prophet had travelled around the Iroquois reservations preaching, but his words were not written down. After his death, oral reconstructions of the teachings were begun, and eventually that of Tonawanda came to be regarded as something of a standard. This version was recorded, though not published, by Ely S. Parker in 1845 and 1848, and according to Wallace "agrees remarkably well in many details with the Allegany-Cattaraugus version, which was formulated, according to tradition, at a council at Cold Spring about 1860, at which all speakers of the Code came together to compare versions and decide on an official one" (1972:368, n. 63). That 1860 version was subsequently published by Arthur C. Parker (1913), and has been used throughout this volume. It cannot be assumed, however, that the Code even in its "standard" versions represents the *ipsissima verba* of the prophet. Wallace's conclusion is rather that "the existing Code includes both the words of Handsome Lake and the exhortations, historical introduction and commentary by later speakers, and miscellaneous interpretations, applications, and perhaps new prophetic material" (1972:368, n. 63).

Deardorff reported that among his Seneca friends there was a conviction that the Code as recited was the same in all the longhouses, and noted Parker's inference (quoted in the following texts) that the Cold Spring meeting resulted in a fixed and canonized text. Against these views he contended that:

> There is no one text of the Good Message. Versions vary from preacher to preacher; from one longhouse to another; and from time to time. Parker's Good Message took 3 days for recitation. The common allotment now is 4; but at Sour Springs in 1949 the preacher found 5 necessary to complete his version, which contained material that the delegates there from Cold Spring had never heard before.

Nor is the version printed by Parker the only one that has been certified by what Deardorff calls "the Sanhedrin of chiefs at Tonawanda" for use on the circuit of Six Nations meetings (1951:98–101). Furthermore, besides these Six Nations meetings for which an individual preacher of the Code must be certified at Tonawanda, there are more frequent local "chiefs' conventions" at which the Code is recited by locally-chosen preachers who have only to satisfy their present audience.

Having sketched something of what is known about the development of the Handsome Lake tradition, we can now address those specific questions about the "sociology of storytelling" outlined above. First, there is the matter of how the stories were preserved. Initially, they were reconstructed by persons who had heard Handsome Lake. Timothy Alden, the president of Allegheny College and a frequent visitor among the Seneca, attended a council at Tonawanda in July, 1818, three years after the prophet's death. According to this account, the purpose of that council was to revive Handsome Lake's "moral instructions," on the subject of which John Sky, a Tonawanda chief, spoke for three hours. On this occasion Alden also witnessed a public confession and other activities, all of which Deardorff observes are "still the essential ingredients of a general 'Six Nations Meeting'" (1951:97–8).

In the early years some of those involved in preserving the Handsome Lake stories were themselves acting as prophets. Reports of such activity come from Allegany (1825–7), Tonawanda (1838), and Buffalo Creek (1838). The prophet at Tonawanda claimed that four angels came to him annually from the Great Spirit, and, according to a contemporary report, spoke "as though Handsome Lake himself were speaking" (Deardorff, 1951:98). Gradually, specially trained and recognized "preachers" emerged as the primary bearers of the tradition.

As to the form in which the tradition was preserved, it is clear that a written text came into existence within the first generation. We know that Ely S. Parker wrote down Jimmy Johnson's version of the Code, recited at Tonawanda in 1845 (Deardorff, 1951:98). In fact over the years the Code was committed to writing several times, motivated in part by concern for its preservation (cf. "1" under "Texts," below).

But it is important to notice that the existence of written text(s) did not halt the oral transmission of the tradition or the creative handling of it in performance, and the first of the texts reprinted below witnesses to a remarkably relaxed attitude about safeguarding an early written version. In fact Shimony shows that there is a general bias against the "white man's writing" going back to Handsome Lake himself and continuing down to the present. At Six Nations Reserve, for example, there is "a strong feeling that imparting information by mail or leaving a note is not the 'Longhouse way'," and families therefore want to live as close as possible to their own Longhouse, so as not to miss messengers with news of ceremonies. In addition "the strongest ritualists and preachers think it is wrong to use any sort of written aid in learning to preach or in learning any ritual." Some preachers at Six Nations Reserve do own copies of Parker's version of the Code, but they will not admit to using them in the instruction of new preachers (Shimony, 1961:39–40).

Second, a class of official storytellers, or preachers of the Code, emerged in the Longhouse Religion, and "Handsome Lake preacher" is today one of three formal speaking roles specifically identified by the Iroquois (Foster, 1974:30). The process by which these persons are selected and trained seems quite informal. Much of the learning in effect takes place secretly, younger Longhouse members just "picking it up" while listening and watching at Code recitations and other ceremonies (Shimony, 1961:128–9). Their "public stance . . . is one of humility," since from the Iroquois point of view their abilities are "a matter of 'luck,' of natural endowment, rather than accomplishment," and their learning, therefore, "more or less automatic." The actual "sources" of their learning seem to be repeated hearing of speeches at ceremonies, combined with "informal consultation with experienced speakers" (Foster, 1974:31). The eventual vadidation of a Six Nations preacher at Tonawanda is based on his successful recitation from memory of a complete, orthodox version of the Code, usually lasting four days (Shimony, 1961:193–4). The social status of speakers, as well as of other ritualists, within the community is very high (Shimony, 1961:72–3).

Of course, the Handsome Lake traditions exist as part of the popular culture as well. Ordinary people know and cite them, doubtless with varying degrees of comprehensiveness and "accuracy" (as measured by the verbal performance of the Code preachers and the various written texts). Several of Fenton's informants told him of how Handsome Lake had instituted certain changes in traditional ceremonies which persist down to the present. One chief's wife on the Onondaga Reservation said, "Before Handsome Lake came here the Onondagas used liquor at the dances; since then they have food to eat" (Fenton, 1953:68).

A third question has to do with how the stories are told. It appears that at least some Iroquois hold the belief that there is but one version of the Code, but as we have seen, this view does not square with the facts. Rather, there is local autonomy with respect to versions of the Code, and it is even acknowledged that established preachers, "when they got old," added to or subtracted from it (Deardorff, 1951:101). Shimony says that when reciting the Code, "the preacher interpolates and extemporizes upon the standard text" (1961:14; cf. 196–7, and also Foster, 1974:171–85).

There is a great deal of formality in Iroquois speech events. W. Chafe has identified distinct speaking styles for chanting, preaching, and conversation, and speaks of a "fixed pattern" for dealing with all the items in a traditional Thanksgiving Address (1961:7, 147–8). There are certain "criteria of speaking well" (of "effective delivery" as over against "mere recitation") which are recognized and insisted upon by the audience. These include "a feeling for balance of content" (the speaker includes "everything," but doesn't go on at too great length), "memory," "discretion" (a "general cultural theme," including "good judgment, care and modesty in public behavior," and "self-effacement and suppression of private interest") and the like (Foster, 1974:32–3).

Because it has such expectations, the audience exerts some control over the performance. In addition certain members of the audience ("deacons") may become more directly involved by serving as "prompters" during ceremonials (Shimony, 1961:74). It is also the case that the specific situation has an effect on what the preacher says, interpolations often being aimed in the direction of local problems and needs (cf. Shimony, 1961:14–5, 159–60, 195–7; also, Tooker's interpretation of Handsome Lake's accomplishment, 1968).

Fourth, there are several occasions during which one can find formal mention of the Handsome Lake tradition. The tradition has in fact been incorporated into the Iroquois ritual cycle, and although the Code in its entirety is preached only at special "conventions," excerpts from it may also be preached during the Midwinter and Green Corn ceremonies and at the Strawberry Festival. At the latter the preacher "gives several passages from the Code verbatim as 'texts,' but he is free to develop these in a homily of his own" (Foster, 1974:126). The two occasions on which the primary purpose is the recitation of the Code itself are the Six Nations conventions and the chiefs' conventions. The latter are the more frequent, being scheduled locally "to satisfy a variety of needs." Such a meeting may be called if the leaders of a congregation feel that the people need "a spiritual stimulus—that people 'are slipping,' or absent from the Longhouse too much, or sinful, or demoralized"—in order to "'bring them back to the Longhouse way.'" The most common reason for calling a chiefs' convention is "to provide an opportunity for spiritual purging before participating in the major Longhouse ceremonials." They may also be called occasionally to show "respect to Handsome Lake and the Creator" and afford the people an opportunity "to hear the sacred words." The term "Six Nations conventions" refers to a biennial circuit of Code recitations that begins at Tonawanda and proceeds to other Longhouses in New York and Canada (Shimony, 1961:191–203). And of course, informal use of the tradition will be more or less frequent in the culture, as suggested above.

Fifth, the recitation of the Handsome Lake traditions has played a major role in the preservation of Iroquois culture. According to Shimony, the Longhouse has "emerged as the central social institution of the conservative culture, and each of the four Longhouses at Six Nations functions not only as a religious organization, but as a pulpit for moral education, an irredentist society for defending Indian rights, a cooperative for mutual aid, a medical center, and a social club" (1961:16).

Finally, it is possible to say something about the relationship of the Handsome Lake tradition to the wider life of the community. We may begin with the observation that while not all nonChristian Iroquois approve of Handsome Lake, he has nevertheless had a recognizable influence on traditional Iroquois ceremonialism (cf., for example, Snorer's statement to Fenton, 1953:108). In effect Handsome Lake usurped traditional religion by abolishing (or, attempting to abolish) the medicine societies, introducing fundamental changes in various ceremonials and in cultural values, replacing the recitation of the creation myth with the recitation of the Code, and the like (in addition to references already cited, cf. Parker, 1909:162–4; McElwain, 1978:9). At the same time he was taken up into traditional Iroquois religion, which in the process was adapted to changing social conditions (cf. Tooker, 1968). Shimony comments that today the ritual calendar of the Longhouse fuses two traditional "complexes," viz. "the ethical and moral system of Handsome Lake" and "the older agricultural calendric rites," although the fusion is not an altogether harmonious one. Still, "today Gaihwi'yo (sic) has been so assimilated into the generalized Iroquoian religion that the entire religious complex is designated as 'Gaihwi'yo!'" (1961:132, 192).

One particularly interesting feature of all this is how the tradition *of* Handsome Lake became a tradition *about* him. To illustrate this point we may look at the Thanksgiving Address, which is closely related in structure to other ritual narrations and is a very important "speech event" in the Iroquois ceremonial cycle. According to Foster (1974:3–4), now that "myth-narration has fallen into disuse" in the Longhouse religion, it is the Thanksgiving Address and related speeches "whose context and structure are the most explicit expressions of the cosmological sequence of the spirit forces." These forces are arranged in the Address in a definite hierarchical pattern, beginning with those on the earth (people, grasses, fruit, etc.) and extending next to those in the sky (wind, Thunderers, sun, moon, stars) and, finally, those beyond the sky (the Four Beings, Handsome Lake, and the Creator). The prophet has been incorporated into the pantheon of spirits.

The texts in Chapter II, Section 5, show that the Code itself contains considerable biographical information about Handsome Lake, and refers to him frequently in the third person. The references to him in the Thanksgiving Address have two foci: 1. biography (he was once alive; he had a long sickness, during which he repented; he received a revelation through the Four Beings that the Creator perceived that humans were without guidance and was sending Handsome Lake on a mission to tell them what they should do; he carried this message to the people and taught them until his death), and 2. an expression of gratitude that the preaching has continued down to the present (cf. Corbett Sundown's version of the Address, recorded in Chafe, 1961).

Foster remarks that the Handsome Lake section of the Address "stands out from previous sections . . . in tone and structure," precisely because he is treated biographically, and not just as another spirit. This suggests a more recent inclusion of the prophet into the hierarchic sequence (1974:80–3). Chafe agrees, noting that prior to 1900 only the Cattaraugus version of the Address (1896) contains a reference to the prophet (1961:13). Be that as it may, the move to take the prophet up into the tradition must have been begun long before the turn of the century. F. Speck traces the impetus for it back to Handsome Lake himself (he ". . . taught that after his death he would abide next to the Creator, and this accounts for his name being listed in this position in the tabulation"; 1949:29), and E. Johnson, a Tuscarora chief, reports the contents of a Code recitation by the prophet's grandson in the course of which he mentions that at the beginning of the second morning's narration "thanks" were "returned to" Handsome Lake and the Creator (1881:195).

These, then, are some of the dynamics of the preservation of the Handsome Lake tradition. This tradition was not preserved in any one form or version. But it *was* preserved, and in closing we would point again to the utility of that process. In the beginning the teachings of the prophet enabled a considerable number of conservative Iroquois to steer a course between assimilation and fanatical nativism. Initially, this consolidation of their views caused a sharper division between Christian and nonChristian Iroquois, but "in the long run it reduced antagonism. More secure in their faith, and focused upon the image of the prophet as their great leader, the pagans were less sensitive to slight and more tolerant of their Christian neighbors." And this despite the "lurid and distorted" stories which the latter circulated about Handsome Lake and his teachings (Wallace, 1972:333). Above all, the Code became the focal point for the crystallization of a new religion, which has been instrumental in enabling many Iroquois to maintain a satisfactory sense of identity in a time of tremendous cultural pressure and change.

Texts

> The following texts are all taken from Arthur C. Parker, *The Code of Handsome Lake, the Seneca Prophet* (1913). The first is part of Parker's own introduction to the Code. The second is from Edward Cornplanter's preamble to the Code, "How the White Race Came to America and Why the Gaiwiio became a Necessity," and contains a pedigree for the version of the Code which Cornplanter recites. The third is from the Code itself, and includes the last section of the Code proper and the closing words of the preacher, Edward Cornplanter.

1. (Parker, 1913:7–8)

The Gaiwiio is the record of the teachings of Handsome Lake, the Seneca prophet, and purports to be an exact exposition of the precepts that he taught during a term of sixteen years, ending with his death in 1815. It is the basis of the so-called "new religion" of the Six Nations and is preached or recited at all the annual mid-winter festivals on the various Iroquois reservations in New York and Ontario that have adherents. These reservations are Onondaga, Tonawanda, Cattaraugus and Allegany in New York and Grand River and Muncytown in Ontario.

There are six authorized "holders" of the Gaiwiio among whom are John Gibson (Ganiodaiio; "Handsome Lake," a sachem name formerly held by the prophet) and Edward Cornplanter (Sosondowa), Senecas, and Frank Logan (Adodarho), Onondaga. Chief Cornplanter is by far the most conservative though Chief Gibson seems to have the greater store of explanatory matter, often interpolating it during his exposition. Chief Logan is a devout adherent of his religion and watches the waning of his prophet's teachings with grave concern . . .

> There follows a description of the times and circumstances under which Gaiwiio is recited, and of its appeal. . . .

The present form of the Gaiwiio was determined by a council of its preachers some fifty years ago (ca. 1860). They met at Cold Spring, the old home of Handsome lake, and compared their versions. Several differences were found and each preacher thought his version the correct one. At length Chief John Jacket, a Cattaraugus Seneca, and a man well versed in the lore of his people, was chosen to settle forever the words and the form of the Gaiwiio. This he did by writing it out in the Seneca language by the method taught by Rev. Asher Wright, the Presbyterian missionary. The preachers assembled again, this time, according to Cornplanter, at Cattaraugus where they memorized the parts in which they were faulty. The original text was written on letter paper and now is entirely destroyed. Chief Jacket gave it to Henry Stevens and Chief Stevens passed it on to Chief Cornplanter who after he had memorized the teachings became careless and lost the papers sheet by sheet. Fearing that the true form might become lost, Chief Cornplanter in 1903 began to rewrite the Gaiwiio in an old minute book of the Seneca Lacrosse Club. He had finished the historical introduction when the writer discovered what he had done. He was implored to finish it and give it to the State of New York for preseration. He was at first reluctant, fearing criticism, but after a council with the leading men he consented to do so. He became greatly interested in the progress of the translation and is eager for the time to arrive when all white men may have the privilege of reading the "wonderful message" of the great prophet.

The translation was made chiefly by William Bluesky, the native lay preacher of the Baptist church. It was a lesson in religious toleration to see the Christian preacher and the "Instructor of the Gaiwiio" side by side working over the sections of the code, for beyond a few smiles at certain passages, in which Chief Cornplanter himself shared, Mr. Bluesky never showed but that he reverenced every message and revelation of the four messengers.

2. (Parker, 1913:18–9)

> The gist of the story about the necessity of the Gaiwiio is that "the evil one" tricked a young English preacher into taking "five things" (rum, playing cards, coins, a violin, and a decayed leg bone) across the ocean, in order to corrupt a people who until his coming had been virtuous and honest and had had "no unnatural evil habits." He accomplished this with the aid of Columbus.

Now all this was done and when afterward he saw the havoc and the misery his work had done he said, "I think I have made an enormous mistake for I did not dream that these people would suffer so." Then did even the devil himself lament that his evil had been so great.

So after the swarms of white men came and misery was thrust upon the Ongweoweh ("real men," the Iroquois) the Creator was sorry for his own people whom he had molded from the soil of the earth of this Great Island, and he spoke to his four messengers and many times they tried to tell right men the revelations of the Creator but none would listen. Then they found our head man sick. Then they heard him speak to the sun and to the moon and they saw his sickness. Then they knew that he suffered because of the cunning evils that Hanisseono (the "evil one") had given the Ongweoweh. So then they knew that he was the one. He was the one who should hear and tell Gaiwiio. But when Ganiodaiio (Handsome Lake) spoke the evil being ceased his lament and sought to obstruct Gaiwiio, for he claimed to be master.

The Gaiwiio came from Hodianokdoo Hediohe, the Great Ruler, to the Hadioyageono, the four messengers. From them it was transmitted to Ganiodaiio, Handsome Lake who taught it to Skandyogwadi (Owen Blacksnake) and to his own grandson, Sosheowa (James Johnson). Blacksnake taught it to Henry Stevens (Ganishando), who taught it to Sosondowa, Edward Cornplanter. "So I know that I have the true words and I preach them," adds Cornplanter.

3. (Parker, 1913:79–80)

Now shortly after he (Handsome Lake) said a few words. To the numbers gathered about him to hear his message he said, "I will soon go to my new home. Soon I will step into the new world for there is a plain pathway before me leading there. Whoever follows my teachings will follow in my footsteps and I will look back upon him with outstretched arms inviting him into the new world of our Creator. Alas, I fear that a pall of smoke will obscure the eyes of many from the truth of Gaiwiio but I pray that when I am gone that all may do what I have taught."

This is what he said. This is what Ganiodaiio, our head man, said to his people. Eniaiehuk ("It was that way"; a rubric with which virtually all the sections of the Code end).

(Then the preacher says:) "Relatives and friends: His term of ministry was sixteen years. So preached our head man, Ganiodaiio.

"Let this be our thanks to you and to the four messengers also. I give thanks to them for they are the messengers of our Creator. So, also, I give thanks to him whom we call Sedwagowane, our great teacher (a title applied to Handsome Lake). So, also, I give thanks to our great Creator.

"So have I said, I, Sosondowa (Great Night), the preacher."

(Signed) Edward Cornplanter, Sosondowa

CHAPTER IV
ANTHROPOLOGICAL MATERIALS AND THE OLD
TESTAMENT

Until now I have generally avoided dealing specifically with the Old Testament, while assuming throughout the possibility of making comparisons between it and materials of the kind presented in chapters II and III. Chapter I suggested a general approach to such comparisons, arguing that larger patterns rather than culture-specific details should be the focus of attention. In this chapter I will turn to some actual examples of anthropologically-informed interpretations of biblical prophecy, and then take up the question of what we can hope to learn from such comparisons.

Some Anthropological Perspectives on Old Testament Prophecy

In recent years an increasing number of biblical scholars have made use of theories, methods, and materials from the social sciences in their own work. The case studies which I will briefly discuss represent only a sampling of these, even if we limit ourselves to essays whose primary tie to the social sciences is through anthropology. I have chosen them because they are relatively brief and make systematic use of comparative materials. They provide, therefore, convenient examples of how comparison might work.

R. Wilson's paper, "Prophecy and Ecstasy: A Reexamination" (1979), addressed the problem of is how we are to understand the role of ecstasy in Israelite prophecy, particularly in the writing prophets. Stated in a slightly different way, the question is how ecstasy relates to "the relatively rational forms of prophetic action and speech that form critics have seen in the biblical literature" (1979:321).

The first question we might ask is why Wilson should want to turn to comparative materials in his effort to suggest a solution to this problem. The answer is clear: evidence within the Old Testament is insufficient in both quantity and clarity to allow a consensus which satisfactorily accounts for all the evidence to emerge.

What, then, does he gain from consulting anthropological studies on this topic? One thing is added precision in the use of terms. For example, "ecstasy" (anthropologists usually prefer the term "trance") is defined as a type of behavior, and not a form of divine-human communication. "Possession" and "soul travel" are the main modes of such communication associated with ecstasy. Furthermore, these studies show that possession does not always imply trance. Possession is positively valued in some societies, is characterized by stereotypical behavior and speech patterns which can be socially validated, and may even be expected of individuals within certain groups in the society. From these observations Wilson derives principles to be employed when assessing Old Testament evidence on "ecstasy": 1. One should not be "too quick to generalize about the nature of possession behavior in Israel" (e.g., by assuming that it was always the same from group to group, that all prophets were subject to possession, that possession behavior would be by definition uncontrolled or incoherent; 1979:328). 2. The possibility should be entertained that Israelite prophets exhibited stereotypical behavior (perhaps in speech patterns), and that, if so, different groups in the society reacted differently to them (1979:328–9).

Turning to the Old Testament, Wilson first lists a group of phrases ("the hand of the Lord fell upon me," "the spirit rested on them" and the like) which seem to indicate that Yahweh was thought of as communicating with prophets "by means of possession" (1979:325). The real focus of his attention, however, is a discussion of the semantic differences between the niphal and hithpael forms of the root *nb' in the course of which he concludes that the latter was used "to describe characteristic prophetic behavior," which varied among groups and over the course of Israelite and Judean history. Sometimes the reference is to trance behavior, but increasingly it is to recognizable patterns of speech (1979:336).

In this discussion he makes use of anthropological data in the following ways: 1. A particular view of the semantic development from hithpael to niphal is rejected because on the basis of anthropological studies it can be seen to depend on an oversimplified view of ecstasy (1979:329–30). 2. He appeals to anthropological studies to support an alternative view according to which the hithpael means "to act like a prophet," and refers to observable behavior (1979:330). 3. He also draws on such studies in proposing an interpretation of a specific passage, 1 Sam 10:10–3 (the inquiry about the "father" of the prophetic band in v. 12 suggests that the speaker felt the need for professional validation of the genuineness of the spirit possession he was witnessing, while the absence of intelligible speech does not necessarily mean the absence of "genuine divine-human communication"; 1979:333).

Wilson concludes that when prophets were possessed, they behaved in recognizable ways; that such behavior was not static, but differed among groups and changed over time; and that not all groups within Israel viewed ecstasy in the same way.

This study contributes to a solution to the problem of ecstasy and the biblical prophets in two ways. First, it provides a definition of ecstasy which allows prophetic speech to be seen within the realm of possession behavior. Second, it shows how operating with this definition enables a single notion of divine-human communication to reconcile a variety of data (phrases referring to possession, uncontrolled possession behavior, rational speeches, resistance of some persons to some of the prophets).

What is new here? Most obviously, a coherent view of the dynamics of a social process or situation. This view rests on the assumption that if possession occurs in ancient Israel, it will be analogous to that in other cultures. The implied criterion is that the best solution to the problem at hand will be one that is compatible with both the biblical data and known social processes. This implies further that while Israel can (even must) be seen as a unique social, religious, and political entity, its uniqueness is more likely to be found in specifics of behavior and in the content of what a prophet says than in the overall pattern characteristic of trance and possession.

For our second example we turn to an essay by B. Long, "Social Dimensions of Prophetic Conflict" (1981). The problem with which Long deals may be stated as follows: because the Old Testament has a point of view "which champions an impeccable Yahwistic faith," it tends to view conflicts between prophets "almost exclusively in ideological terms" (1981:31–2). As a result, it ignores or suppresses "the societal aspects of conflict—those personal, political, social, and economic factors that would have been a part of any public display of rivalry." Instead it presents us with a simplistic stereotype of any opposition to one of the canonical prophets as "anti-prophetic, anti-Yahwistic, (and) misguided" (1981:32). In addition modern interpreters have tended to accept this biblical point of view and to treat the problem of inter-prophetic conflict as a theological problem (1981:32–3).

Long turns to anthropological materials out of a desire to obtain a "fuller historical understanding" of a situation when, because of its theological bias, the text gives us only hints of the "social, economic, and political currents" that must have been present in such conflicts. Anthropological studies are useful because they provide an access to particular cultures which is not limited to literary texts, allowing us to view instances of conflict in considerable detail. What we gain from them is not "directly comparable data," but an "enriching stimulus to historical and sociological imagination." Specifically with respect to prophetic conflict, we get a "heightened sense of the relative place of ideology (or theology) along side of other forms of social expression" (1981:33–4).

Examples of conflicts that formed part of the functioning of Siberian, North American Eskimo, and African intermediaries reveal it to have been a complex social phenomenon which is "normal" to "the mediational process," though highly situational in its social function. Some instances of conflict may, for example, "reinforce both the clan's world view

and the shaman's central postion in society" (1981:35), and/or be part of
the dynamics by which one mediator established his relative position and
status vis-a-vis another. Conflict may undermine community solidarity.
However, it does not always "undermine public acceptance of the media-
tion process," though it may affect a given individual's credibility among
his peers. Clearly, such conflict has both ideological and social aspects.

When he turns to the Old Testament, Long focuses his attention on
the conflicts mirrored in Jer 26, 27–29, and 37–38. These texts in their
present form reveal the point of view of the "latest editors," the Deuter-
onomists, whose purpose was to explain the exile and present a homily
or warning for the benefit of a later generation. But there are also hints
about Jeremiah's actual situation, including his relative status with respect to the king, princes, and other prophets, and the alliances which
had in his day formed on the basis of family ties, political commitments,
and religious views. The context for Jeremiah's conflicts with other
prophets was a real struggle over the future of the nation. The exact role
of ideology (or theology) in this conflict is difficult to determine exactly,
though "both factions evidently sought support in prophetic oracles"
(1981:49).

What is new in Long's analysis is clearly not the recognition that
Jeremiah and his opponents can be identified with rival political positions in an actual historical situation. Rather, Long sees the anthropological materials as suggesting that the traditional interpretation of this situation has been skewed by virtue of its isolation of "religious ideology
from other forms of social expression." To avoid this trap, it is necessary
to acknowledge "that conflict is a vital element in prophetic activity, and
that it is both deeper and broader than disputes over religious beliefs"
(1981:50). Here, too, we see at work an assumption about the underlying
similarity of certain social patterns among a variety of different cultures.

We turn next to B. Lang's analysis of "The Social Organization of
Peasant Poverty in Biblical Israel" (1982). Lang sets out to explain the
origin and operation of the economic stratification reflected in the Book
of Amos (see, for example, 6:4, 5:11). In attempting to shed light on this
problem he is faced with a familiar set of circumstances: While evidence
in Amos makes the existence of an oppressive social system clear, little
is said about how the system as such functioned. Furthermore, previous
formulations of a solution have been oversimplified (1982:47–8).

Given this state of affairs, Lang turns to anthropological studies for
an overview of the kinds of relationships that have existed between peasants and elites, and for a fuller description of one such system, "rent
capitalism" (1982:48–52). He then returns to Amos and shows how the
prophet's references to "social and economic conditions" fit the model of
rent capitalism. Of this analysis he says, ". . . I am well aware that I am
going slightly beyond the information given in the biblical sources. But

read in the light of anthropology, the scattered bits of economic and social information fit into a definite and clear picture known as rent capitalism. Everything finds, so to speak, its natural place" (1982:59).

In what way has Lang gone "slightly beyond" the evidence? Presumably, in suggesting a specific economic system into which the evidence
fits. And while it would be too much to claim that he has provided proof
for the existence of "rent capitalism" in the Israel of Amos's day, it would
certainly be fair to say that he has demonstrated a coherent fit between
the main features of that system and the prophet's remarks about his own
socio-economic situation. What is new here is the identification of a system, based largely on observations of contemporary peasant societies
and not possible in such a thorough-going way without them. One important feature of such an analysis is that it focuses our attention on the
Israelite socio-economic system as part of its ancient Near Eastern environment (a necessity articulated earlier by Loretz, 1975), rather than on
heavily theological considerations (such as a supposed special constitu-
tion under which Israel was supposed to function; cf. Koch, 1971).

We take as our fourth example M. Buss's essay, "An Anthropological
Perspective Upon Prophetic Call Narratives" (1981). Hoping to achieve
a more comprehensive understanding of the prophetic call experiences,
Buss turns to anthropological materials, motivated partly by the incom-
pleteness of biblical and ancient Near Eastern data and partly by methodological convictions. Comparison is, he believes, an inevitable aspect
of any investigation. Further, comparison is useful in addressing the
question of whether a given phenomenon may "fit a certain kind of psychological or sociological context" (1981:10). What he hopes is that ultimately this comparative data will contribute to "a theoretical understanding of the nature of a call" (1981:11).

His is a short paper with as many pages of bibliography as of text. It
differs from the others so far discussed in not having a separate section
for the discussion of Old Testament data. Instead, Buss includes references to the Old Testament in his general discussion of various specific
aspects of the call experience. The latter include "induction into a social
role" (differentiation among various roles in a society, divine designation,
and the logic of the designee's "reluctance" to assume a role), "communication" (the importance of the role-bearer's special knowledge, personality characteristics associated with creativity and decision-making, and
the contribution which the social isolation characteristic of prophets
makes to both of these), and the "logic and practical implications of a
belief that a call by a spiritual reality has taken place" (the nature of the
prophet's responsibility to society; cf. 1981:16).

Buss concludes "that major features of prophetic call accounts appear
throughout the world and can be understood in terms of sociopsycholog-
ical categories." As a result, he is able to suggest that these "calls" fit

within the realm of human experiences, and need not be "dismissed as a superstition" or viewed as violating "common processes" (1981:17).

We note again the presence of an assumption about the universality of human experience.

As a final example of this turn toward anthropology, let me make some comments about several of my own papers, beginning with a series of three written during 1973–74 and revised and published over the next few years. The first (1974) makes no reference to biblical materials, the second (1977) is devoted entirely to a discussion of Jeremiah, and the last (1981) attempts a systematic comparison of Jeremiah and Handsome Lake. All focus on what I referred to as the "prophetic process," and seek to describe "the dynamics of the prophetic act itself" (1974:38).

The specific problem which motivated these studies was how to compare figures like Wovoka, Handsome Lake, and the Old Testament prophets who seemed in some respects so similar, but who were separated from each other by differences of time, place, and culture. If comparisons were to be made, it was clear they could not be based upon the specific content of the prophets' messages, which were conditioned by cultural traditions and historical situations (cf. 1977:129–31).

How, then, could one proceed? The tack taken by these studies was to propose a model of the prophetic process as a "feedback system" (the phrase is N. Gottwald's; 1981:104). This model, which was presented in diagrammatic form, is a framework which outlines the major components of prophetic activity (God, prophet, audience, and—sometimes—disciples) and specifies the interrelationships among them (cf. 1974:38–40, 1977:131–4, 1981:58–60; on models cf. Carney, 1975:1–43). It has been typical for Old Testament scholars to view prophetic activity as essentially a one-way flow of information: God speaks to the prophet, who then conveys that message to his audience (cf. 1977:134–5). The model suggests that the matter is rather more complicated than this. And since it attempts to isolate the underlying structure of prophetic activity, it allows us to make cross-cultural comparisons. These enrich our knowledge of prophecy in general, and suggest possible interpretations of features partially obscured by the Old Testament's dominant theological interests.

So, for example, the view of the prophetic process which the model conceptualizes has implications for the question of the nature of a prophet's "authority." If the prophetic process is a "feedback system," then full authorization of a prophet would necessarily entail two things: some sort of contact with a deity ("revelation"), and acknowledgment by a group of people (cf. 1974:38; 1977:132, 144–5; 1981:59–69). Such a view takes seriously the social realities of prophetic activity. It follows logically from the need of every intermediary to have a support group, and is in line with current efforts to redress the imbalance in the direction of individualism which has characterized the use of Weber's category, "charisma" (cf. Overholt, 1984). However, the tendency of interpreters to stress the content of the Old Testament prophets' messages (thereby focusing on theological, rather than sociological, concerns) has rendered this observation less than self-evident to some.

The problem, then, is to describe the authority of a prophet in terms of social interaction, that is, as (in at least one of its aspects) an essentially observable social process. For example, Amos 2:11–12 and 7:10–17 imply the social reality of persons or groups attempting to exert control over the activity of prophets, but they reveal little about the basis for such "commanding the prophets." In order to illustrate the importance of this kind of interaction, I cited (1979) three examples drawn from anthropological literature (the Ghost Dances of 1870 and 1890, and Yali; cf. Chapter II, sections 6 and 15) showing the decisive effect an audience can have on a prophet's activity. "The hearers assume" I concluded, "that they know how real prophets ought to function, and they accept or reject a given prophet on the basis of these preconceptions. My contention is that this authorizing process is the social reality that lies behind Amos 2:11–2 and 7:10–7" (1979:532; cf. also 1981:71–2).

Finally, I have suggested (1982) that this view of prophecy and the cross-cultural comparisons integral to the model help us better understand "miracles" which the Old Testament narratives attribute to Elijah and Elisha. The diagram of the prophetic process makes a great deal of the feedback relationship between deity and the prophet and the prophet and his or her audience. However, it also postulates a direct interaction between deity and audience. My earlier discussion of the model refer to this element as "expectations of confirmation," but a better designation would be "supernatural confirmations." This rubric refers to certain experiences which tend to independently confirm the god-given task of the prophet and strengthen people's conviction about his or her authenticity (cf. 1974:47–8, 1981:68–9). "Miracles" would fall into this category.

Now the Old Testament contains a number of examples of prophetic "acts of power," and so I set out to make a special study of these (1982). The biblical data itself allowed several observations. First, two types of such acts could be identified. On the one hand, there were actions quite within the capabilities of any human being to perform, for example, breaking a pot (Jer 19) or walking about naked and barefoot (Isa 20). On the other, there were actions which seemed to be "miracles," to abrogate natural regularities, for example, bringing a dead person back to life (1 Kgs 17, 2 Kgs 4). The latter are found almost exclusively in narratives about Elijah and Elisha. Second, after examining occurrences of the second type within the Elijah-Elisha narratives, one could catch a glimpse of their social function, viz. to legitimate the prophets in the exercise of their role (cf. 1982:6–11). As usual, however, there was need to suggest more concretely the actual social process that may have been involved. In an attempt to do so I discussed case studies from western North America and Siberia which showed how acts of power of this type can function as socially-sanctioned proofs of a shaman's power and authority. On the basis of this evidence I concluded it was reasonable to assume "that the accounts of Elijah's and Elisha's acts of power, whatever else they may 'mean' in the tradition and in the present form of the text, give us a glimpse of the process by which these early Israelite prophets were authorized" (1982:21). It should be noted that the comparison of biblical and non-biblical materials did not focus on the similarity of the acts themselves (e.g., raising the dead), but on how the acts fit a larger social structure or pattern.

Concluding Thoughts on Method

All of the case studies just discussed had recourse to comparative materials in order to treat specific problems for which there was insufficient information within the Old Testament texts. In each case the inquiry was related to a particular social structure or pattern. Even when the discussion addressed some seemingly narrow point (e.g., bizarre ecstatic behavior, conflict among intermediaries), the explanation set it in the context of some social process (e.g., trance and possession, the social dynamics of intermediation). It is important to notice the absence of evolutionary assumptions. To the contrary, these authors assume that certain social processes have been present in a wide variety of cultures, from preliterate hunters and herders to urban, agriculturally-based civilizations, though the forms and even the occasions of their manifestation may be markedly different from society to society. Finally, one may sense that these assemblages of comparative data suggest new possibilities for the interpretation of Old Testament prophecy. Sometimes there are new questions, or a new way of formulating old questions. One thinks of the evidence on the social complexity of storytelling discussed in Chapter III. Sometimes one has the impression that the Old Testament texts are better known because the comparison was undertaken.

But impressions may be deceiving, for "comparison is, at base, never identity" (J. Smith, 1982:35). The question is, can we learn anything new *about the Old Testament* from our comparative materials? Can we ever feel confident that such studies have actually filled in gaps in our knowledge about the social world of the Old Testament?

This is a difficult question on at least two levels. First, variability among cultures means it is not safe to assume that all elements identifiable as part of, say, the structure of divine-human intermediation must necessarily exist in each culture where intermediation is found. However, similarities observed in a study of many cultures give rise to some confidence in the pattern, and when the Old Testament provides us with hints that point in a similar direction, we can make inferences and claim some degree of probability (cf., for example, on the problem of "prophetic authority").

Second, important vested interests are at stake. There is the matter of disciplinary "turf," of the ability (some would even say, of the "right") of a researcher trained in one specialty to employ materials and methods which are in the domain of another. Probably more important in the present instance are theological convictions. The study of the Bible has always been to some extent the province of a believing community. As a result, many engaged in it have had a perception of the Bible's uniqueness (based, it would seem, on convictions about the uniqueness of the Bible's God), and have been inclined to resist comparisons with other cultures. (Lewis points out that anthropologists sometimes harbor similar feelings about their "own" people; 1981:29). In the study of Amos cited above I wrote, "The problem we face is that while the OT hints there is more to the process by which prophetic activity is authorized than the reception of Yahweh's word, this additional 'something' remains for the most part hidden behind a veil of theology" (Overholt, 1979:526). This "veil" confronts *anyone*, believer or not, who approaches the text, because of the particular interests and intentions of its authors and editors. But many times there is an additional veil of our own making in the form of assumptions about God and humanity, the "proper" way to address (or be addressed by) the text, and the like.

Obviously, much of what we say about the Bible is under any circumstances hypothesis. Our studies have more or less probability (usually, assessments of the degree change over time, as the subsequent history of M. Noth's notions about an Israelite amphictyony conveniently illustrates). The many "assured results" of scholarship which have come into question prevent one from claiming that much is "proven." Comparative studies are no different in this respect. If they help interpret certain biblical texts, if they suggest new or altered conceptions of institutions, roles, or situations, if they help us imagine some new configuration for our sparse data or some bridge over a relative gap in our knowledge, then like other methods of investigation they will contribute to our overall enterprise.

How does one go about this? As J. Smith points out (1982:21), we are not blessed with a handy set of "rules for the production of comparisons." One must, of course, attempt to be knowledgeable and cautious in one's actual use of social scientific tools and data (cf. the first four of Wilson's methodological "guidelines," 1980:15–16). Beyond that, one pursues hunches and tries to cultivate an openness to new questions about the viewpoints on familiar material. One tries to be systematic, since ad hoc comparisons may focus on the wrong things (details) and suggest questionable "answers" to problems (like diffusion, reduction [A is "just like" B], and the like). One should cultivate an eye for blind alleys, and a willingness to quit while one is "ahead." Chapters II and III of this book provide some of the raw material for such an enterprise.

BIBLIOGRAPHY

Abbreviations

AA	*American Anthropologist*
CBQ	*Catholic Biblical Quarterly*
HR	*History of Religions*
HTR	*Harvard Theological Review*
JAAR	*Journal of the American Academy of Religion*
JAFL	*Journal of American Folklore*
JBL	*Journal of Biblical Literature*
JRAI	*Journal of the Royal Anthropological Institute of Great Britain and Ireland*
JSOT	*Journal for the Study of the Old Testament*
SWJA	*Southwestern Journal of Anthropology*
ThR	*Theologische Rundschau*
VT	*Vestus Testamentum*
ZAW	*Zeitschrift für die alttestamentliche Wissenschaft*

Sources Cited

Abraham, D.P.

1966 "The Roles of 'Chaminuka' and the *Mhondoro*-Cults in Shona Political History." Pp. 28–46 in *The Zambesian Past: Studies in Central African History.* Eds. E. Stokes and R. Brown. Manchester: Manchester University Press.

Abrahams, Roger D.

1972 "Folklore and Literature as Performance." *Journal of the Folklore Institute* 9:75–94.

Ackroyd, Peter R.

1962 "The Vitality of the Word of God in the Old Testament." *Annual of the Swedish Theological Institute* 1:7–23.

Ahlström, G. W.

1966 "Oral and Written Transmission." *HTR* 59:69–81.

Alban, A.H.

1940 "Gwek's Pipe and Pyramid." *Sudan Notes and Records* 23:200–01.

Amiotte, Arthur

1976 "Eagles Fly Over." *Parabola* 1, no. 3:28–41.

Amoss, Pamela T.

1977 "The Power of Secrecy Among the Coast Salish." Pp. 131–40 in

The Anthropology of Power. Eds. Raymond D. Fogelson and R. N. Adams. New York: Academic Press.

1978   "Symbolic Substitution in the Indian Shaker Church." *Ethnohistory* 25:225–50.

Andreasen, Niels-Erik A.
1983   "The Role of the Queen Mother in Israelite Society." *CBQ* 45:174–94.

Andrzejewski, B. W.
1972a   "Allusive Diction in Galla Hymns in Praise of Sheikh Hussein of Bale." *African Language Studies* 13:1–31.
1972b   "Sheikh Hussen of Bali in Galla Oral Tradition." Pp. 463–80 in *Problemi Attuali di Scienza e di Cultura* (= iv Congresso Internazionale di Studi Etiopici, vol. I). Rome.
1974   "The Veneration of Sufi Saints and Its Impact on the Oral Literature of the Somali People and on Their Literature in Arabic." *African Language Studies* 15:15–53.

Anisimov, A. F.
1963a   "The Shaman's Tent of the Evenks and the Origin of the Shamanistic Rite." Pp. 84–123 in *Studies in Siberian Shamanism.* Ed. H. N. Michael. Toronto: Arctic Institute of North America.
1963b   "Cosmological Concepts of the Peoples of the North." Pp. 157–229 in *Studies in Siberian Shamanism.* Ed. H. N. Michael. Toronto: Arctic Institute of North America.

Bahr, Donald
1977   "Breath in Shamanistic Curing." Pp. 29–40 in *Flowers of the Wind: Papers on Ritual, Myth and Symbolism.* Ed. Thomas C. Blackburn. Socorro, NM: Ballena Press.

Balázs, J.
1968   "The Hungarian Shaman's Technique of Trance Induction." Pp. 53–75 in *Popular Beliefs and Folklore Tradition in Siberia.* Ed. V. Diószegi. Bloomington: Indiana University Press.

Balikci, Asen
1963   "Shamanistic Behavior Among the Netsilik Eskimo." *SWJA* 19:380–96.
1970   *The Netsilik Eskimo.* New York: Natural History Press.

Barnouw, Victor
1977   *Wisconsin Chippewa Myths and Tales and Their Relation to Chippewa Life.* Madison: University of Wisconsin Press.

Barrow, G. L.
1951   "The Story of Jonfrum." *Corona* 3:379–82.

Basilov, V.
1976   "Shamanism in Central Asia." Pp. 149–57 in *The Realm of the Extra-Human: Agents and Audiences.* Ed. A. Bharati. The Hague: Mouton.

Bastide, Roger
1978   *The African Religions of Brazil: Toward a Sociology of the Interpenetration of Civilizations.* Baltimore: John Hopkins University Press.

Bauman, Richard
1975   "Verbal Art as Performance." *AA* 77:290–311.
Beattie, John
1964   *Other Cultures: Aim, Methods and Achievements in Social An-thropology.* New York: Free Press.
Beattie, John and John Middleton, eds.
1969   *Spirit Mediumship and Society in Africa.* London: Routledge and Kegan Paul.
Beidelman, T. O.
1971   "Nuer Priests and Prophets: Charisma, Authority and Power Among the Nuer." Pp. 375–415 in *The Translation of Culture.* Ed. T. O. Beidelman. London: Tavistock.
1981–82   "The Nuer Concept of *Thek* and the Meaning of Sin: Explanation, Translation, and Social Structure." *HR* 21:126–55.
Belshaw, Cyril S.
1965   "The Significance of Modern Cults in Melanesian Development." Pp. 517–22 in *Reader in Comparative Religion,* 2 edn. Eds. W. Lessa and E. Vogt. New York: Harper & Row.
Ben-Amos, Dan
1975   *Sweet Words: Storytelling Events in Benin.* Philadelphia: Institute for the Study of Human Issues.
Benz, Ernst and Karl W. Luckert
1973   "The Road of Life: Report of a Visit by a Navajo Seer." *Ethnome-dezin* 2:405–16.
Berkhofer, Robert F.
1965   "Faith and Factionalism among the Seneca." *Ethnohistory* 12:99–112.
1979   *The White Man's Indian.* New York: Vintage.
Bernardi, Bernardo
1959   *The Mugwe, a Failing Prophet: A Study of a Religious and Public Dignitary of the Meru of Kenya.* London: Oxford University Press.
Bernstein, Basil
1972   "A Sociolinguistic Approach to Socialization; With Some Reference to Educability." Pp. 465–97 in *Directions in Sociolinguistics.* Eds. J. J. Gumperz and D. Hymes. New York: Holt, Rinehart and Winston.
Blenkinsopp, Joseph
1983   *A History of Prophecy in Israel.* Philadelphia: Westminster Press.
Boaz, Franz
1930   *The Religion of the Kwakiutl Indians.* Part I, Texts; Part II, Translations. New York: Columbia University Press.
1966   *Kwakiuti Ethnography.* Ed. by Helen Codere. Chicago: University of Chicago Press.
Bourdillon, M.F.C.
1977   "Oracles and Politics in Ancient Israel." *Man* 12:124–40.
Bourguignon, E.
1965   "The Self, the Behavioral Environment, and the Theory of Spirit

Possession." Pp. 39–60 in *Context and Meaning in Cultural Anthropology*. Ed. M. E. Spiro. New York: Free Press.

1968 "World Distribution and Patterns of Possession States." In *Trance and Possession States*. Ed. R. Prince. Montreal: R. M. Bucke Memorial Society.

1976 "Spirit Possession Belief and Social Structure." Pp. 17–26 in *The Realm of the Extra-Human: Ideas and Actions*. Ed. A. Bharati. The Hague: Mouton.

Bourguignon, E. and L. Pettay

1964 "Spirit Possession, Trance, and Cross-Cultural Research." In *Symposium on New Approaches to the Study of Religion*. Ed. J. Helm. Seattle: American Ethnological Society.

Brewster, A. B.

1922 *The Hill Tribes of Fiji*. Philadelphia: J. B. Lippincott Co.

Brown, Joseph Epes

1953 *The Sacred Pipe: Black Elk's Account of the Seven Rites of the Oglala Sioux*. Norman: University of Oklahoma Press.

Burridge, Kenelm O. L.

1953–54 "Cargo Cult Activity in Tangu." *Oceania* 24:241–54.

1957 "Social Implications of Some Tangu Myths." *SWJA* 12:415–31.

1960 *Mambu: A Study of Melanesian Cargo Movements and Their Social and Ideological Background*. New York: Harper and Row.

1969 *New Heaven, New Earth: A Study of Millenarian Activities*. New York: Schocken.

1981 "Reflections on Prophecy and Prophetic Groups." *Semeia* 21:99–102.

Buss, Martin J.

1981 "An Anthropological Perspective Upon Prophetic Call Narratives." *Semeia* 21:9–30.

Campbell, Joseph

1959 *The Masks of God: Primitive Mythology*. New York: Viking.

Carney, T. F.

1975 *The Shape of the Past: Models and Antiquity*. Lawrence, KA: Coronado Press.

Carroll, Robert P.

1979 *When Prophecy Failed: Cognitive Dissonance in the Prophetic Traditions of the Old Testament*. New York: Seabury.

Casagrande, Joseph B.

1956 "The Ojibwa's Psychic Universe." *Tomorrow* 4:33–40.

Casanowicz, I. M.

1925 "Shamanism of the Natives of Siberia." Pp. 415–34 in *Annual Report of the Smithsonian Institute, 1924*. Washington, D.C.: Government Printing Office.

Chafe, Wallace L.

1961 *Seneca Thanksgiving Rituals*. Bureau of American Ethnology, Bulletin 183. Washington, D.C.: Government Printing Office.

Chaney, Marvin L.

1983 "Ancient Palestinian Peasant Movements and the Formation of

Premonarchic Israel." Pp. 39–90 in *Palestine in Transition: The Emergence of Ancient Israel*. Eds. D.N. Freedman and D.F. Graf. Sheffield: Almond.

Chinnery, E.W.P. and A.C. Haddon
1916–17   "Five New Religious Cults in British New Guinea." *The Hibbert Journal* 15:448–63.

Clements, R. E.
1982   "The Ezekiel Tradition: Prophecy in a Time of Crisis." Pp. 119–36 in *Israel's Prophetic Tradition*. Eds. Richard Coggins, *et al.* Cambridge: Cambridge University Press.

Coleman, Sr. M. Bernard
1937   "The Religion of the Ojibwa of Northern Minnesota." *Primitive Man* 10:33–57.

Colson, Elizabeth
1969   "Spirit Possession Among the Tonga of Zambia." Pp. 69–103 in *Spirit Mediumship and Society in Africa*. Eds. J. Beattie and J. Middleton. London: Routledge and Kegan Paul.

Cooper, John M.
1944   "The Shaking Tent Rite among Plains and Forest Algonquians." *Primitive Man* 17:60–84.

Coote, Robert B.
1976a   "The Application of the Oral Theory to Biblical Hebrew Literature." *Semeia* 5:51–64.
1976b   "Tradition, Oral, OT." Pp. 914–16 in *Interpreter's Dictionary of the Bible*, Supplementary Volume. Nashville: Abingdon.
1981   *Amos Among the Prophets*. Philadelphia: Fortress.

Copway, George
1850   *The Traditional History and Characteristic Sketches of the Ojibwa Nation*. London: Charles Gilpin.

Coriat, P.
1939   "Gwek, the Witch-Doctor and the Pyramid of Dengkur." *Sudan Notes and Records* 22:221–38.

Culley, Robert C.
1963   "An Approach to the problem of oral tradition." *VT* 13:113–25.
1976   "Oral Tradition and the OT: Some Recent Discussion." *Semeia* 5:1–33.
1981   "Anthropology and the Old Testament: An Introductory Comment." *Semeia* 21:1–5.

Daneel, M. L.
1970   *The God of the Matopo Hills: An Essay on the Mwari Cult in Rhodesia*. The Hague: Mouton.

Dangberg, Grace M.
1957   "Letters to Jack Wilson, the Paiute Prophet, Written Between 1908 and 1911." Bureau of American Ethnology, Bulletin 164. Washington, D.C.: Government Printing Office.
1968   "Wovoka." *Nevada Historical Society Quarterly* 11:1–53.

Darnell, Regna
1975   "Correlates of Cree Narrative Performance." Pp. 315–36 in *Explo-*

        rations in the Ethnography of Speaking. Eds. R. Bauman and J. F. Sherzer. Cambridge: Cambridge University Press.

Deardorff, M. H.

1951   "The Religion of Handsome Lake: Its Origin and Development." Pp. 79–107 in *Symposium on Local Diversity in Iroquois Culture*. Ed. W. N. Fenton. Bureau of American Ethnology, Bulletin 149. Washington, D.C.: Government Printing Office.

Dégh, Linda

1958   "Some Questions of the Social Function of Story-telling." *Acta Ethnographica* 6:91–146.

Densmore, Frances

1918   *Tenton Sioux Music*. Bureau of American Ethnology, Bulletin 61. Washington, D.C.: Government Printing Office.

1932   "An Explanation of a Trick Performed by Indian Jugglers." *AA* 34:310–14.

Despres, L.A.

1968   "Anthropological Theory, Cultural Pluralism, and the Study of Complex Societies." *Current Anthropology* 9:3–16.

Donaldson, Mara E.

1981   "Kinship Theory in the Patriarchal Narratives: The Case of the Barren Wife." *JAAR* 49:77–87.

Drucker, Philip

1955   *Indians of the Northwest Coast*. Garden City: Natural History Press.

Eaton, John

1982   "The Isaiah Tradition." Pp. 58–76 in *Israel's Prophetic Tradition*. Ed. Richard Coggins, *et al.* Cambridge: Cambridge University Press.

Eckert, Georg

1937   "Prophetentum in Melanesien." *Zeitschrift für Ethnologie* 69:135–40.

Eliade, Mircea

1964   *Shamanism: Archaic Techniques of Ecstasy*. New York: Pantheon.

Elwin, Verrier

1939   *The Baiga*. London: John Murray.

1955   *The Religion of an Indian Tribe*. London: Oxford University Press.

Emmet, D.

1956   "Prophets and Their Societies." *JRAI* 86:13–23.

Epstein, Arnold L., ed.

1967   *The Craft of Social Anthropology*. London: Tavistock.

Evans-Pritchard, E. E.

1940   *The Nuer*. New York: Oxford University Press.

1956   *Nuer Religion*. Oxford: Oxford University Press.

1964   "Social Anthropology." Pp. 1–134 in *Social Anthropology and Other Essays*. New York: Free Press.

Fenton, William N.

1953   *The Iroquois Eagle Dance: An Offshoot of the Calumet Dance*.

Bureau of American Ethnology, Bulletin 156. Washington, D.C.: Government Printing Office.

1968   *Parker on the Iroquois*. Syracuse: Syracuse University Press.

Feraca, S. E.

1961   "The Yuwipi Cult of the Oglala and Sicangu Teton Sioux." *Plains Anthropologist* 6:155–63.

Fergie, Deane

1977   "Prophecy and Leadership: Philo and the Inawai'a Movement." Pp. 147–73 in *Prophets of Melanesia*. Ed. Garry Trompf. Port Moresby: Institute of Papua New Guinea Studies.

Finnegan, Ruth

1967   *Limba Stories and Story-Telling*. London: Oxford University Press.

1970   *Oral Literature in Africa*. New York: Oxford University Press.

1977   *Oral Poetry: Its Nature, Significance and Social Context*. Cambridge: Cambridge University Press.

1978   *A World Treasury of Oral Poetry*. Bloomington: Indiana University Press.

Firth, Raymond

1969   "Foreword." Pp. ix-xiv in *Spirit Mediumship and Society in Africa*. Eds. J. Beattie and J. Middleton. London: Routledge and Kegan Paul.

Fisher, Lawrence E. and Oswald Werner

1978   "Explaining Explanation: Tension in American Anthropology." *J. of Anth. Research* 34:194–218.

Flannery, Regina

1939   "The Shaking-tent Rite among the Montagnais of James Bay." *Primitive Man* 12:11–6.

Fohrer, G.

1961   "Remarks on Modern Interpretation of the Prophets." *JBL* 80:309–19.

1962   "Zehn Jahre Literatur zur alttestamentlicher Prophetie." *ThR* 28:1–75, 235–97, 301–74.

1980   "Neue Literatur zur alttestamentlichen Prophetie." *ThR* 45:1–39, 109–32, 193–225.

Fontana, Bernard L.

1973   "Introduction to the New Edition" of Mooney (1896). Glorieta, NM: Rio Grande Press.

Foster, Michael K.

1974   *From the Earth to Beyond the Sky: An Ethnographic Approach to Four Longhouse Iroquois Speech Events*. National Museum of Man Mercury Series, Canadian Ethnology Service, Paper no. 20.

Fry, Peter

1976   *Spirits of Protest: Spirit-Mediums and the Articulation of Consensus Among the Zezuru of Southern Rhodesia (Zimbabwe)*. Cambridge: Cambridge University Press.

Fugle, Eugene
1966   "The Nature and Function of the Lakota Night Cults." *Museum News* (Vermillion, S. Dakota) 27 (no. 3–4):1–38.

Gager, John G.
1975   *Kingdom and Community: The Social World of Early Christianity.* Englewood Cliffs: Prentice-Hall.

Garbett, G. Kingsley
1966   "Religious Aspects of Political Succession Among the Valley Korekore." Pp. 137–70 in *The Zambesian Past: Studies in Central African History.* Eds. Eric Stokes and Richard Brown. Manchester: Manchester University Press.
1969   "Spirit Mediums as Mediators in Valley Korekore Society." Pp. 104–27 in *Spirit Mediumship and Society in Africa.* Eds. J. Beattie and J. Middleton. London: Routledge and Kegan Paul.

Geertz, Clifford
1973   "Thick Description: Toward an Interpretive Theory of Culture." Pp. 3–30 in *The Interpretation of Cultures.* New York: Basic Books.

Gill, Sam D.
1977–78   "Prayer as Person: The Performative Force in Navajo Prayer Acts." *HR* 17:143–57.
1982a   *Native American Religions: An Introduction.* Belmont, CA: Wadsworth.
1982b   *Beyond "the Primitive": The Religions of Nonliterate Peoples.* Englewood Cliffs: Prentice-Hall.

Gitay, Yehoshua
1983   "Reflections on the Study of the Prophetic Discourse." *VT* 33:207–21.

Goldammer, K.
1972   "Elemente des Schamanismus im alten Testament." *Ex Orbe Religionum: Studies in the History of Religions,* Supplements to *Numen,* 22:266–85. Leiden.

Goldman, Irving
1975   *The Mouth of Heaven: An Introduction to Kwakiutl Religious Thought.* New York: John Wiley & Sons.

Gottwald, Norman K.
1979   *The Tribes of Yahweh.* Maryknoll: Orbis.
1981   "Problems and Promises in the Comparative Analysis of Religious Phenomena." *Semeia* 21:103–12.
1983a   Editor. *The Bible and Liberation.* Maryknoll: Orbis.
1983b   "Sociological Method in Biblical Research and Contemporary Peace Studies." *American Baptist Quarterly* 2:142–56.

Granzberg, Gary, Jack Steinbring and John Hunter
1977   "New Magic for Old: TV in Cree Culture." *Journal of Communication* 27:154–57.

Grim, John A.
1983   *The Shaman: Patterns of Siberian and Ojibway Healing.* Norman: University of Oklahoma Press.

Guariglia, G.
1958   "Prophetismus und Heilserwartungsbewegungen in niedern Kulturen." *Numen* 5:180–98.
Guiart, Jean
1951   "John Frum Movement in Tanna." *Oceania* 22:165–75.
1956   "Culture Contact and the 'John Frum' Movement on Tanna." *SWJA* 12:105–16.
Gunn, David M.
1976   "On Oral Tradition: A Response to John Van Seters." *Semeia* 5:155–63.
Gunneweg, A.
1959   *Mündliche und schriftlich Tradition der vorexilischen Prophetenbucher.* Göttingen: Vandenhoeck & Ruprecht.
Haeberlin, Herman
1918   "SBETETDA'Q, A Shamanistic Performance of the Coast Salish." *AA* 20:249–57.
Hajdú, P.
1968   "The Classification of Samoyed Shamans." Pp. 147–73 in *Popular Beliefs and Folklore Tradition in Siberia.* Ed. V. Diószegi. Bloomington: Indiana University Press.
Halifax, Joan
1979   *Shamanic Voices: A Survey of Visionary Narratives.* New York: E. P. Dutton.
Hallowell, A. Irving
1934   "Some Empirical Aspects of Northern Saulteaux Religion." *AA* 36:389–404.
1942   *The Role of Conjuring in Saulteaux Society.* Philadelphia: University of Pennsylvania Press.
Hallpike, C. R.
1971   "Some Problems in Cross-Cultural Comparison." Pp. 123–40 in *The Translation of Culture.* Ed. T. O. Beidelman. London: Tavistock.
Harris, Marvin
1968   *The Rise of Anthropological Theory.* New York: T. Y. Crowell.
Herskovits, Melville J. and Frances S.
1936   *Suriname Folk-lore.* New York: Columbia University Press.
1958   *Dahomean Narrative: A Cross-Cultural Analysis.* Evanston: Northwestern University Press.
Hill, W. W.
1935   "The Hand Trembling Ceremony of the Navaho." *El Palacio* 38:65–8.
1938   "Navajo Use of Jimsonweed." *New Mexico Anthropologist* 3:19–21.
Hultkrantz, Åke
1967   "The Spirit Lodge, A North American Shamanistic Seance." Pp. 32–68 in *Studies in Shamanism.* Ed. Carl-Martin Edsman. Stockholm: Almqvist & Wiksell.
1968   "The Aims of Anthropology: A Scandinavian Point of View." *Current Anthropology* 9:289–310.

1973   "A Definition of Shamanism." *Temenos* 9:25–37.
Hurt, Wesley R.
1960   "A Yuwipi Ceremony at Pine Ridge." *Plains Anthropologist* 5:48–52.
Hurt, Wesley R. and James H. Howard
1952   "A Dakota Conjuring Ceremony." *SWJA* 8:286–96.
Hymes, Dell
1971   "The 'Wife' who 'Goes Out' Like a Man: Reinterpretation of a Clackamas Chinook Myth." Pp. 49–80 in *Structural Analysis of Oral Tradition*. Eds. Pierre Maranda and Elli K. Maranda. Philadelphia: University of Pennsylvania Press.
1972   "Models of the Interaction of Language and Social Life." Pp. 35–71 in *Directions in Sociolinguistics: The Ethnography of Communication*. Eds. J. J. Gumperz and D. Hymes. New York: Holt, Rinehart and Winston.
1975   "Breakthrough into Performance." Pp. 11–74 in *Folklore: Performance and Communication*. Eds. Dan Ben-Amos and Kenneth S. Goldstein. The Hague: Mouton.
Inglis, Judy
1957   "Cargo Cults: The Problem of Explanation." *Oceania* 27:249–63.
Jackson, H. C.
1923   "The Nuer of the Upper Nile Province." *Sudan Notes and Records* 6:59–107, 123–89.
Jarvie, I. C.
1963   "Theories of Cargo Cults: A Critical Analysis." *Oceania* 34:1–31, 108–36.
Jenness, Diamond.
1935   *The Ojibwa Indians of Parry Island, Their Social and Religious Life*. Canadian Department of Mines, Bulletin 78; Anthropological Series, No. 17. Ottawa.
Jojoga, Willington
1977   "The PEROVETA of Buna." Pp. 212–37 in *Prophets of Melanesia*. Ed. Garry Trompf. Port Moresby: Institute of Papua New Guinea Studies.
Johnson, Elias
1881   *Legends, Traditions and Laws of the Iroquois, or Six Nations, and History of the Tuscarora Indians*. Lockport, NY: Union Printing and Publishing Co.
Jules-Rosette, Bennetta
1978   "The Veil of Objectivity: Prophecy, Divination, and Social Inquiry." *AA* 80:549–70.
Kane, Steven M.
1974   "Ritual Possession in a Southern Appalachian Religious Sect." *JAFL* 87:293–302.
Kapelrud, Arvid S.
1967   "Shamanistic Features in the Old Testament." Pp. 90–96 in *Studies in Shamanism*. Ed. Carl-Martin Edsman. Stockholm: Almqvist and Wiksell.

Kee, Howard C.
1980   *Christian Origins in Sociological Perspective.* Philadelphia: West-
          minster Press.
Kehoe, Alice B.
1968   "The Ghost Dance in Saskatchewan." *Plains Anthropologist*
          19:296–304.
Kelley, William Fitch
1971   *Pine Ridge 1890: An Eye Witness Account of the Events Surround-
          ing the Fighting at Wounded Knee.* San Francisco: Pierre Bovis.
Kemnitzer, Luis S.
1970   "The Cultural Provenience of Objects Used in Yuwipi: A Modern
          Teton Dakota Healing Ritual." *Ethnos* 35:40–75.
1978   "Yuwipi." *Indian Historian* 11 (no. 2):2–5.
Kluckhohn, Clyde
1939   "Some Personal and Social Aspects of Navaho Ceremonial Prac-
          tice." *HTR* 32:57–82.
1944   *Navaho Witchcraft.* Boston: Beacon Press.
Kluckhohn, Clyde and Dorothea Leighton
1962   *The Navaho.* Rev. edn. Garden City, NY: Anchor.
Knoll-Greiling, U.
1952–53   "Berufung und Berufungserlebnis bei die Schamanen." *Tribus* n.s.
          2–3:227–38.
Köbben, A. J. F.
1960   "Prophetic Movements as an Expression of Social Protest." *Inter-
          national Archives of Ethnography* 44:117–64.
Koch, Klaus
1971   "Die Entstehung der sozialen Kritik bei den Profeten." Pp. 236–
          57 in *Probleme biblischer Theologie.* Ed. H. W. Wolff.
          München: Chr. Kaiser Verlag.
1983   *The Prophets: The Assyrian Period.* Trans. by Margaret Kohl. Phil-
          adelphia: Fortress Press.
1984   *The Prophets: The Babylonian and Persian Periods.* Trans. by Mar-
          garet Kohl. Philadelphia: Fortress Press.
Koppers, W.
1959   "Prophetismus und Messianismus als völkerkundliches und uni-
          versalgeschichtliches Problem." *Saeculum* 10:38–47.
1960   "Prophetism and Messianic Beliefs as a Problem of Ethnology and
          World History." *Proceedings of the IXth International Congress
          for the History of Religions, Tokyo and Kyoto, 1958.* Tokyo.
Kopytoff, Igor
1971   "Ancestors as Elders in Africa." *Africa* 41:129–41.
LaBarre, Weston
1971   "Materials for a History of Studies of Crisis Cults: A Bibliographic
          Essay." *Current Anthropology* 12:3–44.
Lambert, Richard S.
1955   *Exploring the Supernatural: The Weird in Canadian Folklore.*
          London: Arthur Barker.
1956   "The Shaking Tent." *Tomorrow* 4:113–28.

Lame Deer, John (Fire) and Richard Erdoes
1972   *Lame Deer Seeker of Visions.* New York: Simon and Schuster.
Lang, Bernhard
1982   "The Social Organization of Peasant Poverty in Biblical Israel."
          JSOT 24:47–63. (= 1983a: 114–27)
1983a   *Monotheism and the Prophetic Minority.* Sheffield: Almond Press.
1983b   "Old Testament and Anthropology: A Preliminary Bibliography."
          Biblische Notizen 20:37–46.
1984   "Spione im gelobten Land: Ethnologen als Leser des Alten Testa-
          ments." Pp. 158–77 in *Ethnologie als Sozialwissenschaft.* Eds.
          E. W. Müller, R. König, K.-P. Koepping, and P. Drechsel.
          Wiesbaden: Westdeutscher Verlag.
Lanternari, Vittorio
1962–63   "Messianism: Its Historical Origin and Morphology." *HR* 2:52–72.
1963   *The Religions of the Oppressed: A Study of Modern Messianic
          Cults* New York: Mentor.
1965   *The Religions of the Oppressed* (CA* book review). *Current An-
          thropology* 6:447–65.
1974   "Nativistic and Socio-Religious Movements: A Reconsideration."
          Comparative Studies in Society and History 16:483–503.
1976   "Dreams as Charismatic Significants: Their Bearing on the Rise of
          New Religious Movements." Pp. 321–35 in *The Realm of the
          Extra-Human: Ideas and Actions.* Ed. A. Bharati. The Hague:
          Mouton.
Lawrence, Peter
1964   *Road Belong Cargo: A Study of the Cargo Movement in the South-
          ern Madang District New Guinea.* Manchester: Manchester
          University Press.
Leeson, I.
1952   *Bibliography of the Cargo Cults and Other Nativistic Movements
          in the South Pacific.* Sydney.
Lehtisalo, T.
1937   "Der Tod und die Wiedergeburt des kunftigen Schamanen." *Jour-
          nal de la Societe Finno-Ougrienne* 48:1–34.
Leighton, Alexander H. and Dorothea C.
1949   *Gregorio, The Hand-Trembler: A Psychobiological Personality
          Study of a Navaho Indian.* Cambridge: Peabody Museum Pa-
          pers, 40:1.
Lessa, William A. and Evon Z. Vogt, eds.
1965   *Reader in Comparative Religion: An Anthropological Approach.*
          New York: Harper and Row, 2 edn.
Lesser, A.
1933   "Cultural Significance of the Ghost Dance." *AA* 35:108–15.
Levi-Strauss, Claude
1963   *Structural Anthropology.* Garden City: Anchor.
Lewis, B. A.
1951   "Nuer Spokesmen: A Note on the Institution of the *Ruic.*" *Sudan
          Notes and Records* 32:77–84.

Lewis, I. M.
1971   *Ecstatic Religion: An Anthropological Study of Spirit Possession and Shamanism.* Baltimore: Penguin.
1981   "What is a Shaman." *Folk* 23:25–35.
Limburg, James
1978   "The Prophets in Recent Study." *Interpretation* 32:56–68.
Lincoln, Bruce
1981   *Priests, Warriors, and Cattle: A Study in the Ecology of Religions.* Berkeley: University of California Press.
Long, Burke O.
1976a   "Recent Field Studies in Oral Literature and the Question of Sitz im Leben." *Semeia* 5:35–49.
1976b   "Recent Field Studies in Oral Literature and their Bearing on O.T. Criticism." *VT* 26:187–98.
1981a   "Social Dimensions of Prophetic Conflict." *Semeia* 21:31–53.
1981b   "Perils General and Particular." *Semeia* 21:125–28.
1982   "The Social World of Ancient Israel." *Interpretation* 36:343–55.
Long, C.
1974   "Cargo Cults as Cultural Historical Phenomena." *JAAR* 42:403–14.
Loretz, O.
1975   "Die prophetische Kritik des Rentenkapitalismus." *Ugarit-Forschungen* 7:271–8.
Luckert, Karl W.
1975   *The Navajo Hunter Tradition.* Tucson: University of Arizona Press.
Lynd, J. W.
1889   "The Religion of the Dakotas." *Collections of the Minnesota Historical Society* 2:150–74.
McBride, S. Dean
1983   "The Polity of Ezekiel 40–48." Paper delivered at the Annual Meeting of the Society of Biblical Literature. Dallas, TX, December.
McElwain, Thomas
1978   *Mythological Tales and the Allegany Seneca: A Study of the Socio-Religious Context of Traditional Oral Phenomena in an Iroquois Community.* Stockholm: Almqvist and Wiksell.
MacGaffey, Wyatt
1977–78 "Cultural Roots of Kongo Prophetism." *HR* 17:177–93.
McKane, W.
1979   "Prophecy and the Prophetic Literature." Pp. 163–88 in *Tradition and Interpretation.* Ed. G. W. Anderson. Oxford: Oxford University Press.
1982   "Prophet and Institution." *ZAW* 94:251–66.
Manning, R. O.
1976   "Shamanism as a Profession." Pp. 73–94 in *The Realm of the Extra-Human: Agents and Audiences.* Ed. A. Bharati. The Hague: Mouton.

Matthews, Washington
1902   *The Night Chant, A Navaho Ceremony.* Memoirs of the American Museum of Natural History, vol. 6. New York.
Meeks, Wayne A.
1983   *The First Urban Christians: The Social World of the Apostle Paul.* New Haven: Yale University Press.
Meggitt, M. J.
1973–74 "The Sun and the Shakers: A Millenarian Cult and its Transformations in the New Guinea Highlands." *Oceania* 44:1–37, 109–26.
Mendelsohn, I.
1962   "Dream, Dreamer." P. 868 in *Interpreter's Dictionary of the Bible,* vol. A-D. Nashville: Abingdon.
Messenger, J. C.
1959   "The Role of Proverbs in a Nigerian Judicial System." *SWJA* 15:64–73.
Middleton, John
1963   "The Yakan or Allah Water Cult among the Lugbara." *JRAI* 93:80–108.
1967   Editor. *Magic, Witchcraft, and Curing.* New York: Natural History Press.
Mikhailovski, V. M.
1895   "Shamanism in Siberia and European Russia." *JRAI* 24:62–100, 126–58.
Mooney, James
1896   *The Ghost-Dance Religion and the Sioux Outbreak of 1890.* Annual Report of the Bureau of American Ethnology, 14. Washington, D.C.: Government Printing Office.
Morgan, W.
1931   "Navaho Treatment of Sickness: Diagnosticians." *AA* 33:390–405.
Morriseau, Norval
1965   *Legends of My People, The Great Ojibway.* Ed. by Selwyn Dewdney. Toronto: Ryerson Press.
Mowinckel, S.
1946   "Prophecy and Tradition: The Prophetic Books in the Light of the Study of the Growth and History of the Tradition." *Avhandlinger utgitt av det Norske Videnskaps-Akademe I Oslo* II:1–88.
1962   "Tradition, Oral." Pp. 683–85 in *Interpreter's Dictionary of the Bible,* vol. R-Z. Nashville: Abingdon.
Myerhoff, Barbara G.
1974   *Peyote Hunt: The Sacred Journey of the Huichol Indians.* Ithaca: Cornell University Press.
1976   "Balancing Between Worlds: The Shaman's Calling." *Parabola* 1, no. 2:22–9.
Nachtigall, Horst
1976   "The Cultural-Historical Origin of Shamanism." Pp. 315–22 in *The Realm of the Extra-Human: Agents and Audiences.* Ed. A. Bharati. The Hague: Mouton.

Napier, B. D.
  1962   "Vision." P. 791 in *Interpreter's Dictionary of the Bible*, vol. R-Z.
             Nashville: Abingdon.
Neihardt, John G.
  1961   *Black Elk Speaks.* Lincoln: University of Nebraska Press.
Neumann, P. H. A., ed.
  1979   *Das Prophetenverstandnis in der deutschsprachigen Forschung
             seit Heinrich Ewald.* Darmstadt: Wissenschaftliche Buchgesell-
             schaft.
Newcomb, Franc J.
  1938   "The Navaho Listening Rite." *El Palacio* 45:46–9.
Nielsen, Eduard
  1954   *Oral Tradition.* London: SCM.
Oden, Robert A.
  1983   "Jacob as Father, Husband, and Nephew: Kinship Studies and the
             Patriarchal Narratives." *JBL* 102:189–205.
Ohnuki-Tierney, Emiko
  1976   "Shamanism and World View: The Case of the Ainu of the North-
             west Coast of Southern Sakhalin." Pp. 175–200 in *The Realm of
             the Extra-Human: Ideas and Actions.* Ed. A. Bharati. The
             Hague: Mouton.
O'Reilly, P.
  1950   "'Jonfrum' is New Hebridean 'Cargo Cult'." *Pacific Islands
             Monthly* 20(no. 6):67, 69–70 and (no. 7):59–61, 63–5.
Orlinsky, Harry M.
  1971   "Whither Biblical Research?" *JBL* 90:1–14.
Overholt, Thomas W.
  1974   "The Ghost Dance of 1890 and the Nature of the Prophetic Pro-
             cess." *Ethnohistory* 21:37–63.
  1977   "Jeremiah and the Nature of the Prophetic Process." Pp. 129–50
             in *Scripture in History and Theology.* Eds. A. L. Merrill and T.
             W. Overholt. Pittsburgh: Pickwick Press.
  1978   "Short Bull, Black Elk, Sword, and the 'Meaning' of the Ghost
             Dance." *Religion* 8:171–95.
  1979   "Commanding the Prophets: Amos and the Problem of Prophetic
             Authority." *CBQ* 41:517–32.
  1981   "Prophecy: The Problem of Cross Cultural Comparison." *Semeia*
             21:55–78.
  1982   "Seeing is Believing: The Social Setting of Prophetic Acts of
             Power." *JSOT* 23:3–31.
  1984   "Thoughts on the Use of 'Charisma' in Old Testament Studies." Pp.
             287–303 in *In the Shelter of Elyon.* Eds. W. Boyd Barrick and
             John R. Spencer. Sheffield: JSOT Press.
Overholt, Thomas W. and J. Baird Callicott
  1982   *Clothed-in-Fur and Other Tales: An Introduction to an Ojibwa
             World View.* Washington, D.C.: University Press of America.
Parker, Arthur C.
  1909   "Secret Medicine Societies of the Seneca." *AA* 11:161–85.

1913   *The Code of Handsome Lake, The Seneca Prophet*. Albany, NY:
            State Museum.

Parker, Simon B.
1978   "Possession Trance and Prophecy in Pre-Exilic Israel." *VT* 28:271–
            85.

Peters, Larry G. and Douglass Price-Williams
1980   "Towards an Experiential Analysis of Shamanism." *American Eth-
            nologist* 7:397–418.

Petersen, David L.
1981   *The Roles of Israel's Prophets*. Sheffield: Journal for the Study of
            the Old Testament.

Popov, A. A.
1968   "How Sereptie Djaruoskin of the Nganasans (Tavgi Samoyeds) Be-
            came a Shaman." Pp. 137–45 in *Popular Beliefs and Folklore
            Tradition in Siberia*. Ed. V. Diószegi. Bloomington: Indiana
            University Press.

Powers, William K.
1977   *Oglala Religion*. Lincoln: University of Nebraska Press.
1984   *Yuwipi: Vision and Experience in Oglala Ritual*. Lincoln: Univer-
            sity of Nebraska Press.

Pressel, Esther
1974   "Umbanda Trance and Possession in Sao Paulo, Brazil." Pp. 113–
            225 in *Trances, Healing and Hallucination* by Felicitas D. Good-
            man, Jeannette H. Henney, and Esther Pressel. New York:
            Wiley.

Rahmann, Rudolf
1959   "Shamanistic and Related Phenomena in Northern and Middle In-
            dia." *Anthropos* 54:681–760.

Ranger, Terence
1966   "The Role of Ndebele and Shona Religious Authorities in the Re-
            bellions of 1896 and 1897." Pp. 94–136 in *The Zambesian Past:
            Studies in Central African History*. Eds. Eric Stokes and Rich-
            ard Brown. Manchester: University Press.

Rasmussen, Knud
1927   *Across Arctic America*. New York: Putnam's.
1932   *Intellectual Culture of the Copper Eskimos*. Report of the Fifth
            Thule Expedition 1921–24, vol. 9. Copenhagen: Gyldendalske
            Boghandel, Nordisk Forlag.

Ray, Verne F.
1941   "Historic Backgrounds of the Conjuring Complex in the Plateau
            and the Plains." Pp. 204–16 in *Language, Culture and Person-
            ality: Essays in Memory of Edward Sapir*. Eds. L. Spier, *et al.*
            Menasha: Sapir Memorial Publication Fund.

Reichard, Gladys
1950   *Navaho Religion: A Study of Symbolism*. Princeton: Princeton
            University Press.

Ridington, Robin
1971   "Beaver Dreaming and Singing." *Anthropologica* 13:115–28.

Rigby, Peter
1975   "Prophets, Diviners, and Prophetism: The Recent History of Ki-
        ganda Religion." *Journal of Anthropological Research* 31:116–
        48.
Ringgren, Helmer
1950   "Oral and Written Transmission in the OT." *Studia Theologica*
        3:34–59.
1982   "Prophecy in the Ancient Near East." Pp. 1–11 in *Israel's Prophetic
        Tradition*. Eds. Richard Coggins, *et al.* Cambridge: Cambridge
        University Press.
Rogerson, John W.
1978   *Anthropology and the Old Testament*. Atlanta: John Knox Press.
Ruby, Robert H.
1966   "Yuwipi, Ancient Rite of the Sioux." *Montana, the Magazine of
        Western History* 16:74–9.
Sapir, Edward and Harry Hoijer
1942   *Navaho Texts*. Iowa City: Linguistic Society of America.
Schaeffer, Claude S.
1969   *Blackfoot Shaking Tent*. Calgary: Glenbow-Alberta Institute.
Schapera, I.
1962   "Should Anthropologists Be Historians?" *JRAI* 92:143–56.
Scheff, Thomas J.
1966   *Being Mentally Ill: A Sociological Theory*. Chicago: Aldine.
Schlosser, K.
1950   "Prophetismus in niederen Kulturen." *Zeitschrift für Ethnologie*
        75:60–72.
Seitel, Peter
1980   *See So That We May See: Performance and Interpretations of Tra-
        ditional Tales from Tanzania*. Bloomington: Indiana University
        Press.
Shack, William A. and H. M. Marcos
1974   *Gods and Heroes: Oral Traditions of the Gurage of Ethiopia*. Lon-
        don: Oxford University Press.
Shimony, Annemarie A.
1961   *Conservatism Among the Iroquois at the Six Nations Reserve*. New
        Haven: Yale University Publications in Anthropology, No. 65.
Shirokogoroff, S. M.
1935   *Psychomental Complex of the Tungus*. London: Kegan Paul,
        Trench, Trubner.
Silver, Morris
1983   *Prophets and Markets: The Political Economy of Ancient Israel*.
        Boston: Kluwer-Nijhoff.
Simmons, Leo W., ed.
1942   *Sun Chief: The Autobiography of a Hopi Indian*. New Haven: Yale
        University Press.
Smith, A. Donaldson
1897   *Through Unknown African Countries*. London: Edward Arnold.

Smith, Jonathan Z.
1971–72   "*Adde Parvum Parvo Magnus Acervus Erit.*" *HR* 11:67–90.
1982   "In Comparison a Magic Dwells." Pp. 19–35 in *Imagining Religion: From Babylon to Jonestown.* Chicago: University of Chicago Press.
Smith, Marian
1954   "Shamanism in the Shaker Religion of Northwest America." *Man* 54:119–22.
Speck, F. G.
1949   *Midwinter Rites of the Cayuga Long House.* Philadelphia: University of Pennsylvania Press.
Spencer, Dorothy M.
1970–71   "The Recruitment of Shamans among the Mundas." *HR* 10:1–31.
Spencer, Robert F.
1977   "Shamanism in Northwestern North America." Pp. 351–63 in *The Anthropology of Power.* Eds. R. D. Fogelson and R. N. Adams. New York: Academic Press.
Spier, Leslie
1935   *The Prophet Dance of the Northwest and its Derivatives: The Source of the Ghost Dance.* Menasha: George Banta Publishing Co.
Stanner, W. E. H.
1958   "On the Interpretation of Cargo Cults." *Oceania* 29:1–25.
Sutherland, W.
1910   "The 'Tuka' Religion." *Transactions of the Fijian Society, 1908–1910.* Pp. 51–7.
Suttles, Wayne
1957   "The Plateau Prophet Dance among the Coast Salish." *SWJA* 13:352–96.
Tamoane, Matthew
1977   "Kamoai of Darapap and the Legend of Jari." Pp. 174–211 in *Prophets of Melanesia.* Ed. Garry Trompf. Port Moresby: Institute of Papua New Guinea Studies.
Thomson, Basil
1895   "The Kalou-Vu (ancestor-gods) of the Fijians" and "A New Religion: The Tuka Cult." *JRAI* 24:340–59.
1908   *The Fijians. A Study of the Decay of Custom.* London: William Heinemann.
Thompson, E. P.
1972   "Anthropology and the Discipline of Historical Context." *Midland History* 1:41–55.
Thwaites, Reuben G., ed.
1896–1901 *The Jesuit Relations and Allied Documents.* 73 vols. Cleveland: Burrows.
Toelken, J. Barre
1969   "The 'Pretty Language' of Yellowman: Genre, Mode, and Texture in Navaho Coyote Tales." *Genre* 2:211–35.

Tooker, Elizabeth
  1968   "On the New Religion of Handsome Lake." *Anthropological Quarterly* 41:187–200.
Trimingham, J. Spencer
  1952   *Islam in Ethiopia.* London: Oxford.
Trompf, G. W.
  1977a   Editor. *Prophets of Melanesia.* Papua: Institute of Papua New Guinea Studies.
  1977b   "'Bilalaf'." Pp. 20–107 in *Prophets of Melanesia.* Ed. G. W. Trompf. Port Moresby: Institute of Papua New Guinea Studies.
Turner, Harold W.
  1978   *Bibliography of New Religious Movements in Primal Societies* Vol. 2, North America. Boston: G. K. Hall.
Turner, Victor W.
  1967   "Aspects of Saora Ritual and Shamanism: An Approach to the Data of Ritual." Pp. 181–204 in *The Craft of Social Anthropology.* Ed. Arnold L. Epstein. London: Tavistock.
Tuza, Esau
  1977   "Silas Eto of New Guinea." Pp. 108–46 in *Prophets of Melanesia.* Ed. G. W. Trompf. Port Moresby: Institute of Papua New Guinea Studies.
Utley, Robert M.
  1963   *The Last Days of the Sioux Nation.* New Haven: Yale University Press.
Van Seters, John
  1976   "Oral Patterns or Literary Conventions in Biblical Narrative." *Semeia* 5: 139–54.
Vasilevich, G. M.
  1963   "Early Concepts about the Universe among the Evenks (Materials)." Pp. 46–83 in *Studies in Siberian Shamanism.* Ed. Henry N. Michael. Toronto: University of Toronto Press.
  1968   "The Acquisition of Shamanistic Ability among the Evenki (Tungus)." Pp. 339–49 in *Popular Beliefs and Folklore Tradition in Siberia.* Ed. V. Diószegi. Bloomington: Indiana University Press.
Vdovin, I. S.
  1976   "The Study of Shamanism among the Peoples of Siberia and the North." Pp. 261–73 in *The Realm of the Extra-Human: Agents and Audiences.* Ed. A. Bharati. The Hague: Mouton.
Vecsey, Christopher
  1983   *Traditional Ojibwa Religion and Its Historical Changes.* Philadelphia: American Philosophical Society.
Voget, F. W.
  1960   "Man and Culture: An Essay in Changing Anthropological Interpretation." *AA* 62:943–65.
Walens, Stanley
  1981   *Feasting With Cannibals: An Essay on Kwakiutl Cosmology.* Princeton: Princeton University Press.

Wallace, Anthony F. C.
1956   "Revitalization Movements." *AA* 58:264–81.
1959   "Cultural determinants of response to hallucinatory experience."
        A.M.A. Archives of General Psychiatry 1:58–69.
1972   *The Death and Rebirth of the Seneca.* New York: Vintage.
Waterman, T. T.
1930   "The Paraphernalia of the Duwamish Spirit Canoe Ceremony." *Indian Notes* 7:129–48, 295–312, 535–61.
Watson, Elmo S.
1943   "The Last Indian War, 1890–91—A Study of Newspaper Jingoism." *Journalism Quarterly* 20:205–19.
Watson-Franke, M.-B. and Lawrence C. Watson
1975   "Understanding in Anthropology: A Philosophical Reminder."
        Current Anthropology 16:247–62.
Widengren, Geo
1948   *Literary and Psychological Aspects of the Hebrew Prophets.* Uppsala.
Williams, F. E.
1923   *The Vailala Madness and the Destruction of Native Ceremonies in the Gulf Division.* Port Moresby: Papuan Anthropology Reports, No. 4.
1934   "The Vailala Madness in Retrospect." Pp. 369–79 in *Essays Presented to C. G. Seligman.* Eds. E. E. Evans-Pritchard, *et al.* London: Routledge and Kegan Paul.
Willis, C. A.
1928   "The Cult of Deng." *Sudan Notes and Records* 11:195–208.
Willis, R. G.
1970   "Kaswa: Oral Tradition of a Fipa Prophet." *Africa* 40:248–56.
Wilson, Robert R.
1977   *Genealogy and History in the Biblical World.* New Haven: Yale University Press.
1979   "Prophecy and Ecstasy: A Reexamination." *JBL* 98:321–37.
1980   *Prophecy and Society in Ancient Israel.* Philadelphia: Fortress Press.
1984   *Sociological Approaches to the Old Testament.* Philadelphia: Fortress Press.
Worsley, Peter
1968   *The Trumpet Shall Sound: A Study of "Cargo" Cults in Melanesia.* New York: Schocken.
Wyman, Leland C.
1936a   "Navaho Diagnosticians." *AA* 38:236–46.
1936b   "Origin Legends of Navaho Divinatory Rites." *JAFL* 49:134–42.
1950   "The Religion of the Navaho Indians." Pp. 343–61 in *Ancient Religions.* Ed. Vergilius Ferm. New York: Philosophical Library.
1970   *Blessingway.* Tucson: University of Arizona Press.
1975   *The Mountainway of the Navajo with a myth of the Female Branch recorded and translated by Father Berard Haile, OFM.* Tucson: University of Arizona Press.

Wyman, Leland C. and Franc J. Newcomb
1963   "Drypaintings Used in Divination by the Navajo." *Plateau* 36:18–
          24.

SUBJECT INDEX

INDEX TO MARGINAL NOTATIONS

An explanation of the system of marginal notations is found on pages 21–2.